The Law of Internal Armed Conflict

Laws regulating armed conflict have existed for centuries, but the
bulk of these provisions have been concerned with wars between
States. Relatively little attention has been paid to the enormously
important area of internal armed conflict. At a time when
international armed conflicts are vastly outnumbered by domestic
disputes, this book seeks to redress the balance through a
comprehensive analysis of those rules which exist in international law
to protect civilians during internal armed conflict. From regulations
in the nineteenth and early twentieth centuries according to the
doctrine of recognition of belligerency, this book traces the
subsequent development of international law by the Geneva
Conventions and their additional Protocols, as well as through the
more recent jurisprudence of the Yugoslav and Rwandan tribunals.
The book also considers the application of human rights law during
internal armed conflict, before assessing how effectively the applicable
law is, and can be, enforced.

LINDSAY MOIR is Lecturer in Law at the University of Hull Law
School. His research interests include humanitarian law and human
rights.

CAMBRIDGE STUDIES IN INTERNATIONAL AND COMPARATIVE LAW

This series (established in 1946 by Professors Gutteridge, Hersch Lauterpacht and McNair) is a forum for studies of high quality in the fields of public and private international law and comparative law. Although these are distinct legal sub-disciplines, developments since 1946 confirm their interrelation. Comparative law is increasingly used as a tool in the making of law at national, regional and international levels. Private international law is now often affected by international conventions, and the issues faced by classical conflicts rules are frequently dealt with by substantive harmonisation of law under international auspices. Mixed international arbitrations, especially those involving state economic activity, raise mixed questions of public and private international law, while in many fields (such as the protection of human rights and democratic standards, investment guarantees and international criminal law) international and national systems interact. National constitutional arrangements relating to 'foreign affairs', and to the implementation of international norms, are a focus of attention.

Professor Sir Robert Jennings edited the series from 1981. Following his retirement as General Editor, an editorial board has been created and Cambridge University Press has recommitted itself to the series, affirming its broad scope.

The Board welcomes works of a theoretical or interdisciplinary character, and those focusing on new approaches to international or comparative law or conflicts of law. Studies of particular institutions or problems are equally welcome, as are translations of the best work published in other languages.

A list of books in the series can be found at the end of this volume

The Law of Internal Armed Conflict

Lindsay Moir

CAMBRIDGE
UNIVERSITY PRESS

PUBLISHED BY THE PRESS SYNDICATE OF THE UNIVERSITY OF CAMBRIDGE
The Pitt Building, Trumpington Street, Cambridge, United Kingdom

CAMBRIDGE UNIVERSITY PRESS
The Edinburgh Building, Cambridge CB2 2RU, UK
40 West 20th Street, New York, NY 10011-4211, USA
477 Williamstown Road, Port Melbourne, VIC 3207, Australia
Ruiz de Alarcón 13, 28014 Madrid, Spain
Dock House, The Waterfront, Cape Town 8001, South Africa

http://www.cambridge.org

First published 2002

Printed in the United Kingdom at the University Press, Cambridge

Typeface Swift 10/13 pt.   *System* LaTeX 2_ε [TB]

A catalogue record for this book is available from the British Library

Library of Congress Cataloguing in Publication data
Moir, Lindsay, 1970–
The law of internal armed conflict / Lindsay Moir.
        p.   cm. – (Cambridge studies in international and comparative law; [19])
Includes bibliographical references and index.
ISBN 0 521 77216 8 (hardback)
1. Humanitarian law.   2. War victims – Legal status, laws, etc.   3. Civil
war – Protection of civilians.   I. Title.   II. Cambridge studies in international and
comparative law (Cambridge, England: 1996); 19.
KZ6515.M65   2002
341.6'7 – dc21   2001037351

ISBN 0 521 77216 8 hardback

Contents

Preface and acknowledgements   *page* vii

Table of cases   x

Table of treaties and other international instruments   xvi

1   The historical regulation of internal armed conflict   1

The customary laws of war and belligerent practice   3

*The development of humanitarian law for internal
    armed conflict*   21

The drafting history of common Article 3   23

2   Article 3 common to the Geneva Conventions   30

Scope of application   31

The elements of internal armed conflict   34

The binding nature of common Article 3 for insurgents   52

The content of common Article 3   58

Common Article 3 in practice   67

3   Additional Protocol II of 1977   89

The drafting process of Additional Protocol II   91

The binding nature of Protocol II for insurgents   96

Scope of application   99

The content of Additional Protocol II   109

Additional Protocol II in practice   119

**4   Customary international law and internal
    armed conflict**   133

The Tadić jurisprudence   134

*The Statute of the International Criminal Court:
    confirming custom*   160

Contribution of the Tadić Case to international law   188

5	**Human rights during internal armed conflict**	193
	Human rights and humanitarian law	193
	Human rights law and common Article 3	197
	Human rights law and Additional Protocol II	210
6	**Implementation and enforcement of the laws of internal armed conflict**	232
	Sanctions against lawbreakers	233
	Alternative means of securing compliance	243
	Enforcement of human rights law	255
	Summary and conclusions	273
	Bibliography	278
	Index	298

Preface and acknowledgements

In 1993, the world was shocked by the terrible events unfolding in the former Yugoslavia and in Rwanda. As a postgraduate student at the University of Cambridge, about to embark on a PhD, I was aware of those laws which existed for the regulation of 'traditional' wars, fought between sovereign States. Much less of my legal education, however, had been devoted to the rules which exist to regulate civil war, and in particular, to protect the civilian population from the atrocities being routinely committed in Bosnia-Herzegovina and elsewhere, as reported daily by the media. Undertaking an examination of the laws protecting civilians during internal armed conflict therefore seemed to be both a valuable and a timely exercise, especially as the detailed content of those laws and attempts at their enforcement was an area undergoing such rapid development, largely as a result of the conflicts mentioned. This book therefore represents the culmination of the work started in October 1993, and continued throughout my time as a lecturer in the University of Hull Law School. Previous versions of chapters 1 and 6 have appeared in volume 47 (1998) of *International and Comparative Law Quarterly* and volume 3 (1998) of the *Journal of Armed Conflict Law* respectively.

Of course, many developments have taken place since the commencement of this project, perhaps most notably the adoption in the summer of 1998 of a Statute for the International Criminal Court. The International Criminal Tribunals for the former Yugoslavia and Rwanda have also continued to produce important statements on the law through their jurisprudence. Those have been incorporated into the text, and this book provides an account of the legal position as at October 2000. Hopefully international law will continue to develop to the point where civilians routinely receive the necessary protection during armed conflict, and where States consistently demonstrate the political will necessary to achieve the effective enforcement of international law against those who would violate its provisions.

Any undertaking such as this necessarily requires assistance from many individuals, only some of whom can be thanked here, but my gratitude is due first and foremost to my PhD supervisor, Christopher Greenwood, now Professor of International Law at the London School of Economics, for his guidance, support and encouragement throughout my studies at Cambridge. Special thanks are also due to Vaughan Lowe, now Chichele Professor of Public International Law at the University of Oxford, who stepped manfully into the role of supervisor during 1994–1995, and whose unstinting encouragement was equally invaluable. John Hopkins of Downing College, Cambridge, and Professor Peter Rowe of Lancaster University proved to be both supportive and insightful examiners, and I am particularly indebted to James Crawford, Whewell Professor of International Law at the University of Cambridge and Series Editor, for his comments on various drafts. I hope that all of the constructive criticisms and suggestions received have enabled me to make this book an improvement upon the original thesis.

Thanks are due to Cambridge University Press, for their acceptance of my manuscript, and for all of their help which has gone towards its publication in this form. Thanks in particular go to Finola O'Sullivan, Diane Ilott and the Press's independent readers. Their support and suggestions for improvement were invaluable and are, I hope, reflected in the final text. Thanks also to Denise Plattner, Véronique Ziegenhagen and Jean Perrenoud of the International Committee of the Red Cross, and to the Press Offices of the International Criminal Tribunals in The Hague and Arusha.

Special thanks must go to Stephen Neff, Bill Gilmore and Adnan Amkhan of the University of Edinburgh who, through their marvellous teaching, first stimulated my interest in international law as a young student, and who encouraged me to go on to postgraduate study. A PhD student's existence can be a solitary one, and so many thanks are due to all of my friends at Pembroke College, Cambridge, for making sure that that was not the case, and for making my time there so rewarding. I would also like to thank all of my colleagues and students, past and present, in the University of Hull Law School, particularly the late Professor Hilaire McCoubrey, for making the transition from student to academic a relatively painless and enjoyable one.

The Scottish Education Department (subsequently the Student Awards Agency for Scotland) provided the financial support to undertake my studies at Cambridge. Without their generous assistance, this book would have been impossible.

Finally, and above all, I would like to thank my parents, Gina and Andy Moir, and my wonderful wife, Alison, for their constant love, patience and support. This book is dedicated to them.

Table of cases

A-G of the Government of Israel v *Eichmann* 36   *page* 157, 233
    ILR 5

Abella v *Argentina*, Report No. 55/97, Annual   44, 59, 200, 267
    Report of the Inter-American Commission
    on Human Rights 1997 (17 February 1998)

Advisory Opinion on the Legality of the Threat   196, 199, 238, 255
    or Use of Nuclear Weapons [8 July 1996]
    35 ILM 809 (1996)

Akdivar v *Turkey* 23 EHRR 143   265

Aksoy v *Turkey* 23 EHRR 553   265

Alabama Claims, in Moore (ed.), *History and Digest*   11, 16
    of the International Arbitrations to which
    the US has been a Party (Washington, 1898),
    vol. I, 495

Aloeboetoe et al. v *Surinam* (1993) 14 HRLJ 413   268

Altesor v *Uruguay* 70 ILR 248   262

Aydin v *Turkey* ECHR Reports 1997-VI,   217, 218
    No. 50, 1866

Barcelona Traction Light and Power Company Limited,   57, 245
    Judgment, ICJ Reports (1970) 4

Bleier v *Uruguay* 70 ILR 259   262

Cakici v *Turkey*, Application No. 23657/94,   265
    Judgment of 8 July 1999

Case 6717 (El Salvador), Annual Report of the   266
    Inter-American Commission on Human Rights
    1983–1984 (24 September 1984), OAS Doc.
    OEA/Ser.L/V/II.63, doc.10, 35

Case 6718 (El Salvador), Annual Report of the   266
    Inter-American Commission on Human Rights
    1983–1984 (24 September 1984), 36
Case 6719 (El Salvador), Annual Report of the   266
    Inter-American Commission on Human Rights
    1983–1984 (24 September 1984), 37
Case 6720 (El Salvador), Annual Report of the   266
    Inter-American Commission on Human Rights
    1983–1984 (24 September 1984), 38
Case 6724 (El Salvador), Annual Report of the   266
    Inter-American Commission on Human Rights
    1984–1985 (1 October 1985), OAS Doc.
    OEA/Ser.L/V/II.66, doc.10, rev.1, 1
Corfu Channel Case (Merits), ICJ Reports (1949) 4   245
Cyprus v *Turkey* 4 EHRR 482   196, 263–265

Decision of the Constitutional Court of the Russian   193–194
    Federation, 31 July 1995, available at
    http://www.icrc.org/ihl-nat/
Denmark v *Turkey*, Application No. 34382/97,   265
    Judgment of 5 April 2000 (Friendly
    Settlement)
Denmark, Norway, Sweden and Netherlands v *Greece*   202
    (1969) Ybk ECHR 186
Dermit v *Uruguay* 71 ILR 354   262
Drescher Caldas v *Uruguay* 79 ILR 180   262

Ergi v *Turkey* ECHR Reports 1998-IV, No. 81, 1751   265
Estrella v *Uruguay* 78 ILR 40   262

Fals Borda v *Colombia*, Comm. No. 46/1979, UN   204
    Doc. A/37/40, 193
Farrell v *United Kingdom* 5 EHRR 466   265–266
Fédération Nationale des Déportés et Internés   151, 233
    Résistants et Patriotes and Others v *Barbie* 78 ILR
    124
Fernando and Raquel Mejia v *Peru* Report No. 5/96,   218
    Annual Report of the Inter-American
    Commission on Human Rights 1995
    (28 February 1996)

Güleç v *Turkey* ECHR Reports 1998-IV, No. 80, 1698   265

Kaya v *Turkey* ECHR Reports 1998-I, No. 65, 297 265, 266
Kiliç v *Turkey*, Application No. 22492/93, 265
    Judgment of 28 March 2000

Lawless v *Ireland* (Merits) 1 EHRR 15 195, 206
Loizidou v *Turkey* 23 EHRR 513 265, 273
López v *Uruguay* 68 ILR 29 262

Mahmut Kaya v *Turkey*, Application No. 22535/93, 265
    Judgment of 28 March 2000
McCann and Others v *United Kingdom* ECHR Series 265, 266
    A, Vol. 324 (1996)
Military and Paramilitary Activities In and 18, 31, 42, 47, 48,
    Against Nicaragua (*Nicaragua* v *US*) 49–50, 56, 69, 87,
    (Merits) 76 ILR 5 138, 140, 240, 245,
    247, 255, 273

Naulilaa Arbitration (*Germany* v *Portugal*) 2 Int. 238
    Arb. Awards 1013

Ogur v *Turkey*, Application No. 21594/93, 265
    Judgment of 20 May 1999

Perdoma and De Lanza v *Uruguay* UN Doc. A/35/40, 111 86
Pius Nwaoga v *The State* 52 ILR 494 146
Prize Cases (1862) 2 Black 635, 17 L 459 16
Prosecutor v *Akayesu*, Case No. ICTR-96-4-T, 35, 123, 137, 141,
    Judgment of 2 September 1998, 144, 148, 149, 151,
    37 ILM 1399 (1998) 152, 160, 168, 173,
    175, 181, 182,
    201, 217, 233

Prosecutor v *Aleksovski*, Case No. IT-95-14/1-T, 233
    Judgment of 25 June 1999
Prosecutor v *Aleksovski*, Case No. IT-95-14/1-A, 50, 181, 233
    Judgment of the Appeals Chamber, 24 March
    2000
Prosecutor v *Blaskić*, Case No. IT-95-14, Judgment of 181, 233
    3 March 2000
Prosecutor v *Delalić, Mucić, Delić and Landžo*, 45, 49, 137, 141, 157,
    Case No. IT-96-21-T, Judgment of 160, 168, 172, 173, 180,
    16 November 1998 181, 182, 191, 192, 201,
    217, 218, 233

Prosecutor v *Erdemović*, Case No. IT-96-22-T*bis*,   187, 233
   Sentencing Judgment of 5 March 1998,
   37 ILM 1182 (1998)
Prosecutor v *Furundžija*, Case No. IT-95-17/1-T,   45, 135, 141, 144,
   Judgment of 10 December 1998, 38 ILM   172–173, 201,
   317 (1999)   216, 217, 218
Prosecutor v *Furundžija*, Case No. IT-95-17/1-A,   233
   Judgment of the Appeals Chamber, 21 July
   2000
Prosecutor v *Jelisić*, Case No. IT-95-10, Judgment of   233
   14 December 1999
Prosecutor v *Kambanda*, Case No. ICTR-97-23-S,   182, 233
   Judgment of 4 September 1998, 37 ILM 1411
   (1998)
Prosecutor v *Karadžić and Mladić* (Rule 61),   48, 126, 127,
   Cases IT-95-5-R61 and IT-95-18-R61, 108   136, 137, 190
   ILR 86
Prosecutor v *Kayishema and Ruzindana*, Case No.   155, 181, 182,
   ICTR-95-1; ICTR-96-10, Judgment of   183, 233
   21 May 1999
Prosecutor v *Kupreškić et al.*, Case No. IT-95-16,   57, 108, 151, 155,
   Judgment of 14 January 2000   175–176, 233, 241
Prosecutor v *Martić* (Rule 61), Case   136, 137, 144,
   No. IT-95-11-R61, 108 ILR 40   145, 240–241
Prosecutor v *Mrksić, Radić and Sljivancanin*   48, 126, 135, 137,
   (Rule 61), Case No. IT-95-13-R61,   151, 152, 190
   108 ILR 53
Prosecutor v *Musema*, Case No. ICTR-96-13,   181, 182, 233
   Judgment of 27 January 2000
Prosecutor v *Nikolić* (Rule 61), Case   48, 126, 127, 135,
   No. IT-94-2-R61, 108 ILR 21   137, 150, 153,
                                                                         190, 217
Prosecutor v *Rajić* (Rule 61), Case No. IT-95-12-R61,   48, 126, 137,
   108 ILR 142   144, 190
Prosecutor v *Ruggiu*, Case No. ICTR-97-32,   233
   Judgment of 1 June 2000
Prosecutor v *Rutaganda*, Case No. ICTR-96-3,   45, 233
   Judgment of 6 December 1999, 39 ILM 557
   (2000)

Prosecutor v *Serushago*, Case No. ICTR-98-39-S,   182, 233
Judgment of 5 February 1999, 38 ILM 854 (1999)

Prosecutor v *Tadić*, Indictment, 34 ILM 1028   201, 217, 234
(1995)

Prosecutor v *Tadić*, Case No. IT-94-1-AR72,   32, 42–43, 47, 51, 57,
Appeal on Jurisdiction of 2 October   80, 120, 121, 126,
1995, 35 ILM 32 (1996)   127, 134–149,
                                                       157–160, 164, 166,
                                                       188–192, 248, 275

Prosecutor v *Tadić*, Case No. IT-94-1-T,   45, 48–49, 57, 59, 127,
Opinion and Judgment of 7 May 1997   134, 135, 136, 141,
(excerpts also available at 36 ILM 908   148, 149, 150–156,
(1997))   160, 168, 172,
                                                     173, 190–191

Prosecutor v *Tadić*, Case No. IT-94-1-A,   46, 47–48, 49–50, 127, 134,
Judgment of Appeals Chamber,   136, 141, 149, 150, 152,
15 July 1999, 38 ILM 1518 (1999)   154–156, 191, 233

Public Prosecutor v *Oie Hee Koi* [1968] 2 WLR 715 (PC)   189

R v *Bartle and the Commissioner of Police for the*   177–179, 236
Metropolis and Others, ex parte Pinochet; *R* v *Evans*
and Another and the Commissioner of Police for the
Metropolis and Others, ex parte Pinochet [1999] 2 All
ER 97

Re Yamashita (1946) 327 US 1   180

Republic of Ireland v *United Kingdom* 2   87, 202, 206
EHRR 25

Sevtap Veznedaroglu v *Turkey*, Application   265
No. 32357/96, Judgment of 11 April 2000

Short v *Iran* (*US* v *Iran*) 16 Iran-US Claims Tribunal   55
Reports 76

Stewart v *United Kingdom*, Comm. 10044/82,   266
European Commission of Human Rights
Decisions and Reports, No. 39 (1984) 162

Tanrikulu v *Turkey*, Application No. 23763/94,   265
Judgment of 8 July 1999

Timurtas v *Turkey*, Application No. 23531/94,   265
Judgment of 13 June 2000

Trial of German Major War Criminals: Proceedings   158
    of the International Military Tribunal Sitting at
    Nuremberg Germany, Part 22 (HMSO, London, 1950)

Tyrer v *United Kingdom* 2 EHRR 1   215

US v *The Three Friends* (1896) US 1, 41 L 897   8

Velásquez Rodríguez Case (1988) 9 HRLJ 212, (1990)   268
    11 HRLJ 127

Table of treaties and other international instruments

See also individual entries in the index.

1856 Paris Declaration Respecting Maritime Law   18
1863 Instructions for the Government of Armies of the United States in the Field (Lieber Code)   12, 19
1864 Geneva Convention for the Amelioration of the Condition of the Wounded in Armies in the Field   19
1899 Hague Convention (II) with Respect to the Laws and Customs of War on Land, and its Annex: Regulations Concerning the Laws and Customs of War on Land   19
1907 Regulations Respecting the Laws and Customs of War on Land, Annexed to Hague Convention (IV) Respecting the Laws and Customs of War on Land   19, 135, 213, 215, 218
1925 Geneva Protocol for the Prohibition of the Use of Asphyxiating, Poisonous or Other Gases, and of Bacteriological Methods of Warfare   84, 145
1926 International Convention with the Object of Securing the Abolition of Slavery and the Slave Trade   218
1928 Havana Convention on Rights and Duties of States in the Event of Civil Strife   19
1929 Geneva Convention Relative to the Treatment of Prisoners of War   19, 72
1945 Charter of the United Nations   76, 110, 203, 234, 238, 249, 251–255, 256
     Control Council for Germany Law No. 10   148, 153, 177
1948 Convention on the Prevention and Punishment of the Crime of Genocide   148, 174, 177
     Universal Declaration of Human Rights   62, 197

1949 Geneva Convention I for the Amelioration of the Condition of the
      Wounded and Sick in Armed Forces in the Field   27, 28, 116,
      157, 239
      Geneva Convention II for the Amelioration of the Condition of
      Wounded, Sick and Shipwrecked Members of Armed Forces at
      Sea   27, 28, 116, 157, 239
      Geneva Convention III Relative to the Treatment of Prisoners of
      War   27, 28, 60, 112, 113, 114, 157, 207, 215, 221, 222, 223, 239
      Geneva Convention IV Relative to the Protection of Civilian
      Persons in Time of War   24, 26, 27, 111, 112, 114, 157, 203,
      207, 211, 213, 215, 216, 218, 219, 220, 221, 222, 223, 225, 226,
      239, 264, 267
1950 European Convention for the Protection of Human Rights and
      Fundamental Freedoms   37, 44, 62, 195, 196, 198, 199, 200,
      202, 204–206, 208, 212, 216, 218, 220, 222, 223, 225, 229, 263–
      266
      1952   First Protocol   218, 219, 265
      1963   Second Protocol   220
             Fourth Protocol   208, 230
      1984   Seventh Protocol   226
1954 Hague Convention for the Protection of Cultural Property in the
      Event of Armed Conflict   118, 138, 188, 239
1956 Supplementary Convention on the Abolition of Slavery, the Slave
      Trade and Institutions and Practices Similar to Slavery   218
1966 International Covenant on Civil and Political Rights   37, 44, 62,
      92, 110, 112, 114, 195, 196, 197–198, 199, 200, 202–203, 204–
      209, 211, 212–213, 216, 218, 219, 221–222, 225, 226, 229, 230,
      258–263, 267, 269
      (First) Optional Protocol to the International Covenant on Civil
      and Political Rights   261–263
      International Covenant on Economic, Social and Cultural Rights
      219, 222, 223, 228, 229
1969 American Convention on Human Rights   37, 44, 195, 196, 197,
      198, 199, 202, 204–206, 208, 209, 210, 212, 215, 216, 218,
      219, 222, 223, 225, 229, 230, 266–268
      Vienna Convention on the Law of Treaties   52–53, 57
1973 International Convention on the Suppression and Punishment of
      the Crime of Apartheid   148, 163
1977 Geneva Protocol I Additional to the Geneva Conventions of
      12 August 1949, and Relating to the Protection of Victims of

International Armed Conflicts   1, 47, 66, 69, 71, 79, 89–93, 99, 100, 103, 106, 110, 114, 116–119, 133, 136, 147, 157, 159, 163–164, 190, 200, 203, 207, 215, 216, 219, 239, 241–242, 246, 274, 276

Geneva Protocol II Additional to the Geneva Conventions of 12 August 1949, and Relating to the Protection of Victims of Non-international Armed Conflicts   14, 32, 38, 39, 84, 86, 89–132, 133, 136, 137, 142, 143–144, 147, 157, 159, 160, 164, 165–167, 176, 188, 194, 196, 200, 207–208, 210–231, 232, 237, 239–240, 243–246, 265, 273–276

1978   Vienna Convention on the Succession of States in Respect of Treaties   55

1979   International Convention Against the Taking of Hostages   203

1980   United Nations Convention on Prohibitions or Restrictions on the Use of Certain Conventional Weapons Which May be Deemed to be Excessively Injurious or to Have Indiscriminate Effects   270

1981   African Charter on Human and Peoples' Rights   268–271

1984   Convention Against Torture and Other Cruel, Inhuman or Degrading Treatment or Punishment   62, 178, 200–201, 212, 236

1985   Inter-American Convention to Prevent and Punish Torture   201

1987   European Convention for the Prevention of Torture and Inhuman or Degrading Treatment or Punishment   201

1989   United Nations Convention on the Rights of the Child   219, 220

1992   United Nations Declaration on the Protection of All Persons from Enforced Disappearances   163

1993   Convention on the Prohibition of the Development, Production, Stockpiling and Use of Chemical Weapons and on their Destruction   146

Statute of the International Tribunal for the Prosecution of Persons Responsible for Serious Violations of International Humanitarian Law Committed in the Territory of Former Yugoslavia Since 1991   50, 134, 135, 136, 137, 147–150, 152–155, 156, 158, 161, 164, 167–168, 179, 180, 183, 185, 186, 189–192, 201, 217–218

1994   Statute of the International Tribunal for Rwanda   134, 136, 149, 152, 153, 154, 157–158, 162, 165, 175, 179, 180, 181, 183, 185, 186

ILC Draft Statute for an International Criminal Court   163, 184

1995   Turku Declaration on Minimum Humanitarian Standards   145
1996   ILC Draft Code of Crimes Against the Peace and Security of
         Mankind   153, 163, 164, 169, 172–173, 175, 179, 180
       ILC Draft Articles on State Responsibility   241
       Protocol on Prohibitions or Restrictions on the Use of Mines,
         Booby-traps and Other Devices to the 1981 United Nations
         Convention on Prohibitions or Restrictions on the Use of
         Certain Conventional Weapons Which May be Deemed to be
         Excessively Injurious or to have Indiscriminate Effects   146
1997   Ottawa Convention on the Prohibition of the Use, Stockpiling,
         Production and Transfer of Anti-Personnel Mines and on Their
         Destruction   271
1998   Statute of the International Criminal Court   32, 90, 152, 160–188,
         189, 233, 235, 236, 255, 271, 277

1 The historical regulation of internal armed conflict

It is perhaps trite to observe that non-international, or internal, armed conflicts have been commonplace throughout history. They have occurred for a variety of reasons, such as the desire to overthrow one government and replace it with another, or the desire of one or more parts of a State to secede from the rest and achieve independence. Particularly relevant for two reasons, however, was the demise of colonial rule in Africa and Asia.[1] First, colonised peoples frequently rose up against the colonial power in an effort to gain independence,[2] and secondly, upon achieving independence, violent internal struggles for power frequently ensued, often along tribal, ethnic and religious lines.

The legal regulation of internal armed conflict has continued to grow in importance in the post-colonial era. Since 1945, the vast majority of armed conflicts have been internal rather than international in character.[3] Kofi Annan, Secretary-General of the United Nations, has stated that 'wars between sovereign States appear to be a phenomenon in distinct decline'.[4] Unfortunately, this is not true of internal armed conflict and, to make matters worse, time has witnessed an apparent diminution in the application of the laws of war to internal armed conflicts, from their general observance in the 1861–1865 American Civil

---

[1] Many similar characteristics have been seen more recently in the demise of Soviet influence and Communist rule in Eastern Europe.
[2] As Algeria did against France in 1954, for example. Such conflicts would now be classed as international rather than internal under Article 1(4) of Additional Protocol I of 1977. See below at pp. 89–90.
[3] Statistics compiled by the International Peace Institute in Oslo suggest that in the period 1990–1995, seventy-three States were involved in armed conflicts, of which fifty-nine were involved in internal conflict or civil war. See Dan Smith, *The State of War and Peace Atlas*, 3rd edn (London, 1997), 90–95.
[4] Preface to UNHCR, *The State of the World's Refugees* (Oxford, 1997), ix.

1

War, to their blatant disregard in more recent conflicts, such as those in Bosnia-Herzegovina and Rwanda, typified by atrocities, ethnic cleansing and genocide. That so many such conflicts continue to arise clearly underlines the need for their effective legal regulation, while the pattern of many of these conflicts further demonstrates that those most in need of legal protection are civilians, i.e. those not directly involved in hostilities.

Given that these conflicts are *internal*, however, why should they be subject to *international* regulation at all? There are several reasons why this should be so. First, despite their non-international character, internal armed conflicts can have a profound effect on international peace and security. Hostilities can spill over into neighbouring States which may also be subject to influxes of refugees fleeing the war zone. There is also the risk that third States will intervene on behalf of one side or another, causing an escalation of hostilities.[5] Secondly, international law is no longer concerned only with States and their mutual relations. Perhaps best exemplified by the development of human rights law following the Second World War, individuals are now also seen as being the holders of rights and obligations under international law. Just as a government's treatment of its own citizens in that sphere is now regulated by international law, so the humanitarian protection of its citizens in situations of armed conflict is equally a matter of concern for the entire international community. Thirdly, international law protects those not involved in hostilities in the context of international armed conflict, and there is no reason why this should not also be the case merely because the conflict is characterised as internal. It is warfare nonetheless, and experience has shown that the civilian need for protection is often even greater where the conflict is internal.

That humanitarian rules were applicable in armed conflicts was accepted long before the nineteenth century, but the fact that internal armed conflicts were regarded as beyond the ambit of international regulation meant that the application of such norms to them was certainly not a matter of course. The traditional laws of war rely on the ability and willingness of the contending parties to distinguish between civilians and combatants, and between military and non-military targets. During internal armed conflict, however, such clear distinctions may

---

[5] This was particularly common at the height of the Cold War, where the United States and Soviet Union, fearful of nuclear war, chose instead to become involved (either directly or indirectly) in non-international conflicts in smaller but strategic States, using them as a battleground for their rival ideologies.

be impossible. Insurgents, often bereft of the military hardware and manpower available to government forces, frequently feel compelled to resort to guerrilla warfare and indiscriminate attacks. They are unlikely to have many of the facilities required to take care of prisoners, the sick and wounded. Using their fellow citizens as cover, insurgents frequently escape identification, forcing the government to wage war against virtually an entire civilian population.

Towards the end of the eighteenth century there had been a distinct move towards the application of the laws of warfare to internal as well as international armed conflicts,[6] but this was based almost exclusively on the character of the conflicts and the fact that both were often of a similar magnitude, rather than any overriding humanitarian concern to treat the victims of both equally. Not until the late nineteenth century did the application of the laws of war to internal armed conflict become a widespread and pressing issue in international law. It is here that the examination of their effect must begin.

The customary laws of war and belligerent practice

Prior to the nineteenth century, internal uprisings were commonly believed to be purely a matter of domestic security. The existing authority in the State treated rebels as criminals unworthy of any legal protection, a view still espoused by some legal scholars well into the twentieth century.[7] By the nineteenth century, however, the sharp theoretical

[6] Emmerich de Vattel, for example, in *The Law of Nations* (London, 1760), book III, chapter 18, 109–110, argued that, 'A civil war breaks the bands of society and government, or at least it suspends their force and effect; it produces in the nation two independent parties, considering each other enemies, and acknowledging no common judge: therefore of necessity these two parties must, at least for a time, be considered as forming two separate bodies, two distinct people, though one of them may be in the wrong in breaking the continuity of the state, to rise up against lawful authority, they are not the less divided in fact; besides, who shall judge them? Who shall pronounce on which side the right or the wrong lies? On earth they have no common superior. Thus they are in the case of two nations, who having a dispute which they cannot adjust, are compelled to decide it by force of arms. Things being thus situated, it is very evident that the common laws of war, those maxims of humanity, moderation and probity... are in civil wars to be observed by both sides.'

[7] See, for example, Thomas Baty and John H. Morgan, *War: Its Conduct and Legal Results* (London, 1915), 289; Pasquale Fiore, *International Law Codified*, trans. E. M. Borchard (New York, 1918), 533; Wyndham L. Walker, *Pitt Cobbett's Leading Cases on International Law*, 5th edn (London, 1937), vol. II, 6; and Hans Wehberg, 'La Guerre civile et le droit international' (1938-i) 63 *Rec des Cours* 7 at 9.

distinction traditionally drawn between internal and international armed conflict was not necessarily adhered to in practice, and the legal status of internal armed conflicts could be fundamentally altered by invoking the doctrine of recognition of belligerency.[8]

Traditional international law and the recognition of belligerency

In classical international law, an armed or violent challenge to the established authority within a State was characterised by reference to three different stages, depending upon the scale and intensity of the conflict: rebellion, insurgency and belligerency.[9] Rebellion was a modest, sporadic challenge by a section of the population intent on attaining control. Provided the uprising could be dealt with swiftly and effectively in the normal course of internal security, the conflict remained fully domestic. No international restraints on conduct were applicable, and the rebels had no rights or protection in international law, remaining instead punishable under municipal law.[10]

Insurgency, on the other hand, referred to a more substantial attack against the legitimate order of the State,[11] with the rebelling faction being sufficiently organised to mount a credible threat to the government. Foreign States were thus forced to acknowledge the factual situation pertaining in the country in order to protect their own interests:[12]

Insurgency, so far as foreign States are concerned, results, on the one hand, from the determination... not to recognise the rebellious party as a belligerent on the ground that there are absent one or more of the requirements of belligerency. On the other hand, recognition of insurgency is the outcome both of the unwillingness of foreign States to treat the rebels as mere lawbreakers, and of the desire of those States to put their relations with the insurgents on a regular, although clearly provisional basis... It may prove expedient to enter into contact with the insurgent authorities with a view to protecting national interests in the territory occupied by them, to regularizing political and commercial

---

[8] Those authors mentioned above in n. 7 did, however, accept that such recognition removed the conflict from purely internal regulation.

[9] See Heather A. Wilson, *International Law and the Use of Force by National Liberation Movements* (Oxford, 1988), 22–29.

[10] *Ibid.*, 23–24. See also Richard A. Falk, 'Janus Tormented: The International Law of Internal War' in James N. Rosenau (ed.), *International Aspects of Civil Strife* (Princeton, 1964), 185 at 197, and R. P. Dhokalia, 'Civil Wars and International Law' (1971) 11 *Indian JIL* 219 at 224–225.

[11] Dhokalia, 'Civil Wars', 225–226.

[12] Ordinarily these were of an economic character, the third States accepting that certain areas and resources might be controlled by the insurgents.

intercourse with them, and to interceding with them in order to ensure a measure of humane conduct of hostilities.[13]

A recognition of insurgency conferred no formal status on either party, and was certainly not regarded as according belligerent rights,[14] although certain international rights and duties were then brought into play.[15] The requirements necessary for insurgency to be recognised, however, were not settled:

> any attempt to lay down conditions of recognition of insurgency len[t] itself to misunderstanding. Recognition of insurgency create[d] a factual relation in the meaning that legal rights and duties as between insurgents and outside States exist[ed] only in so far as they [were] expressly conceded and agreed upon for reasons of convenience, of humanity, or of economic interest.[16]

The final stage was reached when the insurgents were extended recognition as a belligerent party. This amounted to a declaration by the recognising party that the conflict had attained such a sustained level that both sides were entitled to be treated in the same way as belligerents in an international armed conflict, and could be granted either by the parent government or by some third State.[17] Recognition, whether of insurgency or belligerency, was however, different from recognition of the insurgent party as the legitimate government of the afflicted State. It was simply recognition of the fact of the existence of war: 'It [did] not involve recognition of any government or political regime, nor ... any expression of approbation or disapprobation or indicate any sympathy

---

[13] Hersch Lauterpacht, *Recognition in International Law* (Cambridge, 1947), 270–271.

[14] Norman J. Padelford, *International Law and Diplomacy in the Spanish Civil Strife* (New York, 1939), 196–200.

[15] The foreign State's shipping was secure through the belligerents' duty not to blockade ports, to visit and search foreign ships on the high seas or to capture those vessels; both sides gained the rights to prevent supplies from abroad destined for their opponents from entering the country where the conflict was taking place and to requisition lawfully the property of foreigners and nationals; and, although the government ultimately represented the State, insurgents were permitted to enter into agreements on 'routine matters' and make arrangements with the ICRC, etc. See Erik Castren, *Civil War* (Helsinki, 1966), 216–223; Morris Greenspan, *The Modern Law of Land Warfare* (Berkeley, 1959), 620; Herbert W. Briggs, *The Law of Nations*, 2nd edn (New York, 1952), 1000–1003; Georg Schwarzenberger, *International Law* (London, 1968), vol. II, 693; and Wilson, *National Liberation Movements*, 24–25.

[16] Lauterpacht, *Recognition*, 276–277. See also Greenspan, *Modern Land Warfare*, 619; Evan D. T. Luard, 'Civil Conflicts in Modern International Relations' in Evan D. T. Luard (ed.), *The International Regulation of Civil Wars* (London, 1972), 7 at 21; and Castren, *Civil War*, 214.

[17] Although there was a significant distinction between the two, on account of its implications.

for or prejudice against the cause for which either side [was] fighting nor [did] the refusal to recognise carry any such implications.'[18] Nevertheless, some commentators claimed that recognition of the insurgent government *must* follow belligerent recognition. While accepting that belligerent recognition related to the existence of war (a question of fact) rather than to the recognition of a government, Smith, for example, maintained that, 'if we recognise the fact that a war is being carried on, then the recognition of the insurgent government follows as a necessary consequence. Wars can only be carried on by governments, and there must be at least two parties to every war.'[19] This may be true as regards the practice of equating internal armed conflicts with international armed conflicts following a recognition of belligerency, but the fundamental assertion that recognition of belligerency is separate from the recognition of an insurgent government remains unaffected. One may have been a logical consequence of the other, but they were not the same – to claim otherwise would accept that a State could have two governments. States may have taken notice of the *de facto* position of the insurgents and dealt with them accordingly, but this stopped short of actual *de jure* recognition.[20]

The doctrine of belligerent recognition took shape, at least for Great Britain and the United States, in the early nineteenth century through practice arising from the conflict in the Spanish-American colonies.[21] The United States had granted belligerent rights to the South American States in 1815, proclaiming a strict neutrality.[22] Britain also had a policy of 'neutrality' throughout the conflict, or, rather, a policy of

[18] James W. Garner, 'Recognition of Belligerency, (1938) 32 *AJIL* 106 at 111–112.

[19] Herbert A. Smith, 'Some Problems of the Spanish Civil War' (1937) 18 *BYIL* 17 at 18.

[20] In the context of the Spanish-American colonies' revolt in the early nineteenth century, the American position was that, 'So long as a contest of arms, with a rational or even remote prospect of eventual success, was maintained by Spain, the United States could not recognize the independence of the colonies as existing *de facto* without trespassing on their duties to Spain by assuming as decided that which was precisely the question of the war.' See John B. Moore, *A Digest of International Law* (Washington, 1906), vol. I, 89. Britain did not reject intercourse with the Spanish provinces, but was careful to avoid any formal recognition of the governments thereof. See F.O. 72/108 in Herbert A. Smith (ed.), *Great Britain and the Law of Nations* (London, 1932; reprinted New York, 1975), vol. I, 118. At one point in the early twentieth century, the USA even had a policy of not recognising governments which came to power via revolution. See Green H. Hackworth, *Digest of International Law* (Washington, 1940), vol. I, 185.

[21] For an outline of the development of the concept see Smith, *Law of Nations*, 261–333, and Moore, *Digest*, 164–205.

[22] *Dip. Corr.* 1865, I, 536 at 540. Reproduced in Moore, *Digest*, 172.

non-interference whilst still affording certain benefits to the Spanish.[23] In 1819, however, the Foreign Office took the necessary steps to place Spain and her colonies on the same footing, at least in so far as the export of munitions was concerned.[24] This was effectively Britain's first recognition of belligerency, although the consequences of the decision were not fully accepted until 1822.[25]

Recognition of belligerency by third States rendered the customary international law of neutrality applicable between those States and the parties to the conflict.[26] Of course, there was no requirement upon third States to be neutral. Neutrality only becomes possible in the event of an armed conflict, however, and internal conflict could only be considered as such if the insurgents were recognised as belligerents. Consequently, if third States wished to have the rights attached to neutrality, in particular for their shipping, then a recognition of belligerency was required.

[23] Both neutrality and non-interference reflect the desire to remain detached from a conflict, but whereas neutrality as an international legal concept provides that a State may not, by virtue of any governmental measure, intervene in a conflict to the benefit of one of the belligerent parties, a policy of non-interference, by contrast, is merely an expression of political attitude and the aim not to become directly involved in the conflict, while retaining the possibility of treating one side more advantageously. Several official opinions between 1814 and 1819 illustrate the fact that Spain was still seen by Britain as entitled to a measure of favour, contrary to the strict impartiality required by neutrality in international law. A paper of 22 September 1817 stated that 'the declarations alluded to, must be understood . . . in the most limited sense, and as conveying only an intimation that Great Britain would not afford direct assistance to either Party. In any other sense the term neutrality would scarcely preserve its proper signification towards both Parties – Because the Antecedent relations with Spain, or rather with the Spanish Government, must continue, and to elevate the Insurgent Provinces to the same conditions of Amity could not but affect the pretensions and the interests of Spain; and however competent it might be to a State to form such relations, by separate and specific engagements, it would be a result that could not be implied in the profession of neutrality between both Parties.' (F.O. 83/2365, reproduced in Smith, *Law of Nations*, 273–274.)

[24] For some time the export of arms and munitions to South America and Africa had been prohibited, except under royal licence. This prohibition was now extended to include Spain.

[25] Following the recognition of belligerency, the F.O. Legal Officer was still undecided as to the competency of the insurgent Government of Peru to declare a blockade. In 1822, however, he stated that, 'Considering the principles of neutrality that have been professed on the part of this Country, the asserted independent Governments would have a right to exercise the ordinary privileges of War in maritime capture.' (F.O. 83/2366, reproduced in Smith, *Law of Nations*, 279.)

[26] Axel Möller, *International Law in Peace and War* (Copenhagen, 1935), part II, 157; James L. Brierly, *The Law of Nations*, 6th edn, edited by Humphrey Waldock (Oxford, 1963), 141; Castren, *Civil War*, 168.

This imposed no duty or requirement on the established authority in the State concerned to recognise the belligerents, but widespread recognition of belligerency by foreign States would undoubtedly have influenced the parent government to follow suit. Equally, if recognition by the parent government had already taken place, it could hardly then complain of interference should other States do the same.

Recognition appeared to work against the third State, however, in that it then became legitimate prey for both sides should they engage in commercial warfare.[27] Its freedom of action was also severely curtailed, as neutrality demands. In contrast, recognition of belligerency was most beneficial to the insurgents:

> They gain[ed] the great advantage of a recognized status, and the opportunity to employ commissioned cruisers at sea, and to exert all the powers known to maritime warfare, with the sanction of foreign nationals. They [could] obtain abroad loans, military and naval materials, and enlist men, as against everything but neutrality laws; their flag and commissions [were] acknowledged, their revenue laws... respected, and they acquire[d] a quasi-political recognition.[28]

Third States were prohibited from providing assistance to the legitimate government, eliminating to some degree the latent inequality between the parties to the conflict, and furthermore, the act of recognition was open to interpretation as an expression of moral support for the insurgents.

With so little advantage apparently accruing to third States recognising the belligerency of insurgents abroad, why should they take such action? The most obvious reason could be that the recognising State *did* in fact support the aims for which the rebels were fighting. Political motives and self-interest are, after all, the foundation upon which much of State practice has historically been built. In this respect, it may also have made good sense since victorious insurgents may well be influenced by any recognition afforded when deciding on future foreign relations. Such an act of recognition would clearly be damaging to the recognising State's relations with the legitimate government, but relations to protect its nationals or property in any territory under insurgent control would

---

[27] For details of how belligerency could affect the interests of third States upon the sea, see *US v The Three Friends* (1896) 166 US 1, 41 L 897, where the Supreme Court held at 918 that, 'the recognition of belligerency involves the right of blockade, visitation, search and seizure of contraband articles on the High Seas, and abandonment of claims for reparation on account of damages suffered by our citizens from the prevalence of warfare'.

[28] Henry Wheaton, *Elements of International Law*, 8th edn, edited by R. H. Dana (London, 1866), n. 15 at 37.

become correspondingly easier. Recognition might also have been influential in tempering the hostilities on humanitarian grounds.[29]

The geographical location of the conflict was also vital. Should the contest be conducted entirely on land, with the third State far away and in no immediate danger of involvement, then it is difficult to imagine any real need to recognise insurgents as a belligerent party. In the absence of any effects on national interests, recognition by third States was simply an expression of open support for the insurgents which could rightly be regarded by the parent State as an unfriendly act.[30] The position was different where the conflict extended to the seas:

> Where the insurgents and the parent state are maritime, and the foreign nation has extensive commercial relations and trade at the ports of both, and the foreign nation and either or both of the contending parties have considerable naval force, and the domestic contest must extend itself over the sea ... the liability to political complications, and the questions of right and duty to be decided at once, usually away from home, by private citizens or naval officers, seem to require an authoritative and general decision as to the status of the three parties involved.[31]

Recognition of belligerency by third States therefore occurred most commonly in maritime situations, often following the institution of a blockade upon insurgent ports by the legitimate authority. An excellent example is that of the recognition afforded to the Confederate States in the American Civil War, most importantly by Great Britain.[32]

---

[29] By leading the insurgents to suspect that a recognition of belligerency and all that entailed might follow if the laws of war were applied to the conflict. Wheaton, for example, stated in *Elements of International Law*, 35, that a prerequisite for such recognition was the 'actual employment of military forces on each side, acting in accordance with the rules and customs of war'.

[30] As stated in Wheaton, *Elements of International Law*, 34: 'The reason which requires and can alone justify this step [i.e. the recognition of belligerency] by the government of another country is that its own rights and interests are so far affected as to require a definition of its own relations to the parties.'

[31] *Ibid.*, 35.

[32] On 13 May 1861. This was done implicitly, however, through a declaration of neutrality, rather than by any express statement of recognition in favour of the South. France, Spain, the Netherlands and Brazil also declared their neutrality in 1861. See John B. Moore, *History and Digest of the International Arbitrations to which the US has been a Party* (Washington, 1898), vol. I, 595. Other examples of such recognition include that granted to the Spanish colonies in America during their war of independence by the United States and Great Britain (see above); that afforded to the Greeks in their insurrection of 1821–1829 by Russia, France, Great Britain, etc.; and possibly that afforded by some Latin American States to the Cuban insurgents during the Civil War of 1868–1878 (although this is a matter of some debate, see below p. 18 n. 68).

Recognition of belligerency by the parent State brought into effect the *jus in bello* in its entirety between it and the rebels.[33] The overriding problem was that such recognition was commonly believed to be entirely at the discretion of the government, which was unlikely to take that step until it was clear that the insurrection could not be put down quickly or effectively.[34] Recognition tended then to come late if at all, and only once reciprocity had become an issue.

Again, such recognition was clearly more beneficial to the insurgents than to the government, which was no longer in a position to put down the insurrection in any manner which it saw fit, treating the rebels as mere criminals at the mercy of domestic law. Rather, it found that the rebels had rights and duties analogous to its own which served to eliminate the inequalities between the sides to some extent, imposing obligations on both. Only those means permitted by international law could be employed in suppressing the conflict from then on. That was (and is) always the position in theory, but where a government used all of the power at its disposal to crush an insurrection, at least the conflict would be over quickly and before it received widespread international attention. Recognition could, then, serve to prolong the conflict.[35] It might also have been regarded as a concession to the insurgents and a sign of weakness.

It is not wholly true, however, that the government itself would not benefit from the act of recognition. Certainly the members of its armed forces would benefit (at least theoretically), in that they were then entitled to expect improved treatment both during the course of hostilities and in the event of capture.[36] It was therefore desirable from a humanitarian standpoint that the government recognise the insurgents as belligerents as soon as possible, although this was seldom considered important. Rather, there may have been other factors inducing a government to recognise the belligerency of insurgents – upon recognition

---

[33] See Thomas J. Lawrence, *The Principles of International Law*, 7th edn (London, 1923), 64; Castren, *Civil War*, 135–137; Julius Stone, *Legal Controls of International Conflict* (London, 1959), 305; and Lassa F. L. Oppenheim, *International Law* (London, 1906), vol. II, 66.

[34] Recognition by the established government in a State was, in fact, very rare.

[35] The use of severe violence by the legitimate authority could itself tend to prolong the hostilities, however, provoking the insurgents into an even more desperate struggle, a point well made in Castren, *Civil War*, 145.

[36] Although breaches of the laws of war are inevitable in reality. Even where belligerency was recognised, the treatment of enemy soldiers often fell well short of what could be considered acceptable, e.g. the treatment of prisoners by both sides in the American Civil War, which included placing them in strategic military targets as human shields.

the government gained certain rights against third States, particularly as regards foreign shipping,[37] whereby it was 'relieved from responsibility for acts done in the insurgent territory; its blockade of its own ports [was] respected; and it acquire[d] a right to exert, against neutral commerce, all the powers of a party to a maritime war'.[38]

State practice and the recognition of belligerency

Before any conclusions can be drawn on the question of the recognition of belligerency, a study of the actual practice and *opinio juris* of States in the nineteenth century as regards the doctrine is essential.[39]

The prevailing view was still that the laws of war were inapplicable to internal armed conflict in the absence of recognition of belligerency, although this opinion was by no means unanimous. Indeed, some legal scholars from the turn of the century seemed to give the impression that the laws of war were, or at least ought to have been (morally as much as legally), applicable during all armed conflicts irrespective of whether they were internal or international, at least once the struggle had reached a certain stage.[40] These writers tended to be American, however, and hugely influenced by the Civil War of 1861–1865. Their views may

---

[37] See, for example, the *Alabama Claims*, concerning the rights of the United States following Great Britain's failure to act as neutrality demanded during the American Civil War, in Moore, *History and Digest of Arbitrations*, 495 at 653.

[38] Wheaton, *Elements of International Law*, 37. See also US Diplomatic Correspondence on this point, *Dip. Corr.* 1861, 105: 'If the foreign state recognizes belligerency in the insurgents, it releases the parent state from responsibility for whatever may be done by the insurgents, or not done by the parent state where the insurgent power extends.' (Reproduced in Francis Wharton (ed.), *A Digest of the International Law of the United States*, 2nd edn (Washington, 1887), vol. I, 518.)

[39] For detailed analysis of some important historical case studies, see Castren, *Civil War*, 38–66, where he draws heavily on the following works: P. Sadoul, *De la Guerre civile en droit des gens* (Nancy, 1905); J. Siotis, *Le Droit de la guerre et les conflits armés d'un caractère non international* (Paris, 1958); J. P. Weber, *Problèmes de droit international public posés par les guerres civiles* (Geneva, 1940); and H. Wehberg, 'La Guerre civile'. Evidence of the *opinio juris* of the United States and Great Britain is to be found in texts such as Wharton, *Digest*; Moore, *Digest*; Arnold D. McNair, *International Law Opinions* (Cambridge, 1956), vol. I; and Smith, *Law of Nations*.

[40] They drew on more humanitarian arguments than Vattel for such an application of the laws of war, e.g. Theodore D. Woolsey, *Introduction to the Study of International Law*, 4th edn (London, 1875), 168: 'The same rules of war are required in such a war as in any other – the same ways of fighting, the same treatment of prisoners, of combatants, of non-combatants, and of private property by the army where it passes; so also natural justice demands the same veracity and faithfulness which are binding on the intercourse of all moral beings.' See also Wheaton, *Elements of International Law*, 374.

therefore have been unrepresentative, a typical expression stating that, 'it is all war, whatever its cause or object, and should be conducted in a civilised way...There is no distinction from a military view between a civil war and a foreign war until after the final decisive battle.'[41]

Whilst it might be argued that the relevant stage to be reached in order for the laws of war to apply was analogous to that where belligerency would customarily be recognised, by no means all of these writers felt that some concrete form of recognition had to take place. Even those advocating the view that a recognition of belligerency was necessary before the laws of war could apply simply stated that in civil war recognition of belligerency was 'usually' afforded to the insurgents, as if virtually automatic,[42] begging the question whether recognition of belligerency was so readily or automatically afforded as to mean that the laws of war were essentially applicable to internal armed conflicts *per se.*

An examination of some major internal conflicts of the nineteenth and early twentieth centuries shows that, in those cases where the laws of war were accepted and applied by opposing forces, some form of recognition of belligerency *had* invariably taken place. Although appearances might suggest otherwise, and that humanitarian law was accepted without a recognition of belligerency in some cases, further examination tends to indicate that, at some stage, there had been an act by the parent government showing an intention to be bound by the laws of war.[43] In the American Civil War, for example, the blockade declared on Confederate States on 19 April 1861, followed by the Lieber Code, under which the laws of war were to be observed,[44] could clearly be considered

---

[41] Hannis Taylor, *A Treatise on International Public Law* (Chicago, 1901), 454. Most continental European jurists were still firmly of the opinion that only a recognition of belligerency made the international laws of war applicable. See, for example, A. Merignhac, *Droit public international* (Paris, 1912), vol. III, 19, and Fiore, *International Law Codified*, 533.

[42] E.g. H. W. Halleck, *International Law* (San Francisco, 1861), vol. II, 333; George B. Davis, *The Elements of International Law*, 3rd edn (New York, 1908), 275; and Walker, *Pitt Cobbett's Leading Cases*, vol. II, 6.

[43] As in the American War of Independence (1774–1783), the Wars of Independence by the Spanish-American Colonies (1810–1824), the American Civil War (1861–1865) and the Greek insurrection (1946–1949).

[44] Although the Lieber Code was an order to Unionist armies, its standards appear to have been generally observed by both sides. See Quincy Wright, 'The American Civil War, 1861–65' in Richard A. Falk (ed.), *The International Law of Civil War* (Baltimore, 1971), 30 at 56. There was only one trial leading to execution for a breach of the laws of war at the conclusion of hostilities – that of Captain Henry Wirtz, the Commander responsible for the maltreatment of Union prisoners at the Andersonville Stockade. See Wright, 'The American Civil War', 73 and Samuel E. Morison, *The Oxford History of*

tacit recognition of belligerency by the Government.[45] By contrast, where recognition of belligerency was not afforded by the government,[46] the laws of war tended not to be applied, often leading to barbaric conduct by both sides. Admittedly, violations can occur in any armed conflict, but one may conclude that a recognition of belligerency tended to encourage the observance of the humanitarian rules of warfare, whereas an absence of recognition had the opposite effect.[47]

That recognition of belligerency was not always afforded in wide-ranging conflicts suggests that the act of recognition (and hence the application of humanitarian law) was a purely discretionary matter for States. It was largely accepted, however, that certain conditions had to be met before recognition could properly be accorded:[48] first, the armed

the American People (London, 1965), 705. For a more sympathetic view of Captain Wirtz's responsibility, however, see Donald A. Wells, *War Crimes and Laws of War*, 2nd edn (Lanham, 1991), 95, where it is suggested that Wirtz 'had actually done his best under abysmal conditions for which he was not responsible [but that the public required a] "scapegoat"'. It would, of course, be naive to assume that this single execution means that there were no other serious breaches of the laws of war.

[45] There was no requirement for recognition to be express, and in the other conflicts mentioned above in n. 43 some act of tacit recognition also took place. The American Civil War can be highlighted further in that Lincoln later criticised certain States for failing to observe neutrality as regards the conflict. The Greek insurrection was possibly different in that the laws of warfare were applied through persuasion by the ICRC. Agreement by the Greek Government was nevertheless at least a tacit recognition of belligerency. Lauterpacht, however, seemed opposed to the idea of tacit recognition of belligerency, claiming that, 'so-called implied recognition is often an exhibition of wishful political thinking, and might well disappear from the dictionary of international law. The fact that international practice has developed the intermediate instrument of recognition of insurgency is an additional reason for avoiding the fiction of implied recognition of belligerency.' See *Recognition*, 271.

[46] As in the Greek revolt against the Ottoman Empire (1821–1829), the Hungarian Civil War (1848–1849), the Cuban Wars of Liberation against Spain (1868–1878 and 1895–1898) and the Spanish Civil War (1936–1939).

[47] Where there was no recognition of belligerency, the humanitarian laws of war were inapplicable, States retaining their right to counter any revolt in the fashion which they perceived to be the most effective, no matter how severe that might be.

[48] There is much writing to support this view, e.g. Garner states in 'Recognition of Belligerency', 112, that, 'recognition is a matter entirely within the discretion of foreign states in the sense that they are free to judge for themselves whether the struggle has attained the proportions of a war, and, if so, whether they can recognise it as such without impairing their own rights or prejudicing the general interests of the community of states. But there are certain generally accepted tests by which the existence of a state of war [is] to be determined, and recognition prior to this stage is premature and may justly be regarded by the parent state as an unfriendly act.' Of course, even if the criteria were objectively satisfied, the recognition of belligerency could still be regarded by the parent government as unfriendly. See the attitude of the United States to Britain's recognition of belligerency in the American Civil War, as discussed below at pp. 15–16.

conflict within the State must have escalated from one of a purely local character, involving the actions of only a small section of the State and population, to that of a general character, resembling a traditional international war and involving a large proportion of the population;[49] secondly, the insurgents had to occupy and administer a substantial portion of the national territory;[50] thirdly, the insurgents had to conduct hostilities in accordance with the laws of war, through armed forces under a responsible authority;[51] and finally, the hostilities must have reached such a magnitude that foreign States found it necessary (either diplomatically or economically) to define their attitude towards the contesting factions by according them belligerent status.[52]

These criteria[53] would seem to suggest that the question of belligerency was one of fact, not to be decided according to political support for one side or another,[54] a view strongly reflected in the nineteenth century *opinio juris* of both the United States and Great Britain. In a statement of general principle given by the British Law Officers[55] in the context of the 1867 Cretan Insurrection, it was said that:

It is always a question of fact to be determined by the Government of the Neutral State, whether the Insurrection has or has not assumed the dimensions of War, and whether the legitimate interests of the Neutral State do or do not require

---

[49] Lauterpacht, *Recognition*, 176; Charles C. Hyde, *International Law Chiefly as Interpreted and Applied by the United States*, 2nd edn (Boston, 1945), vol. I, 198; Lawrence, *Principles of International Law*, 329; Hackworth, *Digest*, 385; Schwarzenberger, *International Law*, vol. II, 708; Rosalyn Higgins, 'International Law and Civil Conflict' in Luard, *Civil Wars*, 169 at 170.

[50] Lauterpacht, *Recognition*, 176; Werner Levi, *Contemporary International Law: A Concise Introduction* (Boulder, 1979), 71; Luard, 'Civil Conflicts', 20; Higgins, 'Civil Conflict', 170.

[51] Lauterpacht, *Recognition*, 176; Schwarzenberger, *International Law*, vol. II, 708; Higgins, 'Civil Conflict', 170; Luard, 'Civil Conflicts', 20.

[52] Lauterpacht, *Recognition*, 176; Lawrence, *Principles of International Law*, 329; Luard, 'Civil Conflicts', 20; Higgins, 'Civil Conflict', 170; Hyde, *International Law*, 198.

[53] Interestingly, bearing a close resemblance to the criteria for the application of Additional Protocol II of 1977. Protocol II might therefore be considered a retrograde step, containing as it does only limited regulation of a small class of internal armed conflicts, whilst a recognition of belligerency brought into play the whole of humanitarian law. Of course, Additional Protocol II applies automatically (at least in theory), whereas recognition of belligerency was discretionary. On Additional Protocol II, see chapter 3 below.

[54] Indeed, Lauterpacht clearly stated that, 'recognition is not in the nature of a grant of a favour or a matter of unfettered political discretion, but a duty imposed by the facts of the situation . . . [and provided the requirements are met, then the contesting parties are] legally entitled to be treated as if they are engaged in a war by two sovereign States'. See *Recognition*, 175.

[55] Karslake, Selwyn and Phillimore.

that she should claim from both parties the performance towards her of the obligations incident to the Status of a belligerent.[56]

Indeed, by the end of the nineteenth century, common opinion was that the practice of Europe and the United States had been to look upon belligerency as fact rather than principle.[57] But while belligerency itself may well have been a fact, affording recognition was quite different: 'While recognition is the legal attestation of an established condition of existing facts, the decision as to whether it is to be accorded, and the method by which it is accomplished, are political questions decided by the political branch of each interested government, and intimately associated with national policy.'[58] Thus, provided certain requirements regarding the intensity of the conflict had been met, showing the hostilities to be equivalent to a state of war in that respect, a State whose interests were affected (or were liable to be affected) to such an extent as to make a determination of their position necessary was free to decide whether it wished to be neutral in the conflict or not. Where the decision was made to be a neutral party, an act of recognition of the belligerency of both sides would follow.

Great Britain and the United States were diametrically opposed, however, on the rights and wrongs of Britain's recognition of the belligerency of the Confederate States in the American Civil War. As stated above, Britain recognised the Confederates as belligerents relatively early in the conflict, based on the opinion that the conflict amounted to a war in the international law sense, so that such an act was completely justified, especially in view of the possible effects on British shipping. As the British Law Officers[59] stated on 14 February 1867:

This recognition was in accordance with principle and practice; – that it was within the scope of the undoubted privilege of the Neutral State, – and lastly that the course pursued by the declaration of Blockade on the part of the Government of the United States, had rendered this recognition both necessary and inevitable. – The right of blockade which pressed so severely upon the interests of Neutral States, was a right incident, and incident only, to a state of war in which two or more belligerents were engaged, – and never before, in the history of States, was the recognition of so extensive a blockade required by a Neutral State . . .

[56] F.O. 83/2396, reproduced in Smith, *Law of Nations*, 263.
[57] John T. Abdy (ed.), *Kent's Commentary on International Law*, 2nd edn (Cambridge, 1866), 105, quoting *Hansard* CLXII, 1565.
[58] Padelford, *Spanish Civil Strife*, 23–24.
[59] Phillimore, Karslake and Selwyn.

...For the United States to demand the exercise of these belligerent rights, and at the same time to refuse a belligerent status to the enemy, was plainly contradictory. In truth the position is as novel and unsound in International Law and clearly propounded for the first time for the obvious purpose of giving the United States the advantage of being exclusively recognized by the Neutral State as Belligerent.[60]

The American Government, however, felt that the British recognition had been afforded so early as to constitute an international wrong, which it sought to have submitted to international arbitration,[61] and steadfastly refused to accept that the Declaration of Blockade had left Britain with no alternative but to recognise the belligerency of the Confederates. In essence, the blockade had been an admission by the United States that war existed – a recognition of belligerency by the US Government itself. Great Britain, by recognising the belligerency of the Confederacy, had simply been insisting that the consequences of the US Government's act be accepted. Indeed, when the matter came before the US Supreme Court, it was the British view which found favour: 'The proclamation of blockade is, itself, official and conclusive evidence to the court that a state of war existed which demanded and authorized a recourse to such a measure, under the circumstances peculiar to the case.'[62] Thus, one American jurist asserted that, 'if the British Government erred in thinking that the war began as early as Mr Lincoln's proclamation in question, they erred in company with our Supreme Court'.[63]

A clearer vindication of Britain's position is difficult to imagine, and its influence shaped much future thought on the matter. When, for example, San Domingo revolted against Spain in 1864, and the Spanish authorities proclaimed a blockade on Dominican ports which was accepted by the British Government, the Law Officers[64] were asked for their opinion as to the status of the insurgents. They stated clearly that the Government could not refuse to recognise the Dominican insurgents

---

[60] F.O. 83/2225, reproduced in Smith, *Law of Nations*, 309–310.

[61] There is a great deal of writing on this dispute. See Moore, *Digest*, 184–193 and Smith, *Law of Nations*, 302–312 for an outline and directions towards more detailed treatments.

[62] *Prize Cases* (1862) 2 Black 635, 17 L 459 at 477.

[63] Woolsey, *Introduction to International Law*, appendix III, n. 19, at 359. The Arbitral Panel for the *Alabama Claims* also accepted that 'the circumstances out of which the facts constituting the subject-matter of the present controversy arose were of a nature to call for the exercise on the part of Her Britannic Majesty's government of all possible solicitude for the observance of the rights and the duties involved in the proclamation of neutrality issued by Her Majesty on the 13th day of May, 1861'. See Moore, *History and Digest of Arbitrations*, 654–655.

[64] Palmer, Collier and Phillimore.

as belligerents since the acceptance of the blockade had accorded the Spanish Government belligerent rights – rights incident only to a state of war.[65] Lord McNair saw this as evidence of an emerging doctrine in international law – namely that where a parent government proclaims a blockade and claims the right to enforce it against third States, recognition of belligerency for both sides ceases to be discretionary.[66] This may go too far. That recognition of belligerency was a matter of choice for the affected State is clear. Provided the criteria mentioned above were met, along with some effect on the third States' interests, the *possibility* of recognition arose. To say that following a proclamation of blockade States lost this free choice is not strictly true, although their interests may then have been affected to such an extent as to leave them with no practical alternative.

The position with regard to both the parent government and foreign States therefore was that belligerency was recognised first out of self-interest, and secondly on a factual basis. The factual existence of a state of war in international law was necessary before the discretionary implementation of the political tool of recognition. Such recognition was effective only for the purpose of the armed conflict and in relation to the recognising State, making it constitutive in character. It had lasting effect only if the insurgents managed to defeat the existing authorities and establish their independence.[67] State practice and *opinio juris* were fairly uniform in accepting that the laws of war applied only where the insurgents had been recognised as belligerents. Even those writers advocating humanitarian law's more routine application to civil war tied their idea closely to the status of belligerency. Civil war is, after all, the very situation in which the struggle has attained such proportions as to make both parties analogous to belligerents in the international law sense.

The laws of war were *not* automatically applicable to internal armed conflicts in the nineteenth and early twentieth centuries. States may have observed them in some cases through the doctrine of recognition of belligerency (either tacit or express), but this was done out of self-interest and for practical purposes, rather than through the belief that they were so bound by international law. Even on the occasions when recognition was afforded, it was a *concession* to the insurgents, certainly

---

[65] F.O. 83/2373, reproduced in Smith, *Law of Nations*, 318.

[66] McNair, *Opinions*, vol. I, 141.

[67] Oppenheim, *International Law*, vol. II, 66. Smith wrote in *Law of Nations*, 262, that:
'In truth, belligerent recognition is merely a particular form of *de facto* recognition, provisional in its nature and limited to the duration of the war from which it results.'

not a legal entitlement.[68] Had State practice been uniform, it might
have demonstrated an emerging customary law trend to apply humanitarian law automatically to internal conflicts, but States clearly did not
feel any legal obligation to recognise belligerency.[69] Without the discretionary recognition of belligerency by foreign States or, more rarely, by
the parent government, the laws of war were of no application to internal conflicts. When they did apply, it was on a purely reciprocal basis,
resulting more from convenience and a fear of reprisals than from any
overriding concern for humanity.

Humanitarian rules of armed conflict prior to the 1949 Geneva Conventions

If recognition of belligerency invoked the *jus in bello*, what then were the
applicable laws of war, and how did they relate to internal armed conflict? Not until rather late in the development of international law did
any question of the observance of multilateral conventions regulating
the conduct of international hostilities arise, and even this came long
before any convention seeking to regulate internal armed conflict.

Codification of the laws of armed conflict did not begin until 1856,
with the Paris Declaration dealing with aspects of maritime law. The
laws of war were therefore customary, having developed from the practice of States. This body of rules contained such fundamental principles
as proportionality and distinction, and regulated the selection of targets,
means of injuring the enemy, etc. The subsequent codification of these
principles, however, did not serve to displace customary law, which continues to exist alongside the conventions.[70] Virtually all of the previous
customary law of armed conflict has now been codified.

---

[68] Despite the common occurrence of internal armed conflicts in Latin America in the
nineteenth and early twentieth centuries, there is little documented State practice as
regards the recognition of belligerency, perhaps because those States were generally
not navally powerful. In the Cuban insurrection of 1868 it was alleged that the rebels
had been recognised as insurgents by Peru, Mexico and Chile, but the USA found
that there was no evidence of Chile having acted at all, and that Mexico had not
recognised belligerency, merely authorising the Cuban flag to be accepted in its
ports. See Moore, *Digest*, 194.

[69] It is unclear from much of the nineteenth-century literature how much importance
was placed on *opinio juris*, with many works concentrating on practice and usage.
Oppenheim, writing in 1905 and taking due account of previous opinion,
nevertheless stressed the fact that customary law required a practice which was
believed to be legally necessary or right. See *International Law*, vol. I, 22–23.

[70] For an explanation of the relationship between customary and conventional
international law, see *Military and Paramilitary Activities In and Against Nicaragua
(Nicaragua v US)* (Merits), 76 ILR 5, paragraphs 172–179.

The first real attempt at the codification of the laws of land warfare was drawn up during the American Civil War by Dr Francis Lieber, in the form of a military manual for the forces in the field which became known as the 'Lieber Code'.[71] Such manuals are often useful evidence of the law,[72] but must always be treated with considerable caution, often being drawn up from a military viewpoint rather than a strictly legal one.[73]

With the age of codification underway, several international agreements were concluded, such as the Geneva Convention of 1864 dealing with the wounded and sick on land (revised in 1906 and 1929), Hague Convention II of 1899, Hague Convention IV of 1907 and its Regulations dealing with general land warfare, and the Geneva Convention of 1929 dealing with prisoners of war. Before the mid-twentieth century, however, no international agreement applied to anything other than purely international conflicts (although regional agreements could deal with internal conflicts[74]), and although customary law provided that the rules of international armed conflict could apply to internal armed conflicts through the recognition of belligerency, that doctrine was rapidly becoming obsolete.[75] By the time civil war broke out in Spain in 1936,

---

[71] *Instructions for the Government of Armies of the United States in the Field*, prepared by Francis Lieber, promulgated as General Orders No. 100 by President Lincoln, 24 April 1863. Reproduced in Dietrich Schindler and Jirí Toman (eds.), *The Laws of Armed Conflicts. A Collection of Conventions, Resolutions and Other Documents*, 3rd edn (Dordrecht, 1988), 3.

[72] Baxter saw them as particularly valuable evidence of the practice of States. See Richard R. Baxter, 'Multilateral Treaties as Evidence of Customary International Law' (1965–1966) 41 *BYIL* 275 at 282–283.

[73] For criticism of the Code see Percy Bordwell, *The Law of War Between Belligerents* (Chicago, 1908), 74. Rosemary Abi-Saab finds it ironic that the Code was thought of as providing an example of how the laws of war could be codified to apply to international conflicts, whereas today it is sought to apply the laws of international war to internal conflict. See 'Humanitarian Law and Internal Conflicts: The Evolution of Legal Concern' in Astrid J. M. Delissen and Gerard J. Tanja (eds.), *Humanitarian Law of Armed Conflict: Challenges Ahead: Essays in Honour of Frits Kalshoven* (Dordrecht, 1991), 209 at 210–211.

[74] E.g. the Convention on Duties and Rights of States in the Event of Civil Strife, signed at Havana on 20 February 1928, between the American States. Reproduced in Schindler and Toman, *The Laws of Armed Conflicts*, 893–896.

[75] Even by the late nineteenth century recognition of belligerency was becoming less common, largely due to the fact that third States were anxious to protect their own shipping from the exercise of belligerent rights. The United States certainly opted not to recognise belligerency in the conflicts in Cuba, Colombia, Haiti and Brazil. The decision not to recognise may have been dressed up as being because of the failure of the insurgents to meet certain criteria, but self-interest undoubtedly played a major role. Gasser states that the last recognition of belligerency granted by a government to insurgents within its territory was during the Boer War in 1902. See Hans-Peter

recognition of belligerency had fallen into such decline that it is difficult to equate the action of any State with the recognition of General Franco's forces as belligerents, despite the proportions of the struggle. Several States (e.g. Germany, Italy and Portugal) recognised Franco's regime as the *de jure* government, but it is unclear whether this entailed an implicit recognition of belligerency. The military intervention and aid afforded by those States would certainly have been contrary to the neutrality required by such recognition. Other European States, led by the United Kingdom, came to a non-intervention agreement, which may have given the impression of neutrality as required by the recognition of belligerency. Although they did offer some concessions to the Franco junta, all of the signatories explicitly denied, however, that the agreement was a recognition of belligerency, refusing to grant belligerent rights to either side.[76] Foreign States were prepared to recognise the existence of the insurrection, and many of their acts were clearly a recognition of insurgency,[77] but belligerency was denied[78] in order to prevent either side (especially the navally stronger insurgents) from exercising belligerent rights on the high seas.[79] The absence of a recognition of belligerency meant that the international laws of war were not necessarily applicable to the conflict, and a continuation of this policy (i.e. of not recognising

---

Gasser, 'International Humanitarian Law' in Hans Haug (ed.), *Humanity for All: The International Red Cross and Red Crescent Movement* (Berne, 1993), 491 at 559.

[76] For analyses of the attitude of third States to the Spanish Civil War see, for example, Luard, 'Civil Conflicts', 20–21; Hugh Thomas, 'The Spanish Civil War' in Luard, *Civil Wars*, 26; Castren, *Civil War*, 53 ff.; Ann van W. Thomas and A. J. Thomas Jr, 'International Legal Aspects of the Civil War in Spain, 1936–1939' in Falk, *Civil War*, 111; Herbert W. Briggs, 'Relations Officeuses and Intent to Recognise: British Recognition of Franco' (1940) 34 *AJIL* 47; Vernon A. O'Rourke, 'Recognition of Belligerency in the Spanish Civil War' (1937) 31 *AJIL* 398; and Smith, 'Spanish Civil War', 18.

[77] Lauterpacht states, in *Recognition*, 270–271, that, 'The two principal cases of recognition of insurgency as distinguished from recognition of belligerency ... are the cases of the Cuban War of Independence and the Spanish Civil War of 1936–9.'

[78] Padelford confirms, in *Spanish Civil Strife*, 18, that 'the fact of insurgency was generally admitted, but [that] recognition of belligerency was withheld by foreign states'. The policy of the United States included 'refusal to recognise belligerency and to countenance interference with American shipping on the high seas', whereas UK policy was that, whilst under normal circumstances recognition of belligerency may well have been afforded to the parties, the circumstances were not normal. The UK stated that 'recognition of the belligerency of the insurgents was withheld on the part of Great Britain and many other states'. See Padelford, *Spanish Civil Strife*, 187–188 and Lauterpacht, *Recognition*, 272.

[79] Charles De Visscher, *Theory and Reality in Public International Law*, trans. P. E. Corbett (Princeton, 1957), 237.

belligerency in situations where to do so would have been perfectly acceptable) would have held many dangers for the protection of those
embroiled in internal hostilities. The situation as regards the legal regulation of internal armed conflicts was therefore far from satisfactory.

This decline in the recognition of belligerency in State practice was
largely welcomed by States, who appeared unconcerned at the resultant
lack of any real legal regulation in such conflicts. Fortunately for those
in need of protection, however, other actors exist on the international
plane, capable of influencing both States and the future direction of
international law itself. The development of humanitarian law as applicable during internal armed conflict was thus able to continue, and it
is to this evolution that we now turn.

The development of humanitarian law for internal armed conflict

The question of the protection of victims and civilians is particularly
acute during internal armed conflict, since the established authorities
usually find it impossible to accept either regulation or help from out-
siders in favour of their own rebellious nationals. Apart from the con-
sensual recognition of belligerency, States were strongly opposed to any
compulsory international regulation of internal armed conflict. This did
not mean, however, that attempts were not still made to help such victims on humanitarian, rather than legal, grounds. No international body
has exerted as much influence in this direction as the Red Cross movement, and particularly the International Committee of the Red Cross
(ICRC). The institution has had a vital role to play in codifying the laws
of war, and although draft rules, regulations, reports, etc. as produced
and adopted by the ICRC are not legally binding on governments, they
are important in both clarifying the existing law and influencing its
future development.

The development of Red Cross interest

Even before the First World War, the ICRC had made appeals for the
international regulation of civil wars. Unfortunately, applications by the
ICRC or foreign Red Cross societies to engage in humanitarian relief
work were often regarded by States as an unfriendly attempt to interfere
in their domestic affairs, and this was still the prevailing attitude in 1912
when the Red Cross International Conference in Washington refused to

consider a draft suggesting that Red Cross societies provide aid for both sides during civil conflict. Several States were strongly opposed to this, particularly Russia, believing that it would be improper for the Red Cross to impose any duty upon itself to work for the benefit of rebels regarded as criminals by the laws of their land.[80]

The ICRC (along with national societies) was able, however, to take limited action in some subsequent internal conflicts,[81] and by 1921 had adopted a modest resolution affirming the right of all victims of civil wars to relief in conformity with the general principles of the Red Cross.[82] This was recognised in the 1928 revision of the Statute of the ICRC,[83] and enabled the organisation for the first time to induce both sides in the conflicts in Upper Silesia and Spain to give limited undertakings to respect the principles of the Geneva Conventions. Encouraged by this, a more substantial resolution was passed in 1938,[84] anticipating the application of all essential principles of the Geneva Conventions to internal armed conflicts. The Spanish Civil War had already served to underline the inadequacy of this extra-legal approach, however, and a conference to address the problem was in preparation as war broke out in 1939.

The path to the Conventions of 1949

After the Second World War, the ICRC again considered internal armed conflicts, striving towards the codification of legal principles for their regulation, and at the Preliminary Conference of National Red Cross Societies in 1946, a draft provision was considered which stated that, 'In case of armed conflict in the interior of a State, the Convention shall be equally applied by each of the adverse Parties, unless one of these

---

[80] Anton Schlögel, 'Civil War' (1970) 108 *Int Rev of the Red Cross* 123 at 125. See also Jean S. Pictet, *Commentary on the Geneva Conventions of 12 August 1949, Volume III* (Geneva, 1960), 29.

[81] Most notably those in Russia and Hungary, Pictet, *Commentary III*, 29; see also Schlögel, 'Civil War', 125 and Georges Abi-Saab, 'Non-international Armed Conflict', in UNESCO, *International Dimensions of Humanitarian Law* (Dordrecht, 1988), 217 at 219. On ICRC action in the Russian Revolution, see André Durand, *History of the International Committee of the Red Cross, Volume I: From Sarajevo to Hiroshima* (Geneva, 1984), 97–108.

[82] Resolution XIV of the 10th International Red Cross Conference, Geneva, 1921. See Schlögel, 'Civil War', 125–126.

[83] Article 4 of the Statute was revised to read as follows: 'The special role of the ICRC shall be . . . (d) to take action in its capacity as a neutral institution, especially in case of war, civil war or internal strife . . .'

[84] Resolution XIV of the 16th International Red Cross Conference, London, 1938. See Schlögel, 'Civil War', 126–127.

expressly declares its refusal to conform thereto.'[85] This attempted to place the practice of reciprocity on a legal footing and, despite well-founded fears that governments would object strongly to the idea, the 1947 Conference of Government Experts gave it a measure of support.[86] Their recommendation fell short of the Red Cross proposal, speaking only of applying the 'principles' of the Convention, and even then only on a reciprocal basis. But the proposal was not rejected out of hand, and on the strength of this the ICRC came up with a new draft for the 1948 International Conference in Stockholm. Based, perhaps naturally, more upon the 1946 Red Cross text than that of the Government Experts, it read as follows:

In all cases of armed conflict which are not of an international character, especially cases of civil war, colonial conflicts, or wars of religion, which may occur in the territory of one or more of the High Contracting Parties, the implementing of the principles of the present Convention shall be obligatory on each of the adversaries. The application of the Convention in these circumstances shall in nowise depend on the legal status of the parties to the conflict and shall have no effect on that status.[87]

This was altered slightly during the course of the Conference, the phrase 'especially cases of civil war, colonial conflicts, or wars of religion' being deleted, a provision on reciprocity being inserted, and the term 'provisions' replacing 'principles'. It was in this amended form that the draft provision finally came before the Diplomatic Conference of 1949.[88]

The drafting history of common Article 3

The original text before the 1949 Diplomatic Conference therefore stated that:

In all cases of armed conflict not of an international character which may occur in the territory of one or more of the High Contracting Parties, each of the

---

[85] Schlögel, 'Civil War', 127.

[86] The text adopted at the meeting of Government Experts was as follows: 'In case of civil war, in any part of the home or colonial territory of a Contracting Party, the principles of the Convention shall be equally applied by the said Party, subject to the adverse Party also conforming thereto.' See Schlögel, 'Civil War', 127.

[87] Pictet, *Commentary III*, 31.

[88] The Official Red Cross Commentaries fail to mention this third change – an important one, returning to the original proposal of the Preliminary Conference. (See Pictet, *Commentary III*, 31.) This oversight is pointed out by David A. Elder, 'The Historical Background of Common Article 3 of the Geneva Convention of 1949' (1979) 11 *Case W Res JIL* 37 at 43, and n. 18 therein. See also *Final Record of the Diplomatic Conference of Geneva of 1949* (Berne, 1951), vol. I.

Parties to the conflict shall be bound to implement the provisions of the present Convention, subject to the adverse Party likewise acting in adherence thereto. The Convention shall be applicable in those circumstances, whatever the legal status of the Parties to the conflict and without prejudice thereto.

The Joint Committee charged with studying the common Articles immediately split into two bodies of opinion, reflecting the conflict between State sovereignty and humanitarianism.[89] The first[90] was opposed to the draft Article in this form, fearing that it was too wide in application and failed to protect the rights of States adequately in favour of individual rights. It was felt that the Article would cover all forms of insurrection, rebellion and civil disorder, compelling a government in the throes of internal conflict to apply conventions concluded for the regulation of war, granting belligerent status to insurgents who may be no more than a small group of rebels. In addition, it was feared that criminals might form themselves into organisations in order to claim the protection of the Conventions on the pretext that their crimes were 'acts of war', hampering the government in legitimate measures of repression. There were also apparent problems in seeking to apply all provisions of the Conventions to internal armed conflicts, particularly with regard to Convention IV.[91]

The second body of opinion[92] accepted that the Article might be less than perfect, but supported its attempt to make humanitarian protection as complete as possible during internal armed conflict, suggesting that so-called 'bandits' might actually be disaffected patriots fighting for their independence and dignity – goals sanctioned by the international community. Their behaviour in the field would show whether they were mere criminals or true combatants complying with humanitarian principles, and therefore entitled to the protection of the

[89] Pictet, *Commentary III*, 32–33. For a comprehensive study and analysis of the arguments, proceedings and outcome of the Diplomatic Conference, see R. Abi-Saab, *Droit humanitaire et conflits internes. Origines et évolution de la reglementation internationale* (Paris, 1986); Elder, 'Historical Background', 41–54; and *Final Record of the Diplomatic Conference of Geneva of 1949* (Berne, 1951), vol. II-B.

[90] Including Australia, Canada, China, France, Greece, Italy, Spain, the United Kingdom and the United States.

[91] See the fears of the UK in *Final Record II-B*, 10, and Canada, who argued at 13 that, 'It would be inconceivable to suggest that even in a large-scale civil war supporters of the rebels could justifiably demand from the lawful Government that they be treated as protected persons under the Civilian Convention, although they were not living in the part of the country controlled by rebels. No lawful Government would be able to quell a rebellion under these circumstances.'

[92] Including Denmark, Hungary, Mexico, Norway, Romania and the USSR.

Conventions. It was also felt that the adoption of the proposal would not prevent a legitimate government from taking measures under its own laws for the repression of acts considered illegal, or dangerous to the order and security of the State.

The Swiss delegate therefore suggested that a sub-committee should deal with the definition of 'armed conflict' and draft a text seeking to reconcile the different viewpoints. A Special Committee was duly established, comprising Australia, Burma, France, Greece, Italy, Monaco, Norway, the Soviet Union, Switzerland, the United Kingdom, the United States and Uruguay. Several proposed amendments were placed before it,[93] many favouring some formal or factual criteria to be met before the Conventions were applicable to internal conflict,[94] fearing that States would otherwise be compelled to apply humanitarian obligations in cases of mere banditry and disorder. In contrast, supporters of the Stockholm Draft felt that the text already implied armed conflicts similar to those of international character, and not mere internal strife. The Special Committee thus took two votes before continuing, the first pronouncing in favour of extending the Convention to internal armed conflict, the second rejecting the Stockholm text in order to define more clearly those cases of internal armed conflict to which the Conventions should apply.[95]

Two options were then available to the Committee[96] – either to limit the cases of internal conflict to which the Conventions were to apply, or else to limit the provisions of the Conventions to be applied in those conflicts. This question was submitted to a working party,[97] which produced a draft[98] requiring each party to the conflict to apply all provisions of the Convention (except those dealing with the protecting power), the observance of which neither depended on, nor had any effect on, the

---

[93] By Australia, Canada, France, Greece, Hungary, Italy, Spain and the United States.

[94] Those by Australia, France, Spain and the United States. Italy, in contrast, proposed that, where the conflict was not covered by the French amendment (i.e. where the conflict did not resemble international conflict), only the principles of humanitarian law should apply to internal conflict, with no requirement of factual preconditions. For a brief summary of these positions, see *Final Record II-B*, 121, and Elder, 'Historical Background', 44–46.

[95] See records of the 3rd and 4th meetings of the Special Committee in *Final Record II-B*, 45. This clearer definition was never arrived at, leading to the problems outlined below in chapter 2, pp. 34–52.

[96] *Final Record II-B*, 122.

[97] Consisting of Australia, France, Norway, Switzerland and the United States.

[98] Reproduced as Annex A to the 7th Report of the Special Committee, *Final Record II-B*, 124.

legal status of the parties. Application depended on the formal criterion that the established government had recognised the belligerency of the adverse party,[99] or else that the adverse party could exhibit the characteristics of an engaged belligerent force.[100] Where those conditions were not met, the parties were to strive to reach agreement to bring into force some or all of the provisions of the Conventions, whilst at least respecting their underlying humanitarian principles at all times. The ICRC's right to offer humanitarian assistance was also explicitly included. The question of reciprocity was left unresolved, although the obligation presupposed that the adverse party had declared itself bound by the Conventions and the laws and customs of war in general.

This Draft was submitted to the Special Committee for consideration, but received little support.[101] In particular, France and the United Kingdom felt that it was impossible to extend automatically all of the provisions of the Conventions to internal conflicts as the Draft sought to do (again seeing particular problems with respect to Convention IV), whilst the ICRC delegate stated that, in his opinion, the draft text could not have applied in any recent internal conflict. The Soviet Union felt that it would only serve to make the application of the Conventions to internal conflict even more difficult, and Monaco argued not only that the text was too involved and indefinite, but that the initial aim of the Stockholm Draft to apply the complete Conventions to civil war had been unsound. Its delegate therefore proposed, with the support of the United Kingdom, that the Working Party be asked to redraft the text, determining which provisions were applicable in civil war.

The second draft of the Working Party comprised two draft Articles, the Civilians Convention (No. IV) receiving its own due to the difficulties involved in its application to internal armed conflicts.[102] Only one obligation was imposed upon the parties in this case, that of complying at all times with the humanitarian principles of the Convention. An appeal was included, however, to reach agreements to put into effect all or part of the Convention. With regard to the other three Conventions, the new Draft retained many of the features of the original: it still sought to bind each party to the conflict to apply all provisions of the Conventions in

---

[99] Based upon the Australian amendment.

[100] Those were the factual criteria suggested by France and the United States: for example, the possession of an organised military force under the control of a responsible civilian authority, with the capacity to ensure respect for the provisions of the Conventions.

[101] *Final Record II-B*, 46–50.

[102] See n. 91 above.

the case of conflicts sufficiently close to international conflicts (determined by the formal criteria outlined above); it still presupposed that the adverse party recognised its duty to comply with the Convention and the laws and customs of war; and, in cases where the criteria were not met, the parties were to seek to apply all or part of the Conventions by special agreement, whilst at all times being bound to respect at least the underlying humanitarian principles. The ICRC right of initiative was retained, and the application of the provision neither depended on nor affected the legal status of the parties.

This Draft again received an unsympathetic reception from the Special Committee:[103]

the sub-division of non-international conflicts into two categories would raise interminable discussions at the beginning of each civil, colonial, or other war as to whether it belonged to one or the other category; no jurisdiction had been provided for to determine whether the conditions for full application of the Conventions had been met in a specific case; ... in reality such a decision was left to the discretion of the *de jure* government; and ... the conditions in question would very seldom be fulfilled.[104]

It is certainly true that the object of the Conventions was to provide for their immediate and automatic application in cases of internal conflict, and not to leave the question of application up to the parties to the conflict.[105] As a result, several amendments were submitted, with only the French one receiving a significant level of support. It provided that:

In the case of an armed conflict not of an international character occurring in the territory of one of the High Contracting Parties, each Party to the conflict shall apply the provisions of the Preamble to the Convention for the Protection of Civilian Persons in Time of War. The Parties to the conflict should further endeavour to bring into force, by means of special agreements, all or part of the other provisions of the Convention for the Protection of Civilian Persons, likewise those of the Convention for the Relief of Wounded and Sick, the Convention Relative to the Treatment of Prisoners of War, and the Maritime Convention. The application of the foregoing provisions shall not affect the legal status of the Parties to the conflict.[106]

This was submitted to a second Working Party (consisting of France, Italy, Monaco, the Soviet Union and the United Kingdom) for examination, and, on the basis of the text, another draft Article was drawn up and

---

[103] 23rd and 24th meetings of the Special Committee, *Final Record II-B*, 76–79.
[104] *Final Record II-B*, 123.
[105] Despite the end result. See the opinion of the Soviet delegate, *Final Record II-B*, 79.
[106] Reproduced in 7th Report of the Special Committee, *Final Record II-B*, 123.

placed before the Special Committee. It again sought to bind each party to the conflict, retained the ICRC right of initiative, and provided that application of the provisions had no effect on the legal status of the parties. There were, however, some fundamental differences: the parties were bound to apply only the Conventions' most basic humanitarian principles rather than all provisions, their application set out in the form of a general requirement of humane treatment followed by a series of specific prohibitions, with the parties then being called upon to try to bring into force all or part of the other provisions through special agreements. A new provision also called expressly on the parties to the conflict to collect and care for the wounded and sick.

On presenting the text to the Special Committee, the French delegate pointed out that it offered in all cases the advantage of allowing automatic implementation of concrete and precise provisions which were the essence of the humanitarian rules to be observed during internal conflicts.[107] The main criticism was that it failed to take into account conflicts which were akin to international conflicts, and to which all of the provisions of Conventions I, II and III could reasonably be applied, although this was by no means accepted by all delegates.[108] The Soviet delegate furthermore felt that it was impossible to summarise in a few lines all of the provisions offering protection to war victims which were applicable in civil war, as the Working Party had tried to do, and instead put forward a proposal seeking to bind each party to an internal conflict to apply all provisions in each Convention guaranteeing humane treatment for victims without discrimination (although without clearly defining exactly which provisions were to be applied). Following a vote, however,[109] the Special Committee did make several minor amendments to the second Working Party's draft. The amended Article (now reading as common Article 3 does today) was nevertheless rejected when put to the vote.[110] The Special Committee therefore reverted to the second proposal of the first Working Party, and the amendments proposed thereto, but both were rejected, as was the original Stockholm Draft. Thus, despite agreement that protection should be extended to cover internal armed conflicts, no text outlining this had been found to be acceptable.

---

[107] 28th meeting of the Special Committee, *Final Record II-B*, 82.

[108] See *Final Record II-B*, 124.

[109] The proposal was rejected by one vote for to nine against.

[110] Five votes for to five against. The Uruguayan delegate felt that, as Chairman, he ought to refrain from voting, although he later made a statement that he was in support of the amended Article. See Annex G to 7th Report of the Special Committee, *Final Record II-B*, 127.

The Special Committee reported back to the Joint Committee accordingly, drawing its attention to three texts – the second draft of the first Working Party, the amended draft of the second Working Party, and the Soviet Proposal. The Joint Committee approved the amended draft of the second Working Party[111] and, when placed before the Plenary Meeting, it was adopted by thirty-four votes to twelve, with one abstention. The outcome was a compromise between those delegations (e.g. the Soviet Union) which felt that the humanitarian protection offered by the Article did not go far enough, and those delegations (e.g. Burma[112]) which feared either that the Article went too far, covering even minor disturbances, or else that it would act as an incitement to violence and conflict. The ICRC accepted that such compromise had been inevitable, but nevertheless gave the Article its full support,

because this text is simple and clear and has the merit of ensuring, in the case of civil war, at least the application of the humanitarian rules which are recognised by all civilized peoples. This text, therefore, without being a complete expression of the ideal which the International Committee has in view, ensures a minimum protection and – which is still more important – gives impartial humanitarian bodies, such as the International Committee of the Red Cross, means of intervention.[113]

Had the Conventions failed completely to mention civil war, the natural conclusion might have been that the Conference had not wished to draw up any regulations at all for the protection of victims of such conflicts. Despite the vehemence of the Burmese delegate, this was certainly not the case, and in the end common Article 3 was adopted by a large majority. It may not have fulfilled the hopes of all delegations but, as the Swiss delegate pointed out, 'half a loaf is better than no bread. A comparatively modest solution is certainly better than none.'[114]

[111] By twenty-one votes to six, with fourteen abstentions. The other two texts were rejected.
[112] Burma had consistently opposed the extension of the Conventions to insurgents who sought by undemocratic means to overthrow a legally constituted government by force, objecting to the legal status which it perceived them as being granted.
[113] *Final Record II-B*, 336–337.
[114] 19th Plenary Meeting, *Final Record II-B*, 335.

2　Article 3 common to the Geneva Conventions

The eventual outcome of the Diplomatic Conference was the first legal regulation of internal armed conflict to be contained in an international instrument – common Article 3. It provides that:

In case of armed conflict not of an international character occurring in the territory of one of the High Contracting Parties, each Party to the conflict shall be bound to apply, as a minimum, the following provisions:

(1) Persons taking no active part in the hostilities, including members of armed forces who have laid down their arms and those placed *hors de combat* by sickness, wounds, detention, or any other cause, shall in all circumstances be treated humanely, without any adverse distinction founded on race, colour, religion or faith, sex, birth or wealth, or any other similar criteria. To this end, the following acts are and shall remain prohibited at any time and in any place whatsoever with respect to the above-mentioned persons:

(a) violence to life and person, in particular murder of all kinds, mutilation, cruel treatment and torture;

(b) taking of hostages;

(c) outrages upon personal dignity, in particular, humiliating and degrading treatment;

(d) the passing of sentences and the carrying out of executions without previous judgment pronounced by a regularly constituted court affording all the judicial guarantees which are recognised as indispensable by civilised peoples.

(2) The wounded and sick shall be collected and cared for.

An impartial humanitarian body, such as the International Committee of the Red Cross, may offer its services to the Parties to the conflict.

The Parties to the conflict should further endeavour to bring into force, by means of special agreements, all or part of the other provisions of the present Convention.

The application of the preceding provisions shall not affect the legal status of the Parties to the conflict.

30

In the absence of a requirement to apply the actual provisions of the Geneva Conventions themselves, common Article 3 is an attempt to impose the underlying humanitarian principles of all four Conventions upon the parties to internal armed conflicts. As a result, it is frequently referred to as a 'Convention in miniature' or as a 'microcosm' of the Conventions as a whole.[1]

Scope of application

The question of which conflicts come within the scope of common Article 3 is clearly pivotal, and yet has been dogged by controversy. Of course this does not render the rules governing such conflicts redundant, but the problem lies as much in the identification of internal armed conflicts as in their legal regulation. The text of the Article itself states that it is applicable 'in the case of armed conflict not of an international character occurring in the territory of one of the High Contracting Parties'. Two separate criteria exist in this provision, one of which is markedly more straightforward than the other. To consider the less problematic element first, there is a positive requirement as regards the geographical location of the conflict, which must take place 'in the territory of one of the High Contracting Parties' (in the sense of being *limited* to the territory of a High Contracting Party). This poses no real difficulty – there are to date 189 States party to the Geneva Conventions,[2] which amounts to a virtually universal level of acceptance. As a result, there is very little territory in the world which does not belong to one of the High Contracting Parties.[3]

---

[1] Georges Abi-Saab, 'Non-international Armed Conflicts' in UNESCO, *International Dimensions of Humanitarian Law* (Dordrecht, 1988), 217 at 221; Gerald I. A. D. Draper, 'Humanitarian Law and Internal Armed Conflicts' (1983) 13 *GaJICL* 253 at 264; James E. Bond, *The Rules of Riot: Internal Conflict and the Law of War* (Princeton, 1974), 80–81; and Jean S. Pictet, *Commentary on the Geneva Conventions of 12 August 1949, Volume I* (Geneva, 1952), 48.

[2] As at 19 April 2001 (ICRC figures). All UN members are parties. The Marshall Islands and Nauru are the only parties to the ICJ Statute not party to the Geneva Conventions.

[3] Where an internal armed conflict does occur on such territory (e.g. the conflict which took place in Yemen in the 1960s, Yemen not being a party to the Geneva Conventions at that time), Article 3 itself is inapplicable, and conduct must be regulated by the customary law governing the hostilities. See Gerald I. A. D. Draper, 'The Geneva Conventions of 1949' (1965-i) 114 *Rec des Cours* 63 at 84. Of course, such wide acceptance would appear to render common Article 3 applicable to the conflict in any event as customary international law. See *Military and Paramilitary Activities In and Against Nicaragua (Nicaragua v US)* (Merits) 76 ILR 5, paragraph 218. This was

Much more important is the second part of the test, which requires that there be an 'armed conflict'. There is, as yet, no universally accepted definition of the term, and common Article 3 helps only in so far as it defines those conflicts to which it applies in a negative way, stating what they must not be (i.e. 'international in character') without offering further guidance as to their precise identification. The vital question is, therefore, what exactly is meant by 'armed conflict not of an international character'?

The lack of an authoritative definition or interpretation may not, however, be a problem after all. It might even be a blessing in disguise. The 'no-definition' school of thought believes that no definition, be it either general or enumerative, can be precise enough to cover all possible manifestations of a particular concept. Furthermore, an overly strict definition might in fact result in consequences far removed from the intentions of the framers, the text becoming more restrictive the more complete the definition tries to be.[4] As Pictet explained when examining the content of 'violence to life' and 'outrages upon personal dignity' prohibited by common Article 3:

it is always dangerous to go into too much detail – especially in this domain. However great the care taken in drawing up a list of all the various forms of infliction, it would never be possible to catch up with the imagination of future torturers who wished to satisfy their bestial instincts; and *the more specific and complete a list tries to be, the more restrictive it becomes.*[5]

It is possible, then, to see the open texture of common Article 3 as a strength rather than as a weakness, permitting humanitarian protection

---

recently reaffirmed by the Yugoslav Tribunal Appeals Chamber in *Prosecutor v Tadić* (Appeal on Jurisdiction) 35 ILM 32 (1996) at paragraph 98.

[4] Additional Protocol II suffers in this respect. See chapter 3, pp. 99–109.

[5] Jean S. Pictet, *Commentary on the Geneva Conventions of 12 August 1949, Volume III* (Geneva, 1960), 39 (emphasis added). See also C. H. M. Waldock, 'The Regulation of the Use of Force by Individual States in International Law' (1952-ii) 81 *Rec des Cours* 455 at 509 for an examination of the idea in relation to the definition of aggression. The Preparatory Committee for the International Criminal Court Statute also encountered this difficulty when discussing how to define the crimes within the Court's jurisdiction, with some delegations expressing 'the view that it might not be possible to envisage all of the various offences, that exhaustive definitions might excessively restrict the jurisdiction of the court and that in some instances it might be useful to retain an element of flexibility to permit the continuing development of the law'. See *Report of the Preparatory Committee on the Establishment of an International Criminal Court*, Volume I, UN Doc. A/51/22 (13 September 1996), at paragraph 55.

in as many situations as possible through a broad interpretation of its provisions.[6] Indeed, the ICRC has used this ambiguity in an effort to push the threshold of application as low as possible, seeking to take action in all situations of civil unrest,[7] particularly as regards access to prisoners and detainees to ensure humane treatment. As part of this strategy, Commissions of Experts have been formed periodically to clarify the law and consolidate humanitarian initiatives, with the Commission established in 1962 to examine the issue of aid for the victims of internal conflicts finding that, 'the existence of an armed conflict, within the meaning of article 3, cannot be denied if the hostile action, directed against the legal government [,] is of a collective character and consists of a minimum amount of organization'.[8]

In addition, the absence of an accepted definition of 'armed conflict' has not tended to cause too many problems in the sphere of international armed conflicts. Although there may be no agreement as to what constitutes an armed conflict, States generally recognise one when they see it. A detailed definition is not absolutely essential to realise that when the troops of different States are engaged in combat, then an armed conflict is in progress.[9] That is not to dispute that there are obviously some situations (e.g. low-intensity border incidents) where it is difficult to say for certain whether an armed conflict is in progress or not. The point is simply that, except at very low levels, it is not normally a problem to determine whether an international armed conflict exists.

Why, then, should there be a problem as regards internal armed conflict? The situation is markedly different in that the position within a State is not analogous to its international relations. It is clearly unusual

---

[6] Castren believed that it was the intention of the framers not to provide a definition. He asserted in *Civil War* (Helsinki, 1966), 85, that 'the Convention *deliberately* avoids [a definition] because this could lead to a restrictive interpretation' (emphasis added). Pictet also stated that there was a 'deliberate avoidance of a definition in Article 3'. See Howard S. Levie (ed.), *The Law of Non-international Armed Conflict* (Dordrecht, 1987), 41.

[7] G. Abi-Saab, 'Non-international Armed Conflicts', 224–225.

[8] ICRC, *Commission of Experts for the Study of the Question of Aid to the Victims of Internal Conflicts*, Geneva, 25–30 October 1962 (Geneva, 1962), 3, reproduced in G. Abi-Saab, 'Non-international Armed Conflicts', 225.

[9] Pictet suggests in *Commentary I* at 32, that, 'Any difference arising between two States and leading to the intervention of armed forces is an armed conflict within the meaning of Article 2 [of the Geneva Conventions], even if one of the Parties denies the existence of a state of war. It makes no difference how long the conflict lasts, or how much slaughter takes place.'

for a State to employ force in its relations with other States. In contrast, force is frequently used within the State's own territory and against its own citizens, ranging from everyday enforcement action against common criminals to large-scale operations aimed at quelling riots or other civil disturbances.[10] In an environment such as this, where force is a constant element, it is necessarily more difficult to determine when an armed conflict has come into being. Given the political factors which are bound to influence these circumstances,[11] and common Article 3's silence as regards the party who is to determine the existence or otherwise of an armed conflict (and indeed the method by which this determination is to be made), decisions on the issue will inevitably be made by the State itself. Naturally reluctant to bind themselves to rules which could be perceived as favouring political opponents, States can therefore hide behind the lack of a definition to prevent the application of humanitarian law by denying the very existence of armed conflict.[12]

This is clearly unsatisfactory from a humanitarian standpoint, and it seems desirable to employ some objective method to make it clear when an Article 3 conflict is in existence, rather than to leave the matter in the hands of national governments and their instincts for self-preservation. In that case, a formal definition of 'armed conflict not of an international character' would appear to be necessary. What criteria might be used to this end?

The elements of internal armed conflict

Several delegations at the Diplomatic Conference had pressed for certain factual criteria to be met before the Article became applicable. This view

---

[10] Taking the United Kingdom as an example, in the year ending 31 March 1998, a total of 6,826 police officers were qualified to carry firearms, and firearms were used in 12,134 operations (although they were discharged on only four occasions, resulting in two deaths). See *Fifth Periodic Report by the United Kingdom of Great Britain and Northern Ireland Under Article 40 of the International Covenant on Civil and Political Rights* (August 1999). These figures exclude Northern Ireland, where the police force is armed.

[11] E.g. the conflict between the right to rebel and the right to maintain public order. See Dan Ciobanu, 'The Concept and Determination of the Existence of Armed Conflicts not of an International Character' (1975) 58 *Rivista di Diritto Internazionale* 43 at 51, and Richard R. Baxter, 'Ius in Bello Interno: The Present and Future Law' in John N. Moore (ed.), *Law and Civil War in the Modern World* (Baltimore, 1974), 518 at 527.

[12] The lack of any method for the determination of the question makes it difficult to take issue with the government's denial of an armed conflict without this being perceived as intervening in the State's internal affairs. Of course, the test of whether an armed conflict exists or not is still objective in theory, so that the State's view ought not to be conclusive.

was eventually abandoned,[13] but the main threads running through the various suggestions can perhaps be useful in determining the issue of when Article 3 ought to apply. Pictet summarised them as follows:

(1) That the Party in revolt against the *de jure* Government possesses an organized military force, an authority responsible for its acts, acting within a determinate territory and having the means of respecting and ensuring respect for the Convention.

(2) That the legal Government is obliged to have recourse to the regular military forces against insurgents organized as military and in possession of a part of the national territory.

(3) (a) That the *de jure* Government has recognized the insurgents as belligerents; or

    (b) that it has claimed for itself the rights of a belligerent; or

    (c) that it has accorded the insurgents recognition as belligerents for the purposes only of the present Convention; or

    (d) that the dispute has been admitted to the agenda of the Security Council or the General Assembly of the United Nations as being a threat to international peace, a breach of the peace, or an act of aggression.

(4) (a) That the insurgents have an organization purporting to have the characteristics of a State.

    (b) That the insurgent civil authority exercises *de facto* authority over persons within a determinate territory.

    (c) That the armed forces act under the direction of the organized civil authority and are prepared to observe the ordinary laws of war.

    (d) That the insurgent civil authority agrees to be bound by the provisions of the Convention.[14]

These criteria are merely guidelines to assist in judging the existence of internal conflict, however, and may in fact set a far higher threshold of application than is actually required by the Article itself. The ICRC has successfully offered its services in situations falling below these requirements,[15] although there has been no indication from either those States concerned, or from the ICRC, that this was a result

---

[13] Rightly so, according to Pictet, *Commentary I*, 49. Perhaps confusingly, however, he goes on to state that they are nevertheless convenient criteria. They were certainly considered useful in the determination of the existence of an armed conflict by the International Criminal Tribunal for Rwanda. See *Prosecutor* v *Akayesu* (Case ICTR-96-4-T), Judgment of 2 September 1998, 37 ILM 1399 (1998) at paragraph 619.

[14] Pictet, *Commentary I*, 49–50.

[15] E.g. in Northern Ireland and Poland. See Hans Haug (ed.), *Humanity for All: The International Red Cross and Red Crescent Movement* (Berne, 1993), 145–162.

of the operation of common Article 3. Nonetheless, there is no question of the application of Article 3 being dependent upon any criteria other than the existence of an armed conflict in the territory of a High Contracting Party.

Organisation of the insurgents

It is widely accepted that a degree of organisation is required on the part of insurgents before an internal armed conflict can be said to exist under common Article 3. This follows from the fact that the insurgents must be a 'party' to an armed conflict – a random group of looters and rioters is undoubtedly difficult to accept as being a party to a serious conflict. The organisational requirement itself is not a controversial proposition, however. The difficulty arises not in stating that it must exist, but rather in determining the necessary level.

General consensus would appear to support the proposition that, in order for insurgents to be a 'party' to an internal armed conflict, the level of organisation required probably must be such that they are capable of carrying out the various obligations imposed upon them by Article 3, which imposes duties and obligations on all sides to the conflict. It is therefore difficult to accept that an armed conflict can exist without the rebels being capable of observing these obligations. This, in turn, seems unlikely without the insurgents being organised (at least to a degree) along military lines, including a responsible command structure and controlling authority.[16]

Despite the assertion that insurgents must be sufficiently organised to be capable of abiding by their humanitarian obligations, there have been suggestions that common Article 3 ought nevertheless to be applied as widely as possible.[17] These claims are based on the premise that it contains only those limited principles which ought to be observed in all conflicts and other cases of violence. Thus, Pictet asked: 'What Government would dare to claim before the world, in a case of civil disturbances which could justly be described as acts of mere banditry, that, Article 3 not being applicable, it was entitled to leave the wounded uncared for, to inflict torture and mutilations and to take hostages?'[18] That may be a reasonable question, but in the situation described, clearly

---

[16] See Draper, 'The Geneva Conventions', 90.

[17] Despite his claim that the proposed criteria were convenient, Pictet further suggested, in *Commentary I* at 49, that the Article ought to apply even where they were not met.

[18] Pictet, *Commentary I*, 50.

not amounting to an armed conflict (and thus outwith the scope of Article 3), international human rights law might impose various obligations upon the State concerned, preventing it from acting in the manner suggested.[19]

The danger with Pictet's viewpoint is that, without sufficient organisation on the part of the insurgents, the net of application would be spread too wide, so that Article 3 would include those conflicts which are too limited or small-scale to have been intended. It is, after all, generally accepted that low-intensity internal disturbances and tensions are excluded from the ambit of the provision.[20] Pictet would appear to have lost sight of the fact that the provisions of common Article 3 are binding on both sides.[21] Are we to expect a disorganised group of rioters to observe even the most basic laws of war in their relations with State authority? The spontaneous nature of the situation and the lack of organisation or responsible control is bound to make this highly improbable.[22] As Bond points out,[23] if, indeed, all Article 3 does is to impose 'a few essential rules which [a government] in fact respects daily, under its own laws, even when dealing with common criminals',[24] then one might wonder why so many scholars have been quite so vocal in its praise, or why so many States are opposed to its application. In fact, common Article 3 only imposes certain obligations, and even then only in certain

---

[19] At least to the extent that human rights obligations have not been derogated from, as permitted in certain circumstances. See Article 4 of the International Covenant on Civil and Political Rights, Article 15 of the European Convention on Human Rights and Article 27 of the American Convention on Human Rights, as discussed in chapter 5 below. Pictet seems to be concerned only with obligations upon the State.

[20] The Committee Report stated that, 'It was clear that this [armed conflict not of an international character] referred to civil war, and not to mere riot or disturbances caused by bandits.' See *Final Record II-B*, 129. Bond concluded that the delegates considered armed conflict not of an international character to be 'civil war by any other name, and voted in favour of applying a limited number of principles to a limited range of conflicts'. See Bond, *Rules of Riot*, 56–57.

[21] See below at pp. 52–58 for an examination of the legal basis for this.

[22] The Los Angeles Riots of 29 April–1 May 1992 are a good example of violence on a large scale, but in a context which was clearly not an internal armed conflict due to the absence of organisation on the part of the rioters, and their lack of any political objective. Although figures vary, during the course of the riots over 50 people were killed, over 2,000 were injured and approximately 13,000 were arrested. Around 10,000 members of the National Guard were deployed, and the total property damage has been estimated at $1 billion. See, for example, James D. Delk, *Fires and Furies: The LA Riots: What Really Happened* (Palm Springs, 1995).

[23] James E. Bond, 'Internal Conflict and Article 3 of the Geneva Conventions' (1971) 48 *Denver LJ* 263 at 270.

[24] Pictet, *Commentary I*, 49–50.

situations – – the Diplomatic Conference would never have accepted any-thing more onerous. In seeking a wide application of Article 3, Pictet seeks to expand its scope further than was intended.[25]

Colonel Draper furthermore suggested that the ability of insurgents to comply with their obligations under Article 3 not only implies a modicum of organisation, but also a degree of possession of national territory.[26] Control of territory also figures prominently in the criteria suggested at the Diplomatic Conference,[27] these suggestions coming al-most thirty years before Additional Protocol II went a step further and explicitly listed territorial control in Article 1 as a prerequisite for its application.[28] There would seem to be no doubt that territorial control would serve to strengthen the case for claiming that an Article 3 con-flict was in progress, as certain aspects of the obligations (e.g. care of the sick and wounded) would be particularly difficult otherwise. That is not to say that it would be impossible, however, and it would not appear that common Article 3 *cannot* apply where insurgents do not control part of the territory of the State. Where the insurgents are organised to the relevant level and in control of some territory, then Article 3 might well become applicable, assuming that any further required criteria are also met. The lack of territorial control, however, need not necessarily preclude its application.

Governmental use of armed forces

A second factor suggested was that, in order for common Article 3 to be applicable to a situation, the government must be forced to have re-course to regular armed forces in an effort to control the situation. On the face of it, this seems perfectly sensible – the very term 'armed con-flict' could easily be perceived as implying that the military are involved in active operations. The use of troops could accordingly be valuable ev-idence in the determination of whether a situation amounted to armed conflict. That might appear especially true from a peculiarly British per-spective, where in the majority of instances the police are unarmed.[29] In

---

[25] As Bond points out in *Rules of Riot* at 54, 'Pictet apparently believes that even one man brandishing a gun in another's face is non-international armed conflict within the meaning of Article 3.'

[26] Draper, 'The Geneva Conventions', 90.

[27] Pictet, *Commentary I*, 49–50.

[28] See chapter 3, pp. 105–107.

[29] Although this is not the case in Northern Ireland, where members of the Royal Ulster Constabulary routinely carry firearms. Northern Ireland, however, has never been treated as an Article 3 situation. See also n. 10 above.

those States which possess an armed police force, however, the question arises as to whether there is any substantial difference between the police using armed force against insurgents and the army doing likewise. Both are, after all, arms of State authority.

In addition, there may be other valid reasons for a State's use of the armed forces rather than the police. Where police resources are overstretched, or where the police force is engaged in industrial action, for example, State authorities may be faced with no option but to employ the armed forces to maintain peace and deal with any major disturbances. This would not, however, necessarily transform the situation into one of internal armed conflict. Equally, if the use of the military were to be accepted as a necessary criterion for the application of common Article 3, what would prevent a State from temporarily transferring troops into the police force, thus ensuring that the police had a vast arsenal with which to counter the insurgency?

The basic idea behind this as a proposed element of internal armed conflict is undoubtedly sound, in that Article 3 certainly ought to apply where an insurgency has become so intense and widespread that the State's armed forces are required to become involved in quelling the hostilities, but the current lack of a universal concept of police or armed forces, alongside the absence of any homogeneity as regards the methods of enforcement at their disposal, creates a problem.

Of even greater importance, however, is that nothing in common Article 3 defines internal armed conflict in terms of the parties involved. It is certainly not the case that, in order for Article 3 to be applicable to a situation, the conflict must simply be between government forces and some rebel organisation.[30] An armed conflict between two or more insurgent factions, whether or not it involves government troops or the police, can thus still be regulated by the Article. The armed conflict in Somalia at the time of writing should therefore be regulated by the provisions of common Article 3, although there have been no explicit statements by any of the parties that they recognise this as being the case.[31]

---

[30] Unlike Additional Protocol II, common Article 3 contains no requirement that the government be a party to the conflict (see chapter 3, pp. 103–105). Of course, in such circumstances the government is still likely to employ either the police or the army in an effort to restore or maintain order, thus eventually becoming involved (assuming that there is a government at all).

[31] The conflict is being fought between a number of armed factions (including the Somali Salvation Alliance, the Somali National Front, the United Somali Congress/Somali National Alliance, the Rahanweyu Resistance Army, the Somali

The fact that a conflict can come under Article 3 even where the government calls on neither the police nor the armed forces, and considering the other circumstances, innocent or otherwise, in which troops may be employed instead of police officers, makes it difficult to accept this as a suitable general indication of Article 3's relevance. The criterion was only intended as one among several, however, and not as a sufficient test on its own.

Recognition of belligerency

The organisation and territorial control aspects are strongly reminiscent of the traditional doctrine of recognition of belligerency, in that where situations existed meeting those requirements, States would previously have considered a grant of belligerency to the insurgent party.[32] Indeed, some delegates at the Diplomatic Conference did appear to have the recognition of belligerency in mind during discussion on Article 3, mentioning it as another possible criterion for the provision's application.[33]

How would a recognition of belligerency impact upon the application of common Article 3? It will be recalled that a recognition of belligerency by the State brought the entire *jus in bello* into operation. It might therefore seem reasonable to assume that where belligerent recognition has been awarded, the conflict becomes subject to all four Geneva Conventions in their entirety, as well as the rest of humanitarian law, and not simply common Article 3. Some scholars certainly support this proposition. Sir Hersch Lauterpacht, for example, writing in the seventh edition of *Oppenheim*, argued that:

> In so far as, in consequence of the recognition of the belligerency of the insurgents by the legitimate government, the conflict has assumed an international complexion, the rules of the Geneva Conventions apply *in toto* if the legitimate Government is a party to them and if the recognised insurgents formally accept and apply the provisions of these Conventions. Failing this the accepted customary rules of war apply as between the parties in this as in other spheres.[34]

National Movement and the Somali Salvation Democratic Front), without the involvement of the government formed in August 2000. See Project Ploughshares, *Armed Conflict Report 2000* (Ontario, 2000), available at http://www.ploughshares.ca/content/ACR/ACR00/ACR00-Somalia1.html.

[32] See above at pp. 5–18.

[33] Pictet, *Commentary I*, 49–50.

[34] Lassa F. L. Oppenheim, *International Law*, 7th edn, edited by Hersch Lauterpacht (London, 1952), vol. II, 211–212. See also Heather A. Wilson, *International Law and the Use of Force by National Liberation Movements* (Oxford, 1988), 45, and Castren, *Civil War*, 86.

The issue was never finally decided at the Diplomatic Conference, however, and this failure of the Conventions to deal with the recognition of belligerency and its consequences leaves us faced with a serious problem. As Colonel Draper explained: 'The root of the difficulty lies in the phrase "armed conflict not of an international character". Does it mean "international" by reference to the parties engaged in the conflict, or by reference to the legal consequences as to which rules of conduct are then brought to bear?'[35]

Two main arguments reject the proposition that a recognition of belligerency brings into operation the whole of humanitarian law rather than the provisions of Article 3 alone.[36] The first is that, although the Conventions themselves may be silent on the subject, the *travaux préparatoires* are clear – civil conflicts in which the rebels have been recognised as belligerents *were* intended to come within the scope of common Article 3. In fact, that situation was used as an illustration of the precise type of conflict which the Article was intended to regulate.[37] The second criticises the opinion advanced by Lauterpacht in *Oppenheim* as being flawed. Colonel Draper argued that it relies firstly on the understanding that the State involved is a party to the Geneva Conventions, and secondly, on the assumption that the insurgents recognised as belligerents are a 'Power which accepts and applies the Conventions', as provided for in common Article 2.[38] Article 2(3) is, however, simply inapplicable to insurgents. The 'Powers' envisaged by that provision are States which are not party to the Conventions but which nevertheless have the requisite capacity to become a party. Insurgents are not in that position, and if the argument in *Oppenheim* were to be accepted in relation to insurgents, then the application of humanitarian law to internal armed conflicts would have returned to the previous position of being reciprocal, instead of unilateral obligations placed on both parties, as required by the Conventions. This would clearly be contrary to the automatic application of common Article 3 as it was intended.[39]

Of course, the recognition of belligerency has fallen into disuse as a legal concept,[40] so the question will arise rarely, if ever. The point nevertheless remains that, even if such recognition were to occur, then

---

[35] Draper, 'Humanitarian Law', 267.

[36] See Gerald I. A. D. Draper, *The Red Cross Conventions of 1949* (London, 1958), 16–17.

[37] *Final Record II-B*, 121.

[38] See Draper, *The Red Cross Conventions*, 16, and 'Humanitarian Law', 266–268.

[39] See the discussion of reciprocity below at pp. 85–86, and also at pp. 107–108 and 175–176.

[40] See above at pp. 19–21.

provided that the State is a party to the Geneva Conventions, common Article 3 and not the Conventions as a whole will apply to the conflict. No other regulation of internal armed conflict exists within the Conventions, absent an agreement under Article 3(2).[41] If an Article 3(2) agreement is needed to render the whole of the Conventions applicable to internal armed conflict, then obviously Article 3 alone is ordinarily applicable. Indeed, the Swiss delegate stated that: 'The provisions embodied in Article [3] are intended to constitute a complete and exhaustive code of the obligations assumed by the contracting States in the event of non-international armed conflicts; apart from this text, no other article of the Conventions applies to civil wars.'[42] Where the State is not a party to the Conventions, a recognition of belligerency would still invoke the customary laws of war, although Article 3 would apply even here, since the International Court of Justice has stated that its provisions represent the 'general principles' of humanitarian law, and are thus applicable in every armed conflict.[43]

A definition at last?

Although the thrust of the above examination has been directed towards the lack of, or the difficulty in arriving at, an internationally accepted definition of 'internal armed conflict', the issue may recently have been settled. The Appeals Chamber of the International Criminal Tribunal for the Former Yugoslavia (ICTY) offered a definition of the term 'armed conflict' in 1997 in *Prosecutor v Tadić* (Appeal on Jurisdiction). It held that:

an armed conflict exists whenever there is a resort to armed force between States or protracted armed violence between governmental authorities and organized armed groups or between such groups within a State. International humanitarian law applies from the initiation of such conflicts and extends beyond the cessation of hostilities until a general conclusion of peace is reached; or, in the

[41] An interesting question arises as to whether a recognition of belligerency could be regarded as equivalent to an agreement under Article 3(2), or indeed whether an Article 3(2) agreement could represent an implicit recognition of belligerency. Both courses of action might ultimately render the whole of the *jus in bello* applicable to the conflict. The question would take on more significance, however, should either concept be used at all frequently in practice, although the parties to the conflict in Bosnia-Herzegovina did reach an agreement to apply common Article 3 and several other provisions of the Geneva Conventions (Agreement No. 1, 22 May 1992, Article 2, paragraphs 1–6). No effort was made, however, actually to put these provisions into practice.

[42] *Final Record II-B*, 336.

[43] As outlined above at n. 3. See also chapter 4, pp. 139–144, and references therein.

case of internal conflicts, a peaceful settlement is achieved. Until that moment, international humanitarian law continues to apply in the whole territory of the warring States or, in the case of internal conflicts, the whole territory under the control of a party, whether or not actual combat takes place there.[44]

The Appeals Chamber therefore took a more inclusive approach to the question, asserting that the threshold for the application of common Article 3 is actually relatively low. It saw the sole requirements for the existence of an internal armed conflict as being a state of protracted armed violence, involving organised non-governmental armed groups. No requirements that the insurgents exercise territorial control or meet their obligations under common Article 3 were included, and it was also felt to be unnecessary that the government be forced to employ its armed forces (or even that the government be a party to the conflict at all), or that the insurgents be recognised as belligerents. The required organisational aspect can probably be taken to equate with that mentioned above (i.e. a responsible command structure and a level of organisation which would allow the rebels to carry out their obligations under Article 3), while the requirement that violence must be protracted hints that it must have reached a certain level of intensity, although expressed in terms of the duration rather than the scale of the violence.[45] This certainly appears to be a fairly wide interpretation of 'internal armed conflict', seeking to ensure that common Article 3 has as broad an application as possible.

The Appeals Chamber's definition still means, however, that Article 3 does not apply as widely as Pictet would have wished.[46] Both requirements would preclude isolated or sporadic acts of violence, such as riots or other internal disturbances, from amounting to internal armed conflict, and so from being subject to the relevant humanitarian regulation. Article 3 itself is therefore irrelevant, but that is not to say that the standard of treatment which it represents is of no consequence in those situations. Pictet's suggestion that Article 3 should apply to situations not amounting to armed conflict cannot be supported, although he may have been right to an extent in that the standards contained within Article 3 remain applicable. As mentioned above, however, obligations to observe these standards would be placed on the State not by common Article 3 itself and thus by humanitarian law, but rather by

---

[44] *Tadić* (Jurisdiction) at paragraph 70.

[45] See chapter 3, pp. 106–107, on the issue of intensity as required by Article 1 of Additional Protocol II.

[46] See above at pp. 36–38.

international human rights law. Whether the content of Article 3 applies *qua* humanitarian law or human rights law is vitally important. It thus remains crucial for two reasons to determine whether an internal armed conflict exists.

First, although the provisions of common Article 3 might apply as human rights law, there is scope for States not to apply all of the protection through the mechanism of derogation, which permits them to avoid certain human rights obligations for reasons such as national security or a declared state of emergency. Of course, the right to derogate does not attach to all human rights provisions,[47] and several of the protections afforded by Article 3 cannot be derogated from.[48] Nevertheless, not all of the Article has non-derogable status,[49] and it is possible for States to make a case for not upholding all of the protection therein.

Secondly, human rights obligations are imposed upon States.[50] Only the humanitarian provisions of common Article 3 are binding equally

[47] See, for example, Article 4 of the International Covenant on Civil and Political Rights, 1966, where paragraph 2 outlines that no derogation is possible from Articles 6 (right to life), 7 (freedom from torture), 8 (prohibition of slavery), 11 (no imprisonment for failure to fulfil contractual obligation), 15 (non-retroactivity of criminal law), 16 (recognition before the law) and 18 (freedom of thought, conscience and religion). See also Article 15 of the European Convention on Human Rights and Article 27 of the American Convention on Human Rights.

[48] The right to life (Article 3(1)(a)), the prohibition of torture and other inhuman or degrading treatment or punishment (Article 3(1)(a) and (c)), and freedom from the retroactive application of penal laws (contained within Article 3(1)(d)).

[49] E.g. the judicial guarantees in Article 3(1)(d). The provision protects only those judicial guarantees which are 'recognised as indispensable', but none of the international human rights instruments make the right to a fair trial non-derogable.

[50] See, for example, *Abella v Argentina* (Report No. 55/97, Case 11.137, Inter-American Commission on Human Rights Annual Report 1997) where the Commission stated in paragraph 174 that 'Unlike human rights law which generally restrains only the abusive practices of State agents, Common Article 3's mandatory provisions expressly bind and apply *equally* to both parties to internal conflicts, i.e., government and dissident forces.' This might appear a backward-looking assertion considering individuals can now be held criminally responsible for war crimes, crimes against humanity and genocide, and the position is actually very difficult, with the Security Council and General Assembly both having been prepared to call for all parties to internal conflicts to observe human rights as well as humanitarian law obligations. In Resolution 1214 of 28 August 1998, for example, the Security Council '*Demands* that the Afghan factions put an end to discrimination against girls and women and other violations of human rights, as well as violations of international humanitarian law' and in Resolution 1270 of 22 October 1999, it '*Calls upon* all parties [to the conflict in Sierra Leone] to ensure safe and unhindered access of humanitarian assistance to those in need ... to guarantee the safety and security of humanitarian personnel and to respect strictly the relevant provisions of international humanitarian and human rights law'. The General Assembly, in the context of the conflict in Sudan, urged all parties 'To respect and protect human rights and

upon the insurgent parties.[51] Although the provisions of Article 3 might therefore be relevant as human rights law in situations not amounting to armed conflict, they are then obligations which only the State bears, and which have no binding force for the insurgents. This addresses the concern for the protection of insurgents at the hands of the State, but it must be unacceptable if international law is equally concerned with the treatment of government troops at the hands of insurgents.

It will be apparent, then, that whether an internal armed conflict has come into being is an important question, and whether the definition proffered by the Yugoslav Tribunal will come to be widely accepted and used by States remains to be seen, although it has been relied upon as authoritative in subsequent ICTY cases.[52] Nonetheless, as the Trial Chamber of the Rwanda Tribunal stated in *Prosecutor v Rutaganda*,[53] the definition of armed conflict offered by the ICTY is still 'termed in the abstract, and whether or not a situation can be described as an "armed conflict", meeting the criteria of Common Article 3, is to be decided upon on a case-by-case basis'. In the absence of an independent authority to decide on such matters, the question whether an internal armed conflict exists or not will be left to the State. It is unrealistic to expect parties involved in the situation to be either willing or capable of assessing the position objectively. Irrespective of how precise, or how general, the accepted definition of 'internal armed conflict' might be, so long as the definition contains certain criteria in order to determine the existence or otherwise of a conflict, it will always be open to States to claim that those criteria have not been met by the insurgents, thus preventing the application of humanitarian law. Until it is in the State's own interests to apply humanitarian law, the likelihood must be that it will be disregarded.

fundamental freedoms, to respect fully international humanitarian law ... and to ensure that those responsible for violations of human rights and international humanitarian law are brought to justice' (GA Resolution 54/182, 17 December 1999), and urged all parties to the Afghan conflict 'To respect fully all human rights and fundamental freedoms' (GA Resolution 54/185, 17 December 1999). International law seems likely to move towards the imposition of human rights obligations upon individuals as human rights in general assume greater horizontal effect. See Andrew Clapham, *Human Rights in the Private Sphere* (Oxford, 1993), in particular chapter 4.

[51] See pp. 52–58 below.

[52] *Prosecutor v Tadić*, Case IT-94-1-T (Judgment of 7 May 1997) 36 ILM 908 at paragraphs 561–568, *Prosecutor v Delalić, Mucić, Delić and Landžo*, Case IT-96-21-T (Judgment of 16 November 1998) at paragraph 183, and *Prosecutor v Furundžija*, Case IT-95-17/1-T (Judgment of 10 December 1998) 38 ILM 317 (1999) at paragraph 59.

[53] ICTR-96-3, Judgment of 6 December 1999, 39 ILM 557 (2000) at paragraph 91.

The upper threshold

Thus far, the focus of discussion has been at the lower end of the spectrum, and the issue of when internal disturbances cease to be just that, and actually become internal armed conflicts. A similar problem, however, arises at the other end of the scale, namely, when does internal armed conflict become *international* armed conflict? This is obviously an especially problematical issue since it requires one to assess the extent of participation in the conflict by one or more outside States. Having already grappled with the term 'armed conflict', what is vital in this situation is an understanding of the term 'not of an international character'. Unfortunately, as Farer points out, 'One of the most assured things that might be said about the words "not of an international character" is that no one can say with assurance precisely what meaning they were intended to convey.'[54] The question of just when third-party interference pushes a conflict beyond the internal threshold and into the sphere of international conflicts is vital in that internal armed conflicts (or conflicts confined to the territory of a single State) often amount to 'wars by proxy'.[55] Even in the post-Cold War international order, outside involvement in internal armed conflicts is still far from uncommon.

Academic opinion supports the proposition that foreign intervention can change the legal character of a conflict.[56] It is certainly difficult to accept that once various States are engaged in military operations against each other it remains a purely internal armed conflict. Hostilities between the armed forces of more than one State are clearly international and, as such, ought to be governed by all four Geneva Conventions, and not simply common Article 3.[57] In contrast, however, it was undoubtedly the intention of the framers of the Conventions that relations between States and insurgents be governed by Article 3 alone, and not the whole of humanitarian law (at least in the absence of an

---

[54] Tom J. Farer, 'The Humanitarian Laws of War in Civil Strife: Towards a Definition of "International Armed Conflict"' (1971) 7 *Rev Belge du Droit International* 20 at 26.

[55] G. Abi-Saab, 'Non-international Armed Conflicts', 222. Such struggles clearly can have characteristics of both internal and international armed conflict. A good example is the civil war fought in Yemen in the early 1960s which, although originally a purely Yemeni conflict, developed into a war essentially between Egypt and Saudi Arabia, fought on Yemeni territory.

[56] See Ciobanu, 'Concept and Determination', 54 and n. 33, where he outlines various bodies which take the view that foreign intervention (especially if military) does indeed transform the conflict.

[57] As the Appeals Chamber in *Tadić*, Case IT-94-1-A (Judgment of Appeals Chamber, 15 July 1999), stated at paragraph 84, 'It is indisputable that an armed conflict is international if it takes place between two or more States.'

Article 3(2) agreement).[58] Given the reluctance of States to accept openly even the limited measure of protection contained in common Article 3, however, it seems unlikely that outside interference on behalf of the insurgents would persuade the authorities to be any more charitable and implement the entire *jus in bello* against enemies within the State.

A solution is to employ the theory of pairings, enabling the application of different legal regimes between various parties according to their relationship with each other.[59] In the *Nicaragua* Case, for example, the International Court of Justice found that the relationship between the *Contras* and the United States was not such that the *Contras* were acting on behalf of the United States. Fighting between the *Contras* and the Nicaraguan Government was accordingly non-international and subject to common Article 3. The involvement of the United States itself, however, attracted the regulation applicable to international armed conflicts, hence the Geneva Conventions as a whole (or else the customary laws of war).[60] Internal conflict can thus co-exist with international conflict, and recent case law from the ICTY tends to confirm this.[61] In *Tadić* (Appeal on Jurisdiction), for example, the Appeals Chamber held that:

To the extent that the conflicts had been limited to clashes between the Bosnian Government forces and Bosnian Serb rebel forces in Bosnia-Herzegovina, as well as between the Croatian Government and Croatian Serb rebel forces in Krajina (Croatia), they had been internal (unless direct involvement of the Federal Republic of Yugoslavia (Serbia and Montenegro) could be proven).[62]

Whether a conflict is characterised as international therefore depends upon the direct involvement of more than one State. As outlined by the Appeals Chamber in the *Tadić* Appeal Judgment,

in case of an internal armed conflict breaking out on the territory of a State, it may become international (or, depending upon the circumstances, be international in character alongside an internal armed conflict) if (i) another State

[58] Or, less likely, a recognition of belligerency. See pp. 40–42 above.
[59] Just as the applicable legal regime between various parties to the conflict following the Iraqi invasion of Kuwait in 1991 was dependent upon whether or not those particular States were parties to Additional Protocol I. See Baxter, 'Ius in Bello Interno', for a discussion of how this theory would have applied in Vietnam.
[60] *Nicaragua* Case at paragraph 219. See also Theodor Meron, *Human Rights in Internal Strife: Their International Protection* (Cambridge, 1987), 47–48; and Hilaire McCoubrey and Nigel D. White, *International Law and Armed Conflict* (Aldershot, 1992), 319. The fact that such intervention is unlawful should not affect the law applicable to it.
[61] See chapter 4 below and Christopher J. Greenwood, 'War Crimes Proceedings Before the International Criminal Tribunal for the Former Yugoslavia' [1997] *Military LJ* 15.
[62] At paragraph 72.

intervenes in that conflict through its troops, or alternatively if (ii) some of the participants in the internal armed conflict act on behalf of that other State.[63]

The level of direct involvement required is, however, a controversial question, especially as regards determining whether insurgents are acting on behalf of another State. In several Rule 61 cases, the Yugoslav Tribunal found that the requisite level did exist, and so considered the constituent conflicts to be international in character.[64] In *Prosecutor v Rajić*, for example, the Tribunal stated that the conflict could be rendered international if Croatian troops had intervened significantly and continuously in the conflict in Bosnia, or if Croatia had exercised such control over Bosnian Croat forces as to make them agents of Croatia, and proceeded to find evidence of both.[65] The Tribunal furthermore held that the degree of control required to be exercised by Croatia over Bosnian Croat troops need not reach that required by the *Nicaragua* Case, since the issue was simply whether the armed conflict was international or internal in character, and not whether the conflict was actually the responsibility of Croatia.[66]

In *Prosecutor v Tadić* (Judgment), however, the Trial Chamber used a strict test of 'effective control', characterising the issue as:

whether, after 19 May 1992, the Federal Republic of Yugoslavia (Serbia and Montenegro), by its withdrawal from the territory of the Republic of Bosnia and Herzegovina and notwithstanding its continuing support for the VRS [Bosnian Serb Army], had sufficiently distanced itself from the VRS so that those forces

---

[63] At paragraph 84.

[64] *Prosecutor v Nikolić* 108 ILR 21 at 35–36; *Prosecutor v Mrksić, Radić and Sljivancanin* 108 ILR 53 at 62–63; *Prosecutor v Karadžić and Mladić* 108 ILR 86 at 131–132, where the Tribunal held that JNA involvement was such as to render the conflict in Bosnia international in its entirety; and *Prosecutor v Rajić* 108 ILR 142.

[65] 108 ILR 142 at 154–158.

[66] *Ibid.* The Appeals Chamber in *Tadić* (Appeal Judgment), in seeking to depart from the *Nicaragua* Case, confused the two issues. See Separate Opinion of Judge Shahabuddeen at paragraph 17, where he states that 'On the question of whether the United States was responsible for the delictual acts of the *contras*, the Appeals Chamber considered that *Nicaragua* was not correct and reviewed the general question of the responsibility of a state for the delictual acts of another. It appears to me, however, that the question does not arise in this case. The question, a distinguishable one, is whether the FRY was using force through the VRS against BH, not whether the FRY was responsible for any breaches of international humanitarian law committed by the VRS.' The test used in *Nicaragua* had been 'whether or not the relationship of the *contras* to the United States Government was so much one of dependence on the one side and control on the other that it would be right to equate the *contras*, for legal purposes, with an organ of the United States Government, or as acting on behalf of that Government'. (*Nicaragua* Case at paragraph 109.)

could not be regarded as *de facto* organs or agents of the VJ [Federal Yugoslav Army] and hence of the Federal Republic of Yugoslavia (Serbia and Montenegro).[67]

It was accepted that prior to 19 May 1992 the conflict had been international in character, but the Chamber decided that after that date the Bosnian Serbs were *not* agents of the Federal Republic of Yugoslavia, and that the conflict was therefore internal.[68] This seemed a dubious decision in light of much of the factual evidence,[69] and Presiding Judge McDonald, dissenting, found that 'at all times relevant to the indictment, the armed conflict ... was international in character'.[70] The Trial Chamber in the *Delalić* Case agreed with Judge McDonald, holding that the creation of the VRS had been merely a legal fiction, and that therefore 'the international armed conflict in Bosnia and Herzegovina, at least from April 1992, continued throughout that year and did not alter fundamentally in its nature'.[71]

The opinion of the majority in the *Tadić* Judgment regarding the character of the armed conflict in Bosnia-Herzegovina was, however, overturned on appeal. The Appeals Chamber accepted that in order for outside interference to transform the legal nature of a conflict, some notion of control was implicit, but felt that confusion reigned on the matter, and that it was therefore 'imperative to specify what degree of authority or control must be wielded by a foreign State over armed forces fighting on its behalf in order to render international an armed conflict which is *prima facie* internal'.[72] In what seems an unnecessary (and indeed dubious) piece of reasoning,[73] the Appeals Chamber decided to use the test of 'overall control',[74] holding that the 'effective control' test, as used

---

[67] Paragraph 587.

[68] Paragraphs 577–608.

[69] See *Tadić* (Appeal Judgment) at paragraphs 151–161.

[70] Dissenting Opinion, paragraph 1. She also questioned whether 'effective control' was indeed the test laid down by the *Nicaragua* Case, as the majority believed, arguing instead that the appropriate test was one of 'dependency and control'. See Part II of the Dissenting Opinion.

[71] *Prosecutor v Delalić* at paragraphs 233–234.

[72] *Tadić* (Appeal Judgment) at paragraphs 88–97.

[73] See *Tadić* (Appeal Judgment), Separate Opinion of Judge Shahabuddeen at paragraph 5: 'I ... appreciate the general direction taken by the judgement of the Appeals Chamber, but, so far as this case is concerned, I am unclear about the necessity to challenge *Nicaragua*. I am not certain whether it is being said that that much debated case does not show that there was an international armed conflict in this case. I think it does, and that on this point it was both right and adequate.' See also n. 66 above and accompanying text.

[74] At paragraph 146.

in the *Nicaragua* Case, was not persuasive for two reasons: first, to use a test of effective control is contrary to the very logic of the international law of State responsibility, and secondly, it is also inconsistent with judicial and State practice, both of which 'envisaged State responsibility in circumstances where a lower degree of control than that demanded by the *Nicaragua* test was exercised'.[75]

Despite doubts over its reasoning on the point, there can be little doubt that the result arrived at by the Appeals Chamber was the correct one. It found that, even after May 1992, the Bosnian Serb Army (VRS) and the Federal Yugoslav Army (VJ) did not amount to 'two separate armies in any genuine sense'.[76] The military objectives, strategies and tactics remained the same, the VJ provided extensive financial, logistical and other assistance, the military structure and ranks of the two armies were identical, several active elements of the VJ continued to be involved in fighting within Bosnia, and JNA operations planned from Belgrade continued to be carried out.[77] In fact, 'the link between the VJ and VRS clearly went far beyond mere coordination or cooperation between allies and in effect, the renamed Bosnian Serb Army still comprised one army under the command of the General Staff of the VJ in Belgrade'.[78] It was therefore finally concluded that 'the armed forces of the *Republica Srpska* were to be regarded as acting under the overall control of and on behalf of the FRY. Hence, even after 19 May 1992 the armed conflict in Bosnia and Herzegovina between the Bosnian Serbs and the central authorities of Bosnia and Herzegovina must be classified as an *international* armed conflict.'[79]

A distinction can be drawn, however, between the situation where foreign troops support rebels against government troops, and that

---

[75] At paragraph 124. For the detailed reasoning of the Appeals Chamber, see paragraphs 115–145. The Appeals Chamber nevertheless disagreed with Judge McDonald's Dissenting Opinion that the 'effective control' test was not the test actually used in the *Nicaragua* Case. It held in paragraph 112 that it was 'unclear whether the Court [in the Nicaragua Case was] propounding "effective control" as an alternative test to that of "dependence and control" set out earlier in paragraph 109, or [was] instead spelling out the requirements of the same test. The Appeals Chamber believes that the latter is the correct interpretation.' The 'overall control' test has since been followed in *Prosecutor v Aleksovski*, Case IT-95-14/1-A (Judgment on Appeal, 24 March 2000) at paragraphs 122–135.

[76] *Tadić* (Appeal Judgment) at paragraph 151.

[77] *Ibid.*

[78] *Ibid.*, at paragraph 152.

[79] *Ibid.*, at paragraph 162. This had important consequences for the accused as regards individual criminal responsibility for grave breaches of the Geneva Conventions under Article 2 of the ICTY Statute. See chapter 4.

where foreign troops support government troops against rebels. The latter is less clear in international law, but an example is the conflict in Afghanistan, where the Soviet Union intervened on behalf of the Government against several *mujahidin* groups. In that instance, the ICRC continued to treat the conflict as internal,[80] which must be correct where two States are not actually in conflict with each other.

To an extent, the question of whether a conflict has passed through the internal ceiling and become international may be losing its significance in any case. Certainly, recent developments have meant that the distinction between internal and international armed conflict is becoming less important. In fact, many of the customary law rules governing both would appear to be essentially the same.[81] This is especially true in light of the case law of the Yugoslav Tribunal which, in outlining the customary international law regulating internal armed conflict in the *Tadić* Case, asked:

Why protect civilians from belligerent violence, or ban rape, torture or the wanton destruction of hospitals, churches, museums or private property, as well as proscribe weapons causing unnecessary suffering when two sovereign States are engaged in war, and yet refrain from enacting the same bans or providing the same protection when armed violence has erupted 'only' within the territory of a single State? If international law, while of course duly safeguarding the legitimate interests of States, must gradually turn to the protection of human beings, it is only natural that the aforementioned dichotomy should gradually lose its weight.[82]

At the upper end of the spectrum, therefore, we would appear to be moving tentatively towards the position whereby the legal distinction between internal and international armed conflict is becoming outmoded. If this trend continues, then there may shortly be a body of international humanitarian law which applies to *all* armed conflicts.[83] What

[80] Hilaire McCoubrey, *International Humanitarian Law* (Aldershot, 1990), 175.
[81] See chapter 4.
[82] *Tadić* (Appeal on Jurisdiction) at paragraph 97. The Appeals Chamber nonetheless stressed at paragraph 126 that this did not result in the regulation of internal armed conflict by humanitarian law in its entirety. Several commentators disagree with the Appeals Chamber on this point. See below at pp. 146–147.
[83] Indeed, Cassese, in the memorandum of 22 March 1996 from the President of the ICTY to the members of the Preparatory Committee for the Establishment of the International Criminal Court, asserted at paragraph 11 that, 'there has been a convergence of two bodies of international law with the result that internal strife is now governed to a large extent by the rules and principles which had traditionally only applied to international conflicts...due largely to the following four factors: (1) the increase in the number of civil conflicts; (2) the increase in the level of cruelty of

will matter as regards legal regulation will not be whether an armed conflict is international or internal, but simply whether an armed conflict *per se* exists or not. This, however, serves only to return us to the initial problem of the lower threshold, in that if there is no armed conflict, humanitarian law is inapplicable.

The binding nature of common Article 3 for insurgents

Common Article 3 states clearly who is bound by its provisions – it is to be observed by 'each Party to the conflict'. There is nothing controversial in the imposition of obligations upon the contracting parties – they have chosen to become parties to the Convention and are bound by its terms accordingly. In contrast, the attempt also to bind insurgent parties poses the question how can common Article 3 impose binding obligations upon non-State parties who have never agreed to the Conventions and who, furthermore, have no capacity to become parties to the Conventions as such? Cassese considered it to be 'undisputed'[84] that Article 3 binds insurgents,[85] while the Belgian representative at the 1974–1977 Diplomatic Conference believed that Protocol II must be binding upon insurgents, since it was intended to develop and supplement common Article 3, which 'is binding on both States and rebels'.[86] There is clearly, then, a general acceptance by both scholars and States that common Article 3 binds States and insurgents alike. But on what basis?

Perhaps the best initial course of action is to turn to the law of treaties, as codified by the Vienna Convention on the Law of Treaties, 1969,[87] in order to examine the question of legal effects on non-parties. The Vienna

---

internal conflicts; (3) the increasing interdependence of States; and, (4) the influence of universal human rights standards'.

[84] Antonio Cassese, 'The Status of Rebels Under the 1977 Geneva Protocol on Non-international Armed Conflicts' (1981) 30 *ICLQ* 416 at 424.

[85] As do other scholars. See, for example, David A. Elder, 'The Historical Background of Common Article 3 of the Geneva Convention of 1949' (1979) 11 *Case W Res JIL* 37 at 55; Dietrich Schindler, 'The Different Types of Armed Conflicts According to the Geneva Conventions and Protocols' (1979-ii) 163 *Rec des Cours* 117 at 147; Jean S. Pictet, *Commentaries on the Geneva Conventions of 12 August 1949, Volumes I–IV* (Geneva, 1952–60); Draper, 'Humanitarian Law', 264, 'The Geneva Conventions', 84 and *The Red Cross Conventions*, 16–17; Baxter, 'Ius in Bello Interno', 527; and Castren, *Civil War*, 85.

[86] Cassese, 'Status of Rebels', 422–423.

[87] 1155 UNTS 331; 8 ILM 679 (1969).

Convention itself deals only with treaties between States,[88] but the general or customary international rules on the subject regulate the effect of treaties on any international subject, and the Convention is therefore still relevant as a codification of this law.[89] Articles 34–36 provide that treaties can impose rights and obligations upon third parties, provided that (a) it was the intention of the parties to the treaty to do so, and (b) the third party assents to these rights or obligations. As far as the first requirement is concerned, irrespective of how much attention was paid to the question of binding third parties in the *travaux préparatoires* of the 1949 Conventions, a clearer expression of the State parties' intentions cannot be found than the actual text of Article 3. It was obviously intended to create duties and rights for both States *and* insurgents. Turning to the second requirement, however, insurgents will not necessarily feel obliged to assent to this imposition and comply with the obligations contained in common Article 3. Obviously there are good reasons for doing so,[90] but the Article is designed to apply where rebels are attacking the established authority and they are unlikely to feel a strong sense of duty towards international obligations agreed to by the very government to which they are so violently opposed. Leaving aside the law of treaties, then, what other bases are there for the binding force of common Article 3 upon insurgents?

The legal justification most commonly advanced is the doctrine of legislative jurisdiction.[91] This provides that insurgents are bound as a result of the parent State's acceptance of the Convention, since upon ratification the Conventions become binding on all of a State's nationals,

---

[88] Article 1.

[89] As Cassese explains: 'this Convention relates only to States, while the customary rules on the matter have a broader scope, in that they govern the effects of treaties on *any international subject* taking the position of a third party vis-a-vis a treaty. However, it is appropriate to rely on the Convention, for two reasons. First, general international law does not differentiate ... between States and other international legal persons, as far as the effect of treaties between States are concerned. Secondly, the Vienna Convention does not deviate from that law; rather it codifies it and spells it out. Although it explicitly refers to treaties between States only ... it does not rule out the applicability of its provisions to other international entities. One can therefore legitimately draw on the Convention in order to ascertain the contents of general principles, to the extent that the Convention does not depart from them.' See 'Status of Rebels', 423.

[90] Reasons of humanity and reciprocity. For example, the rebels would hope to benefit through better treatment of their prisoners, etc. Adherence to Article 3 might also give the insurgents greater credibility in the eyes of the international community.

[91] First advanced by the Greek delegate, Agathocles. See *Final Record II-B*, 94.

the legally constituted government having the capacity to legislate for all nationals. There would certainly appear to be a '"strong indication that State practice assumes that these provisions . . . are binding also for the rebels . . ." and therefore one can point both to "State practice and *opinio juris*" to the effect that the "ratification of Art. 3 of the Geneva Conventions . . . has the effect that also rebels are bound"'.[92] Despite relatively broad acceptance of this argument,[93] it is politically untenable. Cassese remains equally unconvinced of its merits, considering it to be:

based on a misconception of the relationship between international and domestic law. Indisputably, in most States international treaties become part of domestic law upon ratification, but they then bind individuals and State authorities qua domestic law, and indeed benefit from all the judicial guarantees provided for by that legal system. However, what is at stake in the present case is not whether rebels are subjects of domestic law, but their legal standing in international law – their status vis-a-vis both the lawful Government and third States and the international community at large.[94]

It may seem unimportant whether the relevant provisions are applied under the aegis of domestic law or international law, so long as they are in fact applied. If the obligation to observe Article 3 is based upon domestic law, however, difficulties arise. While insurgents may have a commitment to observe certain humanitarian standards, they are unlikely to have any commitment to domestic law. Domestic legislation may even be declared null and void in the territory under insurgent control, including those rules incorporating the Geneva Conventions or common Article 3.[95] In such a situation, one might assume that the Article would no longer bind them, yet faced with clear international

---

[92] Cassese, 'Status of Rebels', 430 n. 34, quoting a letter from Bothe.

[93] See Jean S. Pictet, *Commentary on the Geneva Conventions of 12 August 1949, Volume II* (Geneva, 1960), 34. In this, the last of the ICRC Commentaries to be completed, legislative jurisdiction is cited in addition to the reason contained in the other Commentaries (see n. 96 below and accompanying text). In agreement are Baxter, 'Ius in Bello Interno', 527; Schindler, 'Different Types of Armed Conflicts', 151; Elder, 'Historical Background', 55; Morris Greenspan, *The Modern Law of Land Warfare* (Berkeley, 1959), 623; and Draper, 'The Geneva Conventions', 96, although he had previously held the view that 'When individuals group themselves in a particular way so that they become a party to an internal conflict, then they are given collectively a sufficient legal personality to enable them to be subject to the obligations and to hold rights conferred or imposed on them by these Conventions', as an extension of the conferring of rights and duties upon a *levée en masse*. See *The Red Cross Conventions*, 17.

[94] 'Status of Rebels', 429.

[95] *Ibid.*, 429–430.

opinion that insurgents *are* bound by Article 3, the legislative jurisdiction argument cannot explain the continuing legal impact of Article 3. Cassese's argument that insurgents are not bound by Article 3 under domestic law simply due to their parent State's acceptance of the Conventions therefore seems compelling.

An alternative justification for the binding force of Article 3 upon insurgents must therefore be found, and one possible solution is to assert that treaties entered into by States are binding upon insurgents provided the rebel authority exercises effective control over part of the national territory. Insurgents are then said to be bound by reason of the fact, and to the extent, that they purport to represent the State or part of it.[96] This would appear to follow logically from the fact that treaties are binding for a government which assumes power through revolution (as the insurgents would in case of victory), since the legal personality of the State remains unchanged.[97] It would be anomalous for insurgents to find themselves bound by the obligations of Article 3 on attaining overall control of the State, whereas up to that point the Article had been unconcerned with their actions, leaving them free to disregard even the most basic of obligations despite controlling a sizeable portion of the State's territory. A successor government is, after all, responsible for acts imputable to the revolutionary movement which establishes it, even if those acts occurred prior to the establishment of the government.[98] This possible legal basis would therefore appear to hold more water than the first until one considers that not all rebels

[96] Baxter, 'Ius in Bello Interno', 528; Schindler, 'Different Types of Armed Conflict', 151; and Elder, 'Historical Background', 55, cite this argument as an alternative. Pictet, *Commentary I*, 51 lists this as the only legal basis for the Article's binding force upon insurgents, unlike *Commentary II* (see n. 93 above).

[97] On State succession and treaties generally, see Ian Brownlie, *Principles of Public International Law*, 4th edn (Oxford, 1990), 667–673. Of course, in the case of secession or the gaining of independence by a former colony this may not be the case. It is accepted as part of general international law that the rule of non-transmissibility applies to decolonisation and other appearances of new States by either union or dissolution. See Brownlie, *Principles*, 668; Arnold D. McNair, *The Law of Treaties* (Oxford, 1938), chapter 37 on the position of new States and insurgents with regard to treaties; and the Vienna Convention on Succession of States in Respect of Treaties, 1978 ((1978) 72 *AJIL* 971). Contrary to this, however, the ICRC insisted during the civil war in the Congo that, even though the Congo was not a party to the Geneva Conventions, it was nevertheless bound as a former colony. See Donald W. McNemar, 'The Postindependence War in the Congo' in Richard A. Falk (ed.), *The International Law of Civil War* (Baltimore, 1971), 244 at 259.

[98] See, for example, *Short v Iran (US v Iran)* (1987) 16 Iran-US CTR 76 at paragraph 33 and ILC discussions on the issue (Draft Statutes on State Responsibility, Article 15), in particular the Special Rapporteur's First Report on State Responsibility, UN Doc.

do claim to represent the State. Indeed, the aim in many conflicts may be rather to create a new State, and to bind insurgents on this basis in such circumstances would be absurd.

A third hypothesis therefore holds that insurgents are bound by common Article 3 as individuals under international law. This could occur (provided the parent State is a party) through the Conventions which, 'in keeping with other developments in modern international law, [treat] persons and entities other than States as subjects of international rights and duties'.[99] Alternatively, the insurgents might be bound by customary international law, Article 3 merely being confirmation of the existing law which binds all States,[100] irrespective of their accession or otherwise to the Conventions. There is support for this in the work of several scholars,[101] and it is difficult to argue with the view that Article 3 represents customary international law in light of the judgment in the *Nicaragua* Case, where the International Court of Justice (ICJ) stated that:

Article 3 . . . defines certain rules to be applied in the armed conflicts of a non-international character. There is no doubt that, in the event of international armed conflicts, these rules also constitute a minimum yardstick, in addition to the more elaborate rules which are also to apply to international conflicts; and they are rules which, in the Court's opinion, reflect what the Court in 1949 called 'elementary considerations of humanity'.[102]

To the extent that common Article 3 represents customary law 'elementary considerations of humanity', might it even be *jus cogens*?[103] This is a difficult question, and it must always be remembered that

A/CN.4/490 (24 April 1998), and Report of the ILC on the Work of its 50th Session, GAOR 53rd Session, Supp. No. 10, UN Doc. A/53/10 and Corr. 1 (1998), paragraphs 409–451, in particular paragraphs 416–418 and 430–441.

[99] Oppenheim, *International Law*, vol. II, 211, n. 3.

[100] And thus, following the argument in Oppenheim, *International Law*, vol. II, 211, n. 3, all individuals.

[101] E.g. Greenspan, *Modern Land Warfare*, 624, and Castren, *Civil War*, 86. In this way it is possible for individuals to have obligations stemming directly from international law.

[102] At paragraph 218. See Rosemary Abi-Saab, 'Humanitarian Law and Internal Conflicts: The Evolution of Legal Concern' in Astrid J. M. Delissen and Gerard J. Tanja (eds.), *Humanitarian Law of Armed Conflict: Challenges Ahead: Essays in Honour of Frits Kalshoven* (Dordrecht, 1991), 209 at 223, and 'The "General Principles" of Humanitarian Law According to the International Court of Justice' (1987) 259 *Int Rev of the Red Cross* 367.

[103] This has been asserted by some writers, e.g. Schindler, 'Different Types of Armed Conflicts', 151 and Michael Bothe, 'Conflits armes internes et droit international humanitaire' (1978) 82 *Rev Generale de Droit International Public* 82 at 92. On *jus cogens* in general, see Frederick A. Mann, *Further Studies in International Law* (Oxford, 1990), 84–102; I. M. Sinclair, *The Vienna Convention on the Law of Treaties*, 2nd edn (Manchester, 1984), 203–226; L. Alexidze, 'Legal Nature of Jus Cogens in Contemporary International Law' (1981-iii) 172 *Rec des Cours* 218.

something does not become a peremptory norm simply because it is convenient that it should do so. It has been suggested that three groups of such norms exist: those protecting the foundations of law, peace and humanity; those rules of co-operation protecting fundamental common interests; and those protecting humanity to the extent of human dignity, personal and racial equality, life and personal freedom.[104] Common Article 3 clearly aims at the protection of humanity, and also falls within the definition of obligations *erga omnes* given in the *Barcelona Traction Case*[105] (i.e. those principles and rules governing the basic rights of the human person). This case has been criticised as making an arbitrary distinction between human rights and 'basic' human rights,[106] but those rights contained in Article 3 have nevertheless been authoritatively determined by the ICJ as being the most fundamental.

Article 53 of the Vienna Convention on the Law of Treaties states that a peremptory norm is 'a norm accepted and recognised by the international community of States as a whole as a norm from which no derogation is permitted and which can be modified only by a subsequent norm of general international law having the same character'. Are these criteria met by common Article 3? The answer is probably that they are, and that it is accordingly reasonable to regard Article 3 as a peremptory norm,[107] but the whole issue of *jus cogens* is so complex as to make reliance upon the concept dangerous. It would nevertheless appear that most theoretical difficulties can be overcome if the binding force of Article 3 for insurgents is removed from the domestic law sphere and instead applies directly through customary international law.[108] The

---

[104] Mann, *Further Studies*, 86–87.

[105] *Barcelona Traction Light and Power Company Limited*, Judgment, ICJ Rep (1970) 4, at paragraphs 33–35.

[106] Indeed, it has been suggested that the general law of human rights is now *jus cogens*. See Asbjörn Eide, 'The New Humanitarian Law in Non-international Armed Conflict' in Antonio Cassese (ed.), *The New Humanitarian Law of Armed Conflict* (Naples, 1979), 277 at 299. This assertion cannot be accepted. The right to a fair trial, for example, is implicitly determined to be non-basic by the *Barcelona Traction* Judgment (*ibid.*, at paragraph 91), and is derogable in human rights instruments, despite being listed in common Article 3.

[107] In *Prosecutor v Kupreškić*, Case IT-95-16-T (Judgment, 14 January 2000), the ICTY Trial Chamber expressed the opinion at paragraph 520 that 'most norms of international humanitarian law . . . are also peremptory norms of international law'. To the extent that common Article 3 represents the most fundamental tenets of humanitarian law, this would seem to support the proposition that its provisions do indeed represent *jus cogens*.

[108] Individuals can be, after all, the holders of rights and duties directly under international law, as confirmed by the *Nuremberg Trials* and, more recently, *Prosecutor v Tadić* (Jurisdiction) at paragraph 128 and *Tadić* (Judgment) at paragraphs 661–662.

rights and obligations thus devolve upon both the government and the rebels, neither of whom would have any excuse for failing to abide by them. Common Article 3 can thus be shown to be legally binding on all parties to an internal armed conflict. That being the case, what protection does it actually provide?

The content of common Article 3

Humane treatment

Common Article 3 begins with a wide-ranging requirement that 'Persons taking no active part in the hostilities, including members of armed forces who have laid down their arms and those placed *hors de combat* by sickness, wounds, detention, or any other cause, shall in all circumstances be treated humanely.' Two questions arise from this, the first concerning the personal field of the provision's application or, in other words, just who is covered by its terms. The issue of how to define those not taking part in hostilities was barely discussed by the Diplomatic Conference, although a British proposal to replace 'who' with 'which' in the phrase 'members of armed forces who have laid down their arms', in order to indicate that the armed forces as a whole must lay down their arms, was rejected.[109] Clearly, then, the Conventions refer to individuals rather than bodies of troops, and single soldiers who surrender are entitled to humane treatment whether or not the army of which they are members continues to fight.[110]

It would seem to be uncontroversial to assert that civilians are to receive the full protection of the Article, provided, of course, that they take no actual part in the armed conflict. The natural assumption that civilians are not members of the armed forces, and therefore not involved directly in the hostilities, however, can be a dangerous one in the context of internal armed conflict. In many internal conflicts there is an initial asymmetry between State forces and insurgent troops – government forces ordinarily have access to the full array of military equipment in the State, in contrast to the more limited resources available to the insurgents. To combat this, especially in the early stages of conflict, rebels are often forced to carry out armed operations in the form of a guerrilla war, depending upon the civilian population for support in

---

[109] 38th meeting of the Special Committee, *Final Record II-B*, 100.
[110] Pictet, *Commentary I*, 53, and *Commentary III*, 39.

terms of food, shelter and concealment.[111] It is accordingly difficult to distinguish between civilians and guerrilla fighters. In view of the humanitarian thrust of Article 3, however, the answer to this problem must be that where the insurgents have no recognisable armed forces as such,[112] the protection contained in the Article must be afforded to the entire civilian population.[113] This approach would lead to problems in dealing with insurgents who *have been* involved in hostilities, but who are not at a specific time, and it would be unrealistic to expect government troops not to take measures against rebels simply because they are not involved in an attack at that moment. The State's military equipment and personnel are, after all, easily identifiable and remain legitimate targets throughout the conflict. Nevertheless, where insurgents cannot be differentiated from civilians, they must cease to be legitimate targets. As the Inter-American Commission on Human Rights outlined in *Abella v Argentina*:

Common Article 3's basic purpose is to have certain minimum legal rules apply during hostilities for the protection of persons who do *not* or *no longer* take a *direct or active* part in the hostilities... Individual civilians are... covered by Common Article 3's safeguards when they are captured or otherwise subjected to the power of an adverse party, even if they had fought for the opposing party.
... the persons who participated in the attack on the military base were legitimate military targets only *for such time as they actively participated in the fighting.*[114]

Only those not involved in military operations are to receive the protection of common Article 3. Does it therefore follow that insurgents involved in an attack remain unprotected by the Geneva Conventions?

---

[111] Although, ironically, in Bosnia it was the 'rebels' (i.e. Serbs) who held these advantages rather than the Government.

[112] E.g. a lack of uniforms. Of course, they must still attain a certain level of organisation for there to be an armed conflict at all.

[113] In general terms. The population in such circumstances would not, of course, be entirely 'civilian'.

[114] Paragraphs 176 and 189. The ICTY likewise held with respect to persons held by Bosnian-Serb forces that, 'Whatever their involvement in hostilities prior to that time, each of these classes of persons cannot be said to have been taking an active part in the hostilities. Even... members of the armed forces of the Government of the Republic of Bosnia and Herzegovina otherwise engaged in hostile acts prior to capture... would be considered "members of armed forces" who are "placed *hors de combat* by detention".' See *Tadić* (Judgment) at paragraph 616. Insurgents returning to their village after an attack, for example, can still be considered to be involved in hostilities, however, and can be reasonably targeted – military operations clearly must include travel to and from the attack site, even though no action is taken in transit.

There are certainly no limitations placed upon the right of a State to put down a rebellion beyond those imposed by Article 3. Once rebel soldiers are captured, or otherwise rendered unable to continue fighting, however, they become *hors de combat* and are entitled to the same level of humane treatment as civilians. Their legal status nevertheless remains unchanged, exposing them to the full force of the State's criminal law.

A fear was also expressed by the Czechoslovakian delegate that Article 3 offered no protection for prisoners of war, on the basis that 'members of armed forces who have laid down their arms' does not cover those who have fallen into the hands of the enemy.[115] The Article does indeed fail to guarantee to prisoners of war all of the protections afforded by Geneva Convention III, but it does at least guarantee a minimum of humane treatment.[116] Prisoners of war are, after all, placed *hors de combat* through detention, if not 'any other cause'.

Humane treatment is not only to be afforded 'in all circumstances' (i.e. not reciprocally), but must also be observed 'without any adverse distinction founded on race, colour, religion or faith, sex, birth or wealth, or any other similar criteria'. Despite its inclusion in the corresponding provisions of various human rights instruments, no express mention is made in this context of national origin, and whether an adverse distinction on that basis would be acceptable may well depend on the purpose of the distinction. Whilst not necessarily the same as national origin, the ICRC did propose the inclusion of 'nationality' during the Diplomatic Conference, but met with strong opposition from France and the United States. France in particular felt that nationality could be a perfectly reasonable basis for discrimination, claiming that: 'It might be perfectly legal for a government to treat insurgents who were its own nationals differently from foreigners taking part in a civil war. The latter might be looked on as being more guilty than nationals of the country concerned, or they might, on the other hand, be treated less severely or merely regarded as subject to deportation.'[117] This seems, *prima facie*, a valid argument, and it may be acceptable for nationality to be used as a distinguishing tool in judicial matters, allowing nationals of one State or another to receive a more severe (although always humane) punishment than other nationals participating in the conflict. Such a distinction does not represent adverse discrimination as envisaged by common Article 3, however. There is no suggestion that nationality or

---

[115] *Final Record II-B*, 334.
[116] See the statement of the Swiss delegate, *ibid.*, 336.
[117] *Ibid.*, 94.

national origin be used to discriminate in humanitarian matters.[118] It would indeed be 'the very denial of the spirit of the Geneva Conventions to avail oneself of the fact that the criterion of nationality had been set aside as a pretext for treating foreigners, in a civil war, in a manner incompatible with the requirements of humane treatment, for torturing them, or for leaving them to die of hunger'.[119] As far as the guarantee of humane treatment is concerned, nationality and national origin are thus subsumed in the safety net of 'any other similar criteria'.

The second question to arise concerns the issue of what actually constitutes 'humane treatment'. The *travaux préparatoires* offer little help in determining the extent of this obligation, although the ICRC Commentaries suggest that a definition is unnecessary, the phrase having entered sufficiently into everyday parlance as to be understood.[120] Of course, the concept of humane treatment will not always be an objective one, and might vary according to circumstances such as the climate and the level of treatment practically feasible.[121] The ideological and social backgrounds of the parties to the conflict are also bound to be reflected.[122] An international minimum standard of treatment might therefore seem desirable, but worldwide inter-cultural agreement seems unlikely. Article 3(1) instead takes the easier approach of outlining behaviour which falls short of humane treatment through a list of explicit prohibitions.[123] Those proscribed activities, contained in paragraphs (a) to (d), 'are and shall remain prohibited at any time and in any place whatsoever', illustrating the stringency of the ban – there can be no excuse for such behaviour, and these acts may not be justified even as belligerent reprisals.[124] Paragraph (c), however, prohibiting 'outrages upon personal dignity, in particular, humiliating and

---

[118] Elder, 'Historical Background', 61–62.

[119] Pictet, *Commentary I*, 56.

[120] *Ibid.*, 53.

[121] *Ibid.*

[122] Illustrated by Elder, 'Historical Background', 60.

[123] The Burmese delegate had considered the four prohibitions to be unnecessary, since there could never be any reason to treat those persons taking no part in hostilities other than humanely. This was clearly a minority (and rather idealistic) view, however, and came from the delegate who believed that 'no Government of an independent country can, or will ever, be inhuman or cruel in its actions towards its own nationals'. See 18th Plenary Meeting, *Final Record II-B*, 329.

[124] See Christopher J. Greenwood, 'The Twilight of the Law of Belligerent Reprisals' (1989) 20 *NYIL* 35, reprisals during internal conflicts being covered at 67–68. For a discussion of belligerent reprisals during internal armed conflict, see pp. 237–243 below.

degrading treatment', has been criticised as a strange bedfellow of the other three paragraphs,

[seeming] upon superficial analysis to be an anachronism of chivalry, somewhat out of place in a listing of proscribed inhumane activities. These acts do not endanger the physical or mental health of prisoners. Furthermore they may not be practicably capable of regulation. But is it not somewhat anomalous to proscribe such treatment while allowing the death penalty if not capriciously executed?[125]

It is possible to take issue with the argument that humiliating or degrading treatment has no effect on the mental health of the prisoner and that it may be incapable of regulation, but the thrust of the underlying argument, certainly with respect to executions, is quite correct. To have argued against the provision's inclusion at the Diplomatic Conference on that basis would have been churlish, however, flying in the face of the recently agreed Universal Declaration of Human Rights. Indeed, this attitude has continued through many more recent international treaties (particularly in the field of human rights), all of which outlaw not only torture, but also inhuman or degrading treatment.[126]

Some might also consider the provisions of paragraphs (b) and (d) surprising, in that the ICRC admits that these practices (i.e. the taking of hostages and passing of summary sentences) are common in wartime.[127] Their inclusion is explained by reason of the fact that they are 'nevertheless shocking to the civilised mind' and, like belligerent reprisals, contrary to the modern idea of justice, being based on the principle of collective responsibility.[128] Reprisals *per se* are not shocking, and are not always illegal. The shooting or inhumane treatment of hostages by way of reprisal is, however, unlawful, and it may well be this that the ICRC had in mind.

Paragraph (2), outlining protection for the wounded and sick, elicited virtually no debate at the Diplomatic Conference. The ICRC considered it to be 'concise and particularly forceful. It expresses a categorical obligation which cannot be restricted and needs no explanation.'[129] In

---

[125] Elder, 'Historical Background', 63.
[126] See Universal Declaration of Human Rights, Article 5; International Covenant on Civil and Political Rights, Article 7; European Convention on Human Rights, Article 3; and the Convention Against Torture and Other Cruel, Inhuman or Degrading Treatment or Punishment.
[127] Pictet, *Commentary I*, 54.
[128] *Ibid.*
[129] *Ibid.*, 56.

reflecting the continuing humanitarian ideals of the Red Cross movement, it received no explanation or criticism, the terseness of the
wording serving only to illustrate the absolute nature of a provision
acceptable to all.

The right of humanitarian initiative

This provision was vitally important to the ICRC as well as various delegations, yet it was achieved in relatively minimalist fashion. A proposal by the United States to place the right on a more compulsory
footing was rejected,[130] the ICRC asserting that the strength of the organisation lay in its independence, which would be compromised if
it were to be mentioned in a more mandatory provision. In fact, the
Soviet proposal eventually rejected by the Diplomatic Conference[131]
made no mention of the right of humanitarian initiative whatsoever,
on the basis that the ICRC would always be free to offer its services
in any case.[132] The second sentence of paragraph (2) therefore simply
states that 'An impartial humanitarian body, such as the International
Committee of the Red Cross, may offer its services to the Parties to the
conflict.'

Experience has shown that the offer of humanitarian assistance was
often considered a hostile act of interference, and common Article 3
prevents such an inference by placing the offer on a formal footing.
The ICRC, or any similar organisation, is thus legally entitled to offer
assistance, although States of course are under no obligation to accept,
and may reject any such offer.

Special agreements

The penultimate sentence of Article 3, providing that 'The Parties to
the conflict should further endeavour to bring into force, by means of
special agreements, all or part of the other provisions of the present
Convention', underlines the fact that parties to an internal conflict are

---

[130] The proposal was worded as follows: 'An impartial humanitarian body, such as the
International Committee of the Red Cross, *shall be requested* to furnish its services to
the Parties to the conflict' (emphasis added). *Final Record II-B*, 100–101. The same
delegate had previously suggested that it might be more appropriate to provide that
'the Parties to the conflict *should accept the offer*' of the ICRC. See *Final Record II-B*, 83.
[131] See above at pp. 28–29.
[132] *Final Record II-B*, 98.

bound only to observe Article 3, remaining free to disregard the entirety of the remaining provisions in each Convention.[133]

The Czechoslovakian delegate saw the provision merely as an appeal,[134] and the Soviet delegate had been critical throughout the Conference of such statements as failing to constitute any legal obligation. Pictet's ICRC Commentaries to the Geneva Conventions, however, suggest that the parties are in fact *bound* to seek agreements in this regard. *Commentary I* states that the parties are 'under an obligation' to try to bring about the fuller application of the Conventions,[135] the obligation presumably being to make an effort to reach an agreement in good faith. It is nevertheless accepted that the government remains free with respect to its final decision on the matter.[136] *Commentary III*, however, states that the government '*must* endeavour' to reach such special agreements.[137] This cannot be the case. Stating that the parties 'should' try to reach such agreements is quite different from asserting that they 'must'. At most, it could perhaps be accepted that governments have a moral duty to seek such agreements,[138] but this certainly does not amount to a legal obligation, which was never the intention of the Diplomatic Conference.

The purpose of the provision can be seen as not only to seek an application of the Conventions which is as comprehensive as possible, but also to provide a possible solution to one of the main problems regarding the legal regulation of internal armed conflict – namely that conflict within a State can move through several different phases over time, expanding and contracting in scale and intensity. Small groups of individuals can eventually become parties to full-blown civil war. Agreements as envisaged by Article 3 would thus enable the shifting intensity of hostilities to be met, adapting the legal regime to meet the specific circumstances and harking back to the idea expressed at the Diplomatic Conference that some civil wars are sufficiently close to international armed conflict in severity to merit the application of most, if not all, of the Geneva Conventions. Of course, such agreements are seldom made,

---

[133] Pictet, *Commentary I*, 59. See also the opinion of the Special Committee as expressed by the Swiss delegate, *Final Record II-B*, 36–37.

[134] *Final Record II-B*, 334; Elder, 'Historical Background', 67.

[135] Pictet, *Commentary I*, 59.

[136] *Ibid.*, 60.

[137] Pictet, *Commentary III*, 43 (emphasis added). Castren, *Civil War*, 85, states that the provision 'presupposes' that the parties will endeavour to bring the whole of humanitarian law into force.

[138] As Pictet suggests, *Commentary III*, 42.

especially where one side perceives itself to be in the ascendancy. This is unfortunate, since where a conflict reaches the proportions rendering a special agreement desirable, the final outcome is likely to be uncertain and much could be gained by both sides through the fuller application of humanitarian law in those circumstances.

Effect on legal status

The final clause of common Article 3 asserts that 'The application of the preceding provisions shall not affect the legal status of the Parties to the conflict.' Its inclusion was absolutely vital. The provision was retained throughout the entire drafting history of the Article, and is commonly regarded as the price demanded by the delegates for the Article's adoption, easing the fear that a government's capacity to suppress internal revolt would be interfered with. The application of the Article does not therefore constitute any recognition by the government that the insurgents have any authority, and certainly does not amount to a recognition of belligerency.[139] Insurgents remain insurgents in the context of domestic law, and rebellions may be suppressed and insurgents tried accordingly.[140]

Despite the apparent clarity of this provision, it has been suggested that it might actually fail to realise its objective. Even during the Diplomatic Conference it was seen as:

an attempt to safeguard the legal status of the *de jure* government. I say it is only a bait – but it is a bait – which I hope will fail in its object. Whether or not you safeguard the legal status of the *de jure* government, the mere inclusion of this Article in an international Convention will automatically give the insurgents a status as high as the legal status which is denied to them. It can easily be imagined that this paragraph is going to be an encouragement and an incentive to the insurgents.[141]

Indeed scholars have since argued that, despite the obvious intention of the framers of the Conventions, Article 3 *must* confer a measure of

---

[139] To underline this fact, the Conference agreed a resolution stating that 'The Conference consider that the conditions under which a Party to a conflict can be recognised as a belligerent by Powers not taking part in this conflict, are governed by the general rules of international law on the subject and are in no way modified by the Geneva Conventions.' *Final Record of the Diplomatic Conference of Geneva of 1949* (Berne, 1951), vol. I, 362.

[140] Pictet, *Commentary I*, 60–61; Elder, 'Historical Background', 68; Draper, 'Humanitarian Law', 271, and 'The Geneva Conventions', 93.

[141] Statement of the Burmese delegate, 18th Plenary Meeting, *Final Record II-B*, 330.

international legal personality upon the insurgents, at least to the extent that they become the holders of rights and obligations under the Article.[142] This might explain the general reluctance on the part of governments to admit its applicability. It must be feared that an acceptance of the relevance of Article 3 would send the wrong signals to the rest of the international community – signals that the State is no longer capable of maintaining order, and that the situation has become so serious that the insurgents have achieved some international status or personality akin to that of belligerents. As Greenberg explains, 'In a revolutionary war . . . status is the prize for which fighting is waged. Thus, in spite of the plea contained in Article 3 of the Geneva Conventions to put aside (at least to some extent) questions of status, this politically is impossible.'[143]

In wars of self-determination or secession in particular, rebels are keen to gain some perceived measure of international status, and yet, ironically, it is for that very reason that they are likely to reject the application of Article 3 to the conflict. To accept that the struggle comes within the scope of common Article 3 is to accept that it is *internal* in nature. Insurgents are perhaps more likely to claim the application of all four Geneva Conventions, indicating the belief that the conflict should instead be classed as international.[144] This would be perfectly acceptable should the rebels then make an effort to apply the actual provisions of the Conventions, resulting in greater protection than that offered by Article 3 alone, but such an outcome is unlikely where the State refuses to accept that even Article 3 is applicable. Rebels are understandably prepared to treat the conflict as international in terms of observing humanitarian law only if the State does likewise.

Insurgents are likely to be averse to the acceptance of Article 3 in at least two other respects. As already outlined, the initial position in most internal armed conflicts is weighted against them. The State ordinarily has at its disposal substantial military equipment, firepower and personnel, so that unless rebels are numerous and well equipped their only real option is guerrilla war. If they were to accept the relevance of Article 3, foregoing the use of terror and subversion, they would in

---

[142] G. Abi-Saab, 'Non-international Armed Conflicts', 223–224; Castren, *Civil War*, 87.

[143] Eldon van C. Greenberg, 'Law and the Conduct of the Algerian Revolution' (1970) 11 *Harvard ILJ* 37 at 70–71.

[144] Thus in the Algerian conflict the FLN finally sought the application of all four Conventions. (See below at pp. 69–72.) Of course, wars of national liberation are now classed as international by Additional Protocol I of 1977, Article 1(4).

all likelihood be crushed, but States, perhaps understandably, may be reluctant to adhere to rules which their opponents are blatantly disregarding. Finally, if the insurgents are to receive no international legal personality from common Article 3, they may also be tempted to disregard the terms of the Article given that its observance might in turn be used as evidence against them in a trial under domestic criminal law.[145]

Common Article 3 in practice

The practical application of common Article 3 is widely perceived as having been disappointing, to say the least. One scholar, writing in 1978, even claimed that it had never been applied in any situation to date, despite numerous civil wars exceeding the minimum threshold.[146] Governments are equally aware that Article 3 has failed to fulfil its purpose to a large extent, and during discussions at the Diplomatic Conference of 1974–1977, several delegates condemned the record of application achieved by the Article. An American delegate, for example, believed its non-observance to be 'an almost universal phenomenon',[147]

---

[145] Although politically it may be unwise to prosecute insurgents at the close of hostilities, since this can lead to ill-feeling and tension at a time when reconciliation ought to be paramount. Often some sort of amnesty has been seen as the best option, as in South Africa. Addressing fears that 'the amnesty provision might...encourage impunity because it seemed to sacrifice justice', the South African Truth and Reconciliation Commission's Chairman, Archbishop Desmond Tutu, explained that, 'The amnesty applicant has to admit responsibility for the act for which amnesty is being sought, thus dealing with the matter of impunity. Furthermore, apart from the most exceptional circumstances, the matter is dealt with in a public hearing. The applicant must therefore make his admissions in the full glare of publicity. Often this is the first time that an applicant's family and community learn that an apparently decent man was, for instance, a callous torturer or a member of a ruthless death squad that assassinated many opponents of the previous regime. There is, therefore, a price to be paid. Public disclosure results in public shaming...Certainly amnesty cannot be viewed as justice if we think of justice only as retributive and punitive in nature. We believe, however, that there is another kind of justice – a restorative justice which is concerned not so much with punishment as correcting imbalances, restoring relationships – with healing, harmony and reconciliation.' See 'Foreword by Chairman' in Truth and Reconciliation Commission of South Africa, *Truth and Reconciliation Commission Report* (Basingstoke, 1999), vol. I, 8–9.

[146] K. Edwin Kilgore, 'Geneva Convention Signatories Clarify Applicability of Laws of War to Internal Armed Conflict' (1978) 8 *Ga JICL* 941 at 945.

[147] Mr Reed, *Official Records of the Diplomatic Conference on the Reaffirmation and Development of International Humanitarian Law Applicable in Armed Conflicts, Geneva (1974–1977)* (Berne, 1978), CDDH/III/SR.32; XIV 313 (hereinafter cited as document numbers from the Conference).

whilst an Iraqi delegate felt that, '[Common Article 3] was not yet generally accepted or applied.'[148]

It is true that since the adoption of the Geneva Conventions there has been a multitude of internal armed conflicts, affording many opportunities for the application of Article 3. Instances of acceptance of the Article are difficult to find however, and despite its existence, 'internal war has lost little of its savagery in the observed conflicts in the post-1949 period'.[149] The situation certainly seems rather depressing. Might it not be the case, however, that whilst explicit references to the acceptance and application of Article 3 are largely non-existent, there has nevertheless been at least a partial acceptance of the principles contained therein, leading to an element of humanitarian protection during internal armed conflicts despite the apparent tendency to disregard the terms of common Article 3? An examination of three major post-1949, but pre-1977, internal conflicts may provide a fuller picture as regards the application of the Article in practice.[150]

Algeria

When Algeria sought to attain political independence from France in 1954, armed violence erupted.[151] France had ratified the Geneva Conventions in 1951, so the question arose as to whether the conditions required for the application of common Article 3 were met (i.e. whether the violence amounted to an 'armed conflict'). The FLN (Algerian National Liberation Front) possessed a fair degree of organisation and territorial control, and the length and intensity of the conflict were considerable,[152] all factors which would certainly point to the conclusion that Article 3 was indeed applicable.

---

[148] Mr Al-Fallouji, CDDH/I/SR.29; VIII 288–289.

[149] Howard J. Taubenfeld, 'The Applicability of the Laws of War in Civil War' in John N. Moore (ed.), Law and Civil War in the Modern World (Baltimore, 1974), 499 at 516.

[150] David P. Forsythe, 'Legal Management of Internal War: The 1977 Protocol on Non-international Armed Conflicts' (1978) 72 AJIL 272 at 275–276 sets out a list of internal conflicts from 1949 to 1975, sorting them according to the application or acceptance by the parties of Article 3.

[151] On the conflict generally see Greenberg, 'Conduct of the Algerian Revolution', 70–71; Arnold Fraleigh, 'The Algerian Revolution as a Case Study in International Law' in Richard A. Falk (ed.), The International Law of Civil War (Baltimore, 1971), 179; and Mohammed Bedjaoui, Law and the Algerian Revolution (Brussels, 1961). For an outline of the action taken by the ICRC, and adherence to the Geneva Conventions by the parties, see Haug, Humanity for All, 97–104.

[152] By June 1956, 400,000 French troops were in Algeria – a number which remained fairly constant until the ceasefire came into force on 19 March 1962. French figures state that at the time of the ceasefire, the FLN had 15,000 members inside Algeria,

Of course, all four Geneva Conventions would have been applicable had the conflict been classed as international rather than purely internal,[153] and action did spill over at times into the neighbouring States of Tunisia and Morocco, which also provided the FLN with support ranging from supplies and training to the use of territory for the launching of attacks and as sanctuary from pursuit.[154] It is however difficult to accept that the involvement of those States transformed the character of the conflict, since neither Tunisian nor Moroccan troops became directly involved in hostilities, and it is doubtful that either State had any measure of control over the FLN.[155] The conflict between the FLN and the national authorities thus remained internal in nature.[156] The FLN did actually characterise the conflict as international,[157] yet initially maintained that only common Article 3 was applicable to the hostilities. The rebels were not alone, however, in the belief that the conflict was of more than domestic interest. Thirteen States sought to have the conflict placed on the agenda of the United Nations Security Council,[158] and the Iranian representative argued on their behalf that:

Because of the size of forces engaged and the modern armaments employed, the Algerian struggle is an armed conflict of incontestable gravity . . . Nothing in

with a further 12,000 in Morocco and 25,000 in Tunisia. The number of casualties was high, official French figures stating that 20,500 French troops were killed, 57,200 injured and 198 missing. French figures also stated that 141,000 FLN members were killed in the conflict. See *Keesing's Contemporary Archives of World Events* (London, 1963), 18908–18912.

[153] Today it certainly would be, under Additional Protocol I, Article 1(4). It could be argued that this provision was greatly influenced by the Algerian conflict, the FLN having persuaded the UN General Assembly to adopt a Declaration against colonialism, paragraph 4 of which stated that, 'All armed action or repressive measures of all kinds directed against dependent peoples shall cease in order to enable them to exercise peacefully and freely their right to complete independence', followed within five days by a resolution on Algeria, paragraph 1 of which stated that, 'The General Assembly . . . recognises the right of the Algerian people to self-determination and independence.' Fraleigh, 'Algeria as a Case Study', 191–192.

[154] *Ibid.*, 193.

[155] See the *Nicaragua* Case at paragraph 109, and discussion of the Hague Tribunal Cases above at pp. 47–50.

[156] The fact that the national authorities were largely French made no difference. It was not until Additional Protocol I of 1977 that such conflicts were classed as international.

[157] Fraleigh, 'Algeria as a Case Study', 181; Taubenfeld, 'Applicability of the Laws of War', 509.

[158] Letter dated 13 June 1956 from the Governments of Afghanistan, Egypt, Indonesia, Iran, Iraq, Jordan, Lebanon, Libya, Pakistan, Saudi Arabia, Syria, Thailand and Yemen. *UN Security Council Official Records* (11th Year), Supplement for April/May/June 1956, Doc. S/3609, 74.

international law prevents a civil war from assuming . . . the character of a conflict whose effects go beyond the national level to the international level . . . What is happening in Algeria is actually war, with all its consequences, both national and international.[159]

France, however, steadfastly refused to accept that the situation was of international concern, repeatedly arguing that operations in Algeria were aimed merely at maintaining public order, and therefore free from international restraints.[160] Mr Alphand, the French representative, stated categorically to the Security Council that 'the French Government considers that Algerian affairs are essentially within the domestic jurisdiction of France',[161] and France won the support of the majority of the Security Council, which voted (by seven votes to two, with two abstentions) not to place the issue on their agenda. Other members were, however, like France, colonial powers who would doubtless not have relished United Nations interest or 'outside interference' should a similar problem face them.[162]

Of course, placing the conflict on the agenda of the Security Council, whilst underlining that the situation was of international concern, would not actually have transformed the conflict into an international one. Indeed, Pictet's Commentaries to the Geneva Conventions demonstrate that during the Diplomatic Conference, several delegates had suggested that the placing of a dispute on the agenda of the UN Security Council or the General Assembly as a threat to international peace, a breach of the peace, or an act of aggression was a suitable criterion for the application of Article 3,[163] underlining the internal nature of the conflict.[164] A referral to the Security Council could not render the *jus in bello* applicable – to hold otherwise would be to accept that a

---

[159] *Security Council Official Records* (11th Year), 729th Meeting, 26 June 1956, 10–11; and 730th Meeting, 26 June 1956, 2. Although claiming that it merits international consideration, the assertion nevertheless clearly accepts that it is a civil conflict.

[160] See discussion of this issue in Bedjaoui, *The Algerian Revolution*, 142–152; Fraleigh, 'Algeria as a Case Study', 181; Taubenfeld, 'Applicability of the Laws of War', 509; and Farer, 'Towards a Definition', 35.

[161] *Security Council Official Records* (11th Year), 729th Meeting, 26 June 1956, 5.

[162] Although this was to happen in due course regardless, as far as Belgium was concerned.

[163] See above at p. 35.

[164] The Algerian situation actually serves to demonstrate the problems with accepting such a view, in that, despite the refusal of the Security Council to consider the conflict, there can be little doubt that it had attained the scale and intensity whereby common Article 3 was (or ought to have been) applicable. It is therefore difficult to accept United Nations consideration as being a necessary requirement for the application of common Article 3, which would inevitably place the extent of legal regulation in the political arena.

procedural decision could have substantive legal consequences. Equally, the Security Council's opinion that this was a purely internal matter did not necessarily preclude the application of common Article 3, and it can be convincingly argued that, absent at that time the provisions of Additional Protocol I, the Algerian Revolution did indeed come within the scope of common Article 3. This was certainly not a minority opinion, the ICRC asserting that it was 'an internal conflict in which one of the Parties did not recognise the opposing Party'.[165] Even an eminent French jurist stated in 1957 that 'article 3 of the Geneva Conventions incontestably had in view [occurrences] such as those for which Algeria is the unfortunate theatre'.[166] But it is one thing for legal scholars and the Red Cross to pass judgment on situations such as Algeria. More important for present purposes is the attitude of the parties themselves.

The FLN were more than ready to accept explicitly the applicability of common Article 3 (although evidence suggests that they made no attempt to apply it),[167] and are first reported to have sought its application in February 1956.[168] They reiterated this claim on several occasions[169] before urging a 'special agreement' under Article 3, aiming at a broader application of the laws of war. Eventually the FLN attempted to achieve full observance of the Conventions by depositing an instrument of ratification with the Swiss Government.[170] France, on the other hand, was less willing to admit the application of Article 3, and never explicitly accepted its obligations under the Article. It is nonetheless possible to argue that France implicitly recognised her duty to act in accordance with its provisions. In response to an official question from a member of the French National Assembly in 1955, Premier Fauré expressly acknowledged that Article 3 was applicable to the conflict (although this was never published in the *Journal Officiel*).[171] The ICRC subsequently

---

[165] ICRC, *The ICRC and the Algerian Conflict* (ICRC Doc. D766b; Geneva, 1962), 2.

[166] R. Pinto, 'Le Drame algerien et la Croix-Rouge Internationale', *Le Monde*, 20 November 1957, 5.

[167] See, for example, Alistair A. Horne, *A Savage War of Peace* (London, 1977), chapter 9.

[168] Greenberg, 'Conduct of the Algerian Revolution', 47, citing J. Siotis, *Le Droit de la guerre et les conflits armés d'un caractère non-international* (Paris, 1958), 211, n. 81.

[169] See the statement given by Belkacem Krim, the FLN leader, to *Le Monde*, 24 June 1958, 3. Also Fraleigh, 'Algeria as a Case Study', 194; Greenberg, 'Conduct of the Algerian Revolution', 49; and ICRC, *ICRC and the Algerian Conflict*, 2.

[170] Bedjaoui, *The Algerian Revolution*, 216–217 and 189–199; Fraleigh, 'Algeria as a Case Study', 194–195.

[171] The question was from M. Boutbien, No. 17,250 of 20 June 1955, and the answer was communicated only to him and the ICRC. See Bedjaoui, *The Algerian Revolution*, 213 and nn. 11 and 12 therein.

made an offer of its services expressly based on the right to do so under Article 3,[172] and French Prime Minister Mollet responded by issuing
a communiqué which stated that: 'In conformity with Article 3 of the
Geneva Conventions regarding armed conflicts not of an international
character, which arise in the territory of one of the contracting parties,
the International Committee of the Red Cross has offered its services to
the French Government. The French Government authorised it to send
a mission to Algeria.'[173] This can only be construed as an admission by
France that common Article 3 was indeed applicable to the conflict. The
ICRC certainly considered this to be the case,[174] and yet when it presented both sides with a draft document whereby they would pledge to
observe Article 3, neither party accepted.[175] It nevertheless seems clear
that both France and the FLN effectively accepted that the conflict was
covered by Article 3. Of course, 'To recognise an obligation, legal or
humanitarian, is not the same as abiding by it. It is well to remember
that in the Spanish Civil War both parties agreed at the outset to respect
the principles of the Geneva Convention of 1929 on prisoners of war.
Both parties proceeded to murder prisoners by the truckload.'[176] It therefore falls to examine whether the provisions of Article 3 were applied
in practice by the FLN and the French military.

Many violations of the laws of war occurred throughout the conflict,
and the number of casualties was high.[177] The FLN fought a mainly
guerrilla war using terrorist tactics, including the execution of captured French military personnel, the assassination of French and Muslim
civilians involved in the administration of Algeria, and the fomenting
of riots leading to massive civilian casualties, culminating in the infamous 'Battle of Algiers' of 1956–1957.[178] At the height of the terrorist

[172] The offer was made in February 1956. See Greenberg, 'Conduct of the Algerian
Revolution', 50, and Pinto, 'Le Drame algerien'.
[173] June 1956. See GPRA, *White Paper on the Application of the Geneva Conventions of 1949 to
the French–Algerian Conflict* (May 1960), 20, reproduced in Greenberg, 'Conduct of the
Algerian Revolution'. See also Pinto, 'Le Drame algerien'.
[174] ICRC, *ICRC and the Algerian Conflict*, 3–4.
[175] Greenberg, 'Conduct of the Algerian Revolution', 51; Bedjaoui, *The Algerian Revolution*,
211.
[176] Forsythe, 'Legal Management of Internal War', 276–277.
[177] It is estimated that in total 2.5 million people died, equivalent to a quarter of the
population. See Fraleigh, 'Algeria as a Case Study', 179, and sources mentioned
therein.
[178] E.g. the bombing on 30 September 1956 of the 'Milk Bar' in Algiers where Europeans
gathered, resulting in the large-scale injury and mutilation of women and children.
See *Le Monde*, 2 October 1956, 4. On the conduct of hostilities in general by both sides
see Fraleigh, 'Algeria as a Case Study', 194–203.

campaign the death rate for civilians was 200 per month,[179] and 'by 1957 no civilian in Algeria, Moslem or French, could expect to be immune from either direct or indiscriminate attack'.[180] France sought to use these facts to illustrate how the FLN was blatantly disregarding the laws of war. However, its record was little better. Emergency legislation was introduced which granted the Algerian authorities wide powers to deal with rebels, leading to the commission of many atrocities, and the prevailing policy of French military commanders was to overcome the insurgency through torture and counter-terrorism. As enunciated by Minister of Defence Chevallier on 25 May 1955, 'You do not fight rebels with legal means; you fight rebels with means identical with theirs. It is the *lex talionis* – eye for an eye, tooth for a tooth; it is the law of self-defence on a country-wide scale.'[181] France executed many captured FLN rebels for bearing arms against the State,[182] conducted campaigns of aerial bombardment (including napalm) against FLN strongholds, and pursued a policy of collective responsibility to cut the FLN off from their support base. This involved mass arrests and widespread torture to find terrorists, whilst transferring huge numbers of civilians from their homes to 'concentration camps', where many died through illness and disease.[183]

Despite these breaches, both sides did take steps to ensure at least a measure of humanitarian protection. In April 1958 the FLN command issued a regulation ordering strict observance of the laws of war and provisions of the Geneva Conventions of 1949,[184] and in May sent a telegram to the ICRC assuring them that their troops would not aggravate the situation through the use of inhuman practices.[185] French prisoners were permitted to communicate (to an extent) with their families, and many were repatriated before the hostilities ended.[186] France, for her part, eventually set up prisoner-of-war camps and authorised the ICRC to visit detainees. The courts also recognised a distinct legal status

---

[179] Brian Crozier, *The Rebels* (London, 1960), 202.

[180] Fraleigh, 'Algeria as a Case Study', 202.

[181] Taubenfeld, 'Applicability of the Laws of War', 509, n. 38.

[182] Although this is not prohibited by Article 3 provided they were tried fairly and by a properly constituted court. See Article 3(1)(d) and Taubenfeld, 'Applicability of the Laws of War', 510.

[183] There are still concerns that former French officials may be prosecuted for their conduct during the conflict.

[184] Bedjaoui, *The Algerian Revolution*, 215, and n. 17 therein.

[185] *Ibid.*

[186] Forsythe, 'Legal Management of Internal War', 277.

for Algerian rebels in order to soften the impact of French law upon them.[187] The Council of Ministers even created a special Commission (the Commission de Sauvegarde des Droits et des Libertés Individuels) to investigate alleged army abuses in Algeria. Its findings were leaked and published without authority in 1957,[188] containing what has been described as 'an official admission of responsibility' for many contraventions of humanitarian law by French troops.[189] It also pointed, however, to several real efforts aimed at ameliorating the effects of the conflict, and found that violations of the law were not committed systematically, although without explicitly finding the laws of war to be applicable. French command had repeatedly issued orders prohibiting the use of the population as targets, and there were many cases of soldiers being tried and punished by the authorities for violations of the rules.[190] Given the report's honesty as regards breaches, it must be assumed that this is also true. That each side repeatedly urged the other to observe the laws of war, accusing each other of breaches whilst denying, or else seeking to justify, their own alleged misconduct can be seen as further evidence of their relevance.

Violations of humanitarian law in armed conflict may be inevitable. It must nevertheless be asked whether the conduct of hostilities in Algeria was acceptable. Some scholars do believe that the humanitarian record of both sides was adequate,[191] but the opposite (and rather more convincing) view holds that, considering both sides had accepted the applicability of Article 3, whether expressly or implicitly, the record of compliance with its provisions was disappointing, and even reprehensible.

The Congo

The Congo gained its independence from Belgium in 1960, at the height of the decolonisation movement. The situation in the State immediately

---

[187] Ibid.; see also Fraleigh, 'Algeria as a Case Study', 196.

[188] Le Monde, 14 December 1957, 7.

[189] Greenberg, 'Conduct of the Algerian Revolution', 55 and n. 90 therein, where the Commission likened French police tactics to those of the Gestapo.

[190] E.g. Le Monde, 19 March 1958, 3.

[191] Bond, 'Internal Conflict', 272; and Fraleigh, 'Algeria as a Case Study', 196, where he expresses the opinion that the parties acted 'in certain respects' in accordance with the Conventions. Forsythe, in 'Legal Management of Internal War', 277, detected attempts 'to implement the spirit of Article 3 . . . and not merely to pay lip service to its applicability'.

afterwards was, however, highly unstable and confused.[192] The central Government in Leopoldville was involved in conflicts with the provinces of South Kasai and Katanga (the latter of which sought secession in a long armed struggle), as well as with an alternative Government based in Stanleyville. Added to this were various tribal struggles and the deployment of a United Nations Force (ONUC) in the struggle against Katanga.

The main focus of this examination is the major conflict between the central Government and Katanga, and the first question to be tackled is whether common Article 3 was applicable to the conflict at all. The Congo was not a party to the Geneva Conventions but the ICRC believed that since the former colonial power (i.e. Belgium) had been a party, the Congo was automatically a party also.[193] It is debatable whether this is the case in international law,[194] but the central Government affirmed that they would abide by the Conventions in a declaration sent to Berne in February 1961.[195] Following a request from the ICRC two days later for all parties in the Congo to uphold the humanitarian principles of the Geneva Conventions, Tshombe (the leader of Katanga) informed the ICRC that his troops also would abide by these principles.[196] No express mention was however made by any party as to whether by referring to 'humanitarian principles' they considered themselves to be bound to apply common Article 3. Nevertheless, by accepting the 'humanitarian principles' of the Conventions, they must presumably have accepted the minimal obligations contained therein.[197]

The situation was rendered more complex through the involvement of a United Nations Force. Some scholars believe that the involvement of UN troops changes the character of the conflict from internal to

[192] An overview of the situation can be found in McNemar, 'War in the Congo'. For more comprehensive analyses, particularly as regards United Nations involvement, see Derek W. Bowett, *United Nations Forces* (London, 1964), 153–254, and Rosalyn Higgins, *United Nations Peacekeeping 1946–1967* (Oxford, 1980), vol. III.

[193] 'Participation of newly independent states in the Geneva Conventions can therefore be admitted as implied by virtue of the signature of the former colonial power. It is considered advisable, however, that they officially confirm their participation in the Conventions by notifying the administering State . . . this is a question neither of accession nor of ratification, but of confirmation of participation or of declaration of continuity.' 'The New African States and the Geneva Conventions' (1962) 13 *Int Rev of the Red Cross* 207 at 208.

[194] See above at n. 97 and accompanying text.

[195] 'The Red Cross Action in the Congo' (1962) 10 *Int Rev of the Red Cross* 3 at 7–8; McNemar, 'War in the Congo', 259.

[196] 'The ICRC in the Congo' (1961) *Int Rev of the Red Cross*, Supplement 14, 43–45, reproduced in McNemar, 'War in the Congo', 260.

[197] Article 3 representing those principles.

international,[198] but, as outlined above,[199] it does not appear that outside interference in an internal conflict *necessarily* transforms its character. This must be especially so where the outside action is taken by a
peacekeeping force, present only with the consent of the host State,
following a determined policy of non-involvement in internal questions, and using force only in self-defence.[200] For this reason ONUC's
involvement did nothing to change the underlying regulation of the
conflict through Article 3. The only possible effect which UN involvement might have had was upon the law applicable during hostilities
between Tshombe's Katangan forces and ONUC. If the theory of pairings
is to be employed in the case of outside involvement, then the laws of
war as a whole rather than simply Article 3 should have been employed
in those circumstances.[201] Tshombe had already undertaken to apply
the humanitarian principles of the Conventions, if not the entirety of
their provisions, but what was the situation as regards the application
of the Geneva Conventions to ONUC?[202]

Various arguments could have been advanced against UN forces being bound by the laws of war: first, the UN is not a signatory to the
Conventions; secondly, the troops in the Congo were national contin-
gents, who continued to be subject to the military rules and regulations
of their own States despite being under UN command[203] – the UN could
not therefore enforce the laws of war; and thirdly, since war is outlawed by the UN Charter, the same restraints should not be imposed
upon the United Nations and aggressors.[204] Secretary-General U Thant

[198] E.g. Farer, 'Towards a Definition', 54. Bowett also saw it as difficult to regard
hostilities in which the United Nations is involved as non-international. See *United
Nations Forces*, 509.

[199] See above at pp. 46–52.

[200] On the UN Force see McNemar, 'War in the Congo', 285–296; Bowett, *United Nations
Forces*, 153–254; and Higgins, *United Nations Peacekeeping*, vol. III.

[201] Although the issue of whether UN forces are actually party to an armed conflict is
rarely straightforward.

[202] See Bowett, *United Nations Forces*, 222–224, and, on the question of the applicability of
laws of war to UN Forces in general, at 484–516. See also Hilaire McCoubrey and
Nigel D. White, *International Organizations and Civil Wars* (Aldershot, 1995), 187–198;
Umesh Palwankar, 'Applicability of International Humanitarian Law to United
Nations Peacekeeping Forces' (1993) 294 *Int Rev of the Red Cross* 227.

[203] Regulation 29(c) governing ONUC, ST/SGB/ONUC/1, 15 July 1963. Reproduced in
Higgins, *United Nations Peacekeeping*, vol. III, 75.

[204] This cannot be the case, and in most cases there is unlikely to have been any
designation of the aggressor anyway. Bowett, *United Nations Forces*, 493–496 and
McNemar, 'War in the Congo', 260–263.

nevertheless notified the ICRC that ONUC *would* be bound by the rules of warfare. In a letter to the President of the ICRC he said that:

I am in entire agreement with you in considering that the Geneva Conventions of 1949 constitute the most complete standards granting to the human person indispensable guarantees for his protection in time of war or in the case of armed conflict whatever form it may take. I also wish to confirm that UNO insists on its armed forces in the field applying the principles of these Conventions as scrupulously as possible.[205]

This was confirmed by the ONUC Regulations.[206] Unfortunately the statement is rather ambiguous – the 'principles' of the Conventions are to be applied rather than the 'provisions', and even then only 'as scrupulously as possible', rather than at all times. To take issue with these points may be straining the construction of the statement, but the fact remains that the UN did not explicitly state that its forces would abide by Article 3.[207] The ICRC nonetheless saw this as an acceptance of the minimum rules applicable under common Article 3, although not the totality of the Geneva Conventions.[208] Bowett, on the

---

[205] 'The United Nations and the Application of the Geneva Conventions' (1962) 10 *Int Rev of the Red Cross* 29.

[206] Article 43 of the Regulations states that, 'the Force shall observe the principles and spirit of the general international Conventions applicable to the conduct of military personnel'. Reproduced in Higgins, *United Nations Peacekeeping*, vol. III, 76. The United Nations made similar undertakings much more recently, in the context of UNAMIR (UN Assistance Mission for Rwanda) action in Rwanda. The Status of Forces Agreement between the UN and the Rwandan Government provided that 'The United Nations shall ensure that UNAMIR shall conduct its operations in Rwanda with full respect for the principles and spirit of the general conventions applicable to the conduct of military personnel. These international conventions include the four Geneva Conventions of 12 August 1949 and their Additional Protocols.' See Daphna Shraga, 'The United Nations as an Actor Bound by International Humanitarian Law' in Luigi Condorelli *et al.* (eds.), *The United Nations and International Humanitarian Law* (Paris, 1996), 317 at 325, n. 16. See also Secretary-General's Bulletin: Observance by United Nations Forces of International Humanitarian Law, UN Doc. ST/SGB/1999/13 (6 August 1999).

[207] Although it might be argued that they did to the extent that Article 3 contains the most basic fundamentals of humanity, and thus the humanitarian principles of the Geneva Conventions. For further discussion of these points see Farer, 'Towards a Definition', 38.

[208] Bowett, *United Nations Forces*, 222–223, a view shared by Gerald I. A. D. Draper. See 'The Legal Limitations Upon the Employment of Weapons by the United Nations Force in the Congo' (1963) 12 *ICLQ* 387 at 410. If ONUC was actually a party to the conflict, however, it would appear to be difficult to accept that only the principles, rather than the Conventions in their entirety, were applicable. For more recent considerations of the applicability of humanitarian law to UN forces and related

other hand, felt that the full scope of international regulation was intended.[209]

We are thus faced with a conflict in which no party explicitly accepted the application of common Article 3, preferring instead to make vague statements accepting the humanitarian principles of the Geneva Conventions. One might have assumed that this was unlikely to lead to a more effective observance of the laws of warfare than in Algeria, where the parties involved actually recognised the validity of Article 3, but the record of compliance was in fact rather better. Detainees on all sides were by and large held in acceptable conditions subject to ICRC visits, and although violations did occasionally occur, they were considered 'exceptions'.[210] Inevitably, a number of civilians died in the conflict, but the majority of these deaths occurred through tribal struggles, rather than military offensives.[211] It is estimated that the number killed in ONUC–Congolese clashes was less than 1,000, whereas the number of deaths resulting from tribal fighting and starvation ran into tens of thousands.[212] Political killings did take place (e.g. the execution of Lumumba), and there were instances of attacks on non-military targets and misuse of the Red Cross symbol,[213] but the number of civilians killed never attained the scale where there was no distinction between them and soldiers.[214] In fact, 'The relevance of the laws of war in the Congo was demonstrated by the circumstances that all parties considered themselves bound by these laws; they based claims and counterclaims on these laws; and they restricted their actions in accordance with these laws.'[215] There was perhaps reason to be optimistic as regards the application of Article 3, or the humanitarian principles of the Geneva Conventions, as another civil conflict broke out in Africa.

issues, see, for example, ICRC, *Symposium on Humanitarian Action and Peace-Keeping Operations* (Geneva, 1994); Condorelli *et al.*, *The United Nations and Humanitarian Law*; and Christopher J. Greenwood, 'Protection of Peacekeepers: The Legal Regime' (1996) 7 *Duke JCIL* 185.

[209] *United Nations Forces*, 509–510.
[210] McNemar, 'War in the Congo', 263–265 gives examples of violations perpetrated by both the ANC (Armée Nationale Congolaise) and ONUC.
[211] An example being the massacre of Balubas in South Kasai by Lumumba's ANC. This outlines just how little control the military leaders had over their troops at times.
[212] Ernest W. Lefever, 'The UN as a Foreign Policy Instrument: The Congo Crisis' in Roger Hilsman and Robert C. Good (eds.), *Foreign Policy in the Sixties* (Baltimore, 1965), 153.
[213] On the avoidance of non-military targets in general, see McNemar, 'War in the Congo', 265–269.
[214] *Ibid.*, 265.
[215] *Ibid.*, 271.

Biafra

Fighting in the Biafran struggle for secession from Nigeria broke out in earnest on 6 July 1967, and was armed conflict on a large scale.[216] Common Article 3 was clearly applicable, hostilities having gone far beyond mere internal disturbances. Both sides were well equipped, with substantial organised armies under responsible authorities, in control of territory, etc. Indeed, several factors point to the possibility that humanitarian law as a whole, rather than simply the provisions of Article 3, may have been applicable to the conflict.[217]

On 30 May 1967, the Federal leader of Nigeria, General Gowon, ordered a complete blockade of Biafran ports, to be enforced by the Nigerian Navy.[218] This was traditionally regarded as an act of war which, in the past, would have represented a recognition of belligerency.[219] The doctrine of recognition of belligerency had, however, fallen into disuse by the 1960s, at least as far as third States were concerned, although it could still be argued that acceptance of the laws of war (as in the Spanish Civil War) actually amounted to a tacit recognition of belligerency on the part of the established government.[220] It seems unnecessary, however, to classify such acts as recognition of belligerency, since recognition was

[216] For an overview of the conflict and reasons behind it, see Anthony H. M. Kirk-Greene, *Crisis and Conflict in Nigeria, A Documentary Sourcebook* (2 vols., London, 1971); Walter Schwarz, *Nigeria* (London, 1968); Ntieyong U. Akpan, *The Struggle for Secession 1966–1970* (London, 1971); Clarence C. Clendenen, 'Tribalism and Humanitarianism: The Nigerian–Biafran Civil War' in Robin D. S. Higham (ed.), *Civil Wars in the Twentieth Century* (Kentucky, 1972), 164; and Margery Perham, 'Reflections on the Nigerian Civil War' (1970) 46 *International Affairs* 231.

[217] One author has claimed that 'The Nigerian conflict was not merely an internal armed conflict, but a full-fledged civil war, and since the precedent of the American civil war there can be no doubt that the customary rules of warfare apply to that particular type of armed conflict.' (E. I. Nwogugu, 'The Nigerian Civil War: A Case Study in the Law of War' (1974) 14 *Indian JIL* 13 at 19.) This is a misleading assertion. First, it is unclear exactly what the difference is between internal armed conflict and 'full-fledged civil war', and secondly, there is no State practice to the effect claimed other than the American Civil War (where there was a recognition of belligerency) and the Spanish Civil War (where both sides undertook to respect the Geneva Convention). See Anton Schlögel, 'Civil War' (1970) 108 *Int Rev of the Red Cross* 123 at 126.

[218] Kirk-Greene, *Documentary Sourcebook*, vol. I, 98.

[219] As in the American Civil War. See above at pp. 15–16.

[220] It is an interesting question whether there was any recognition of belligerency in the former Yugoslavia. The Memorandum of Understanding signed on 27 November 1991 between representatives of the Federal Republic of Yugoslavia, the Yugoslav Peoples' Army, Croatia and Serbia agreed to implement the Geneva Conventions and Additional Protocol I. Hostilities between these parties would indeed have been

previously the medium through which the *jus in bello* became applicable, whereas an explicit acceptance of that law was made in Spain. In the case of Biafra, it could be argued that the blockade was an act of war for which the Federal Government had to bear the consequences, those being the applicability of the customary laws of war in their entirety.

It has been suggested that this made the conflict international rather than internal in character.[221] A better view, however, sees the conflict as remaining internal, but subject to the customary laws of war. The conflict could only have been truly international if Biafra was, in fact, a State.[222] It was never recognised as such by the Federal Government, which repeatedly classed the situation as a mere rebellion and stressed that they were fighting to maintain unity. Biafra was actually recognised by only four African States (Tanzania, Gabon, the Ivory Coast and Zambia) in 1968, and by Haiti in 1969. This was clearly insufficient to constitute Biafra as a State in international law.[223] The Federal Government nevertheless appeared to accept that more than Article 3 was applicable. Even before the outbreak of hostilities, the ICRC had managed to obtain assurances from both sides that they intended to apply the Geneva Conventions in the event of an armed conflict,[224] and despite repeated statements that the army was only undertaking 'police action',[225] the Federal Government issued a Code of Conduct to all members of the Nigerian Forces in July 1967 providing that, 'We are in honour bound to observe the rules of the Geneva Convention in whatever action

international. In Bosnia, however, the various factions agreed only to abide by common Article 3 and certain other provisions of the Geneva Conventions (Agreement of 22 May 1992). This clearly stopped short of an application of the entire *jus in bello*: see *Tadić* (Jurisdiction) at paragraph 73. Whether this amounts to a recognition of belligerency or not is open to debate.

[221] Nwogugu, 'The Nigerian Civil War', 25. He feels other factors, which will be highlighted later, confirm this. Michael Bothe, 'Article 3 and Protocol II: Case Studies of Nigeria and El Salvador' (1982) 31 *American University LR* 899, also classes the conflict as international, but based on Biafra's existence as a *de facto* local regime.

[222] Unless third-party control over Biafran forces could be demonstrated along the lines shown in the Yugoslav Tribunal case law.

[223] Bothe, 'Article 3 and Protocol II', 901, categorically states that the recognition afforded was 'not adequate proof of statehood'. See also David A. Ijalye, 'Was "Biafra" at Any Time a State in International Law?' (1971) 65 *AJIL* 551, where he states at 559 that 'it is difficult to establish that Biafra attained statehood in international law'. On Statehood in general, see James Crawford, *The Creation of States in International Law* (Oxford, 1979).

[224] ICRC, *Annual Report* (1967), 36, and 'External Activities: Nigeria' (1967) 79 *Int Rev of the Red Cross* 535 at 536.

[225] E.g. General Gowon's First Wartime Press Conference, Kirk-Greene, *Documentary Sourcebook*, vol. I, 459.

you will be taking against the rebel Lt.-Col. Odumegwu-Ojukwu and his clique.'[226] No express mention was made of whether the 'rules of the Geneva Convention' to be observed were those of the Conventions as a whole or simply Article 3, but the phrase seems to imply more than just Article 3, and although the rules listed following the statement are very similar to the obligations contained therein, some, such as the prohibition on looting, and the protection of churches, property, etc.,[227] clearly go further. The Federal Government also had a strict policy against indiscriminate bombing of civilian areas[228] despite the fact that methods and means of warfare are not regulated by Article 3.

It has therefore been suggested that the Geneva Conventions as a whole were applicable, demonstrating the international nature of the conflict. The Federal Government would thus have been bound to apply all four Conventions through Article 2(3), Biafra being considered a Power under the Conventions which had tacitly accepted their application.[229] As has already been stated, however, Article 2(3) cannot be used as regards an insurgent party to make all of the Conventions applicable to internal conflict.[230] Even the ICRC made explicit reference in 1967 to Article 3 as regards the conflict.[231] The conflict accordingly remained non-international, the Federal Government choosing to apply broader humanitarian rules than Article 3 on a purely voluntary basis. There is certainly evidence that, despite their acceptance of these regulations, the Federal Government never accepted that the conflict was international in status. In fact, the Code of Conduct stated explicitly that: 'You must bear in mind at all times that ... you are not fighting a war with a foreign enemy. Nor are you fighting a religious war or Jihad. You are only subduing the rebellion of Lt.-Col. Odumegwu-Ojukwu and his clique.'[232]

Happily, the record of compliance with humanitarian law was generally satisfactory. There were occasional violations and mutual allegations of atrocities, but no more so than would be expected in any armed conflict.[233] The Federal Government established prisoner-of-war camps

---

[226] Directive to all Officers and Men of the Armed Forces of the Federal Republic of Nigeria on Conduct of Military Operations, paragraph 3. *Ibid.*, 455–457.

[227] E.g. paragraphs 4(d), (f), (g) and (h).

[228] Bothe, 'Article 3 and Protocol II', 903.

[229] Nwogugu, 'The Nigerian Civil War', 29–32.

[230] See above at p. 41.

[231] 'External Activities in Nigeria' (1967) 80 *Int Rev of the Red Cross* 591.

[232] Kirk-Greene, *Documentary Sourcebook*, vol. I, 455–457.

[233] On the conduct of hostilities generally, see Nwogugu, 'The Nigerian Civil War', 40–47.

for detained Biafran soldiers, the Biafrans doing likewise for captured Federal troops. Both sides allowed the ICRC to visit detainees regularly, and provided basic supplies, medical treatment, etc.[234] Biafra in fact proposed an ICRC-overseen exchange of prisoners in 1968, although the Federal Government opted not to take part.[235] One aspect of the conflict which was less satisfactory, however, was the lack of respect shown by Federal troops for the status of the ICRC. Two ICRC delegates were murdered by Government troops,[236] and a Red Cross hospital was bombed in December 1968.[237] The Federal Government condemned these actions and, following ICRC complaints, made assurances that such acts would not be repeated.[238] An ICRC relief plane was nevertheless shot down by Federal forces in June 1969.[239]

As regards the protection of civilians, the record was better than had been feared, especially as the heavy artillery used by both sides had threatened to make it difficult to avoid non-military targets effectively. Most disturbing, however, was the repeated accusation by Biafran authorities that the Federal Government was engaged in a policy of genocide against Biafrans,[240] ranging from indiscriminate bombing attacks to massacres. These accusations eventually became so serious that the Federal Government felt compelled to invite several States to form an Observer Team with the task of examining the governmental troops' conduct of the hostilities.[241] The Observer Team issued a series of reports finding that, on the whole, troops were aware of the Code of Conduct and following it. It found no evidence of genocide, nor of alleged massacres,[242] although it did find that there had been large-scale killings by troops at Afikpo, and that it was impossible to prove that indiscriminate air attacks had not taken place.[243] It nevertheless concluded

---

[234] 'Help to War Victims in Nigeria' (1969) 96 *Int Rev of the Red Cross* 119–122.

[235] Nwogugu, 'The Nigerian Civil War', 31, and ICRC, *Annual Report* (1969).

[236] 'Help to War Victims in Nigeria' (1968) 92 *Int Rev of the Red Cross* 571–572.

[237] 'Help to War Victims in Nigeria' (1969) 94 *Int Rev of the Red Cross* 3 at 4 and 'Help to War Victims in Nigeria' (1969) 95 *Int Rev of the Red Cross* 81 at 83.

[238] See the reply of the Nigerian Federal Government, 'Help to War Victims in Nigeria' (1969) 95 *Int Rev of the Red Cross* 81 at 133–134.

[239] *Ibid.*, 353–363, where details are also given of Nigeria's expulsion of the ICRC Commissioner General for West Africa.

[240] Nwogugu, 'The Nigerian Civil War', 44, and Kirk-Greene, *Documentary Sourcebook*, vol. II, 47–49. Biafra submitted a Memorandum to the UN Secretary-General on the subject of Nigeria's alleged policy of genocide.

[241] On 6 September 1968, Canada, Poland, Sweden, the UK, the UN Secretary-General and the Organisation of African Unity were requested to dispatch observers.

[242] *Report of the Observer Team to Nigeria*, Cmnd 3878 (1969), 31–34.

[243] *The Times*, 16 February 1970, 5, and *Report of the Observer Team*, 31–34.

that, 'Generally, the conduct of the Federal Army was as good as that of any army during and after war.'[244] Unfortunately, the Observer Team refused a similar invitation from Biafra to examine its conduct during the hostilities,[245] leaving a rather one-sided view as regards details of the hostilities. The extent to which humanitarian law had been applied was nevertheless encouraging.

General State practice

Levels of compliance and willingness to undergo careful scrutiny as demonstrated in the Nigeria–Biafra conflict have been all too rare. For every conflict in which the laws of war have been observed to some extent, there have been many more where the laws of war, particularly common Article 3, have failed to alleviate the suffering caused by hostilities.

In Yemen, for example,[246] despite express statements from both sides that they would 'respect the principles' of the Geneva Conventions,[247] it has been said that it was 'difficult to identify ways in which international law played any role in regulating the conduct of the conflict',[248] and atrocities were perpetrated by both sides. Initial Royalist policy was to murder all detained military personnel, often mutilating their corpses, although such behaviour was eventually tempered following their leader's offer to provide financial rewards for all prisoners brought to him alive,[249] and five prisoner-of-war camps were eventually created which the ICRC was allowed to visit. The ICRC also managed to arrange the exchange of a number of prisoners,[250] but conditions of detention were still generally poor, and on one such occasion it was found that leg-irons were being employed.[251] The lack of protection for the civilian population was even more startling, with practically no distinction being drawn between military and non-military targets. This was particularly evident through Republican actions since, aided by Egypt, they had greater access to modern weapons and aerial power. The Royalists fought a mainly guerrilla campaign, conducted by village tribesmen,

[244] *The Times*, 16 February 1970, 5.
[245] Kirk-Greene, *Documentary Sourcebook*, vol. II, 81.
[246] See Kathryn Boals, 'The Relevance of International Law to the Internal War in Yemen' in Falk, *Civil War*, 303; and Dana A. Schmidt, *Yemen: The Unknown War* (London, 1968).
[247] ICRC, *Annual Report* (1963), 16–17; Boals, 'Internal War in Yemen', 315.
[248] Boals, 'Internal War in Yemen', 315. For an examination of the conduct of hostilities see *ibid.*, at 314–317.
[249] ICRC, *Annual Report* (1963), 17.
[250] On the ICRC's activities in general, see the ICRC, *Annual Reports* (1963–1966).
[251] Boals, 'Internal War in Yemen', 315–316.

which rendered their detection virtually impossible. Republicans therefore repeatedly bombed Royalist areas indiscriminately, on occasion re-
sorting to the use of poison gas.[252] Boals concludes that 'international
law was extremely ineffective in regulating the conduct of the parties
in the Yemen internal war, and hostilities went forward largely without
reference to applicable standards of conduct embodied in existing or
evolving legal norms'.[253]

The conflict in Yemen is one example. There are many others – the civil
war fought in El Salvador in the 1980s was characterised by an almost
total disregard for humanitarian protection, highlighted by the activities of the now infamous 'death squads'.[254] The continued pleas of the
ICRC with respect to more recent conflicts, such as those in Angola,[255]
Rwanda,[256] Afghanistan,[257] Chechnya,[258] Bosnia-Herzegovina[259] and Sri
Lanka,[260] illustrate that the humanitarian laws of war, and Article 3 in
particular, are still readily disregarded.

In Rwanda and Bosnia violations of basic humanitarian principles
were widespread[261] and, although in Bosnia the parties did agree to apply Article 3 and various provisions of the Geneva Conventions,[262] case
law from the International Criminal Tribunal shows how little effect this

---

[252] Such action is clearly prohibited by various international instruments, including the
1925 Geneva Protocol for the Prohibition of the Use of Asphyxiating, Poisonous or
Other Gases, and of Bacteriological Methods of Warfare. Egypt had ratified this in
1928 although at the time of the conflict Yemen was not a party. See Boals, 'Internal
War in Yemen', 316 and Schmidt, *The Unknown War*, 272.

[253] 'Internal War in Yemen', 317.

[254] See, among others, Bothe, 'Article 3 and Protocol II'.

[255] ICRC, *Annual Report* (1993), 56–60; ICRC Special Brochure, *Angola*, Doc. 0575/002, 05/94
(Geneva, May 1994).

[256] ICRC, *Annual Report* (1993), 76–80; *Public Statements Issued by the ICRC on its Activities in
Rwanda: Collection of News Releases and Press Communications* (Geneva, 7 December 1994).

[257] ICRC, *Afghanistan*, Special Brochure, Doc. 0579/002 (Geneva, July 1994); ICRC Press
Releases 1783 (16 August 1994) and 1786 (29 September 1994); ICRC *Annual Report*
(1993), 102–109.

[258] ICRC Press Release 1793 (28 November 1994).

[259] *Declarations of the ICRC re the Former Yugoslavia* 29/7/92–25/11/94, Doc. DP (1994) 49
(Geneva, 1994); *Press Releases and Communications to the Press re the Former Yugoslavia*
2/7/91–2/12/94, Doc. DP (1994) 51b (Geneva, 1994); ICRC *Annual Report* (1993), 145–156
on the former Yugoslavia; and ICRC Press Release 1792 (26 November 1994) on Bihać
in particular.

[260] See ICRC Press Releases 99/53 (18 September 1999) 99/64 (8 November 1999), 99/65
(21 November 1999) and 00/13 (11 May 2000), for example, outlining civilian
casualties and a lack of respect for places of worship. Sri Lanka is a party to the
Geneva Conventions, but not to Additional Protocol II.

[261] See also below at pp. 122–127.

[262] Agreement No. 1, 22 May 1992, Article 2, paragraphs 1–6.

had on the conduct of hostilities. The prolonged hostilities in the north-east of Sri Lanka between the Sri Lankan Army (SLA) and the Liberation Tigers of Tamil Eelam (commonly known as the Tamil Tigers) have re-sulted in numerous casualties on both sides.[263] Indeed, the ICRC has referred to the conflict as a 'no-mercy war', with an absence of prison-ers being taken, or concern for the wounded on the battlefield.[264] Such failures are in clear contravention of international humanitarian law as contained in common Article 3. Concern for civilians also seems to have been limited. Although in 1998 the ICRC expressed the opinion that steps had been taken to spare the civilian population where possible,[265] numerous examples exist pointing to the contrary. In 1996, for example, a suicide bomb attack on the Central Bank by the Tamil Tigers resulted in over 90 deaths and 1,400 casualties,[266] while another bomb attack on a minibus in a busy shopping area of Colombo in March 1998 resulted in 32 deaths and 250 injured persons.[267] The SLA was equally guilty of violations, as discovered when a mass grave was exhumed in 1999 at the site where a former soldier claimed that 600 Tamils killed by gov-ernment troops had been buried.[268] By 1999, the ICRC was becoming more concerned at the growing number of civilian casualties, repeat-edly reminding both the SLA and the Tamil Tigers of their obligation to comply with humanitarian law.[269]

The contention that common Article 3 applies automatically to inter-nal armed conflict is simply not accepted in practice,[270] and yet there is absolutely no issue of reciprocity – the ICRC Commentaries state quite clearly that, 'The obligation is absolute for each of the Parties, and

[263] The government estimated in 1999 that a total of 60,000 lives had been lost in the conflict since 1983. See *Keesing's Record of World Events* (London, 1999), 43311. For further information and background to the conflict see, for example, Robert I. Rotberg (ed.), *Creating Peace in Sri Lanka: Civil War and Reconciliation* (Washington, 1999), chapters 1 and 2 in particular, and A. Jeyaratnam Wilson, *Sri Lankan Tamil Nationalism* (London, 1999).

[264] ICRC, *Annual Report 1998* (Geneva, 1999).

[265] *Ibid.*

[266] See *Keesing's Record of World Events* (1998), 42624–42625.

[267] *Ibid.*, 42132.

[268] *Keesing's Record of World Events* (1999), 42998.

[269] See n. 260 above. Civilian casualties are estimated at over 30,000. See Saman Kelegama, 'Economic Costs of Conflict in Sri Lanka' in Rotberg, *Creating Peace in Sri Lanka*, 71 at 79.

[270] At least not in any truly objective manner – the parties may well accept that the Article applies automatically, but will then simply deny that the position constitutes a non-international armed conflict, regardless of the fact that to most outside observers it would certainly appear to be so.

independent of the obligation on the other Party. The reciprocity clause has been omitted intentionally.'[271] *De jure*, the Article binds both parties as soon as an internal armed conflict comes into existence. State reluctance to accept the applicability of common Article 3 may nonetheless indicate a *de facto* issue of reciprocity. As already outlined, States are unlikely to honour obligations under common Article 3 where opposing insurgents fail to, and vice versa.[272] It is very well to state in theory that the Article applies automatically provided the situation qualifies as an internal armed conflict, but such theory often counts for little.

Under traditional international law, there had been much less of a problem in identifying situations for the application of humanitarian law – the laws of armed conflict applied where there had been a recognition of belligerency by the State authorities. In seeking to apply automatically to all internal armed conflict, however, rather than broaden the scope of protection, common Article 3 perhaps made a rod for its own back, allowing States to escape humanitarian obligations by claiming that an internal armed conflict did not in fact exist. Until reciprocity becomes a *de facto* issue, States are therefore unlikely to temper their actions towards rebellious nationals. After all, 'Established governments have a vested interest in making the cost of unsuccessful revolution high; and even the international community...has a considerable interest in shoring up the price levels.'[273]

So what happens where the parties refuse to accept that Article 3 is applicable? Often, despite statements to that effect, or a refusal to acknowledge the relevance of the Article, statements *are* made agreeing to abide by some vague set of 'humanitarian principles' rather than any specific set of rules.[274] This may not necessarily be a bad thing for several reasons.

---

[271] Pictet, *Commentary I*, 51. See also, for example, Schindler, 'Different Types of Armed Conflicts', 146, and Draper, *The Red Cross Conventions*, 15. Reciprocity clauses had been included in some early drafts of common Article 3 – see above at pp. 23–29.

[272] Additional Protocol II of 1977 would seem to reflect this reality in that, under Article 1, it applies only where the insurgents are able to implement its provisions, possibly reintroducing the concept of reciprocity. See the discussion below at pp. 107–109. For an examination of various declarations made by insurgent groups regarding their willingness to accept international humanitarian law, see Denise Plattner, 'La Portée juridique des déclarations de respect du droit international humanitaire qui émanent de mouvements en lutte dans un conflit armé' (1984) 18 *Rev Belge du Droit International* 298 at n. 2 and 303.

[273] Bond, 'Internal Conflict', 283.

[274] E.g. the conflicts in the Congo and Yemen.

First, it can be argued that the underlying principles of humanitarian law are found in common Article 3 so that, in effect, its provisions are applied regardless. The International Court of Justice sees its provisions as representing the minimum set of humanitarian standards.[275] Secondly, it may be possible that, by observing a set of 'humanitarian principles' rather than Article 3 itself, the parties are actually accepting a slightly broader range of humanitarian protection. The underlying principles of the laws of war must, for example, include the customary principles of proportionality and distinction. Proportionality is certainly not mentioned in common Article 3 since it does not regulate the methods and means of warfare, whereas the principle of distinction is present to an extent (as regards humane treatment[276]), although the use of tactics such as indiscriminate bombing is not expressly ruled out. Thirdly, although States may refuse to accept the applicability of common Article 3, they may nevertheless abide by its standards, for example by allowing the ICRC to visit detainees.[277] Bond found that:

Two conclusions emerge from a survey of state practice. First, states that quell riots, insurrections, or even revolts quickly do not feel bound to respect Article 3. In the absence of any widely held expectation that they should conform to Article 3, they act under emergency or martial law. The internal conflict is over before the international community can apprize itself of the facts and generate any pressure on the competing parties to comply with the provisions of Article 3 or humanitarian law in general. States do, second and nevertheless, accept some obligations to treat opposing forces humanely if the conflict drags on beyond several weeks or months. While this recognition seldom takes the form of an explicit acceptance of Article 3, it often manifests itself in acceptance of some Red Cross initiative.[278]

But even where humanitarian principles rather than the strict provisions of Article 3 are accepted, violations are all too frequent. It may well be true that, 'If it were not regarded as wrong to mistreat individuals in internal war, they would be mistreated all of the time instead of only

---

[275] See n. 43 above and accompanying text.

[276] Protection is for those 'taking no part in hostilities' (Article 3(1)).

[277] Forsythe, 'Legal Management of Internal War', 276 lists twenty-one examples of governments refusing to acknowledge Article 3's applicability but allowing ICRC visits, e.g. Northern Ireland – the UK has never accepted it as an Article 3 conflict, but has applied its standards (the violations in *Republic of Ireland* v *UK*, 2 EHRR 25 clearly being an exception).

[278] Bond, *Rules of Riot*, 60.

some of the time',[279] but in light of the virtually uniform acceptance of the Geneva Conventions, such expressions of resignation serve only to highlight the lack of political will on the part of the international community to implement the relevant protection.

It was, perhaps, unrealistic to suppose that common Article 3 would be perfect. The fact is, however, that it has not even been commonly regarded as adequate, with several vital areas of the laws of war, such as the protection of civilians, methods and means of warfare and respect for the Red Cross, finding no place in its provisions. Those are not the major problem, however, and do not detract from the fact that the Article was a revolutionary step forward, without which further progress in this area may not have been possible. The difficulty is that experience has shown those provisions which the Article does contain to have been largely passed over in practice. The failure of the drafters to define the term 'armed conflict not of an international character' allowed States reluctant to hinder their ability to deal with insurrection by accepting any international humanitarian obligations simply to deny the existence of armed conflict, and thus the applicability of international regulation. Article 3 therefore failed in the main to temper the ferocity of civil war, and a more comprehensive system of humanitarian regulation for internal armed conflict was considered necessary.

---

[279] Forsythe, 'Legal Management of Internal War', 277, paraphrasing Telford Taylor's 'If it were not regarded as wrong to bomb military hospitals, they would be bombed all of the time instead of only some of the time', from *Nuremberg and Vietnam: An American Tragedy* (Chicago, 1970), 40.

3 Additional Protocol II of 1977

Common Article 3 stood alone in the sphere of internal armed conflict for twenty-five years, but, as demonstrated, it had become evident that some amendment or clarification of the rules governing internal conflicts was necessary, since:

When put to the test... the rules of protection in [common] Article 3 had been shown to require elaboration and completion. Government and Red Cross experts consulted by the ICRC since 1971 had confirmed the urgent need to strengthen the protection of victims of non-international armed conflicts by developing international humanitarian law applicable in such situations.[1]

The decision was therefore made to improve the law, and following several conferences of Governmental Experts and ICRC representatives, two Additional Protocols were drafted and placed before the Diplomatic Conference on the Reaffirmation and Development of International Humanitarian Law Applicable in Armed Conflicts, held in Geneva from 1974 to 1977.[2]

Although this book is concerned with internal conflict, and so with Protocol II (the 1977 Protocol Additional to the Geneva Conventions of 12 August 1949, and Relating to the Protection of Victims of Non-international Armed Conflicts[3]), Additional Protocol I is still of relevance. The first session of the Diplomatic Conference achieved the inclusion in Protocol I of Article 1(4), which extends the provisions of the instrument beyond international armed conflicts, to include 'armed conflicts

---

[1] Mrs Bujard (ICRC) in *Official Records of the Diplomatic Conference on the Reaffirmation and Development of International Humanitarian Law Applicable in Armed Conflicts, Geneva (1974–1977)* (Berne, 1978) CDDH/I/SR.22; VIII, 201 at 201 (hereinafter citations from this work are by the document reference therein).

[2] For the text of the Draft Protocols see *Official Records*, vol. I, part 3.

[3] UN Doc. A/32/144 (1977); 16 ILM 1391 (1977).

in which peoples are fighting against colonial domination and alien occupation and against racist regimes in the exercise of their right of self-
determination', thus transforming what had traditionally been an important category of internal conflicts into international armed conflicts.[4]
Classifying armed conflict according to the objectives of the parties was
highly controversial, and seen by many as an attempt by Third World
States to strike a political blow against Western imperialism. It has been
maintained since that such conflicts should indeed be contained within
Additional Protocol II rather than Protocol I.[5] Nevertheless, conflicts for
national liberation are now governed by international humanitarian law
in its entirety, Article 1 of Additional Protocol II explicitly accepting
that the conflicts listed in Article 1 of Protocol I are beyond its scope of
application.[6]

[4] At least as regards the legal rules governing hostilities. It could be argued that in the
majority of cases they were actually international in character anyway from the
point of view of at least one party to the conflict. See, for example, the Algerian
conflict of 1954–1962 as discussed above.

[5] Gerald I. A. D. Draper, 'Wars of National Liberation and War Criminality' in Michael
Howard (ed.), *Restraints on War* (Oxford, 1979), 135 at 150.

[6] There are currently 158 States Parties to Additional Protocol I and 150 States Parties
to Additional Protocol II (ICRC figures as at 19 April 2001). Two States – France and
the Philippines – have ratified Additional Protocol II but not Additional Protocol I.
Should a war of national liberation occur in either, clearly a question as to the
applicable legal regulation would arise. Protocol II itself clearly *excludes* such conflicts
from its ambit, and so the question must ultimately turn on the customary status of
Article 1(4) of Protocol I. If Article 1(4) represents customary international law, then
the laws of international armed conflict would apply, despite France and the
Philippines not being parties to the Protocol. The customary status of Article 1(4)
seems doubtful, however. As Christopher J. Greenwood argues in 'Customary Law
Status of the 1977 Additional Protocols' in Astrid J. M. Delissen and Gerard J. Tanja
(eds.), *Humanitarian Law of Armed Conflict: Challenges Ahead: Essays in Honour of Frits
Kalshoven* (Dordrecht, 1991), 93 at 112, 'the considerable body of opposition in State
practice to treating such conflicts, for the purposes of the *ius in bello*, as though they
were conflicts between States suggests that Article 1(4) went well beyond customary
law as it stood in 1974 and has not met the criteria for being absorbed into
customary law since its inclusion in Protocol I'. He also points out in 'Scope of
Application of Humanitarian Law' in Dieter Fleck (ed.), *The Handbook of Humanitarian
Law in Armed Conflicts* (Oxford, 1995), 43, that opinions still differ, but that States do
not regard it as declaratory of custom. The likelihood must therefore be that a war of
national liberation fought in either France or the Philippines would be considered
internal, and subject only to the provisions of common Article 3. An interesting
question is whether those conflicts governed by Article 1(4) are to be considered as
internal or international in terms of the jurisdiction of the International Criminal
Court. The Rome Statute contains no equivalent provision, and merely defines
internal armed conflicts as those involving protracted hostilities between the
government and organised armed groups. See the discussion by Andreas Zimmerman
in Otto Triffterer (ed.), *Commentary on the Rome Statute of the International Criminal Court*
(Baden-Baden, 1999), 173 at 266–267.

The drafting process of Additional Protocol II

Having achieved the inclusion of struggles for national liberation in Protocol I, the interest of many delegations in a second Protocol to cover internal conflicts greatly diminished. Indeed, some were strongly opposed to any international regulation whatsoever. To avoid Protocol II being neglected, and the consequent risk that no agreement would be reached regarding internal armed conflicts, the provisions of both draft Protocols were discussed at Committee level simultaneously from the second session.[7]

The aims of the ICRC draft Protocol II are widely regarded as having been threefold: first, to develop the existing humanitarian law of internal armed conflict, shoring up any gaps, especially with regard to the conduct of hostilities and methods and means of combat; secondly, to clarify the ambit of humanitarian law with regard to internal armed conflicts, especially the questions of the threshold and ceiling; and thirdly, to safeguard what common Article 3 had already achieved by providing that it would retain its own autonomous existence.[8] The second objective was to be achieved through the adoption of a more detailed definition of 'armed conflict', employing objective criteria. Several possible definitions had been suggested at the Conference of Government Experts, and the ICRC eventually proposed a fairly broad scope for the Protocol's application, requiring the existence of hostilities between armed forces or other organised armed groups under responsible command. The scope of the Protocol was the cornerstone of the whole instrument,[9] and it was therefore in discussions on this issue[10] that the principal divisions of opinion on the very question of the international regulation of internal armed conflicts were to be found.[11]

[7] This led to its own set of problems, as outlined below.
[8] Sylvie S. Junod, 'Additional Protocol II: History and Scope' (1983) 33 *American University LR* 29 at 31–32; Georges Abi-Saab, 'Non-international Armed Conflicts' in UNESCO, *International Dimensions of Humanitarian Law* (Dordrecht, 1988), 217 at 226; and ICRC, *Report on the Work of the Conference of Government Experts on the Reaffirmation and Development of International Humanitarian Law Applicable in Armed Conflict* (Geneva, 1972), vol. II, 33–34.
[9] Mrs Bujard (ICRC), CDDH/I/SR.22; VIII, 201 at 203.
[10] I.e. discussions on draft Article 1.
[11] See David P. Forsythe, 'Legal Management of Internal War: The 1977 Protocol on Non-international Armed Conflicts' (1978) 72 *AJIL* 272 at 279–282; Junod, 'Additional Protocol II', 33; Charles Lysaght, 'The Attitude of Western Countries' in Antonio Cassese (ed.), *The New Humanitarian Law of Armed Conflict* (Naples, 1979), 349; Luigi Condorelli, 'Les Pays afro-asiatiques' in Cassese, *New Humanitarian Law*, 386; Dan Ciobanu, 'The Attitude of the Socialist Countries' in Cassese, *New Humanitarian Law*, 399; and Niccolò Farina, 'The Attitude of the People's Republic of China' in Cassese, *New Humanitarian Law*, 445.

At one extreme were delegations such as Norway, who believed that national sovereignty should be totally subservient to humanitarian protection and that:

the protection of victims of armed conflicts should be the same regardless of their legal or political classification. The Conference should establish identical legislation for all victims of all armed conflicts. The distinction drawn between international and non-international conflicts, and the elaboration of two different protocols with different levels of protection for victims only led to discrimination or what has been called 'selective humanitarianism'.[12]

At the other extreme was a small but vociferous group opposed to the very concept of Protocol II, fearing that it would encourage intervention in their domestic affairs. Mr Sood, the Indian delegate, warned that:

the application of draft Protocol II to internal disturbances and other such situations would be tantamount to interference with the sovereign rights and duties of States. The definition of non-international armed conflicts was still vague and no convincing arguments had been put forward to justify the need for draft Protocol II, the provisions of which would not be acceptable to [his] delegation.[13]

By the time Conference had finally adopted Article 1 of Protocol II, settling its scope, his delegation was even denying the continued validity of common Article 3:

[it] was drafted in an entirely different context when the colonial and imperialist Powers ruled over half the world... the imperial and colonial Powers had, however, a clever pretext that the colonies were overseas parts of their metropolitan empires and hence armed liberation struggles were internal armed conflicts. Fortunately, Article 1 of Protocol I would now cover the wars of national liberation. My delegation is therefore of the view that it is out of context to mention Article 3 common to the Geneva Conventions in connexion with Protocol II.[14]

Most States recognised that the Norwegian view was unrealistic, and draft Article 1 was accompanied by numerous amendments seeking to make its scope more restrictive.[15] This was achieved by raising the threshold of application to cover only high-intensity conflicts, especially as

[12] CDDH/I/SR.23; VIII, 215 at 217.
[13] CDDH/I/SR.23; VIII, 215 at 224. This view is quite consistent with India's restrictive approach to human rights. See India's reservation to the International Covenant on Civil and Political Rights in Liesbeth Lijnzaad, *Reservations to UN-Human Rights Treaties: Ratify and Ruin?* (Dordrecht, 1995), 250–252.
[14] CDDH/SR.49/Annex; VII, 75 at 81.
[15] See G. Abi-Saab, 'Non-international Armed Conflicts', 227–228 and proposed amendments from Romania (CDDH/I/30; IV, 4), Pakistan (CDDH/I/26; IV, 6), Indonesia (CDDH/I/32; IV, 7) and Brazil (CDDH/I/79; IV, 8).

regards territorial control. When Committee I adopted a high-threshold Article 1 in 1975, applying only to conflicts resembling international wars,[16] several delegates were encouraged to demand an even closer parallelism between the two Protocols. Article 1 was, however, adopted by a rather weak consensus, and the Rapporteur for Committee I confirmed that, 'although delegations had not opposed the achievement of a consensus on draft Protocol II, quite a number in fact had serious doubts about it. It would be truer to say that there had been approval by the majority and silence on the part of others.'[17] Even Working Group B, which had originally drawn up draft Article 1, had only a 'very fragile consensus',[18] and some delegations asserted that there was actually no consensus at all.[19]

Despite widespread dissatisfaction, which must have been evident to the delegates, Articles continued to be adopted by weak consensus with large numbers of abstentions, threatening their credibility, until eventually a Protocol closely modelled on Additional Protocol I was adopted by the Committee. More elaborate and detailed even than the ICRC Draft, it clearly had little chance of success, and by the 1977 session the Pakistani delegation:

realized that there was considerable dissatisfaction with the length of the text as well as with the fact that it ventured into domains . . . considered sacrosanct and inappropriate for inclusion in an international instrument. A cross-section of opinion firmly held the view that the text entered into unnecessary details, rendering it not only cumbersome, but difficult to understand and to apply in the peculiar circumstances of a non-international conflict.[20]

Following a multitude of informal meetings, Pakistan presented a series of amendments to the Plenary, constituting a shorter and simplified Protocol II based on the assumption that it 'should not appear to affect the sovereignty of any State Party or the responsibility of its Government to maintain law and order and defend national unity, nor be able to be invoked to justify any outside intervention'.[21] The work of the previous years was thus radically changed and, with a minimum of debate, the Pakistani amendments were accepted by means of a 'gentleman's

---

[16] This text was virtually that finally adopted, and requirements for the threshold being crossed were the same. See CDDH/I/274 and CDDH/219/Rev.1; X, 21 at 40.

[17] CDDH/SR.49; VII, 59 at 67.

[18] Mr Obradović (Yugoslavia, Chairman of Working Group B), CDDH/SR.49; VII, 59 at 66.

[19] Mr Abdine (Syria), CDDH/SR.49; VII, 59 at 67.

[20] CDDH/SR.49; VII, 59 at 61.

[21] *Ibid.*

agreement' – the Draft was curtailed and simplified, in return for which those States opposed to it would not block its adoption. Article 1 was accordingly adopted by fifty-eight votes to five, but with twenty-nine abstentions.[22] That thirty-four States did not vote in favour demonstrates the deep-seated fears of many delegations.[23] Forsythe believes that very little was actually lost in this process, 'because not much, and certainly nothing very revolutionary, was to be found in the draft adopted in committee to begin with'.[24] So just how did the adopted text differ from the original draft prepared and submitted by the ICRC? Essentially three things were left out.[25]

First, Part IV of the ICRC Draft, which dealt with methods and means of warfare, was removed completely, demonstrating the opposition to a 'law of war' approach. The rules which had been contained within these provisions (i.e. the prohibition of unnecessary injury, of perfidy and of the abuse of recognised signs) were not, however, exhaustive of the 'Law of the Hague', and it has been convincingly argued that this omission is therefore of little legal significance.[26] Certainly, vital aspects of the laws of war as regards the protection of civilians survive to a large extent in Articles 13–18 of Additional Protocol II on 'Civilian Population',[27]and draft Article 22 on 'quarter' also survived, being retained in Article 4(1) of the final Protocol. The fact that the Protocol omitted these rules on methods and means cannot in any case prevent them, along with the rest of the provisions of 'Hague Law', from continuing to apply to internal armed conflicts as a matter of customary international law.[28]

The second omission was Part VII of the ICRC Draft, dealing with the execution of Protocol II. This covered such issues as dissemination

---

[22] CDDH/SR.49; VII, 59 at 70.

[23] All of the States not in favour were from the Third World except Norway, although clearly some perceived the Protocol as not going far enough rather than too far, as outlined above.

[24] Forsythe, 'Legal Management of Internal War', 282.

[25] For discussion of the omissions see G. Abi-Saab, 'Non-international Armed Conflicts', 231–233; Forsythe, 'Legal Management of Internal War', 282–283; and a brief mention in Junod, 'Additional Protocol II', 33–34.

[26] G. Abi-Saab, 'Non-international Armed Conflicts', 231–233; Forsythe, 'Legal Management of Internal War', 282–283.

[27] Although much of Part V, Chapter I of the ICRC Draft was condensed into essentially one Article in the final Protocol, the important principles have been retained, along with several additions which will be discussed below. See Forsythe, 'Legal Management of Internal War', 283 and n. 49 therein.

[28] This was nevertheless rather weak given the lack of accepted customary international law in this area, especially in 1977. For an examination of the customary international law applicable to internal armed conflict see chapter 4.

of the Protocol, conclusion of special agreements, and the role of impartial bodies such as the ICRC in helping with the observance of the provisions or in offering their services. Opposition to the last aspect in particular (i.e. draft Article 39) was very strong, and the reluctance to accept such a role for outside organisations again underlines the fear of the developing nations that such provisions would encourage interference in their domestic affairs. In the end, only one Article on relief was retained,[29] referring only to 'relief societies located in the territory of the High Contracting Party, such as Red Cross (Red Crescent [etc.]) organizations'. No mention is made of the ICRC, which accordingly has more standing under common Article 3 than under Additional Protocol II. This is important in theory, as the failure to repeat the right of humanitarian initiative in the Protocol permits States to argue that the ICRC's role is confined to those matters covered by common Article 3. This represents a marked change in direction for many States, and must be viewed as a retrograde step in light of the fact that in 1949 States had been prepared to accept a provision explicitly granting the ICRC the right of initiative. The relationship between common Article 3 and Protocol II, however, means that again the situation remains largely unchanged in practice.[30] Common Article 3 continues to apply to *all* internal armed conflicts, including those within the ambit of Additional Protocol II. It must therefore follow that the removal of draft Article 39 is irrelevant – Article 39 merely reaffirmed the provisions of Article 3, which is clear in its statement that the ICRC does have the right to offer its services to the parties to the conflict.[31]

Finally, any mention of 'the Parties to the conflict' was removed, reflecting the delegations' desire not to bestow any perceived legal recognition or status upon insurgents. As a result, 'the ... Protocol reads like a series of injunctions addressed exclusively to governments, or rather of unilateral undertakings subscribed to only by them'.[32] That such an instrument was intended is not inconceivable. Italy certainly believed that:

In ratifying this instrument, the High Contracting Parties will assume obligations, not towards rebel forces (which are neither subjects of international law nor Parties to Protocol II), but towards the other Contracting Parties, the in-

---

[29] Article 18 of Protocol II.
[30] Again see Forsythe, 'Legal Management of Internal War', 282–283 and G. Abi-Saab, 'Non-international Armed Conflicts', 231–233.
[31] Although the role may be limited, as outlined above.
[32] G. Abi-Saab, 'Non-international Armed Conflicts', 231.

ternational community and world opinion. Clearly, therefore, each Contracting Party's obligation to respect Protocol II cannot be conditioned or modified by the conduct of rebel forces,[33]

and Zaire agreed that:

Only a sovereign State can claim to have international legal personality and, as such, it enjoys all the prerogatives of sovereignty, including that of entering into international agreements and conventions, that is to say, of becoming a party to them. Accordingly, dissident armed forces are . . . rebels with no international legal personality. Their only legal status is that granted them under the domestic laws of their national State. To claim otherwise is to place a sovereign State on the same footing as a rebel movement, and that would imply *de facto* recognition of the movement.[34]

It may be true that only States can become party to Protocol II, but that does not mean that their obligations are owed only to each other, nor indeed that insurgents cannot be bound by the Protocol, and some States at the Conference were prepared to accept this.[35] For reasons discussed below, however, the purging of the phrase 'parties to the conflict' was in fact purely cosmetic, and had no effect on the legal structure of the instrument.[36] Additional Protocol II is clearly intended to apply equally to States and insurgents, although as outlined with regard to common Article 3, the legal basis for this requires further examination.

The binding nature of Protocol II for insurgents

The same justifications have commonly been advanced regarding the binding nature of Protocol II as presented above in relation to common Article 3.[37] For the reasons outlined therein, however, the legal basis for the binding nature of Protocol II on insurgents would appear to turn

---

[33] CDDH/SR.51/Annex; VII, 107 at 122.

[34] CDDH/SR.50/Annex; VII, 85 at 104.

[35] E.g. Belgium and the Soviet Union, who felt that, 'Once adopted, the text would become a national law imposing an obligation on all persons within the territory of the State in question. Any international instrument signed by a Government was binding on all those within its territory . . . Some delegations had thought that the text in question would impose an obligation on Governments only. That would be a serious mistake. The obligation was in fact valid for all citizens.' CDDH/III/SR.32; XIV, 309 at 314.

[36] It nevertheless demonstrates the importance of outward appearances to governments.

[37] I.e. the principle of legislative jurisdiction. See also the Soviet statement, CDDH/III/SR.32; XIV, 314.

on the effects of a treaty for third parties.[38] In order for the Protocol to have any legal effect for insurgents, two criteria must accordingly be met: (a) the High Contracting Parties must have *intended* the Protocol to bind insurgents, and (b) the insurgents must, in turn, *accept* the rights and obligations thereby conferred upon them.

The intention of the delegations at the Diplomatic Conference is difficult to determine objectively since some States clearly accepted the Protocol on the understanding that rebels would neither be bound by, nor receive rights through, its operation, whereas others took the opposite view. Cassese therefore suggested that the intention of the parties be discovered from examining the actual text of Protocol II, and he proceeded to set out three heads under which the objective intention to bind insurgents can be clearly demonstrated.[39] The first of these concerns the relationship between Additional Protocol II and common Article 3. Protocol II 'develops and supplements' common Article 3, which retains its own autonomous existence. In those situations where Protocol II is applicable, therefore, Article 3 necessarily continues to apply. Common Article 3 *does* bind both parties to internal armed conflict, so Protocol II must do likewise. It would, after all, be bizarre if Article 3 conferred rights and obligations upon insurgents, while Protocol II, which merely develops the provisions of that Article, were to be denied such an application. Article 1(1) of Additional Protocol II certainly suggests that the 1974–1977 Conference therefore intended to follow the approach of Article 3 and the 1949 Conference.[40]

Cassese's second argument rests on the fact that Article 1(1) of Protocol II outlines certain conditions which must be met before the Protocol becomes applicable. These relate to responsible command and territorial control on the part of the insurgents, enabling them to 'carry out sustained military operations and to implement [the] Protocol'. It is unclear whether the condition that insurgents be able to implement the provisions of Protocol II further requires that they actually do so,[41] but

---

[38] Especially in light of doubts as to whether Additional Protocol II represents customary international law to any real extent. The best text on the subject is Antonio Cassese, 'The Status of Rebels Under the 1977 Geneva Protocol on Non-international Armed Conflicts' (1981) 30 *ICLQ* 416.

[39] *Ibid.*, 424–430.

[40] This argument is not necessarily straightforward, however, in that it would appear to rule out the possibility that international law-making can be regressive in nature, rather than progressive and developmental.

[41] Thus rendering the Protocol's application based on reciprocity. See the discussion below at pp. 107–109.

it would be absurd were rebels required to comply with Protocol II in order for its provisions to apply, and yet gain no rights or duties from this compliance:

> If that were so, the insurgents would clearly never begin to keep the rules of the Protocol, aware that in any case they would not gain in the least from such behaviour. If the activation of the Protocol is made conditional on their respecting it, this of necessity must entail that once they prove able to implement the Protocol, its provisions become legally binding on them. A contrary interpretation would render the whole Protocol nugatory; it should therefore be discarded as contrary to the principle of 'effective interpretation'.[42]

A contrary argument claims that it is nevertheless in the interests of insurgents to apply the Protocol regardless, in that they would still benefit from its humanitarian protection, the State having a duty to the other High Contracting Parties to apply the Protocol whether the insurgents continue to abide by it or not.[43] Two problems arise from this. First, to assert that the parent State remains bound even where insurgents desist from applying the Protocol is untenable. The rebels *must* apply Protocol II to make it operational.[44] Should they cease to abide by their obligations under it, it necessarily ceases to apply. It is very well to say that a State becomes bound to apply Protocol II automatically upon the satisfaction of the conditions in Article 1(1) by insurgents, but it cannot be accepted that the State remains bound for the duration of the conflict should the insurgents modify their behaviour. To insist on this would ignore the transient nature of civil war. Secondly, as Cassese explains, the argument naively places the Protocol in a world where insurgents are happy to observe standards which they have not accepted, where States are keen to live up to their international obligations through a sense of humanitarianism, and where, should they fail to do so, the international community is quick to round on them, pressuring them to comply. This is sheer fantasy, and were the argument to prevail, the Protocol would die, being reliant on actions by Contracting Parties which are never likely to be forthcoming. 'States are presumed not to undertake exercises in futility',[45] and so insurgents must be bound by, and have rights under, Protocol II.

---

[42] Cassese, 'Status of Rebels', 425.
[43] *Ibid.*, 425–426. The argument was advanced by Italy: see above at text accompanying n. 33.
[44] Article 1(1).
[45] Cassese, 'Status of Rebels', 427.

Cassese's third argument turns on Article 6(5) of the Protocol, which provides that:

At the end of hostilities, the authorities in power shall endeavour to grant the broadest possible amnesty to persons who have participated in the armed conflict, or those deprived of their liberty for reasons related to the armed conflict, whether they are interned or detained.

By imposing a duty on 'the authorities in power' once the conflict is over, the paragraph clearly refers to both the government *and* the insurgents – to do otherwise would assume that insurgents will always be defeated. While this may indeed be an assumption that governments are more than ready to make, it seems inconsistent for the Protocol to afford legal status to insurgents at the end of the conflict, and yet to ignore them while hostilities are in progress. It might be logical to argue that when, and only when, insurgents actually form the government they can have duties imposed upon them, but it does not appear that this was the intention of the majority of delegates.

Turning to the second aspect necessary for a treaty to bind third parties (i.e. the assent of the third party), the willingness of insurgents to abide by Protocol II must be ascertained in each individual conflict, and might take the form of a unilateral declaration to that effect, or perhaps a request to a body such as the ICRC to guarantee respect for the provisions of the Protocol. That no mechanism provides for unilateral declarations (in contrast to Article 96(3) of Protocol I, under which the authority representing a national liberation movement can undertake to apply the Protocol by addressing a unilateral declaration to the depositary) can be explained by the fact that Protocol II only comes into effect where the rebels can and actually do apply its provisions anyway. The best show of willingness to be bound by the Protocol is thus to observe it, so that the conditions in Article 1(1) are met and the instrument can be applied by both sides.

Scope of application

The scope of application of Protocol II is outlined in Articles 1 and 2. Article 2 deals only with the personal field of application, providing that all persons affected by an armed conflict as defined in Article 1 are to receive the protection of the Protocol, without any adverse distinction founded on 'race, colour, sex, language, religion or belief, political or other opinion, national or social origin, wealth, birth or other status, or any other similar criteria'. More important is Article 1, which deals with the material field of application, in that it defines the conditions which must be present for an internal armed conflict to be regulated by Additional Protocol II. It provides that:

1. This Protocol, which develops and supplements Article 3 common to the Geneva Conventions of 12 August 1949 without modifying its existing conditions of application, shall apply to all armed conflicts which are not covered by Article 1 of the Protocol Additional to the Geneva Conventions of 12 August 1949, and relating to the Protection of Victims of International Armed Conflicts (Protocol I) and which take place in the territory of a High Contracting Party between its armed forces and dissident armed forces or other organized armed groups which, under responsible command, exercise such control over a part of its territory as to enable them to carry out sustained and concerted military operations and to implement this Protocol.

2. This Protocol shall not apply to situations of internal disturbances and tensions, such as riots, isolated and sporadic acts of violence and other acts of a similar nature, as not being armed conflicts.

The relationship between Additional Protocol II and common Article 3

Article 1 of the Protocol is clearly much more detailed than common Article 3, especially in its explicit list of conditions which must be met in order to render the Protocol applicable. Additional Protocol II in fact 'develops and supplements' common Article 3, and its other provisions are also more comprehensive and numerous.[46] One Commentary on the 1977 Additional Protocols states, however, that this phrase is not to be taken too literally since, 'it is the idea behind Article 3 which is developed and supplemented, not the provisions of the article itself'.[47] Of course in some situations the Protocol can have an indirect effect on common Article 3, setting out with greater clarity and precision the protections afforded therein. As Georges Abi-Saab has explained:

both Part II on 'Humane Treatment' and Part III on 'Sick, Wounded and Shipwrecked' elaborate in greater detail and more concrete terms the general principles enunciated in common article 3, and can legitimately be considered as an authoritative interpretation of these principles. Part III on the protection of 'civilian population'... can also be taken into consideration in the interpretation

---

[46] Junod nevertheless lists several characteristics shared by Article 1 of Protocol II and Article 3 of the 1949 Conventions. See 'Additional Protocol II', 35–36.

[47] Michael Bothe, Karl J. Partsch and Waldemar A. Solf, *New Rules for Victims of Armed Conflicts: Commentary on the Two 1977 Protocols Additional to the Geneva Conventions of 1949* (The Hague, 1982), 623.

of common article 3, which, being a part of a law-making multilateral treaty of humanitarian import, has to be interpreted in the light of its unfolding object and purpose, and according to the principle of inter-temporal law of its evolving legal environment of which the Protocol is a part.[48]

The fact remains, however, that the Protocol fails to provide guidance with respect to the main stumbling block of common Article 3 – namely, the determination of whether an armed conflict not of an international character actually exists.[49] Additional Protocol II may contain a more concrete set of provisions outlining when an armed conflict comes within the scope of its terms, but the scope of Additional Protocol II is clearly narrower and more restrictive than that of common Article 3. The conditions contained in Article 1 of the Protocol mean that it applies only to the most intense and large-scale conflicts.

This has important consequences. For Protocol II to have completely superseded or replaced Article 3 would have been very dangerous in light of this, and 'the safeguard of the autonomy of common Article 3 [therefore] became a matter not of precaution but of necessity'.[50] The stipulation that common Article 3 was being developed and supplemented 'without modifying its existing conditions of application' was therefore vital, and ensured that the protection already afforded by Article 3 could not be diminished. It follows from this that there must be different types of internal conflict.[51]

First, there are internal disturbances and tensions which, although conflicts of a kind, are regarded by Article 1(2) as being 'not armed conflicts',[52] and so beyond the ambit of common Article 3 and Additional Protocol II. Article 1(2) was lifted almost *verbatim* from the 1973 ICRC Draft,[53] which had stated that the Protocol would not apply to 'internal disturbances and tensions, such as riots, isolated or sporadic acts of violence and other acts of similar nature'. The final text, however, states that this is because these are 'not . . . armed conflicts'. The addition of this

[48] G. Abi-Saab, 'Non-international Armed Conflicts', 237.

[49] *Ibid*. This must be the case, as the Protocol covers only one such type of conflict.

[50] *Ibid*., 229.

[51] Four categories are set out in Bothe, Partsch and Solf, *Commentary on the 1977 Protocols*, 623–624.

[52] These are clearly not governed by humanitarian law, except perhaps to the extent that it coincides with human rights law. The application of human rights law is an interesting question which will be discussed in due course. See Theodor Meron, *Human Rights in Internal Strife: Their International Protection* (Cambridge, 1987), and the discussion below at pp. 230–231.

[53] Bothe, Partsch and Solf, *Commentary on the 1977 Protocols*, 628.

qualification may appear innocuous,[54] but it was nonetheless supported in very strong terms by several delegations,[55] and it is often claimed that the denial of armed conflict status for these situations was in fact directed at common Article 3 rather than Protocol II. The suggested aim was thus definitively to enshrine the threshold for internal armed conflict, and in turn to prevent the application of common Article 3 to less intense situations.[56] This was refuted, however, by several other delegations[57] on the basis of the autonomy granted to common Article 3 by Article 1 of the Protocol, and the Commentary confirms that Article 1(2) 'should not be interpreted as an attempt to change the sense of common Article 3, whose "existing terms of application" are not modified by Article 1 of Protocol II'.[58] In any case, it does not appear to cause any difficulties even if Article 1(2) *is* taken to say that riots and other isolated acts of violence do not amount to armed conflicts under common Article 3.

Secondly, there are those internal armed conflicts which meet the standards for the application of common Article 3, but which fall below the threshold of Protocol II. These continue to be governed by common Article 3.[59] Thirdly, there are those armed conflicts which meet the more restrictive conditions of Additional Protocol II. They are governed by the provisions of the Protocol, but as a subset of internal armed conflicts in general. Common Article 3, its sphere of operation left unchanged by the Protocol, therefore continues to apply alongside it. Finally, there are those internal armed conflicts which are fought for the purpose of national liberation from colonial or oppressive regimes. They are now governed by international humanitarian law as a whole, rather than that portion relating solely to internal armed conflict.[60]

---

[54] Rosemary Abi-Saab suggests that the provision was accepted 'almost inadvertently'. See 'Humanitarian Law and Internal Conflicts: The Evolution of Legal Concern' in Delissen and Tanja (eds.), *Humanitarian Law of Armed Conflict*, 209 at 216.

[55] Particularly (although not exclusively) the Eastern European States. The view was typified by the German Democratic Republic – see the statement by Mr Graefrath at CDDH/I/SR.29; VIII, 285 at 293.

[56] G. Abi-Saab,'Non-international Armed Conflicts', 229; R. Abi-Saab, 'Internal Conflicts', 216–217.

[57] E.g. Italy, CDDH/I/SR.29; VIII, 285 at 290; West Germany, CDDH/I/SR.29; VIII, 285 at 286, and CDDH/SR.49/Annex; VII, 75 at 79–80. See G. Abi-Saab, 'Non-international Armed Conflicts', 230.

[58] Bothe, Partsch and Solf, *Commentary on the 1977 Protocols*, 628.

[59] Junod, 'Additional Protocol II', 35; G. Abi-Saab, 'Non-international Armed Conflicts', 229.

[60] See above at pp. 89–90.

Several delegates at the 1974–1977 Diplomatic Conference expressed the personal view that, in time, common Article 3 and Additional Protocol II would come to be regarded, or treated, as coterminous: 'They thought state practice would effectively redefine common Article 3 "upwards", giving that article the same material application as the Protocol.'[61] There is, however, little evidence to support the proposition that such a shift in scope has taken place to date. While the issue remains to be resolved, any discernible shift has in fact been in the opposite direction, through efforts (largely on the part of the ICRC) to push the threshold of common Article 3 down as low as possible.[62] Greenwood has also argued for a downward shift in the threshold of Protocol II, suggesting that:

> it is difficult to find any justification today for the higher threshold for the application of Additional Protocol II. The provisions of Additional Protocol II are exclusively humanitarian in character. The provisions on the care of the wounded and sick should be uncontentious in any conflict, irrespective of its level of intensity. Those relating to fundamental guarantees are drawn in large part from human rights provisions, which are intended to apply in circumstances of normality, and the principles of common Article 3, which apply at the lower threshold in any event. The provisions on the conduct of hostilities are somewhat different, since these are derived from those of Additional Protocol I. Nevertheless, they are intended exclusively for the benefit of the civilian population and the limitations which they would impose upon government forces seeking to suppress a rebellion are minimal. There is no reason why a government should be obliged to observe these restraints towards its civilian population only in the circumstances specified in Article 1 of Additional Protocol II and not in all those to which common Article 3 applies and which are closer to a situation of normality within a State.[63]

The parties to the conflict

In order to come within the scope of Additional Protocol II, an internal armed conflict must involve hostilities between the armed forces

---

[61] Forsythe, 'Legal Management of Internal War', 286.

[62] See above at p. 33. The USA has actually sought to redefine the threshold of Protocol II downwards to make it coterminous with common Article 3, proposing in a declaration of understanding that Protocol II be applied whenever common Article 3 is applicable. See Hans-Peter Gasser, 'An Appeal for Ratification by the United States' (1987) 81 AJIL 912. Of course the USA is unlikely to face internal armed conflict.

[63] Christopher J. Greenwood, *International Humanitarian Law and the Laws of War* (Preliminary Report for the Centennial Commemoration of the First Hague Peace Conference 1899, pursuant to UN GA Res. 52/154 of 15 December 1997 and UN Doc. A/C.6/52/3) (The Hague, 1999), paragraph 137.

of a High Contracting Party and dissident armed forces or other organised armed groups. This represents one of the major deficiencies of
the Protocol in that, quite unlike common Article 3 (and indeed unlike
the definition of internal armed conflict offered by the International
Criminal Tribunal for the Former Yugoslavia), it does *not* apply where
two or more separate groups confront each other in any State, with no
active part in hostilities being played by government troops. Such situations are clearly possible, e.g. where an existing government is too
weak to intervene, or where the government of a State has collapsed
completely.[64] Indeed, as Greenwood points out: 'In cases of civil war it
is frequently difficult to determine which, if any, group can properly be
regarded as the government of the State concerned . . . Moreover, some of
the most vicious internal conflicts of recent years have occurred between
factions none of which could plausibly be regarded as the government of
a State.'[65] In those cases, rather than come under the more detailed regulation of Protocol II, the conflict must be governed solely by common
Article 3.

The issue of what exactly constitute 'organised armed groups' or
'armed forces' was raised at the Diplomatic Conference, where it was
considered that the phrase 'organised armed groups' implied a level
of organisation similar to that of regular armed forces.[66] It remained
to outline what represented 'armed forces', but an explanatory note
inserted into the Report of Committee I merely described them, rather
unhelpfully, as the following:

all the armed forces – including those which under some national systems might
not be called regular forces – constituted in accordance with national legislation

---

[64] Academic opinion certainly perceives this as being a serious fault. The tone taken by
Junod, 'Additional Protocol II', 36–37 and G. Abi-Saab, 'Non-international Armed
Conflicts', 228–229, suggests their disappointment. Bothe's similar feelings are
underlined in Géza Herczegh, 'Protocol Additional to the Geneva Conventions on the
Protection of Victims of Non-international Armed Conflicts' in György Haraszti (ed.),
Questions of International Law (Budapest, 1981), 71 at 77, n. 13. The ICRC had proposed
the inclusion of a provision to deal with such situations, but this was rejected by the
Conference: 'Such a situation, it appeared to the Conference, was merely a
theoretical textbook example and the provision was dropped, even though the ICRC
had already been confronted with this type of situation.' See Yves Sandoz, Christophe
Swinarski and Bruno Zimmerman (eds.), *Commentary on the Additional Protocols of 8 June
1977 to the Geneva Conventions of 12 August 1949* (Geneva, 1987), 1351. Conflicts such as
those in Angola, Somalia, the Lebanon and Liberia illustrate how real this problem is.
See Hilaire McCoubrey and Nigel D. White, *International Organizations and Civil Wars*
(Aldershot, 1995), 67.
[65] Greenwood, *International Humanitarian Law*, paragraph 138.
[66] According to a statement given by the ICRC in Working Group B of Committee I. See
Bothe, Partsch and Solf, *Commentary on the 1977 Protocols*, 626.

under some national systems; according to the views stated by a number of delegations, the expression would not include other governmental agencies the members of which may be armed; examples of such agencies are the police, customs and other similar organisations.[67]

It is obviously inadequate to define 'armed forces' as including 'all armed forces', and grey areas therefore remain, e.g. an armed police force organised in a military structure.[68]

The dissident armed forces or other organised armed groups must be under 'responsible command', which seems superfluous given that a certain level of organisation is already required on the part of armed groups. Nevertheless, this means that sporadic acts of individuals cannot bring a conflict under the scope of Additional Protocol II. Something more collective in character is required,[69] although it seems unlikely that responsible command must take the form of 'a rigid military hierarchy'.[70] It may well be that all that is required is some 'de facto authority sufficient both to plan and carry out concerted and sustained military operations and to impose the discipline required for the rules of the Protocol to be applied'.[71]

Territorial control and the nature of hostilities

The requirement of territorial control by the insurgents in Protocol II is very restrictive, being based not on the proportion or duration of such control, but rather on its inherent quality, which must be sufficient firstly to allow the rebels to mount concerted and sustained military operations, and secondly, to allow the insurgents to implement the provisions of the Protocol.[72] This raises several problems, and the provision

[67] CDDH/219/Rev. 1; X, 19 at 40; Bothe, Partsch and Solf, *Commentary on the 1977 Protocols*, 626.
[68] See the discussion above at pp. 38–40.
[69] Junod, 'Additional Protocol II', 37; McCoubrey and White, *International Organizations*, 65–66.
[70] Junod, 'Additional Protocol II', 37.
[71] *Ibid.* On this criterion, as well as those of territorial control, sustained and concerted military operations and the ability or will to implement the Protocol, the activities of the IRA in Northern Ireland and ETA in the Basque area of Spain can be excluded from the scope of the Protocol. See Hilaire McCoubrey, *International Humanitarian Law* (Aldershot, 1990), 172; Hilaire McCoubrey and Nigel D. White, *International Law and Armed Conflict* (Aldershot, 1992), 318; and *International Organizations*, 21. It could equally be argued that those situations are beyond the scope of Protocol II anyway, not being armed conflicts.
[72] G. Abi-Saab, 'Non-international Armed Conflicts', 228; Junod, 'Additional Protocol II', 37; Bothe, Partsch and Solf, *Commentary on the 1977 Protocols*, 627.

has been roundly criticised, with many scholars suggesting that it would be virtually impossible for rebels to achieve such effective territorial control until the situation was one of civil war in the classic sense.[73] Indeed, in only the second session of the Diplomatic Conference, Georges Abi-Saab warned that the provision was:

> too restrictive in view of the nature of modern, and particularly guerrilla, warfare. In armed conflict situations characterised by high mobility, territorial control continuously changes hands, sometimes altering between day and night, to the point of becoming meaningless. Other forms of intense armed conflict, such as urban guerrilla armed conflict, would not fulfill the requirement of territorial control. Such a requirement would then exclude from the ambit of Protocol II many, if not most, of the contemporary types of internal armed conflict and would confine it to the relatively rare cases of characterised civil war; it would thus severely limit its real significance and usefulness.[74]

Territorial control is not required by Article 1(4) of Additional Protocol I for national liberation movements to be able to meet the more onerous provisions of that instrument, and Abi-Saab has since suggested a more flexible approach whereby the quality of territorial control is assessed not in isolation, but in relation to the other party. His suggestion was made in the context of Article 1(4) of Additional Protocol I, but if this approach were to be applied by analogy to Additional Protocol II, then it would be sufficient that insurgents undermine the territorial control of the government whilst controlling the population and commanding its allegiance, without necessarily exercising complete or continuous control over an area.[75]

Finally, and despite the difficulty in arriving at an objective criterion for assessing the scale of a conflict, the Diplomatic Conference decided that (in contrast to common Article 3) some cut-off point was required to show that conflicts must have reached a critical point before Protocol II applies. Criteria such as duration and intensity were passed over as too subjective, possibly leading to restrictive interpretations and thus a consequent failure to apply, or delay in applying, the provisions of the Protocol. Instead the terms 'sustained and concerted'

---

[73] R. Abi-Saab, 'Internal Conflicts', 216; Herczegh, 'Protocol Additional', 77.

[74] CDDH/I/SR.24; VIII, 229 at 235. Herczegh, 'Protocol Additional', 78: 'The . . . government may be restricted to towns with garrisons and to . . . principal highways, whereas . . . insurgents may control the countryside.'

[75] G. Abi-Saab, 'Wars of National Liberation in the Geneva Conventions and Protocols' (1979–iv) 165 *Rec des Cours* 353 at 410–411.

were preferred – still implying duration and intensity, although suppos-edly on a more objective basis.[76]

Quite how much of an improvement this is remains to be seen. Granted, it is difficult to come up with a strict definition of intensity, but the terms chosen are still open to interpretation, and States will still be free to assert that the operations of insurgents are neither sustained nor concerted. It is, however, difficult to see how this problem can be effec-tively remedied without the creation of an independent body competent to adjudicate on such matters. Objective criteria may seem reasonable in theory, but the ability of involved parties to make objective decisions must be doubtful.

Ability to implement the Protocol

Once the other material requirements have been met by the insurgent party, the necessary structure and capacity would seem to be in place which might reasonably lead one to expect that the Protocol will be applied. Where insurgents follow this course, then the Protocol does indeed come into operation. For reasons already stated however,[77] they may decide not to apply the Protocol even if it is within their capa-bility to do so. It was therefore suggested by several delegations at the Diplomatic Conference that there should be some obligation on the in-surgents to apply the Protocol first, as an inducement for the State to do likewise.[78] The fear was that, otherwise, States would be expected to observe the provisions of the Protocol whilst their opponents opted not to. Whereas States had been reluctant to apply common Article 3 in the absence of *de facto* reciprocity,[79] the requirement that rebels be able to implement the Protocol before it becomes operational seems to introduce *de jure* reciprocity – the State is required to observe the law

---

[76] Junod, 'Additional Protocol II', 37; McCoubrey and White, *International Organizations*, 66. See also comments of Belgian delegate Mr de Breucker, CDDH/I/SR.29; VIII, 285 at 291.

[77] Such as a lack of commitment to, or respect for, international standards agreed by the government to which they are opposed.

[78] Forsythe, 'Legal Management of Internal War', 285. Although it would appear that all insurgents are required to demonstrate is the capacity to implement the Protocol, rather than the implementation of its provisions in practice, it is not clear how States would be persuaded that this capacity existed, and hence that the Protocol was applicable, without evidence in the form of either actual adherence to the obligations, or else a statement to the effect that the insurgent party would abide by its obligations under the Protocol.

[79] See the discussion above at pp. 85–86.

only to the same extent as the insurgents. This is highly controversial in two respects.

First, the principle of reciprocity is utterly alien to the Geneva Conventions and common Article 3, which are regarded as unilateral obligations applying automatically, and thus remaining unaffected by the conduct of the other party.[80] Suggestions that international humanitarian law is reciprocal in nature have been vehemently rejected by the Yugoslav Tribunal, which held that 'The defining characteristic of modern international humanitarian law is... the obligation to uphold key tenets of this body of law regardless of the conduct of enemy combatants.'[81] Humanitarian law is not based on a system of bilateral relations, instead laying down a set of absolute and unconditional obligations, to which the principle of reciprocity is irrelevant.[82]

Secondly, this seems to build a dangerous circularity into the application of the Protocol[83] – whether Protocol II is applicable or not depends on whether the insurgent party is able to implement it, but that in itself depends on the content of the Protocol. The actual provisions of the Protocol thus have a major effect on the threshold of its application, confusing the issue of the Protocol's threshold with the contents. The provision therefore seems to shift the onus unnecessarily onto the dissidents, instead of both sides being obliged to afford maximum protection to non-combatants at all times.

Article 1 of Protocol II represents a high threshold for application, preventing the application of its rules to all but the most severe internal armed conflicts, and leaving the majority governed by common Article 3, as they were previously. It has been claimed, however, that the threshold of Protocol II is in fact nothing more than an 'exercise in irrelevance'[84] since:

It would seem very strange if any State claimed that it would go below the level of protection contained in these provisions because the conflict had not reached the level provided for in Article 1. In fact, it must be immaterial what level the conflict has reached – these provisions contain nothing more than what follows

---

[80] Charles Lysaght, 'The Scope of Protocol II and its Relation to Common Article 3 of the Geneva Conventions of 1949 and Other Human Rights Instruments' (1983) 33 *American University LR* 9 at 22. See also the discussion above at p. 41.

[81] *Prosecutor v Kupreskić*, Case IT-95-16-T (Judgment of 14 January 2000) at paragraph 511.

[82] *Ibid.*, at paragraph 517.

[83] Bothe, Partsch and Solf, *Commentary on the 1977 Protocols*, 625.

[84] Asbjörn Eide, 'The New Humanitarian Law in Non-international Armed Conflict' in Cassese, *New Humanitarian Law*, 277 at 299.

from the general law of human rights, which today must be considered part of *jus cogens*.

In the same way, the question of the 'threshold' is irrelevant also for those few provisions of combat law which were adopted in the plenary. The actions prohibited in Protocol II, Articles 14–17, must be considered illegal under all circumstances, and can hardly be justified by the claim that the level of conflict has not reached the threshold of Article 1.[85]

This argument is reminiscent of that put forward by Pictet with respect to common Article 3 and, like Pictet's argument, is ultimately unconvincing. It is doubtful whether much of Additional Protocol II represents even customary international law, let alone *jus cogens*. Eide does seem to accept, however, that the provisions of Additional Protocol II could apply as human rights law, an assertion which turns on the relationship between humanitarian law and human rights law,[86] and on the provisions of the Protocol and the protection which they provide.

The content of Additional Protocol II

Before an examination of the substantive content of Additional Protocol II as contained in Part II on 'Humane Treatment',[87] Part III on 'Wounded, Sick and Shipwrecked'[88] and Part IV on 'Civilian Population',[89] Article 3 merits some consideration. It is a saving provision, reflecting the fear of several delegations that the instrument would be used as a basis for interference in the domestic affairs of States party. Article 3(1) therefore provides that the Protocol cannot be invoked to affect a State's sovereignty, its responsibility to maintain or re-establish law and order or its defence of national unity and territorial integrity. Article 3(2) provides that the Protocol cannot justify any intervention, either direct or indirect, in the conflict itself or in the internal or external affairs of the State. Both paragraphs are addressed not only to other States, but in absolute terms. Does the prohibition also apply, then, to international organisations?

Certainly some delegations feared that Article 3(2) would prohibit the United Nations from taking action to preserve international peace and

---

[85] *Ibid.*, 299–300.
[86] See above at pp. 43–45 and chapter 5 below.
[87] Articles 4–6.
[88] Articles 7–12.
[89] Articles 13–18. Despite the title of Part IV, Parts II and III are of course equally applicable to civilians.

security.[90] This is not the case, however – although Article 3 of Protocol II prohibits the Protocol from being used as a justification for intervention, the Security Council is unaffected. The legal basis for UN action is found in the Charter of the United Nations itself, rather than in the Additional Protocols, and United Nations action therefore remains permissible. Article 3 simply means that Additional Protocol II does not add to the possible grounds of intervention – it does not exclude those which already exist.[91]

Humane treatment

Protocol II deals with humane treatment in three lengthy and detailed Articles: Article 4 on fundamental guarantees; Article 5 on persons whose liberty has been restricted; and Article 6 on judicial guarantees.[92] These Articles are based to a large extent on international human rights instruments (in particular the 1966 International Covenant on Civil and Political Rights), and the relationship between human rights and humanitarian law will be examined in chapter 5 below. For the time being it is enough to point out that this aspect of humanitarian protection exists.

Fundamental guarantees

Article 4 contains what have been described as 'the most general accepted principles of civilisation',[93] and clearly applies to civilians, who must be 'persons who do not take a direct part or who have ceased to take part in hostilities'. The Article requires that non-combatants be treated humanely at all times, and proceeds to outline several illustrations, dealing with essentially the same issues as paragraph 1 of common Article 3. Much is added to the protection contained therein, however, with Article 4 bearing a close resemblance to the corresponding provision of Additional Protocol I.[94]

---

[90] Bothe, Partsch and Solf, *Commentary on the 1977 Protocols*, 633, and fears of the delegates of Yugoslavia at CDDH/I/SR.29; VIII, 285 at 295 and Canada at CDDH/I/SR.30; VIII, 299 at 300.

[91] Even if it purported to do so, Articles 2(7) and 103 of the UN Charter would become relevant.

[92] On these areas see G. Abi-Saab, 'Non-international Armed Conflicts', 233–236; Eide, 'New Humanitarian Law', 283–287; Herczegh, 'Protocol Additional', 80–82; and relevant sections of the Commentaries mentioned above.

[93] Eide, 'New Humanitarian Law', 283.

[94] Article 75.

Despite common Article 3 being the basis of the provision, there are several innovations in Article 4(2). Collective punishments,[95] terrorism,[96] slavery,[97] pillage,[98] rape, enforced prostitution and indecent assault[99] are missing from common Article 3's provisions, but all are prohibited by Protocol II, as are threats to commit any of the acts outlawed by Article 4.[100] Where Article 4 really succeeds in breaking new ground, however, is in the detailed protection afforded to children outlined in Article 4(3). Children are to continue to receive an education throughout the armed conflict, to be reunited with their families where possible, to be prevented from taking part in hostilities below the age of fifteen (although even if they do, the special protection contained in Article 4(3) remains applicable where they are captured), and they are to be temporarily removed from the area of hostilities if necessary. None of these provisions have any basis in common Article 3, and are modelled instead on rules contained in Geneva Convention IV,[101] which offers a series of protections for children under the ages of fifteen or eighteen.

Finally, it is interesting to note that one provision of Article 4 actually seeks to protect persons not covered by the first sentence of Article 4(1).[102] The final sentence of paragraph 1 provides that 'It is prohibited to order that there shall be no survivors.' Unlike the rest of Additional Protocol II (and indeed common Article 3), this clearly must concern people who have *not* ceased to take part in the hostilities.[103] It is the only remnant of the otherwise deleted draft section dealing with the methods and means of warfare, and whilst its inclusion is welcome, its physical placement in the Protocol might appear dubious. A self-contained Article located in Part I of the Protocol would in all likelihood, however, have been politically impossible.

Persons whose liberty is restricted

Common Article 3 contains nothing to regulate conditions of internment or detention specifically, the standard of humane treatment

---

[95] Article 4(2)(b).
[96] Article 4(2)(d).
[97] Article 4(2)(f).
[98] Article 4(2)(g).
[99] Found in the second half of Article 4(2)(e).
[100] Article 4(2)(h).
[101] Such as those contained in Articles 24 and 50.
[102] Which provides that humane treatment is only to be afforded to those 'who do not take a direct part or who have ceased to take part in hostilities'.
[103] Bothe, Partsch and Solf, *Commentary on the 1977 Protocols*, 640.

contained in Article 3(1) simply applying to all those not involved in hostilities, including detainees. Article 5 of Protocol II is therefore a valuable addition to the law, with several of its standards being based on the more rigorous provisions of Conventions III and IV, as well as the International Covenant on Civil and Political Rights. It applies in addition to the more general restraints of Article 4, and provides protection for those persons 'deprived of their liberty for reasons related to the armed conflict, whether they are interned or detained'. Again, the provisions are not solely applicable to military personnel in that a civilian interned for reasons of support of one side or another is covered by Article 5, as is the civilian who has committed an ostensibly ordinary criminal act, but one committed whilst taking advantage of the peculiar situation created by the conflict.[104]

The level of protection required to be provided by the detaining power is divided into two distinct categories. The first, contained in paragraph 1, covers those aspects of treatment which must be observed as a minimum in all cases, including such basic needs as medical treatment for the sick, the provision of food and water, the availability of relief, freedom of religion, etc. Paragraph 2, in contrast, deals with what are clearly considered less vital issues (e.g. accommodation, communication and location), and which need only be respected by those responsible for the detainees 'within the limits of their capabilities'. Surprisingly in this regard, paragraph 2(e), which appears to be aimed at the prohibition of medical experiments on those detained or interned, has been placed in the second category.[105] It has been claimed that this need not, however, represent a major problem, since 'The formula "within the limits of their capabilities" should in no case be understood as enabling to deny arbitrarily to the victims the enjoyment of the rights mentioned in Article 5 paragraph 2.'[106] It is nevertheless difficult to see how this could be enforced without independent assessment by some outside body.

The standard of treatment required for detainees is, in addition, linked to the conditions of the local civilian population.[107] Several delegations at the Diplomatic Conference had believed that it would be

---

[104] Bothe, Partsch and Solf give the example of the pillage of abandoned houses, *ibid.*, 645.

[105] *Ibid.*, 646.

[106] *Ibid.*, 647.

[107] See Article 5(1)(b) dealing with the provision of food, water, healthcare, etc., and Article 5(1)(e) covering working conditions.

unreasonable to demand a higher standard of treatment for detainees than that enjoyed by local civilians and the Article was therefore '[d]rafted giving due regard to the difficult conditions of a non-international armed conflict'.[108] This approach may seem *prima facie* reasonable, but it has been criticised as 'misleading': 'the local population whose liberty is not restricted has some possibilities on their own initiative to improve their conditions when in severe difficulty, while the detained or imprisoned people entirely rely on the conditions provided for them by the detaining power'.[109] That may be true, but if the local population is able to improve its living conditions, then the conditions of detention must improve correspondingly. Detainees have less opportunity to improve their own conditions and surroundings, but provided they are treated in a similar manner to the local population, their suffering should be minimised. It was certainly considered more appropriate to link standards of detention with civilian conditions rather than those of combatants, who may well be living in the most extreme circumstances.[110] Of course, it is naive to expect the civilian population always to enjoy better conditions than combatants – civilians may well be penned in by hostilities, with combatants preventing supplies from reaching them and hijacking food or aid for themselves. In such cases, the conditions of any detainees held in the area are inevitably bound to suffer also.

Article 5 has no provision corresponding to Article 126 of Geneva Convention III, referring to visits by an impartial body,[111] and it has therefore been claimed that there is nothing to prevent a detaining power from 'establishing a complete cloak of secrecy' around the treatment being afforded to detainees.[112] That may be true, but the right of humanitarian initiative contained in common Article 3 remains operative regardless. There may be no requirement to accept the offer of services from the ICRC or anybody else, but such offers often are accepted,[113]

---

[108] Bothe, Partsch and Solf, *Commentary on the 1977 Protocols*, 646.

[109] Eide, 'New Humanitarian Law', 284.

[110] This is especially true of guerrilla fighters. See Bothe, Partsch and Solf, *Commentary on the 1977 Protocols*, 647.

[111] Article 126 states: 'Representatives or delegates of the Protecting Powers shall have permission to go to all places where prisoners of war may be, particularly to places of internment, imprisonment and labour... The delegates of the International Committee of the Red Cross shall enjoy the same prerogatives.'

[112] Eide, 'New Humanitarian Law', 285.

[113] Various editions of the ICRC *Annual Reports* illustrate situations, not necessarily armed conflicts under common Article 3, where ICRC help has been readily accepted. See also Forsythe, 'Legal Management of Internal War', 275–276.

and detainees are certainly no worse off under Protocol II in this regard than under common Article 3 (and considerably better off in others).[114]

Penal prosecutions

Article 6 protects those judicial guarantees which are an essential part of any humane legal system. Safeguards include the principle that the accused must be informed of the details of the alleged offence;[115] that conviction must be on the basis of individual responsibility;[116] the principles of *nullum crimen sine lege* and non-retroactivity of penalty;[117] the presumption of innocence;[118] and the right of the accused to be present at trial[119] without being forced to testify.[120] Some of the provisions clearly elaborate in greater detail the measures contained in common Article 3(1)(d),[121] further influenced by Geneva Conventions III and IV,[122] the International Covenant on Civil and Political Rights[123] and Article 75(4) of Additional Protocol I, most of which is accepted as being equally applicable to internal armed conflicts. Besides those provisions covering the actual trial process, three new provisions found in Article 6(3)–(5) deal with advice regarding judicial and other remedies for those convicted, the prohibition of the death sentence for children and pregnant women or the mothers of young children, and encouraging the granting of amnesty at the close of hostilities.

Article 6, unlike Article 75(4)(h) of Protocol I however, does not contain the principle of *non bis in idem*.[124] One possible explanation advanced for this is that, during internal armed conflict, different laws may be

---

[114] Human rights monitoring bodies, such as the UN Human Rights Committee or Amnesty International, might also take an interest in detainees' conditions.

[115] Article 6(2)(a).

[116] Article 6(2)(b).

[117] Article 6(2)(c).

[118] Article 6(2)(d).

[119] Article 6(2)(e).

[120] Article 6(2)(f).

[121] It is relatively basic, however, simply prohibiting at all times 'the passing of sentences and the carrying out of executions without previous judgement pronounced by a regularly constituted court, affording all the judicial guarantees which are recognised as indispensable by civilized peoples'.

[122] Chapter III of Convention III and Chapter IX of Convention IV.

[123] Articles 14 and 15, much of which is taken over either verbatim or at least in principle.

[124] I.e. that nobody shall be liable to be prosecuted or punished for an offence for which he has already been finally acquitted or convicted.

promulgated by both parties to the conflict, and that consequently the application of this principle is difficult.[125] During periods of national emergency, clearly encompassing armed conflict, legislation is furthermore prone to deterioration into vagueness, so that although Article 6(2)(c) on non-retroactive penalties is an important provision, it fails to prevent someone being found guilty of an offence under vague and unreasonable laws promulgated after the conflict broke out, but before the act was committed.[126] Eide has therefore suggested that only those laws in existence prior to the conflict should be used as a basis for punishment,[127] but this would appear to be unworkable. First, it would penalise liberal societies, and secondly, it would also prevent everyday legislation from being available, not to mention legislation which may have to be passed as a genuine response to circumstances arising from the conflict, such as a curfew, or rationing in order to preserve adequate food stocks. It is also misguided to assert that vague legislation is inevitable simply because of conflict. Poor legislation is passed equally in peacetime, and States are naturally cautious about criticising each other's domestic laws, lest their own come under examination. Eide's proposition would furthermore be unpopular with the party controlling the State apparatus, who would thereby be prevented from using it fully to their advantage.[128] Of course, this is not in itself a reason to permit vague laws as a basis for punishment, but it does perhaps illustrate why the alternative suggestion is unlikely to be accepted by the international community.

The wounded, sick and shipwrecked

Common Article 3 contains only a cursory instruction that 'the wounded and sick shall be collected and cared for', without providing any guidance on how this is to be achieved. Articles 7 and 8 of Additional Protocol II elaborate extensively on common Article 3, including a requirement to take all possible measures to search for victims. Part III is applicable to 'all the wounded, sick and shipwrecked, whether or not they have taken part in the armed conflict', again making it plain that these standards are equally relevant to civilian and military casualties.

---

[125] Eide, 'New Humanitarian Law', 286; Bothe, Partsch and Solf, *Commentary on the 1977 Protocols*, 650.
[126] Eide, 'New Humanitarian Law', 285–286.
[127] *Ibid.*
[128] Recognised by Eide: *ibid.*

If Articles 7 and 8 merely elaborate the provisions of Article 3(1)(2) however,[129] Articles 9–12 represent new law in terms of internal armed conflict, and a clear improvement. Corresponding to the relevant provisions of Additional Protocol I,[130] they provide protection for medical and religious personnel engaged in missions of humanitarian concern in the field of the conflict, as well as requiring respect for the distinctive emblem of the Red Cross, none of which was included in common Article 3.

The civilian population

'Pre-existing rules of conventional international law applicable in non-international armed conflict did not provide explicit protection for the civilian population against attacks or the effects of attacks.'[131] Common Article 3 requires humane treatment at all times for those not involved in hostilities. Interpreted broadly, this would preclude attacks on the civilian population as a whole, in which case Article 13 of Additional Protocol II would be yet another provision of common Article 3 set out in more detailed form rather than constituting a new provision.[132] Article 3(1)(a), however, was largely intended to protect *individual* civilians in the power of an enemy party, rather than the civilian population as a whole.[133] In contrast, the provisions of Protocol II appear to be addressed not simply to the party in control of the civilians, but to all parties involved in the conflict, perhaps especially those *not* in control of the civilians.[134] This places these provisions within the realm of Hague Law (i.e. a 'law of war' approach) rather than Geneva Law,[135] and to this extent it is possible to see this as new law, although the principle of distinction contained in the Hague Rules must have been part of customary

---

[129] Corresponding incidentally to Article 10 of Additional Protocol I and certain provisions of Geneva Conventions I and II – Article 8 on search corresponds in general terms to Article 15(1) of Convention I and Article 18(1) of Convention II.

[130] Article 9 corresponds to Article 15 of Protocol I, Article 10 to Article 16, Article 11 to Articles 12 and 13, and Article 12 to Articles 18(4) and 38(1) as well as Articles 38, 39 and 44 of Convention I of 1949.

[131] Bothe, Partsch and Solf, *Commentary on the 1977 Protocols*, 667.

[132] See Herczegh, 'Protocol Additional', 82.

[133] Bothe, Partsch and Solf, *Commentary on the 1977 Protocols*, 667.

[134] G. Abi-Saab, 'Non-international Armed Conflicts', 235. In general, see McCoubrey and White, *International Organizations*, 104–108.

[135] The basis of Article 13 would appear to be Article 51 of Protocol I, which sets out the protection to be afforded to the civilian population in international conflicts, such as freedom from attack and reprisals.

international law to the extent that it applied to non-international armed conflicts.[136] Herczegh has actually argued that since the Second World War the question of distinction had become so blurred as to be ignored in practice, and that one of the main purposes of the Diplomatic Conference was therefore to reinforce the principle. Achieving this through Article 13 and its corresponding provision in Protocol I[137] means that Article 13 can be considered innovative, having as its object the prevention of growth in the number of victims rather than, as under the existing law, the protection of those who have already fallen into enemy hands.[138]

Although the various drafts of Additional Protocol II contained more, and more detailed, provisions in the area of civilian protection which were omitted from the final text, the general principle that the civilian population must be protected remains. There are certainly gaps – e.g. the lack of specific protection against indiscriminate or disproportionate attacks, or against the use of civilians as 'human shields' to deter military operations[139] – but it is possible to argue that the 'general protection' provided in Article 13(1) is broad enough to cope, such acts falling outside the 'humane treatment' which must be afforded at all times under both common Article 3 and Article 4 of Protocol II.[140]

Articles 14–17 are new provisions for internal armed conflict, having no source in common Article 3. They correspond to similar provisions contained in Additional Protocol I (except Article 17), and represent an improvement in the protection of civilians from the effects of conflict. Article 14 prohibits the starvation of civilians as a method of combat,

---

[136] See chapter 4.
[137] Article 48.
[138] Herczegh, 'Protocol Additional', 82–83.
[139] Bothe, Partsch and Solf, *Commentary on the 1977 Protocols*, 676.
[140] It would appear from discussions at the Conference, however, that the term 'general protection' does not include rules of customary international law requiring precautions in attack and proportionality. This is evident from the fact that Article 51(1) of Protocol I provides: 'The civilian population and individual civilians shall enjoy general protection against the dangers arising from military operations. To give effect to this protection, the following rules, which are additional to other applicable rules of international law, shall be observed in all circumstances', whereas Article 13(1) of Protocol II omits the reference to 'other applicable rules of international law'. This was explained as being because 'there is very little *conventional* international law with respect to non-international armed conflicts other than [common] Article 3 ... which contain no provisions pertinent to the subject matter of this Article of ... Protocol II'. CDDH/215/Rev. 1, paragraph 124; Bothe, Partsch and Solf, *Commentary on the 1977 Protocols*, 677. Such customary rules can, of course, apply without being incorporated into the Protocol. See chapter 4 below.

protecting objects indispensable to their survival;[141] Article 15 states that works or installations containing dangerous forces (such as dams or nuclear power stations) shall not be attacked if this would endanger the civilian population;[142] Article 16 protects cultural or historical objects and places of worship from attack;[143] and Article 17 prohibits the forced movement of civilians unless strictly required by military reasons or else for their own security.[144]

Finally, Article 18 of Protocol II deals with the issue of humanitarian relief for the civilian population. This was one of the most controversial and keenly debated Articles at the Conference, and the reduction in content of the final version is substantial.[145] Disagreement was the result of two differing views on relief, it being seen as equating to foreign intervention on the one hand, and as being necessary to prevent suffering of the civilian population, often even greater during internal than international conflicts, on the other.[146] Compromise proved difficult to achieve, and what resulted has been criticised as 'a step backwards in humanitarian law',[147] and 'much closer to the position of the opponents of Protocol II'.[148] Article 18(1) permits relief societies located within the territory to offer their services but, as with common Article 3, there is no corresponding duty to accept the offer. The ICRC is, of course, permitted to offer its services under common Article 3, and Bothe *et al.* correctly point out that, through the obligation to collect and care for the sick and wounded contained in Articles 7 and 8, offers made to that effect under paragraph 1 *must* be accepted if the party itself is either unable or unwilling to act itself in this regard.[149]

Paragraph 2 is more controversial, providing that where the civilian population is suffering undue hardship relief actions *shall* be undertaken. It refers to relief from outside agencies, which led those delegates fearful of intervention to insist that this is only possible with the

---

[141] Corresponding to Article 54 of Protocol I.

[142] This is an exact copy of the first sentence of Article 56(1) of Protocol I, but does not extend to attacks on military objects near the installation.

[143] Corresponding to Article 53 of Protocol I, applying alongside Article 19 of the 1954 Hague Convention for the Protection of Cultural Property in the Event of Armed Conflict.

[144] Corresponding to Article 49 of 1949 Convention IV.

[145] Bothe, Partsch and Solf, *Commentary on the 1977 Protocols*, 694.

[146] *Ibid.*

[147] Eide, 'New Humanitarian Law', 294.

[148] Bothe, Partsch and Solf, *Commentary on the 1977 Protocols*, 695. See also above at p. 95.

[149] *Ibid.*, 695–696.

consent of the High Contracting Party.[150] The requirement of consent corresponds to Article 70(1) of Protocol I, although there the consent required is that of the 'party concerned' rather than necessarily the High Contracting Party. The worry is therefore that Additional Protocol II might allow a government to refuse consent for aid to be given to its opponents. It has, however, been suggested that, 'The Party in question has no unfettered discretion to refuse the agreement, it may only do so for valid reasons, not for arbitrary and capricious ones.'[151] This seems reasonable in light of the humanitarian object of the Protocol, but there is little evidence of this intention from the text itself – the Article un-ambiguously states that the consent of the High Contracting Party is required, making no allusion to the fact that their consent is in any way limited.

As a matter of strict interpretation therefore, any consent sought or received from the insurgents would be both unnecessary and irrelevant, even if the relief action were taking place in territory under their control. This approach is unrealistic in practice, and an alternative interpretation would be that, in accordance with the interpretation of Article 70(1) of Protocol I, a party is only 'concerned' if it is either receiving relief, or else has to grant transit for the aid.[152] Consent of the State party would, then, be necessary only where it is receiving relief itself, or where it must grant transit to enable aid to reach the insurgents.[153] Of course, the government may indeed refuse to grant consent for the transit of aid for rebel civilians through its territory, although this ought to be frowned upon by the international community. In any case, where aid is being distributed in rebel-held territory, which does not require transit through government-controlled areas, there is little the High Contracting Party can reasonably do to prevent it, whether it chooses to grant permission or not.

Additional Protocol II in practice

In 1988, eleven years after its adoption and ten years after its entry into force,[154] Georges Abi-Saab thought that it was still 'too early to evaluate

---

[150] Proposed by Finland in an effort to make the provision acceptable, CDDH/435/440.

[151] Bothe, Partsch and Solf, *Commentary on the 1977 Protocols*, 696. See also interpretative statements made to that effect by Belgium and West Germany at CDDH/SR.53/Annex, 156–157.

[152] Bothe, Partsch and Solf, *Commentary on the 1977 Protocols*, 696.

[153] *Ibid.*

[154] Additional Protocol II entered into force on 7 December 1978.

Protocol II in the light of actual practice',[155] and despite the growth in the number of internal conflicts, relatively little has changed in the intervening period with respect to the application of humanitarian law. The main problem in this regard is that many of the States which have been beset by internal armed conflict since 1977 have never indicated any consent to be bound by Additional Protocol II: Angola, Namibia, Mozambique and Somalia in Africa, Afghanistan and Sri Lanka in Asia, and Haiti and Nicaragua in the Americas.[156] Of course common Article 3 is, or was, applicable to all of these conflicts, yet even its acceptance and effectiveness is not often apparent.[157] Four States struck by internal armed conflict which have indicated their willingness to be bound by the provisions of Additional Protocol II, however, are El Salvador, Rwanda, Bosnia-Herzegovina and Russia.

El Salvador

When the five main guerrilla opposition groups unified in 1980, forming the FMLN, with the aim of overthrowing the right-wing Government and creating a Peoples' State, hostilities broke out between the FMLN and Government forces (comprising the regular armed forces and the National Guard), as well as more extremist paramilitary organisations. It is difficult to be certain, however, whether the conditions for the application of Additional Protocol II were fulfilled. There was certainly an armed conflict taking place on the territory of a High Contracting Party, between its armed forces and dissident armed forces. The problem lies in deciding whether the FMLN had responsible command, and exercised such control over territory as to enable them to carry out sustained and concerted military operations and to implement the Protocol. Although the leadership undertook in 1988 to ensure that its combat methods would satisfy both common Article 3 and Additional Protocol II,[158] little, if any, effort was made to meet the standards contained therein.

---

[155] 'Non-international Armed Conflicts', 236.
[156] Forsythe, 'Legal Management of Internal War', 294, stated that those who needed the Protocol were those who would not accept it, and vice versa.
[157] Examples are numerous of violations even of its more basic provisions.
[158] See the FMLN statement cited in *Prosecutor* v *Tadić* (Appeal on Jurisdiction) 35 ILM 32 (1996) at paragraph 107. Waldemar A. Solf had stated in 1982 that up until then no such statement had ever been made, at least of which he was aware. See 'Commentary on International Non-international Armed Conflicts: Case Studies of Afghanistan, Kampuchea and Lebanon' (1982) 31 *American University LR* 927 at 932.

Territorial gains made by the FMLN tended to be only temporary,[159] and in such a situation it is difficult to accept that many of the provisions of Additional Protocol II could be observed. Certainly Solf doubted:

that a movement that does not control a single town and whose political arm is situated in another country, with only loose links to the movement's organized armed groups, has the capability of implementing the Protocol. I question whether it can implement the judicial standards of article 6, the standards established for the treatment of detained persons under article 5, and the standards established under articles 7–12 for the protection of wounded, sick, shipwrecked, and medical personnel units.[160]

It seems likely that the FMLN were unable to implement the Protocol effectively, due to the essentially guerrilla nature of their struggle. Having been one of the first States to accept the Additional Protocols (Protocol II was ratified by El Salvador on 23 November 1978) it might nonetheless have been hoped that the Salvadorean Government would be keen to uphold its underlying principles, if not its provisions. The Government refused to admit that Protocol II was *de jure* applicable, but it did nevertheless accept that it should be applied because its provisions merely developed and completed the provisions of common Article 3.[161]

Despite this, little humanitarian restraint was shown, and the catalogue of atrocities committed by Government troops makes gruesome reading: civilians were tortured and slaughtered by extreme right-wing army 'death squads'; fleeing refugees were bombed by the army and air force; villages suspected of sympathising with the FMLN were destroyed by indiscriminate bombing and their residents massacred.[162] Steps were eventually taken by the Government to curb the number of human rights violations by its troops, and in May 1984 a special commission was set up to eradicate death squads. In 1985 President Duarte

[159] For details of the conflict, and the nature of hostilities/breaches of humanitarian law, the author has relied heavily on the relevant entries in *Keesing's Contemporary Archives of World Events* (London, 1979–1993).

[160] Solf, 'Case Studies', 932.

[161] Greenwood, 'Customary Status of the Additional Protocols', 113, and 'Application of Humanitarian Law' 48; ICRC, *Annual Report* 39 (1989); *Tadić* (Jurisdiction) at paragraph 117.

[162] In December 1981, for example, government troops attacked FMLN strongholds in the north-east of the country, wiping out eight villages. General Garcia later admitted that the area had been the target of 'aerial bombardment', and that 'a lot of people' had been killed. See *Keesing's Contemporary Archives of World Events* (1982), 31618. In March 1992 hundreds of bodies were exhumed from FMLN areas: see *Keesing's Record of World Events* (1992), 39137.

also announced guidelines for aerial attacks, requiring the army High Command to give prior written approval, and to inform pilots if civilians were in the area. This was too little too late however, and it seems likely that only political factors forced even this gesture towards the provisions of Protocol II.[163] Reporting after the cessation of hostilities in March 1993, the Truth Commission stated that the Army had been responsible for most atrocities, and that the majority of the 75,000 victims had been civilians. It concluded that 'the atrocities committed by the security forces were not uncontrolled excesses but the result of a deliberate counterinsurgency strategy by the state'.[164]

For their part, the FMLN concentrated on a policy of sabotage and economic attacks, but were also guilty of numerous violations of humanitarian law (although to a lesser extent than Government troops). In January 1987, for example, the FMLN tortured, raped and killed seven peasants, and embarked on a tactic of indiscriminate use of landmines while, in late 1987, food stocks were attacked under the slogan 'either everyone eats or no-one eats'. In 1988, following the blowing up of a minibus outside San Salvador, killing eight civilians, the FMLN apologised for their tactics and the civilian casualties which they had caused, finally realising that a complete disregard for humanitarian values was counterproductive. The picture to emerge from the conflict in El Salvador, however, is of an astonishing disregard for the most basic human rights and laws of war.

Rwanda

Rwanda acceded to the Additional Protocols of 1977 on 19 November 1984, several years before the conflict of the early 1990s between the Government and the rebel Rwandan Patriotic Front (RPF) tore the country apart. Were the conditions necessary for the application of Protocol II met? There was clearly an armed conflict in progress, taking place in the territory of a High Contracting Party and, although to a large extent tribal, the conflict was indeed between Government armed forces (mainly Hutu) and dissident armed forces (i.e. the mainly Tutsi RPF).

---

[163] The United States had been providing the right-wing Government of El Salvador with a great deal of support in the form of money, military equipment and training/advisers (and would continue to do so). The US Government had, however, become uneasy at the systematic atrocities being committed, and the measures taken by El Salvador may well have been simply to placate America into continued support. If that were the case, then they were quite successful.

[164] *Keesing's Record of World Events* (1993), 39361.

Questions remain as to whether the RPF were under responsible command, or exercised sufficient territorial control to enable them to carry out sustained and concerted military operations and to implement the Protocol, but having initially 'invaded' Rwanda from exile in October 1990, the RPF gained control of the north of the country, and through military operations were able to force a multiparty constitution in 1991 and a peace agreement in 1992. When this peace agreement was broken by the Government, the RPF were strong enough to advance further, taking the capital, Kigali. There was clearly a degree of organisation and command, and sustained and concerted military operations were carried out. In light of this, it seems untenable to argue that the RPF's control over a large proportion of the country still did not permit them to implement the Protocol if they wished to do so, and so it would appear that all of Protocol II's conditions were met. Indeed, the International Criminal Tribunal for Rwanda has held that the conflict was 'an internal armed conflict within the meaning of Additional Protocol II'.[165]

Military intervention by France on behalf of the Hutu Government, and by a United Nations Force (UNAMIR[166]) in a purely peacekeeping operation, providing humanitarian aid, both failed to change the character of the conflict from internal to international.[167] That being the case, how effective was Protocol II in protecting civilians during the conflict? It is now common knowledge that humanitarian law was powerless to prevent the horrific suffering of thousands of civilians in Rwanda. The Hutu army and various militia organisations launched a campaign of genocide against the Tutsis, with huge numbers being massacred, and the full horror of events can be perhaps traced through various descriptions found in ICRC reports and press releases.

---

[165] *Prosecutor* v *Akayesu*, Case ICTR-96-4-T (Judgment of 2 September 1998) 37 ILM 1399 (1998) at paragraph 627: 'in addition to the requirements of Common Article 3 being met,... the material conditions... relevant to Additional Protocol II have been fulfilled. It has been shown that there was a conflict between, on the one hand, the RPF, under the command of General Kagame, and, on the other, the governmental forces, the FAR. The RPF increased its control over the Rwandan territory from that agreed in the Arusha Accords to over half the country by mid-May 1994, and carried out continuous and sustained military operations until the cease fire on 18 July 1994 which brought the war to an end. The RPF troops were disciplined and possessed a structured leadership which was answerable to authority. The RPF had also stated to the International Committee of the Red Cross that it was bound by the rules of International Humanitarian Law.'

[166] United Nations Assistance Mission for Rwanda.

[167] For the reasons outlined above at pp. 75–76.

On 21 April 1994, for example, the ICRC stated that:

The fighting that has raged in central Rwanda since early April has now spread to the entire country, leaving tens of thousands of people dead and as many injured. Hundreds of thousands more have fled their homes to escape the slaughter and are now scattered throughout the country. There is an enormous need for humanitarian assistance.[168]

Tens, maybe hundreds of thousands killed: the exact number of victims of the massacres that have swept Rwanda over the last two weeks will never be known...The human tragedy in Rwanda is on a scale that the International Committee of the Red Cross (ICRC) has rarely witnessed.[169]

The next week, it was reported that:

The extreme violence that has been tearing Rwanda apart is claiming more victims every day. The refugees streaming across the country's borders give horrific accounts of massacres. ICRC delegates who returned to Geneva on 27 April are badly shocked by the terrible events there. 'It was the heart of darkness,' said one. The conflict in Rwanda, which has caused over 100,000 deaths in two weeks, constitutes one of the gravest crises that the ICRC has ever faced. The hundreds of thousands of people displaced throughout the country now face starvation. There is hardly a family in the country that has not been affected by this tragedy, whether because of the death of loved ones, being forced to flee, or hunger. The entire population is suffering.[170]

Despite continued appeals from the ICRC, and the supposed protection of those at risk by the United Nations, the slaughter continued, with nobody safe from attack:

Twenty-one children were killed in Butare on 1 May during an attack on an orphanage...This outrageous act took place in the context of the violence that has swept the Butare area in recent days. Thirteen volunteers of the Rwandese Red Cross – three of them in the orphanage – have also lost their lives in the most atrocious circumstances.[171]

There has been no halt to the massacres in Rwanda. Appalling atrocities are committed every day, in flagrant violation of the most basic principles of humanity, and the number of victims continues to rise. The efforts being made by the ICRC to lessen the suffering of the Rwandan people cannot mask the horror that has the country in its grip.[172]

The number of victims claimed by the wave of murderous violence that has swept Rwanda can no longer be estimated. Continued heavy fighting in Kigali

---

[168] ICRC News 16/21, April 1994.
[169] ICRC Press Release 1772/21, April 1994.
[170] ICRC News 17/28, April 1994.
[171] ICRC Communication to the Press 94/20/3, May 1994.
[172] ICRC News 19/11, May 1994.

and other regions has been accompanied by further massacres and prompted a mass exodus towards the centre of the country...

On 19 May mortar bombs fell on the main hospital in Kigali, killing 30 wounded. This is yet another serious violation of international humanitarian law added to the countless atrocities committed in Rwanda. The ICRC calls on all the parties to the conflict to respect civilians, the wounded and staff of humanitarian organizations who are risking their lives to bring help to this stricken country.[173]

Breaches of Additional Protocol II, along with every other humanitarian law and human rights instrument, were committed systematically and continually in Rwanda. There was quite simply no humane treatment. Civilians and the wounded were attacked and murdered, along with relief workers and medical staff. Thousands of people were forced to flee their homes in fear of their lives. Genocide was committed on a huge scale. The widespread perpetration of atrocities makes it unnecessary to list individual breaches of Additional Protocol II – the new humanitarian law failed utterly.

Bosnia-Herzegovina

The conflict in Bosnia-Herzegovina began when fighting broke out between Bosnian Muslims and Serbs in March 1992 following a referendum affirming the declaration of independence from Yugoslavia, supported by the Muslims and Croats, but opposed by Serbs. The mainly Serb Yugoslavian National Army intervened on the side of the Serbs, leaving the poorly equipped Muslims dependent upon Croat aid. By May 1992, Serb forces had overrun the majority of Bosnia and Croat forces much of the rest, leaving the Bosnian Muslim Government stranded and besieged in Sarajevo and a few other areas. Space does not permit a detailed examination of the background to the conflict[174] – rather, the main questions to be studied in the present context are the applicability and observance of Additional Protocol II.

Bosnia became a party to Additional Protocol II by succession on 31 December 1992, but whether the conflict met the criteria of Article 1 is a complex and difficult question to answer. There was certainly an armed conflict taking place on the territory of a High Contracting Party, which

---

[173] ICRC Press Release 1776/20, May 1994.

[174] See Edgar O'Ballance, *Civil War in Bosnia, 1992–1994* (New York, 1995); Helsinki Watch, *War Crimes in Bosnia-Hercegovina* (New York, 1992), 19–49; and Laura Silber and Allan Little, *The Death of Yugoslavia* (London, 1995).

'exceed[ed] the intensity requirements applicable to both international
and internal armed conflicts. There ha[d] been protracted, large-scale
violence between the armed forces of different States and between governmental forces and organized insurgent groups.'[175] The second half of
this assertion underlines the main problem: that of assessing the parties
to the conflict, and thus whether the conflict was internal or international in character.[176] To an extent, there was an armed conflict between
the armed forces of the High Contracting Party (i.e. the Bosnian Muslim
Government) and Bosnian Serb dissident armed forces, as required by
Article 1 of Additional Protocol II, but this was only one facet of the
conflict. There was additional involvement on the part of Bosnian Croat
troops, Serbia, Croatia, the United Nations and NATO troops.[177] As already discussed, the involvement of foreign troops can internationalise
a hitherto internal conflict, and much of the academic literature did
regard the situation in former Yugoslavia as comprising a single international conflict.[178] The Hague Tribunal case law also tends to confirm that
many of the constituent conflicts were international,[179] although the degree of outside involvement required was a matter of debate, and where
it is insufficient to render the insurgents agents of another State, then
the conflict must remain internal. Thus, *Tadić* (Appeal on Jurisdiction)
held that while the involvement of the Croatian and Yugoslav Armies
in Bosnia did render the conflict international, '[t]o the extent that
the conflicts had been limited to clashes between Bosnian Government
forces and Bosnian Serb rebel forces in Bosnia-Herzegovina...they had
been internal'.[180] This is clearly correct. The Appeals Chamber accordingly determined that the conflict had both international and internal

---

[175] *Tadić* (Jurisdiction) at paragraph 70.
[176] See above at pp. 47–51.
[177] On the application of humanitarian law to UN forces see the texts cited above
at p. 77, nn. 206 and 208. Christopher J. Greenwood, 'War Crimes Proceedings Before
the International Criminal Tribunal for the Former Yugoslavia' [1997] *Military LJ* 15,
discusses the Tribunal's likely approach to the issue.
[178] Helsinki Watch, *War Crimes in Bosnia*, 5; Theodor Meron, 'International
Criminalization of Internal Atrocities' (1995) 89 *AJIL* 554 at 556. The Commission of
Experts established under Security Council Resolution 780 of 1992 also felt that 'the
character and complexity of the conflicts concerned...justify an approach whereby
it applies the law applicable in international armed conflicts to the entirety of the
armed conflicts in the territory of the former Yugoslavia'. See Interim Report of the
Commission, UN Doc. S/25274 at paragraph 45, a view reiterated in the Final Report,
UN Doc. S/1994/674 at paragraph 44.
[179] See the *Nikolić, Mrksić, Karadžić and Mladić* and *Rajić* Rule 61 Cases, discussed above
at p. 48.
[180] *Tadić* (Jurisdiction) at paragraph 72.

aspects.[181] In *Tadić* (Appeal Judgment), however, the Appeals Chamber found that the conflict in Prijedor was international in character,[182] and should the Rule 61 decisions be confirmed by the Tribunal, little will be considered non-international.

Nonetheless, at least some of the hostilities would have fallen within the scope of Additional Protocol II had either the Bosnian Government or the Bosnian Serbs shown any willingness to apply its provisions. The parties did reach an agreement to apply common Article 3 and several other provisions of the Geneva Conventions,[183] but not Additional Protocol II, and even the more limited provisions of common Article 3 were not applied in practice.[184] Widespread rape, torture, murder and 'ethnic cleansing' demonstrated that the most basic humanitarian and human rights principles had been violated by all sides.

Chechnya

The former Soviet Republic of Chechnya declared its independence in 1991, leading to a conflict between Chechen 'rebels' and Russian forces from 1994 to 1996, which ultimately claimed around 80,000 lives.[185] The agreement finally reached between Moscow and Grozny to end hostilities[186] served only to sidestep the issue, however, and intense fighting broke out again in 1999.

The Russian Federation ratified the Geneva Conventions in 1954, and Additional Protocol II on 29 September 1989. There can therefore be no question that the provisions of international humanitarian law would be applicable, provided the hostilities met the relevant thresholds. Despite Russia's continued assertion that the situation was one of

---

[181] *Ibid.*, at paragraph 77, confirmed by *Prosecutor v Tadić* (Judgment of 7 May 1997) at 209–228, which found the conflict in the Prijedor region to be internal.

[182] See above at pp. 49–50.

[183] Agreement No. 1, 22 May 1992, Article 2, paragraphs 1–6. See *Tadić* (Jurisdiction) at paragraph 73.

[184] As can be seen from the Hague Tribunal's case law, e.g. the offences listed in *Prosecutor v Nikolić* 108 ILR 21 at 24–31 and *Prosecutor v Karadžić and Mladić* 108 ILR 86 at 92–102.

[185] During a television interview on 3 September 1996, General Lebed, the Russian National Security Adviser, stated that between 70,000 and 90,000 people had been killed as a result of the conflict. See *Keesing's Record of World Events* (1996), 41281. For further information and background to the conflict, see Barry Renfrew, 'Chechnya' in Roy Gutman and David Rieff (eds.), *Crimes of War: What the Public Should Know* (New York, 1999), 68, John B. Dunlop, *Russia Confronts Chechnya* (Cambridge, 1998), and Carlotta Gall and Thomas De Waal, *Chechnya* (New York, 2000).

[186] Agreement was reached in August 1996. See *Keesing's Record of World Events* (1996), 41235–41236.

terrorism and anti-terrorist action rather than armed conflict,[187] there can be no realistic doubt that common Article 3 was applicable. A number of experts consulted informally by the Crimes of War Project held unanimously that this was the case,[188] with one of the experts, Tuzmukhamedov, pointing to an implicit recognition by the Russian Government that common Article 3 applied.[189] Agreement was less complete on the question of whether Additional Protocol II was applicable, with four of the six experts leaving the question open.[190] Bassiouni and Turns, however, asserted confidently that this was the case.[191]

The 1994–1996 conflict had been accepted, even within Russia, as an armed conflict. Russian domestic law providing additional compensation for those troops sent on particularly hazardous missions was amended in 1997 to cover those who had 'carried out assignments under the conditions of a non-international armed conflict in the Chechen Republic',[192] and the Russian Constitutional Court held in 1995 that Additional Protocol II was applicable to the Chechen conflict, admitting that its provisions had not been respected due to insufficient steps towards its national implementation.[193] Regardless of whether

---

[187] See, for example, Amelia Gentleman and Ewen MacAskill, 'West Threatens Sanctions against Russia', *Guardian*, 8 December 1999, 15, referring to Vladimir Putin's 'familiar response that Russia is orchestrating an anti-terrorist campaign and not a war against the Chechen people'.

[188] The Crimes of War Project is a collaboration between journalists and academics on the laws of war designed to raise public awareness. See Gutman and Rieff, *Crimes of War*. Their panel of experts consisted of A. P. V. Rogers, Françoise Hampson, H. Wayne Elliott, M. Cherif Bassiouni, David Turns and Bakhtiyar Tuzmukhamedov. See 'Russia's War in Chechnya is an Internal Armed Conflict Governed by International Conventions on War, Top Experts Say', available at http://www.crimesofwar.org/chechnya.

[189] Russian Prime Minister Putin had told the *Financial Times* during an interview that Russia was 'strictly complying with its obligations concerning the provisions of international humanitarian law'. (Tuzmukhamedov, citing the *Financial Times* of 11 December 1999, on-line edition). See http://www.crimesofwar.org/chechnya/tuzmukhamedov.html.

[190] Although Tuzmukhamedov, *ibid.*, tended towards the view that Protocol II was probably not applicable, doubting whether the Chechen armed groups met the necessary requirements of Article 1.

[191] Available at http://www.crimesofwar.org/chechnya/bassiouni.html and http://www.crimesofwar.org/chechnya/turns.html.

[192] Federal Law of the Russian Federation No. 146-FZ (19 November 1997), in *Sobraniye Zakonodatelstva Rossiyskoy Federatsii*, 1997, No. 47, Art. 5343. See Tuzmukhamedov's opinion for the Crime of War Project.

[193] Decision of the Constitutional Court of the Russian Federation on the constitutionality of Presidential Decree No. 2137 of 30 November 1994 on measures for the restoration of the Constitution and the rule of law on the territory of the

Additional Protocol II was applicable in addition to common Article 3 when hostilities recommenced in 1999, violations of humanitarian law have continued to be widespread, with high numbers of civilian casualties.

On 29 October 1999, for example, Russian aircraft attacked a convoy of civilians, killing fifty,[194] leading US Secretary of State Rubin to assert on 8 November 1999 that Russia's 'indiscriminate use of force against civilians [was] not in keeping' with her commitments under humanitarian law.[195] On 6 December 1999, Russian aircraft dropped leaflets over Grozny informing the inhabitants that they had five days to leave, or else face all-out attack:

You are surrounded...All roads to Grozny are blocked. You have no chance of winning. The Russian command is giving you a last chance...Those who remain will be viewed as terrorists and bandits. They will be destroyed by artillery and aviation. There will be no further negotiations. Everyone who does not leave the city will be destroyed. The countdown has started.[196]

Bombardment was stopped on 11 December, with further leaflets being dropped telling civilians of a safe corridor out of Grozny, but shelling recommenced on 13 December.[197] The response of Europe and the United States was swift, although limited. Clearly considering Russia to be in breach of her international legal obligations, the EU issued a communiqué on 10 December condemning the bombardment of Chechnya as 'totally unacceptable', diverting a proportion of technical

---

Chechen Republic, of Presidential Decree No. 2166 of 9 December 1994 on repression of the activities of illegal armed units within the territory of the Chechen Republic and in the zone of the Ossetino-Ingushetian conflict, of Resolution No. 1360 of 9 December 1994 on ensuring the security and territorial integrity of the Russian Federation, the principle of legality, the rights and freedoms of citizens, and disarmament of illegal armed units within the territory of the Chechen Republic and contiguous regions of the northern Caucasus, and of Presidential Decree No. 1833 of 2 November 1993 on the basic provisions of the military doctrine of the Russian Federation. *Sobraniye Zakonodateselstva Rossiyskoy Federatsii*, 1995, No. 33, Art. 3424. The decision is reproduced in part on the ICRC website at http://www.icrc.org/ihl-nat/. See the opinions of Turns and Tuzmukhamedov for the Crimes of War Project.

[194] See Giles Whittell, 'Bomb Raid "Kills 50 Chechnya Refugees"', *The Times*, 30 October 1999, 15.

[195] See Ben MacIntyre, 'UN Accuses Russia of Failing on Rules of War', *The Times*, 9 November 1999, 20. See also US Department of State Daily Press Briefing, 12 November 1999.

[196] See Giles Whittell, 'Chechens Told to Abandon Grozny or Die', *The Times*, 7 December 1999, 16; Amelia Gentleman, 'Flee or Die, Chechens Warned', *Guardian*, 7 December 1999, 1; and *Keesing's Record of World Events* (1999), 43321.

[197] *Keesing's Record of World Events* (1999), 43321.

aid for humanitarian purposes, and suspending a number of provisions of the Partnership and Co-operation Agreement with Russia.[198] The International Monetary Fund postponed a £400m loan,[199] and the United States again accused Russia of violating 'norms of international law'.[200]

Following the entry of Russian troops into Grozny, numerous excesses were committed in clear violation of international humanitarian law, including the creation of 'filtration camps' to separate Chechen rebels from civilians, where reports of rape, torture and murder were widespread.[201] Human rights organisations have also compiled a number of reports detailing the mass murder of civilians and other violations of human rights and humanitarian law.[202] The Kremlin did eventually order official investigations into alleged war crimes,[203] although the impact has been limited to date. In April 2000, the United Nations Commission on Human Rights adopted a resolution in the following terms:

> Guided . . . by the provisions of the International Covenant on Civil and Political Rights, the International Covenant on Economic, Social and Cultural Rights and the Convention against Torture and Other Cruel, Inhuman or Degrading Treatment or Punishment, the Geneva Conventions of 12 August 1949, in particular common article 3 thereof, and Additional Protocol II thereto . . . as well as other instruments of international humanitarian law . . .

[198] M. Fletcher, 'EU Tries War of Words to Help Chechnya', *The Times*, 11 December 1999, 18.

[199] See James Landale, 'Russia Told it Faces Aid Cuts over Grozny', *The Times*, 8 December 1999, 14; Michael Binyon, 'Impact of World Outrage will be Limited', *The Times*, 8 December 1999, 16; and Gentleman and MacAskill, 'West Threatens Sanctions'.

[200] See Ian Traynor, 'US Accuses Russia of Flouting International Law in Chechnya', *Guardian*, 24 December 1999, 9.

[201] See, for example, Paul Wood, 'Chechnya's Civilians Put to the Sword', *Independent*, 6 February 2000, 20, and Patrick Cockburn, 'Russia Rattled by Torture Claims at Chechen Camps', *Independent*, 18 February 2000, 14.

[202] See, for example, the following Reports published by Human Rights Watch: 'Civilian Killings in Staropromyslovski District of Grozny', vol. 12, No. 2(D) (February 2000); 'No Happiness Remains: Civilian Killings, Pillage and Rape in Alkhan-Yurt, Chechnya', vol. 12, No. 5(D) (April 2000); 'February 5: A Day of Slaughter in Novye Aldi', vol. 12, No. 9(D) (June 2000); and 'Welcome to Hell: Arbitrary Detention, Torture and Extortion in Chechnya' (October 2000).

[203] Helen Womack, 'Kremlin Orders Inquiry into Mass Chechen Graves', *Independent*, 26 February 2000, 15. By the end of March, 130 cases had been opened against Russian troops, with the President himself publicising the first officially documented case of rape and murder by a Russian tank commander on national television. See 'Rights and Responsibilities: It is Time for a Real Human Rights Clean-up in Chechnya', *The Times*, 31 March 2000, 23.

Gravely concerned by the continued violence in the Republic of Chechnya of the Russian Federation, in particular reports indicating disproportionate and indiscriminate use of Russian military force, including attacks against civilians...

Gravely concerned also at reports of attacks against civilians and serious crimes and abuses committed by Chechen fighters...

2. *Calls upon* all parties to the conflict to take immediate steps to halt the hostilities and the indiscriminate use of force...

4. *Calls upon* the Government of the Russian Federation to establish urgently... a national, broad-based and independent commission of inquiry to investigate promptly alleged violations of human rights and breaches of international humanitarian law committed in the Republic of Chechnya in order to establish the truth and identity of those responsible, with a view to bringing them to justice and preventing impunity... [204]

By October 2000, Russia had made no apparent progress in the direction required by the Commission.[205]

The position as regards the observance of humanitarian law during internal armed conflict is most disheartening. Despite ample opportunity for the international community to take concrete steps towards the acceptance of the enhanced humanitarian protection contained within Additional Protocol II, applicable as it is in only the most serious of internal conflicts, what has emerged is a pattern of States – indeed all parties – involved in hostilities being unwilling to apply either Protocol II or common Article 3. There have to date been only two internal armed conflicts where both the government and insurgents accepted the application of Additional Protocol II, namely those in El Salvador and the Philippines.[206] It is as if the efforts of so many since the end of the Second World War to ease suffering during hostilities, and indeed to prevent such conflicts from arising, have counted for nothing.

---

[204] Resolution 2000/58 on the Situation in the Republic of Chechnya of the Russian Federation, UN Doc. E/CN.4/RES/2000/58 (25 April 2000).

[205] For condemnation of the Russian Federation in this regard, see Human Rights Watch, *Memorandum on Accountability for Humanitarian Law Violations in Chechnya* (New York, 13 September 2000), and Amnesty International News Release EUR 46/044/2000, 26 October 2000.

[206] Ilene Cohn and Guy S. Goodwin-Gill, *Child Soldiers* (Oxford, 1994), 58. Filipino insurgents told the ICRC on 15 August 1991 of their desire to comply with common Article 3 and Additional Protocol II (ICRC, *Annual Report 1991*, 73), although Asia Watch in 1990 had concluded that, while they were operating under responsible command and capable of launching operations in all provinces, their capacity to implement the due process requirements in Article 6 of the Protocol was doubtful. See Cohn and Goodwin-Gill, *Child Soldiers*, 65.

The conventional humanitarian law to combat atrocities such as those committed in El Salvador, Rwanda, former Yugoslavia and Chechnya is in place, but is proving alarmingly ineffective. International law is not, however, confined to internationally agreed instruments, and so we now turn to consider customary international law, and the role it has to play during internal armed conflict.

4   Customary international law and internal armed conflict

The primary legal bases for the regulation of internal armed conflicts are the conventional rules contained in common Article 3 and Additional Protocol II. During the drafting process of Additional Protocol II there had been a reluctance to accept that any customary rules existed regulating internal armed conflict, and the Martens Clause contained in the Preamble to Protocol II differs from that in Article 1(2) of Protocol I in that it makes no reference to 'the principles of international law derived from established custom'. This has been explained as being due to the fact that 'the attempt to establish rules for a non-international armed conflict only goes back to 1949 and that the application of common Art. 3 in the practice of States has not developed in such a way that one could speak of "established custom" regarding non-international conflicts'.[1]

Meron has nevertheless argued that Additional Protocol II contains a basic core of human rights, many of which have already been accepted as representing customary international law in human rights instruments, and which should therefore continue to have customary law status when stated in humanitarian law instruments.[2] Meron has also

---

[1] Michael Bothe, Karl J. Partsch and Waldemar A. Solf, *New Rules for Victims of Armed Conflicts: Commentary on the Two 1977 Protocols Additional to the Geneva Conventions of 1949* (The Hague, 1982), 620. This is further evidenced by the wording of Article 13(1) of Additional Protocol II compared to Article 51(1) of Protocol I, as outlined above at p. 117, n. 140 and accompanying text. See also Theodor Meron, *Human Rights and Humanitarian Norms as Customary Law* (Oxford, 1989), 72–73.

[2] Meron, *Human Rights and Humanitarian Norms*, 73. He relies on a passage from the ICRC Commentary on the 1977 Protocols which provides that 'Protocol II contains virtually all the irreducible rights of the Covenant on Civil and Political Rights... These rights are based on rules of universal validity to which States can be held, even in the absence of any treaty obligation or any explicit commitment on their part.' See Yves Sandoz, Christophe Swinarski and Bruno Zimmerman (eds.), *Commentary on the*

argued that the failure of the Diplomatic Conference to agree any 'Hague Law' principles for internal conflicts meant that such hostilities would have to be tempered through the advancement of customary law alone, the primary source for which should be principles of humanity. More specifically, he suggested that rules such as proportionality, the prohibition of direct attacks upon civilians, the prohibition of indiscriminate attacks and the prohibition of means and methods of warfare causing unnecessary suffering should be regarded as necessary and proper derivations from those principles.[3]

More recent occurrences, however, have had a profound effect on the development of customary humanitarian law and its application to internal armed conflict. The widespread atrocities committed during conflicts in the former Yugoslavia and Rwanda resulted in the adoption by the United Nations Security Council of Statutes creating International Criminal Tribunals to bring those accused of violations of the relevant law to justice,[4] and amongst the case law of the International Criminal Tribunal for the Former Yugoslavia, *Prosecutor* v *Duško Tadić*[5] is of pivotal importance. The *Tadić* Case was the first to suggest[6] that there is a body of customary international law applicable to internal armed conflict, and that the violation of these rules can involve individual criminal responsibility.

The *Tadić* jurisprudence

The most innovative development regarding the laws of internal armed conflict was brought about by the Appeals Chamber of the ICTY in

Additional Protocols of 8 June 1977 to the Geneva Conventions of 12 August 1949 (Geneva, 1987) at 1340.

[3] Meron, *Human Rights and Humanitarian Norms*, 73–74.

[4] For the Statute of the International Tribunal for the Prosecution of Persons Responsible for Serious Violations of International Humanitarian Law Committed in the Territory of Former Yugoslavia since 1991, see UN Doc. S/25704, Annex, 32 ILM 1192 (1993). For the Statute of the Tribunal for Rwanda, see 33 ILM 1602 (1994).

[5] The jurisprudence can be traced through the following: *Prosecutor* v *Tadić*, Appeal on Jurisdiction, Case IT-94-1-AR72 (2 October 1995) 35 ILM 32 (1996), hereinafter *Tadić* (Jurisdiction); *Prosecutor* v *Tadić*, Opinion and Judgment, Case IT-94-1-T (7 May 1997), excerpts also available at 36 ILM 908 (1997), hereinafter *Tadić* (Judgment); and *Prosecutor* v *Tadić*, Judgment of the Appeals Chamber, Case IT-94-1-A (15 July 1999) 38 ILM 1518 (1999), hereinafter *Tadić* (Appeal Judgment).

[6] Not everybody agreed with the findings. See Rowe in Colin Warbrick and Peter Rowe, 'The International Criminal Tribunal for Yugoslavia: The Decision of the Appeals Chamber on the Interlocutory Appeal on Jurisdiction in the *Tadić* Case' (1996) 45 *ICLQ* 691 at 696 ff. and the debates on the ILC Draft Statute for the International Criminal Court.

Prosecutor v *Tadić* (Appeal on Jurisdiction), and particularly in that part of the judgment dealing with Article 3 of the Tribunal's Statute, which is concerned with 'violations of the laws or customs of war'. Article 3 provides that:

The International Tribunal shall have the power to prosecute persons violating the laws or customs of war. Such violations shall include, but not be limited to:

(a) employment of poisonous weapons or other weapons calculated to cause unnecessary suffering;

(b) wanton destruction of cities, towns or villages, or devastation not justified by military necessity;

(c) attack, or bombardment, by whatever means, of undefended towns, villages, dwellings, or buildings;

(d) seizure of, destruction or wilful damage done to institutions dedicated to religion, charity and education, the arts and sciences, historic monuments and works of art and science;

(e) plunder of public or private property.

The United Nations Secretary-General had stated in his Report[7] that this provision was based on the 1907 Hague Convention No. IV, the Regulations annexed thereto, and the Nuremberg Tribunal's interpretation of those provisions.[8] Article 3 was therefore held by the Appeals Chamber to be a general clause, encompassing all violations of humanitarian law not covered by Articles 2, 4 or 5 of the Tribunal's Statute[9] and, more specifically, violations of the Hague Law on international armed conflicts, infringements of provisions of the Geneva Conventions other than grave breaches, violations of common Article 3 and other customary rules on internal armed conflicts, and violations of agreements binding on the parties to the conflict *qua* treaty law.[10] The Secretary-General believed

---

[7] Secretary-General's Report on Aspects of Establishing an International Tribunal for the Prosecution of Persons Responsible for Serious Violations of International Humanitarian Law Committed in the Territory of the Former Yugoslavia (3 May 1993), UN Doc. S/25704, reprinted in 32 ILM 1159 (1993).

[8] *Ibid.*, paragraphs 41–44. He had also stated at paragraph 34 that, so far as the competence of the Tribunal over subject matter was concerned, application of the principle *nullum crimen sine lege* required that the Tribunal should apply only those rules of humanitarian law which are, beyond any doubt, part of customary law (so that problems over adherence to Conventions do not arise).

[9] Confirmed by *Tadić* (Judgment) at paragraph 609, *Prosecutor* v *Nikolić* (Rule 61) 108 ILR 21 at 36, *Prosecutor* v *Mrksić* (Rule 61) 108 ILR 53 at 62, and *Prosecutor* v *Furundžija* (Case IT-95-17/1-T, Judgment of 10 December 1998), 38 ILM 317 (1999) at paragraphs 132–133. Article 2 of the Statute deals with grave breaches of the Geneva Conventions, Article 4 with genocide and Article 5 with crimes against humanity.

[10] *Tadić* (Jurisdiction) at paragraph 89. In fact, the USA, the UK and France had maintained during Security Council debates on the Tribunal's Statute that Article 3

that since Article 3 of the Statute is concerned only with violations of firmly established customary law, violations of Additional Protocol II were not included. He saw the Rwandan Tribunal as going further in this respect, however, the Security Council having taken a more expansive approach to the choice of applicable law in its Statute by including in the subject-matter jurisdiction international instruments, regardless of whether they were considered to be part of customary law. Article 4 of the Rwandan Statute accordingly also includes violations of Additional Protocol II, despite claims that Protocol II was 'not yet universally recognized as part of customary international law'.[11]

Approach of the Tribunal

Tadić had initially claimed that Article 3 of the Statute (along with Articles 2 and 5) was inapplicable in his case, as it was applicable only to *international* armed conflicts, whereas the conflict taking place in the former Yugoslavia was internal. On appeal against the jurisdiction of the Tribunal, he changed his defence to claim that there was, in fact, no armed conflict taking place in the Prijedor region at the time when the crimes were alleged to have taken place. The Appeals Chamber had no difficulty in dismissing that proposition,[12] furthermore asserting that the jurisdiction of the Tribunal to hear cases under Article 3 of the Statute was nevertheless equally applicable to international and internal armed conflicts.[13] That the Chamber did not find the conflicts to be purely international was vital for the development of the law,[14] in that it

included violations of those provisions of the Geneva Conventions and Additional Protocol I which did not amount to grave breaches, including common Article 3. See Christopher J. Greenwood, 'The International Tribunal for Former Yugoslavia' (1993) 69 *International Affairs* 641 at 650 with n. 33 therein, and n. 120 below.

[11] Report of the Secretary-General Pursuant to Paragraph 5 of Security Council Resolution 955 (1994), UN Doc. S/1995/134, paragraph 12. This is not necessarily the approach taken by the Yugoslav Tribunal itself however. See *Prosecutor v Martić* (Rule 61) 108 ILR 40 at paragraph 8, where it states that 'violations of Additional Protocol II constitute violations of the laws and customs of war and, as such, come under Article 3 of the Statute'.

[12] *Tadić* (Jurisdiction) at paragraph 70.

[13] Confirmed in *Prosecutor v Karadžić and Mladić* (Rule 61) 108 ILR 86 at paragraph 21.

[14] For an outline of the difficulties involved in classifying the conflict, see Greenwood, 'The International Tribunal', 641. The conflict (or indeed conflicts) in the former Yugoslavia was held in *Tadić* (Jurisdiction) at paragraph 77 to have had both internal and international aspects, a stance supported by the Trial Chamber in *Tadić* (Judgment) at paragraphs 578–608, where the conflict in Prijedor was again held to be internal. In *Tadić* (Appeal Judgment), however, the Appeals Chamber instead characterised the conflict as international. The Chamber's initial opinion was contrary to much scholarly literature: see, for example, Theodor Meron,

could then proceed to examine in its entirety the laws of internal armed conflict, with particular emphasis on the customary rules applicable (despite the fact that this was not strictly relevant to a case concerning the validity of the Tribunal's jurisdiction). Such a course of action would have been impossible for the Appeals Chamber had it denied that the conflicts in former Yugoslavia had internal aspects.

The Chamber began by outlining the traditional dichotomy between the regulation of international and internal armed conflicts,[15] but felt that the approach of international law had, over time, become less State-oriented, inevitably leading to the following question:

Why protect civilians from belligerent violence, or ban rape, torture or the wanton destruction of hospitals, churches, museums or private property, as well as proscribe weapons causing unnecessary suffering when two sovereign States are engaged in war, and yet refrain from enacting the same bans or providing the same protection when armed violence has erupted 'only' within the territory of a sovereign State? If international law, while of course duly safeguarding the legitimate interests of States, must gradually turn to the protection of human beings, it is only natural that the aforementioned dichotomy should gradually lose its weight.[16]

Rules of international law for the regulation of internal armed conflicts have therefore developed in two ways: first through treaty law

'International Criminalization of Internal Atrocities' (1995) 89 AJIL 554 at 556, mirroring the view of the Commission of Experts (see above at p. 126, n. 178). Indeed the Prosecutor claimed that the Security Council had determined the conflicts to be international upon adoption of the Statute (Tadić (Jurisdiction) at paragraph 65), a sentiment apparently endorsed by the International Criminal Tribunal for Rwanda in Prosecutor v Akayesu 37 ILM 1399 (1998) at paragraph 606: 'it would appear that, in the case of the ICTY, the Security Council, by making reference to the four Geneva Conventions, considered that the conflict in the former Yugoslavia was an international conflict', continuing to assert that, accordingly, 'when the Security Council added Additional Protocol II to the subject matter jurisdiction of the ICTR, this could suggest that the Security Council deemed the conflict in Rwanda as an Additional Protocol II conflict'. Subsequent cases before the Tribunal have been held to involve international conflict, e.g. the Rule 61 decisions in Nikolić, Martić, Mrksić, Karadžić and Mladić, and Rajić, 108 ILR 142 (see above at p. 48 and n. 64) and the more recent case of Prosecutor v Delalić, Case IT-96-21-T, Judgment of 16 November 1998. The Appeals Chamber's original decision nevertheless received support from Christopher J. Greenwood, 'International Humanitarian Law and the Tadić Case' (1996) 7 EJIL 265 at 270–275; George H. Aldrich, 'Jurisdiction of the International Criminal Tribunal for the Former Yugoslavia' (1996) 90 AJIL 64 at 65–67 and 69; and Theodor Meron, 'The Continuing Role of Custom in the Formation of International Humanitarian Law' (1996) 90 AJIL 238 at 239. See criticism of the decision in Warbrick and Rowe, 'Jurisdiction in the Tadić Case', 696 ff.

[15] Tadić (Jurisdiction) at paragraphs 96–97.
[16] Ibid., paragraph 97.

(as examined in the preceding chapters), and secondly through customary law, to which this chapter is dedicated. The two strands of law
may be separate, but they are nonetheless closely interrelated to the
extent that some rules of treaty law have also become part of customary
law.[17] The Appeals Chamber accordingly undertook a survey of how the
customary law of internal armed conflict has developed, with reference
to those conflicts which had taken place (or indeed were still taking
place) in Spain, the Congo, Biafra, Nicaragua, El Salvador, Liberia, Iraq,
Georgia and Chechnya.

It is settled that the emergence of custom in international law requires both State practice and *opinio juris*, i.e. 'a clear and continuous
habit of doing certain actions ... under the aegis of the conviction that
these actions are, according to International Law, obligatory or right'.[18]
The Tribunal, however, placed much more emphasis upon *opinio juris*
as evidenced by official statements, military manuals and judicial decisions, rather than actual State practice, since:

When attempting to ascertain State practice with a view to establishing the existence of a customary rule or a general principle, it is difficult, if not impossible,
to pinpoint the actual behaviour of the troops in the field for the purpose of
establishing whether they in fact comply with, or disregard, certain standards of
behaviour. This examination is rendered even more difficult by the fact that not
only is access to the theatre of military operations normally refused to independent observers (often even to the ICRC) but information on the actual conduct
of hostilities is withheld by the parties to the conflict; what is worse, often recourse is had to misinformation with a view to misleading the enemy as well
as public opinion and foreign Governments.[19]

This reliance on statements of policy has been criticised, in that without
a detailed examination of actual operational practice it could prove extremely problematical to persuade governments to accept the Tribunal's
opinion on certain aspects of the customary law.[20] The Tribunal seems
to have supported the opposing viewpoint, however, which claims that
military manuals frequently not only state government policy, but also

---

[17] E.g. common Article 3 of the Geneva Conventions and Article 19 of the 1954 Hague
Convention for the Protection of Cultural Property in the Event of Armed Conflict.
This does not mean that they do not continue to apply independently. For further
explanation, see *Military and Paramilitary Activities In and Against Nicaragua*
(*Nicaragua* v *US*) (Merits) 76 ILR 5, at paragraph 179.

[18] Lassa F. L. Oppenheim, *International Law*, 8th edn, edited by Hersch Lauterpacht
(London, 1955), vol. I, 26.

[19] *Tadić* (Jurisdiction) at paragraph 99.

[20] Meron, 'The Continuing Role of Custom', 240.

establish binding obligations upon members of the armed forces, violations of which are punishable under military codes. Such manuals can therefore create mutual expectations of compliance between States, and many of the rules propounded therein are accordingly good evidence of customary law.[21] Baxter certainly believed that 'The firm statement by the State of what it considers to be the rule is far better evidence of its position than what can be pieced together from the actions of that country at different times and in a variety of contexts',[22] and a State's proclamation of its view of the law to its own forces can thus itself be considered a piece of State practice.

Given the inherent difficulties involved in third parties gaining access and reliable information during hostilities, the approach taken by the Appeals Chamber seems sensible, and in this way it was able to set out what it considered to be the principal rules of customary international law governing internal armed conflicts:

[the] protection of civilians from hostilities, in particular from indiscriminate attacks, protection of civilian objects, in particular cultural property, protection of all those who do not (or no longer) take active part in hostilities, as well as prohibition of means of warfare proscribed in international armed conflicts and ban of certain methods of conducting hostilities.[23]

Rules protecting the civilian population from hostilities

The Appeals Chamber determined that, since the Spanish Civil War, rules of international armed conflict protecting civilians from attack have been applied to internal conflicts. As evidence of this, various statements made in the context of the Spanish conflict were cited,[24] including one made by the British Prime Minister, Neville Chamberlain, who had asserted in 1938 that:

there are ... three rules of international law ... which are as applicable to warfare from the air as they are to war at sea or on land. In the first place, it is against international law to bomb civilians as such and to make deliberate attacks upon civilian populations. That is undoubtedly a violation of international law. In the

---

[21] Meron, *Human Rights and Humanitarian Norms*, 41.

[22] Richard R. Baxter, 'Multilateral Treaties as Evidence of Customary International Law' (1965–1966) 41 *BYIL* 275 at 300. See also Christopher J. Greenwood, 'Customary Law Status of the 1977 Additional Protocols' in Astrid J. M. Delissen and Gerard J. Tanja (eds.), *Humanitarian Law of Armed Conflict: Challenges Ahead: Essays in Honour of Frits Kalshoven* (Dordrecht, 1991), 93 at 102–103.

[23] *Tadić* (Jurisdiction) at paragraph 127.

[24] *Ibid.*, at paragraphs 100–101.

second place, targets which are aimed at from the air must be legitimate military objectives and must be capable of identification. In the third place, reasonable care must be taken in attacking those military objectives so that by carelessness a civilian population in the neighbourhood is not bombed.[25]

This clearly assumed that laws of international armed conflict were equally applicable where the conflict was internal,[26] a view echoed in various resolutions passed by the Assembly of the League of Nations.[27] The Tribunal drew upon subsequent State practice to show that the Spanish Civil War was not, however, unique in extending rules of international armed conflict to civil war. Vitally important in this regard was the adoption in 1949 of common Article 3 – especially in view of the International Court of Justice's determination that its provisions have come to constitute 'elementary considerations of humanity', applicable to all armed conflicts as customary international law.[28] The manner in which the ICJ reached this decision has been criticised, however, as 'remarkable . . . for its complete failure to inquire whether *opinio juris* and practice support the crystallization of [Article 3] into customary law . . . Moreover the parties to the Geneva Conventions have built a poor record of compliance with the norms stated in Article 3, and evidence of practice by non-parties is lacking.'[29]

In his Dissenting Opinion in the *Nicaragua* Case, Judge Jennings stated the belief that the Court's view of common Article 3 was 'not . . . free from difficulty',[30] and Judge Ago was furthermore 'reluctant to be persuaded that any broad identity of content exists between the Geneva Conventions and certain "fundamental general principles of international law"'.[31] Only the reasoning behind the Court's conclusion would seem to be in question for most commentators, however, and not the conclusion itself. Indeed, Meron accepts that Article 3 contains norms of such an elementary nature, echoing many other human rights and humanitarian treaties, that they must be regarded as embodying minimum

---

[25] 337 *House of Commons Debates*, cols. 937–938 (21 June 1938). See *Tadić* (Jurisdiction) at paragraph 100.

[26] Although the Spanish Civil War had both international and non-international aspects. See Ann van W. Thomas and A. J. Thomas Jr, 'International Legal Aspects of the Civil War in Spain, 1936–1939' in Richard A. Falk (ed.), *The International Law of Civil War* (Baltimore, 1971), 111.

[27] E.g. League of Nations, OJ Spec. Supp. 183 (1938) at 135–136, reiterating Chamberlain's points. See *Tadić* (Jurisdiction) at paragraph 101.

[28] *Nicaragua* Case, paragraph 218.

[29] Meron, *Human Rights and Humanitarian Norms*, 36–37.

[30] *Nicaragua* Case, 871.

[31] Separate Opinion of Judge Ago, *ibid.*, at 518.

standards of customary international law.[32] This has certainly been the opinion of the International Criminal Tribunals in several subsequent cases, where it has been accepted as being 'clear that the norms of common Article 3 have acquired the status of customary international law'.[33]

Common Article 3 also provides the parties to the conflict with the possibility of reaching an agreement to abide by the broader rules of the Geneva Conventions as a whole, thus applying international humanitarian law in its entirety to internal armed conflict. Although these are rare, agreements to apply certain provisions of the Geneva Conventions were made by parties to the conflicts in the former Yugoslavia[34] and in the Yemeni conflict of the 1960s.[35] Such agreements, however, are not the only way in which international humanitarian law has been applied to internal conflicts, and the Appeals Chamber described several unilateral undertakings (either by States or by insurgents) to apply international humanitarian law during internal hostilities, citing these as evidence of a customary adherence to the basic principles of humanitarian law during internal armed conflict.[36] Thus, a statement made by the Prime Minister of the Congo on 21 October 1964 that:

For humanitarian reasons, and with a view to reassuring, in so far as necessary, the civilian population which might fear that it is in danger, the Congolese

---

[32] Meron, *Human Rights and Humanitarian Norms*, 36–37.

[33] See, for example, *Prosecutor v Akayesu* at paragraph 608 and the following ICTY cases: *Prosecutor v Tadić* (Judgment) at paragraph 617, *Prosecutor v Delalić* at paragraphs 301–306, and *Prosecutor v Furundžija* at paragraph 138. The Constitutional Court of Colombia has, in fact, recently held that the Geneva Conventions and Additional Protocols have passed into customary international law in their entirety (Judgment C-574/92, Section V, B2c, 28 October 1992 and Judgment C-225/95, Section VD, 18 May 1995, both unpublished), although the Trial Chamber in *Furundžija* (paragraph 137 and n. 156 in particular) declined to comment upon whether this was actually the case.

[34] See the agreement reached between the parties to the conflict in Bosnia-Herzegovina on 22 May 1992. This would seem to provide valuable evidence that the conflict was not wholly international in character, since agreement to abide by only certain provisions of the Geneva Conventions is strictly prohibited in international conflict – the entire Conventions apply automatically (see common Article 6/6/6/7). Discussion of this point can be found in *Tadić* (Jurisdiction) paragraph 73, and Greenwood, 'The *Tadić* Case', 272. The Appeals Chamber in *Tadić* (Appeal Judgment) nevertheless considered the conflict to be international in character, due to the relationship between the armed forces of Republika Srpska and the Federal Republic of Yugoslavia. See above at pp. 49–50.

[35] Kathryn Boals, 'The Relevance of International Law to the Internal War in Yemen' in Falk, *Civil War*, 303.

[36] *Tadić* (Jurisdiction) at paragraph 104.

Government wishes to state that the Congolese Air Force will limit its action to military objectives...In this matter, the Congolese Government desires not only to protect human lives but also to respect the Geneva Convention [sic]. It also expects the rebels – and makes an urgent appeal to them to that effect – to act in the same manner,[37]

was considered by the Tribunal to confirm the status of this rule as part of the customary law of internal armed conflicts.[38]

In addition to an examination of State/belligerent practice, the Appeals Chamber also considered as evidence establishing custom various statements made by the ICRC, the UN General Assembly and Security Council, the European Union, instructions in national military manuals, and comments made with respect to Additional Protocol II. Appeals by the ICRC to the parties to internal armed conflicts to respect the basic provisions of international humanitarian law, or at least as a minimum common Article 3, were seen by the Appeals Chamber to have promoted the application of general rules of humanitarian law to internal armed conflicts, with any compliance gained through ICRC persuasion being regarded as State practice.[39] Two General Assembly Resolutions were regarded as further evidence of this development in the law, namely Resolution 2444 of 1968 and Resolution 2675 of 1970. The first recognised 'the necessity of applying basic humanitarian principles in all armed conflicts', and stated that the right of parties to a conflict to adopt means of injuring the enemy was not unlimited, it being prohibited in particular to attack the civilian population, which must at all times be distinguished from those persons taking part in the hostilities.[40] The second resolution elaborated on this somewhat, outlining certain '[b]asic principles for the protection of civilian populations in armed conflicts' (with the term 'armed conflicts' intended to cover those of both international and internal character).[41]

Statements were made by the European Union in the context of the struggles in Liberia and Chechnya, calling for the application of

---

[37] Public Statement of the Prime Minister of the Democratic Republic of the Congo (21 October 1964), reprinted in (1965) 59 AJIL 614 at 616. See *Tadić* (Jurisdiction) at paragraph 105.

[38] Similar examples are given of the Nigerian Federal troops in Biafra and the FMLN in El Salvador, at paragraphs 106–107.

[39] *Tadić* (Jurisdiction) at paragraph 109.

[40] GA Resolution 2444, UN Doc. A/7218 (1968). See *Tadić* (Jurisdiction) at paragraph 110.

[41] GA Resolution 2675, UN Doc. A/C.3/SR 1785 (1970). See *Tadić* (Jurisdiction) at paragraph 111.

international humanitarian law,[42] and the UN Security Council reiterated the EU's call with respect to Liberia,[43] making similar appeals with respect to the conflicts in Somalia and Georgia.[44] In none of these statements or resolutions, however, was common Article 3 mentioned explicitly, the more general term of 'international humanitarian law' being used instead. The Appeals Chamber saw this as 'clearly articulating the view that there exists a *corpus* of general principles and norms on internal armed conflict embracing common Article 3 but having a much greater scope',[45] a view strengthened by the German Military Manual. Bearing in mind that such manuals can provide 'telling evidence' of the practice of States,[46] paragraph 211 of the German Manual was cited, providing that 'German soldiers like their Allies are required to comply with the rules of international humanitarian law in the conduct of military operations in all armed conflicts however such conflicts are characterised.'[47]

As far as the relevance of Additional Protocol II to the customary law is concerned, the Appeals Chamber stated that many of its provisions can now be regarded as declaratory of existing rules or as having crystallised emerging rules of customary law, or else as having been instrumental in their evolution as general principles.[48] It sought to confirm this by citing public statements of the Government of El Salvador which, despite insisting that Additional Protocol II was not *de jure* applicable to the civil war occurring in that country,[49] nevertheless agreed to comply

---

[42] On Liberia see (1990) 6 *European Political Cooperation Documentation Bulletin*, 295, and on Chechnya, Council of the EU – General Secretariat, Press Releases 4215/95 (17 January 1995) and 4385/95 (23 January 1995). Discussed in *Tadić* (Jurisdiction) at paragraphs 113 and 115.

[43] SC Resolution 788 (19 November 1992). See *Tadić* (Jurisdiction) at paragraph 114.

[44] SC Resolutions 794 (3 December 1992) and 814 (26 March 1993) condemn breaches of international humanitarian law in Somalia, and Resolution 993 (12 May 1993) appeals to the parties to comply with international humanitarian law in Georgia. See *Tadić* (Jurisdiction) at paragraph 114.

[45] *Tadić* (Jurisdiction) at paragraph 116.

[46] Baxter, 'Multilateral Treaties', 282–283.

[47] Printed in English with a Commentary as Dieter Fleck (ed.), *The Handbook of Humanitarian Law in Armed Conflicts* (Oxford, 1995), 48. This view, however, would appear to be unique to Germany.

[48] *Tadić* (Jurisdiction) at paragraph 117.

[49] On whether it was objectively or not, see Waldemar A. Solf, 'Commentary on International Non-international Armed Conflicts: Case Studies of Afghanistan, Kampuchea and Lebanon' (1982) 31 *American University LR* 927 at 932; Michael Bothe, 'Article 3 and Protocol II: Case Studies of Nigeria and El Salvador' (1982) 31 *American University LR* 899 at 905–906; and pp. 120–121 above.

with its provisions, considering them merely to develop and supplement common Article 3, 'which in turn constitute[d] the minimum protection due to every human being at any time and place'.[50] The Deputy Legal Adviser of the US State Department, speaking in 1987, also believed that 'The basic core of Additional Protocol II is...reflected in common Article 3 of the 1949 Geneva Conventions and therefore is, and should be, a part of generally accepted customary law.'[51] This is doubtful. While it is too extreme to regard none of the provisions of Additional Protocol II as reflecting, or having attained the status of, customary law, it has nevertheless been convincingly argued that 'most of Protocol II has to be regarded as confined to treaty law in the absence of more substantial State practice evidencing an acceptance of its provisions as customary law'.[52]

Although questions may be raised as regards some of the assertions made by the Tribunal, or at least the value placed upon certain factors in the light of State practice which is replete with examples of humanitarian law failing to be applied to internal armed conflicts, it is nevertheless commonly accepted by States and commentators alike that the protection of civilians and those otherwise not taking part in the hostilities *has* become a part of customary international law. For the International Tribunal to have affirmed this authoritatively is of immense value.[53]

---

[50] Statement forwarded by the Ministry of Defence and Security of El Salvador to the Special Representative of the UN Human Rights Commission (2 October 1987), discussed in *Tadić* (Jurisdiction) at paragraph 117.

[51] (1987) 2 *American University Journal of International Law and Policy* 419 at 430–431. See *Tadić* (Jurisdiction) at paragraph 117.

[52] Greenwood, 'Customary Status of the Additional Protocols', 113. See also Antonio Cassese, 'The Geneva Protocols of 1977 and Customary International Law' (1984) 3 *UCLA Pacific Basin LJ* 55, and opinion of the UN Secretary-General, above at p. 136, n. 11 and accompanying text. There would appear to be broad acceptance of the contention that Article 4 of Additional Protocol II, for example, has attained the status of customary law. This argument was advanced by the Prosecution in *Prosecutor v Furundžija* at paragraph 44, although in that section of the case concerning torture (prohibited by Article 4 of Additional Protocol II) the Trial Chamber held that it need not decide the issue, as a general prohibition against torture has evolved in customary international law (paragraph 137). It was, however, held in the part of the case dealing with rape and sexual assault (also contained in Article 4 of Protocol II) that a prohibition on such conduct had indeed evolved into customary law (paragraph 168), and in *Prosecutor v Akayesu* at paragraph 616, the Rwandan Tribunal held that Article 4 of Additional Protocol II represented fundamental guarantees and was therefore part of customary law.

[53] See also the Rule 61 Decisions in *Prosecutor v Martić* at 45–46, and *Prosecutor v Rajić* at 162–163.

Rules regarding means and methods of warfare

The Tribunal went beyond a simple declaration that civilians were to be protected during non-international armed conflicts, however, and asserted that a body of customary international law has also developed regulating the means and methods of warfare in internal conflict.[54] Taking as its starting point the 1995 Turku Declaration on Minimum Humanitarian Standards,[55] which states in Article 5(3) that 'weapons or other material or methods prohibited in international armed conflicts must not be employed *in any circumstances*',[56] the Appeals Chamber proceeded to assert that:

elementary considerations of humanity and common sense make it preposterous that the use by States of weapons prohibited in armed conflicts between themselves be allowed when States try to put down rebellion by their own nationals in their own territory. What is inhumane, and consequently proscribed, in international wars, cannot but be inhumane and inadmissible in civil strife.[57]

It is certainly difficult to argue with such an eminently sensible (and indeed logical) view, and the determination that a principle of customary law has developed to that effect can be illustrated with particular reference to chemical weapons and their alleged use by the Government of Iraq against its own Kurdish population, condemned as contrary to international law by a number of States. The European Union, for example, made several declarations condemning the use of such weapons and calling for respect of international humanitarian law.[58] Similar statements were made individually by the United Kingdom[59] and by Germany,[60] while the US Government also took a clear stand on the issue, asserting that:

Questions have been raised as to whether the prohibition in the 1925 Geneva Protocol against [chemical weapon] use 'in war' applies to [chemical weapon] use

[54] Confirmed in *Martić* at 45, paragraph 11.
[55] UN Doc. E/CN.4/1995/116 (1995). This emanated from a group of experts, however, and has no binding legal effect. It has nevertheless been endorsed (albeit indirectly) by the Conference on Security and Cooperation in Europe (CSCE) and the UN Sub-commission on Prevention of Discrimination and Protection of Minorities. See *Tadić* (Jurisdiction) at paragraph 119.
[56] Emphasis added.
[57] *Tadić* (Jurisdiction) at paragraph 119.
[58] See, for example (1988) 4 *European Political Cooperation Documentation Bulletin*, 92, as discussed in *Tadić* (Jurisdiction) at paragraph 120.
[59] (1988) 59 *BYIL* at 579. See *Tadić* (Jurisdiction) at paragraph 121.
[60] (1990) 50 *Zeitschrift für Ausländisches Öffentliches Recht und Völkerrecht* at 382–383, and UN Doc. A/C.1/43/PV.31 (1988). See *Tadić* (Jurisdiction) at paragraph 121.

in internal conflicts. However, it is clear that such use against the civilian population would be contrary to the customary international law that is applicable to internal armed conflicts, as well as other international agreements.[61]

Although the Appeals Chamber concentrated upon the use of chemical weapons, they are by no means unique in this regard, and attempts have also been made recently to extend the international prohibition on the use of landmines to include internal armed conflicts,[62] a step urgently needed in light of the horrors caused by these indiscriminate weapons in Angola and many other places.

The Appeals Chamber further asserted that general principles of international law have emerged with respect to methods of warfare and, in order to illustrate the prohibition of perfidy in internal armed conflict, cited the case of *Pius Nwaoga v The State*,[63] where it was held by the Nigerian Supreme Court in the context of the Biafran Civil War that it was illegal to feign civilian status whilst engaging in military operations. This is a rather unhelpful example, however, and cannot in all honesty sustain the conclusion drawn by the Appeals Chamber.[64] The trial in question was in fact for murder under Nigeria's own Criminal Code rather than for a war crime, and the significance of the disguise was not seen as being central to the decision. The Nigerian Court preferred instead to approach the case from the simple outlook that Nwaoga had committed an offence under their Criminal Code, and that he was therefore liable for punishment as a civilian would be.[65] Of course, perfidy should be equally prohibited during internal and international conflicts, and it is unfortunate that the Tribunal could not find a better example of the development of customary law to that effect.

The Appeals Chamber was nevertheless careful to point out that the emergence of the above-mentioned general principles governing internal

---

[61] US Department of State, Press Guidance (9 September 1988), as cited in *Tadić* (Jurisdiction) at paragraph 122. See also now the Convention on the Prohibition of the Development, Production, Stockpiling and Use of Chemical Weapons and on their Destruction, 1993, 32 ILM 800 (1993), Article I of which states that they may 'never [be used] under any circumstances'.

[62] Protocol on Prohibitions or Restrictions on the Use of Mines, Booby-Traps and Other Devices (as amended 3 May 1996) to the Convention on Prohibitions or Restrictions on the Use of Certain Conventional Weapons which may be Deemed to be Excessively Injurious or to Have Indiscriminate Effects, Article 1(2) and 1(3). Doc. CCW/CONF.I/16 (Part I).

[63] 52 ILR 494. In guerrilla conflicts, however, perfidy is commonplace, and it could be argued that the ICTY has lost touch with reality somewhat in their assertion.

[64] See Greenwood, 'The *Tadić* Case', 278.

[65] *Pius Nwaoga v The State* at 496.

armed conflicts does *not* mean that they are regulated by general international law in all its aspects. Two limitations in particular were spelled out:

(i) only a number of rules and principles governing international armed conflicts have gradually been extended to apply to internal conflicts; and

(ii) this extension has not taken place in the form of a full and mechanical transplant of those rules to internal conflicts, rather, the general essence of those rules, and not the detailed regulation they may contain, has become applicable to internal conflicts.[66]

Greenwood nevertheless believes that the rules enumerated by the Tribunal go beyond what had previously been seen as the regulation of internal armed conflict (even beyond the provisions of Additional Protocol II), and come very close indeed to those rules contained in instruments regulating international conflict.[67]

Crimes against humanity

In addition to an examination of the customary laws regulating internal armed conflict, the *Tadić* Case also reaffirmed the customary law status of crimes against humanity, and the fact that they can be committed during internal conflicts. Such crimes are defined in Article 5 of the Yugoslav Tribunal's Statute as:

the following crimes when committed in armed conflict, whether international or internal in character, and directed against any civilian population:

(a)   murder;
(b)   extermination;
(c)   enslavement;
(d)   deportation;
(e)   imprisonment;
(f)   torture;
(g)   rape;
(h)   persecutions on political, racial and religious grounds;
(i)   other inhumane acts.

---

[66] *Tadić* (Jurisdiction) at paragraph 126.

[67] Particularly Additional Protocol I and some weapons agreements. See Greenwood, 'The *Tadić* Case', 278. For even stronger criticism, see Warbrick and Rowe, 'Jurisdiction in the *Tadić* Case', 701, where the interpretation of Article 3 is said to have driven 'a coach and four through the traditional distinctions between an international and a non-international conflict'.

Crimes against humanity were first recognised as imputing individual criminal responsibility in the context of the trials of war criminals
following the Second World War, although the concept itself has arguably been in existence for a much longer period.[68] Such crimes were
traditionally linked to acts committed 'in the execution of or in connection with any crime against the peace or any war crime'.[69] The defence
in *Tadić* therefore argued that crimes against humanity could only be
committed during international armed conflict, and that by seeking to
broaden the scope of their application to include internal armed conflicts, Article 5 of the Tribunal's Statute violated the principle of *nullum
crimen sine lege*.[70]

In fact, the required nexus between crimes against humanity and
either crimes against peace or war crimes was peculiar to the jurisdiction of the Nuremberg Tribunal, and does not exist in contemporary
international law. The Appeals Chamber in *Tadić* (Jurisdiction) found it
to be a 'settled rule of customary international law that crimes against
humanity do not require a connection to international armed conflict',[71]
and that 'there is no question . . . that the definition of crimes against
humanity adopted by the Security Council in Article 5 comports with the
principle of *nullum crimen sine lege*'.[72] Indeed, the requirement of a nexus
between crimes against humanity and any armed conflict has been abandoned completely in State practice, as demonstrated, for example, by the
definition of such crimes in Article II(1)(c) of Control Council Law No. 10
(20 December 1945),[73] and further evidenced by international conventions against genocide and apartheid,[74] both of which class such conduct
as crimes against humanity regardless of their connection to an armed
conflict of any kind. The United Nations Secretary-General's commentary

---

[68] For a discussion of the development of the concept of crimes against humanity,
see *Tadić* (Judgment) at paragraphs 618–623, and *Prosecutor v Akayesu* at paragraphs
563–577, where the Rwandan Tribunal outlines the acceptance of a category of
crimes against humanity dating back to 1874 and even earlier.

[69] Nuremberg Charter, Article 6(2)(c).

[70] *Tadić* (Jurisdiction) at paragraph 139. Of course, the Appeals Chamber of the Tribunal
eventually found that the relevant conflict was international in character in any case.

[71] At paragraph 141.

[72] *Ibid.*

[73] Control Council Law No. 10, Control Council for Germany, *Official Gazette*, 31 January
1946, 50. See *Tadić* (Jurisdiction) at paragraph 140.

[74] Convention on the Prevention and Punishment of the Crime of Genocide,
9 December 1948, 78 UNTS 277, Article 1, and International Convention on the
Suppression and Punishment of the Crime of Apartheid, 30 November 1973, 1015
UNTS 244, Articles 1–2.

on Article 5 of the Statute certainly states that crimes against human-ity can be committed outside any armed conflict, and Article 3 of the Statute of the International Criminal Tribunal for Rwanda (ICTR) as-sumes jurisdiction over crimes against humanity without making any reference to armed conflict.[75] Article 7 of the Statute of the International Criminal Court likewise deals with crimes against humanity without re-quiring an armed conflict,[76] and modern international legal literature tends to support this position.[77]

Article 5 of the Yugoslav Statute nevertheless explicitly requires that crimes against humanity be committed in the context of an armed con-flict, a requirement which the Tribunal itself accepts 'deviates from the development of the doctrine after the Nuremberg Charter'.[78] The Appeals Chamber therefore held it to be:

a settled rule of customary international law that crimes against humanity do not require a connection to international armed conflict. Indeed, as the Pros-ecutor points out, customary international law may not require a connection between crimes against humanity and any conflict at all. Thus, by requiring that crimes against humanity be committed in either internal or international armed conflict, the Security Council may have defined the crime in Article 5 more narrowly than necessary under customary international law.[79]

There can be no doubt that Article 5 was intended to reintroduce this nexus for the specific purposes of the Yugoslav Tribunal. The Appeals Chamber has, however, outlined that the requirement of an armed con-flict (i.e. the existence of an armed conflict at the relevant time and place) is merely a jurisdictional element, and not, therefore, 'a legal ingredient of the subjective element of the crime'.[80]

Besides a reaffirmation of the customary status of crimes against humanity, case law from the ICTY has also made an attempt to clarify further the definition of crimes against humanity. In the Rule 61 Case

---

[75] This view has been endorsed by the Rwandan Tribunal itself, which held in the *Akayesu* Case at paragraph 565 that 'Crimes against humanity... are prohibited regardless of whether they are committed in an armed conflict, international or internal in character.'

[76] Article 7 reads: 'For the purposes of this Statute, "crime against humanity" means any of the following acts when committed as part of a widespread or systematic attack directed against any civilian population, with knowledge of the attack...'

[77] See, for example, Robert Y. Jennings and Arthur Watts (eds.), *Oppenheim's International Law*, 9th edn (London, 1992), vol. I, 996.

[78] *Tadić* (Judgment) at paragraph 627.

[79] *Tadić* (Jurisdiction) at paragraph 141, a view accepted by the Trial Chamber in *Tadić* (Judgment) at paragraphs 623 and 627.

[80] *Tadić* (Appeal Judgment) at paragraph 249.

of *Prosecutor* v *Nikolić*,[81] the Tribunal asserted that crimes against humanity have three distinct components:

First, the crimes must be directed at a civilian population, specifically identified
as a group by the perpetrators of those acts. Secondly, the crimes must, to a
certain extent, be organised and systematic. Although they need not be related
to a policy established at State level, in the conventional sense of the term, they
cannot be the work of isolated individuals alone. Lastly, the crimes, considered
as a whole, must be of a certain scale and gravity.[82]

The Trial Chamber in *Tadić* (Judgment) went on to explain in greater
detail exactly what the various requirements (or elements) of a crime
against humanity are. The first two requirements outlined, i.e. that the
acts or omissions in question be committed in armed conflict and that
there be a nexus between those acts or omissions and the armed conflict,
are specific to the jurisdiction of the Yugoslav Tribunal under Article 5,
and do not apply to crimes against humanity in general under customary international law. As mentioned above, the requirement that the
crimes be committed in armed conflict is satisfied simply by demonstrating that there actually was an armed conflict. It has subsequently been
held that a nexus between the acts of the accused and the armed conflict is not actually required – if that were the case, then crimes against
humanity would necessarily always occur during armed conflicts, and
it is widely accepted that this is not the case.[83]

Attack on a civilian population

Much more important as regards the elaboration of crimes against
humanity in customary international law was the Tribunal's development of the requirement that crimes against humanity be 'directed
against any civilian population'. First, it was held that the word 'any'
demonstrates that crimes against humanity can be committed against
civilians of the same nationality as the perpetrator, as well as civilians
holding a different nationality or who are Stateless. Clearly, then, crimes
against humanity, unlike grave breaches of the Geneva Conventions,[84]
are possible during internal armed conflict. Secondly, it was held that a
wide definition of 'civilian population' is justified. Article 5 of the Statute

---

[81] 108 ILR 21.
[82] *Ibid.*, at paragraph 26.
[83] See *Tadić* (Appeal Judgment) at paragraph 251.
[84] Although see the discussion below at pp. 189–191.

offers no guidance as to the meaning of 'civilian', but the Trial Chamber felt that the requirement would be met where the relevant population was 'predominantly' civilian.[85] The question of just which members of the targeted population qualify as civilians in this regard is less easy to answer, especially in light of the problems outlined above with regard to common Article 3 and the identification of non-combatants during many internal armed conflicts.[86] It was suggested in that context that a broad application of the protection contained in common Article 3 could be justified in light of its humanitarian aims, and this approach would appear to have been followed with respect to the civilian character of the population necessary for an act to constitute a crime against humanity.

The Commission of Experts established by the United Nations pursuant to Security Council Resolution 780 stated that, although Article 5 clearly applied to civilians, meaning non-combatants, this factor 'should not lead to any quick conclusions concerning people who at one point did bear arms'.[87] Relying on this, as well as the *Klaus Barbie* Case[88] and the Tribunal's own decision in the *Mrksić* Rule 61 Decision,[89] the Trial Chamber therefore held that:

the presence of those actively involved in the conflict should not prevent the characterization of a population as civilian and those actively involved in a resistance movement can qualify as victims of crimes against humanity ... although crimes against humanity must target a civilian population, individuals who at one time performed acts of resistance may in certain circumstances be victims of crimes against humanity.[90]

That crimes against humanity must be committed against a 'population' was taken to illustrate their collective nature – they must be

---

[85] *Tadić* (Judgment) at paragraph 638.

[86] See above at pp. 58–59.

[87] Final Report of the Commission of Experts, UN Doc. S/1994/674 at paragraph 78.

[88] *Fédération Nationale des Déportés et Internés Résistants et Patriotes and Others* v *Barbie* 78 ILR 124. There it was held at 140 that 'Neither the driving force which motivated the victims, nor their possible membership of the Resistance, excludes the possibility that the accused acted with the element of intent necessary for the commission of crimes against humanity.'

[89] 108 ILR 53, where patients in the Vukovar hospital, including both civilians and resistance fighters who had laid down their arms, were considered by the Tribunal to have been the victims of crimes against humanity.

[90] *Tadić* (Judgment) at paragraph 643. This approach was also followed by the ICTY in *Prosecutor* v *Kupreskić*, Case IT-95-16 (Judgment of 14 January 2000) at paragraph 548, and by the ICTR: see *Prosecutor* v *Akayesu* at paragraphs 575–576.

widespread or systematic, and the result of an official policy. The defence in *Tadić* had argued that crimes against humanity had to be both widespread *and* systematic, but there is precious little evidence to support that assertion. The text of Article 5 of the Statute is unambiguous on this point, and the Tribunal had no difficulty in holding that widespread and systematic are alternatives. An act is not required to be both in order to be a crime against humanity.[91] The requirement that acts be widespread or systematic, however, raises the question of whether a single isolated act can represent a crime against humanity. Although isolated or random acts were not designed to come within the purview of crimes against humanity, 'that is the purpose of requiring that the acts be directed against a civilian *population*'.[92] Isolated acts can therefore still be crimes against humanity provided there is some nexus between the act and the attack on the civilian population.[93] As the Tribunal held in the *Mrksić* Case: 'Crimes against humanity are to be distinguished from war crimes against individuals. In particular, they must be widespread or demonstrate a systematic character. However, as long as there is a link with the widespread or systematic attack against a civilian population, a single act could qualify as a crime against humanity.'[94]

The fact that crimes against humanity are not isolated acts, but are instead widespread or systematic, is the reason why they are perceived as being so shocking to the conscience of mankind. Such crimes are the result of a conscious and deliberate plan to target a particular population for attack or persecution. Whereas this had previously been assumed to involve some measure of direction on the part of a State, it is now accepted that this is not the case. A policy is still required by

[91] *Tadić* (Judgment) at paragraph 646. The UN Secretary-General stated that crimes against humanity must be committed as part of a 'widespread or systematic attack' (UN Doc. S/1995/134 at paragraph 48). The *Mrksić* Decision at paragraph 30, and Article 3 of the ICTR Statute provide the same, and in the *Akayesu* Decision, at paragraph 579, the Rwandan Tribunal held that '[crimes against humanity] can be part of a widespread or systematic attack and need not be part of both'. The same approach is taken in Article 7 of the Statute of the International Criminal Court.

[92] *Tadić* (Judgment) at paragraph 649.

[93] For discussion of this point, see Part VI of *Tadić* (Appeal Judgment), and in particular paragraph 251.

[94] At paragraph 30. This was vital as regards systematic rape and sexual assaults to intimidate, degrade or terrorise the civilian population, widespread in former Yugoslavia and many other internal conflicts. See Christopher J. Greenwood, 'War Crimes Proceedings Before the International Criminal Tribunal for the Former Yugoslavia' [1997] *Military LJ* 15 at 29.

customary international law, but this need not be a State policy, and furthermore need not be formalised in any sense.[95] In fact, policy can even be 'deduced from the way in which the acts occur. Notably, if the acts occur on a widespread or systematic basis that demonstrates a policy to commit those acts.'[96] This is clearly of great importance to internal armed conflict, where crimes against humanity can therefore be equally well committed in furtherance of insurgent, rather than government, policy.[97]

Discriminatory intent and motive

The final two elements of crimes against humanity elaborated by the Trial Chamber in its *Tadić* Judgment, i.e. that there must be discriminatory intent, and that the act must not be taken for purely personal reasons unrelated to the armed conflict, were highly controversial, and eventually overturned by the Appeals Chamber.

Discriminatory intent is explicitly required by Article 5(h) of the Tribunal's Statute, which deals with 'persecutions on political, racial and religious grounds', but is not mentioned in any other part of Article 5. The Trial Chamber in *Tadić* (Judgment) accepted that discriminatory intent was not a requirement for all crimes against humanity according to the Nuremberg Charter, Control Council Law No. 10, the Tokyo Charter and the ILC Draft Code of Crimes Against the Peace and Security of Mankind. Indeed, it furthermore noted that the Defence had not challenged the exclusion of this requirement in the Prosecution's definition of crimes against humanity, and that although, unlike the Yugoslav Tribunal, the Statute of the Rwandan Tribunal did include discriminatory intent as a requirement for crimes against humanity in general, it had been subject to intense criticism on this very point.[98] Surprisingly in light of this, the Trial Chamber nevertheless went on to hold that discriminatory intent *is* required for all crimes against humanity, because it was 'included in the *Report of the Secretary-General*, and since several

---

[95] *Prosecutor v Nikolić* at paragraph 26, as endorsed by the Trial Chamber in *Tadić* (Judgment) at paragraph 655. See also the 1996 ILC Draft Code of Crimes Against the Peace and Security of Mankind, Article 18, and the commentary thereto.

[96] *Tadić* (Judgment) at paragraph 653.

[97] Indeed, the ILC Draft Code does not even require that the organised group instigating the acts be in control of a portion of national territory. See *Tadić* (Judgment) at paragraph 655.

[98] *Ibid.*, at paragraphs 651–652.

Security Council members stated they interpreted Article 5 as referring to acts taken on a discriminatory basis'.[99]

The Trial Chamber was clearly mistaken on this point. The Appeals Chamber held that both the ordinary meaning and a logical construction of Article 5 lead to the conclusion that *all* crimes against humanity do not have to be perpetrated with discriminatory intent.[100] Furthermore, an examination of the relevant State practice and development of international instruments showed that, equally, 'a discriminatory intent is not required by customary international law for all crimes against humanity'.[101] The Appeals Chamber accepted that the Report of the Secretary-General was, indeed, in conflict with the Statute of the Tribunal on this point, but held that where the two were contradictory the Statute must prevail, especially where, as in this case, the wording of the provision is totally unambiguous.[102] The Secretary-General, like the three States which had made comments in the Security Council,[103] was simply making the observation that crimes against humanity are, in most circumstances, committed on discriminatory grounds. That is undisputably true, but it fails to transform the existence of such discriminatory intent into a legal requirement. As the Appeals Chamber underlined, 'One should not...confuse what happens most of the time...with the strict requirements of law.'[104] Discriminatory intent is not necessary for all crimes against humanity, and by explicitly including the requirement in Article 3 of the Rwandan Statute, the Security Council created a narrower jurisdiction than that existing under customary international law,[105] which requires discriminatory

---

99   *Ibid.*, at paragraph 652. See Report of the Secretary-General, UN Doc. S/1995/134, at paragraph 48, and Provisional Verbatim Record, 11 (French statement including discrimination on national, ethnic, racial and religious grounds as requirements for crimes against humanity), 16 (American statement including nationality, political beliefs, ethnic origin, race, gender and religion), and 45 (Russian statement including nationality, political beliefs, ethnic origin, religion or other grounds).

100   *Tadić* (Appeal Judgment) at paragraphs 282–284.

101   *Ibid.*, at paragraphs 287–292.

102   *Ibid.*, at paragraphs 293–297. The Appeals Chamber further argued at paragraph 297 that the Secretary-General's Report did not purport to be a definitive expression of the position under customary international law, instead merely '*describing* the notion of crimes against humanity in a general way, as opposed to stipulating a technical, legal definition intended to be binding on the Tribunal'.

103   For the Appeals Chamber's discussion of these statements and their importance, see paragraphs 298–304.

104   *Tadić* (Appeal Judgment) at paragraph 302.

105   Just as it did by requiring that crimes against humanity be committed during armed conflict to give the Yugoslav Tribunal jurisdiction.

intent only where the crime against humanity takes the form of persecution.

Finally, the Trial Chamber in *Tadić* (Judgment) held that crimes against humanity could not be committed for purely personal reasons.[106] Again, the Appeals Chamber decided that this is not the case.[107] Nothing in Article 5 of the Statute would suggest that crimes against humanity cannot be committed for purely personal reasons – all that is required is that the crimes must be part of a widespread or systematic attack against a civilian population, and that the accused had knowledge that his acts fitted into such a pattern.[108] The Appeals Chamber explained that the Trial Chamber had gone wrong, first by mistakenly equating the attack on the civilian population with the armed conflict, and secondly by confusing the notion of acts committed for purely personal reasons with acts unrelated to the armed conflict.[109] As outlined with great clarity, and thus meriting quotation:

it conflated two interpretations of the phrase ['purely personal motives']: first, that the act is unrelated to the armed conflict, and, secondly, that the act is unrelated to the attack on the civilian population...The two concepts cannot, however, be identical because then crimes against humanity would, by definition, *always take place in armed conflict*, whereas under customary international law these crimes may also be committed in times of peace. So the two...must be separate notions...A nexus with the accused's acts is required...*only* for the attack on 'any civilian population'. A nexus between the accused's acts and the armed conflict is *not* required...The armed conflict requirement is satisfied by

---

[106] This was derived from the need to prove both the existence of an armed conflict and a nexus between the acts in question and the conflict. Regarding the nexus, it was held that it was sufficient for the act to have been committed during the course of an armed conflict, provided (a) that the act was actually linked to the conflict 'geographically as well as temporally' (*Tadić* (Judgment) at paragraph 633), and (b) that the act was not 'unrelated to the armed conflict' (paragraph 634), taken to mean that the perpetrator knew of the context in which his act occurred, and that it was not committed for purely personal motives. See paragraphs 656–657.

[107] See *Tadić* (Appeal Judgment) at paragraphs 238–272.

[108] See also *Prosecutor* v *Kayishema*, Case ICTR-95-1; ICTR-96-10 at paragraphs 133–134 and *Prosecutor* v *Kupreskić* at paragraph 557.

[109] The Appeals Chamber nevertheless believed that the Trial Chamber had not consciously reached its conclusion. Instead, it was suggested that the Trial Chamber had merely mis-stated the requirement that the acts of the accused be knowingly committed in the context of large-scale crimes as a negative requirement that the accused not be acting for purely personal reasons: 'The Trial Chamber did not, the Appeals Chamber believes, wish to import a "motive" requirement; it simply duplicated the context and *mens rea* requirement, and confused it with the need for a link with the armed conflict, and thereby seemed to have unjustifiably and inadvertently added a new requirement.' See *Tadić* (Appeal Judgment) at paragraph 269.

proof that *there was* an armed conflict; that is all that the Statute requires, and in so doing, it requires more than does customary international law.

The Trial Chamber seems additionally to have conflated the notion of committing an act for purely personal motives and the notion that the act must not be unrelated to the armed conflict... It may be true that if the act is related to the armed conflict, then it is not being committed for purely personal motives. But it does not follow from this that, if the act is unrelated to the armed conflict, it is being committed for purely personal reasons. The act may be intimately related to the attack on a civilian population, that is, it may fit precisely into a context of persecution of a particular group, and yet be unrelated to the armed conflict. It would be wrong to conclude in these circumstances that, since the act is unrelated to the armed conflict, it is being committed for purely personal reasons. The converse is also true; that is, merely because personal motives can be identified in the defendant's carrying out of an act, it does not necessarily follow that the required nexus with the attack on a civilian population must also inevitably be lacking.[110]

A substantial weight of case law was cited by the Appeals Chamber in support of this proposition, demonstrating conclusively that 'under customary law, "purely personal motives" do not acquire any relevance for establishing whether or not a crime against humanity has been perpetrated'.[111]

Individual criminal responsibility

Violations of the laws of internal armed conflict comprising elements contained in Article 5 of the ICTY Statute clearly represent crimes against humanity, and individual criminal responsibility for crimes against humanity is now undisputed. More controversial was the issue of individual criminal responsibility for violations of the laws of armed conflict not amounting to crimes against humanity.

Tadić argued that, even if there are certain general principles applicable to both international and internal armed conflicts, these rules carry no individual criminal responsibility if violations are committed during internal armed conflict. Such an argument was not unheard of – it had even been stated by a member of the ICRC that the 'international humanitarian law applicable to non-international armed conflicts does not provide for individual penal responsibility'.[112] It is certainly true that

[110] *Ibid.*, at paragraphs 251–252.
[111] *Ibid.*, at paragraph 270.
[112] Denise Plattner, 'The Penal Repression of Violations of International Humanitarian Law Applicable in Non-international Armed Conflicts' (1990) 278 *Int Rev of the Red Cross* 409 at 414.

nothing in common Article 3 sets out criminal liability for violations of its provisions. Additional Protocol II is the same, not even containing a provision outlining grave breaches, in contrast to the Geneva Conventions and Additional Protocol I.[113] As the Trial Chamber in *Prosecutor v Delalić* stated, however, 'The fact that the Geneva Conventions themselves do not expressly mention that there shall be criminal liability for violations of common article 3 clearly does not in itself, preclude such liability',[114] and the assertion that those violations of the Conventions which are not grave breaches entail no individual criminal responsibility cannot be supported. Such breaches undeniably cannot be subject to the provisions of the Conventions on jurisdiction (i.e. that all States should either exercise jurisdiction, or else surrender the suspects for trial in another State),[115] but that does not mean that no individual criminal responsibility is involved. Indeed, several national military manuals make the point that all violations of the laws of war not amounting to grave breaches are still war crimes.[116]

Despite this, it has been claimed that violations of common Article 3 have, in fact, never been treated as crimes under international law (although such violations may, of course, still be criminal under the national laws of most States). The International Committee of the Red Cross stated in its comments on the establishing of the ICTY that war crimes are limited to international armed conflict,[117] a view supported by the Commission of Experts established by the Secretary-General.[118] Further weight can be added to this view by the fact that Article 4 of the Statute of the ICTR grants it jurisdiction over individuals accused of war crimes only if they are actually accused of violating common Article 3 and Additional Protocol II, described by the UN Secretary-General

---

[113] Violations of common Article 3 are not grave breaches under the regime of the Geneva Conventions, since they are not committed against protected persons. See Convention I Articles 49 and 50, Convention II Articles 50 and 51, Convention III Articles 129 and 130, Convention IV Articles 146 and 147, and Additional Protocol I Articles 11 and 85. High Contracting Parties are obliged to enact domestic legislation necessary to provide for the imposition of effective penal sanctions on the perpetrators of grave breaches.

[114] *Prosecutor v Delalić* at paragraph 308.

[115] Although even this is of only limited value where a State is unwilling to take such action, as Argentina was in the case of Adolf Eichmann, later tried in Israel. See *A-G of the Government of Israel v Eichmann* 36 ILR 5.

[116] E.g. the manuals of the USA and the UK, discussed in *Tadić* (Jurisdiction) at paragraph 131.

[117] Preliminary Remarks of the ICRC, 25 March 1993, unpublished. See Greenwood, 'The *Tadić* Case', 280 and n. 2 therein.

[118] UN Doc. S/1994/674 at paragraph 52.

as being a provision which 'for the first time criminalises common Article 3'.[119] On adopting the Rwandan Statute, however, the Security Council clearly felt that it was complying with the principle of *nullum crimen sine lege*, which would have been impossible had violations of common Article 3 not already been criminal under international law.

Even at the time of the adoption of the Yugoslav Statute, it was being asserted that breaches of common Article 3 were criminal under international law,[120] and there are clear arguments in favour of the violation of the laws of internal armed conflict entailing criminal responsibility:

> If violations of the international laws of war have traditionally been regarded as criminal under international law, there is no reason of principle why, once those laws came to be extended (albeit in attenuated form) to the context of internal armed conflicts, their violation in that context should not have been criminal, at least in the absence of a clear indication to the contrary.[121]

The Appeals Chamber in *Tadić* (Jurisdiction) felt the same, and by applying the reasoning of the Nuremberg Trials that 'Crimes against International Law are committed by men, not by abstract entities, and only by punishing individuals who commit such crimes can the provisions of International Law be enforced',[122] duly decided that those violations alleged against Tadić resulted in individual criminal responsibility regardless of whether they were committed in the context of an international or an internal armed conflict. Elements of international practice were further cited by the Appeals Chamber, demonstrating that States *do* in

---

[119] UN Doc. S/1995/134 at paragraph 12. See the Dissenting Opinion of Judge Li in *Tadić* (Jurisdiction) (paragraph 13), (1995) 16 HRLJ 466 at 467, who felt that violations of the laws and customs of warfare could be tried only in the context of international conflicts, basing his argument to a large degree on the Rwandan Statute, asking why, if such offences could be committed in either type of conflict, they were not included there.

[120] See US Ambassador Albright's statement to the Security Council, that the 'laws and customs of war' covered by Article 3 of the Tribunal's Statute included all obligations in force in the territory of former Yugoslavia when the alleged acts were committed, including common Article 3 and the Additional Protocols. Similar comments were made by the UK and France. See discussion of this in Meron, 'Criminalization of Internal Atrocities', 560; Greenwood, 'The *Tadić* Case', 267–268; and *Tadić* (Jurisdiction) at paragraph 88.

[121] Greenwood, 'The *Tadić* Case', 280–281. Meron agrees, 'Criminalization of Internal Atrocities', 561, that, 'There is no moral justification, and no truly persuasive legal reason, for treating perpetrators of atrocities in internal conflicts more leniently than those engaged in international wars.'

[122] *The Trial of German Major War Criminals: Proceedings of the International Military Tribunal Sitting at Nuremberg Germany*, Part 22 (1950) at 447. See *Tadić* (Jurisdiction) at paragraph 128.

general intend to criminalise serious breaches of the customary rules and principles of internal armed conflicts.

First, military manuals from Germany, New Zealand, the United States and the United Kingdom were used to establish individual criminal responsibility for violations of humanitarian law as applied to internal conflicts. The German Manual clearly states that breaches of common Article 3 are punishable,[123] while the New Zealand Manual of 1992 states that breaches of common Article 3 would appear to render those responsible liable to trial for war crimes.[124] As already outlined, the manuals of the United States and the United Kingdom consider war crimes to include every violation of the laws of war, including common Article 3.[125]

National legislation implementing the Geneva Conventions can also make it possible for domestic courts to try those responsible for breaches of the law of internal armed conflict. Thus the Tribunal cited the 1990 Criminal Code of the former Yugoslavia, which stated that those provisions dealing with war crimes against the civilian population and the wounded and sick expressly applied 'at the time of war, armed conflict or occupation',[126] which would seem to imply that they apply also to internal conflict. In addition, Article 210 of the Yugoslav Constitution made both Additional Protocols of 1977 directly applicable by the national courts. Likewise the Belgian courts have competence over breaches of Additional Protocol II, as they are deemed to constitute international law crimes.[127]

The Appeals Chamber also saw certain unanimously adopted United Nations Security Council resolutions stating that violations of the humanitarian law of non-international armed conflict carry with them criminal responsibility as being highly relevant to the formation of *opinio juris*. Thus, in two resolutions on Somalia[128] the Security Council

---

[123] Fleck, *Handbook of Humanitarian Law*, paragraph 1209, although this naturally follows from the provision requiring German troops to apply international humanitarian law irrespective of the character of the conflict. See *Tadić* (Jurisdiction) at paragraph 131.

[124] Paragraph 1807. The trial would, however, be held under national criminal law. See *Tadić* (Jurisdiction) at paragraph 131.

[125] See above, n. 116 and accompanying text.

[126] Articles 142 and 143. See *Tadić* (Jurisdiction) at paragraph 132.

[127] Loi de 16 juin 1993 relative à la répression des infractions graves aux Conventions internationales de Genève du 12 août 1949 et aux Protocoles I et II du 8 juin 1977, additionnels à ces Conventions (5 August 1993) Article 7. See *Tadić* (Jurisdiction), at paragraph 132.

[128] SC Resolutions 794 (3 December 1992) and 814 (26 March 1993). See *Tadić* (Jurisdiction) at paragraph 133.

condemned breaches of humanitarian law and asserted that those responsible for the breaches, or indeed those who had ordered them, would be held 'individually responsible', while in Security Council discussions on Resolution 827 (establishing the ICTY) it had been claimed by some States that the Tribunal clearly had jurisdiction over violations of common Article 3.[129] All of these factors enabled the Appeals Chamber to state categorically that 'customary international law imposes criminal liability for serious violations of common Article 3, as supplemented by other general principles and rules on the protection of victims of internal armed conflict, and for breaching certain fundamental principles and rules regarding means and methods of combat in civil strife'.[130]

This stance has since been endorsed by the ICTY in *Tadić* (Judgment)[131] and the *Delalić* Case,[132] and also by the ICTR, which concluded in *Prosecutor* v *Akayesu* that 'the violation of these norms [common Article 3 and Article 4 of Additional Protocol II] entails, as a matter of customary international law, individual responsibility for the perpetrator'.[133]

The Statute of the International Criminal Court: confirming custom

The Rome Statute of the International Criminal Court, adopted in July 1998, represents a vital development in the laws of internal armed conflict. The adoption of the instrument by such a large number of delegates is a clear manifestation of State practice, and affirms a broad view of the customary status given to much of the international law relevant to internal conflict by the Yugoslav and Rwandan Tribunals. This is particularly important in light of the guiding principle that those crimes within the jurisdiction of the Court should be limited to 'the most serious crimes of concern to the international community as a whole',[134] i.e. being reflective of customary international law rather than developing it.

[129] See notes 10 and 120 above, and accompanying text.
[130] *Tadić* (Jurisdiction) at paragraph 134.
[131] At paragraph 613.
[132] At paragraphs 308–316, finding in paragraph 316 that 'the substantive prohibitions in common article 3 . . . constitute rules of customary international law which may be applied by the International Tribunal to impose individual criminal responsibility'.
[133] At paragraphs 611–617, quotation from paragraph 617.
[134] See *Report of the Preparatory Committee on the Establishment of an International Criminal Court*, Volume I, UN Doc. A/51/22 (13 September 1996) at paragraph 51.

In addition, the Rome Statute confirms in the most authoritative manner possible that individual criminal responsibility for such violations is now beyond any measure of doubt.

Crimes against humanity

The inclusion of crimes against humanity within the Statute of the International Criminal Court was not controversial.[135] What was problematic, however, was the issue of what exactly should be included within the list of such crimes, and the circumstances in which they could be committed.[136] States had found the relevant precedents to be 'vague and, in many respects, contradictory'.[137] That crimes against humanity must be committed as part of an attack upon a civilian population was not seriously contested,[138] but fundamental disagreements existed concerning the questions of whether crimes against humanity could only be committed during armed conflict,[139] whether the attack had to be widespread *and* systematic or simply either,[140] and whether the attack had to be discriminatory in nature.[141]

The final text of Article 7, however, supports the statements of the ICTY and ICTR on all of these issues. The chapeau of Article 7(1) spells out the necessary criteria for crimes against humanity, firstly by failing to provide that any nexus to an armed conflict is required. The majority of delegations had supported this view throughout negotiations, explaining that the link required by the Nuremberg and Tokyo Charters, and by the Yugoslav Statute, were peculiar to those Tribunals, and not representative of customary international law.[142] Many of these States were, however, 'surprised when a significant number of delegations argued vigorously that crimes against humanity could only be committed during

---

[135] *Report of the Preparatory Committee*, Volume I at paragraph 82.
[136] For a good discussion of these problems and a commentary on the Article finally adopted, see Machteld Boot, Rodney Dixon and Christopher K. Hall, 'Article 7: Crimes Against Humanity' in Otto Triffterer (ed.), *Commentary on the Rome Statute of the International Criminal Court. Observers' Notes, Article by Article* (Baden-Baden, 1999), 118; and Herman von Hebel and Darryl Robinson, 'Crimes Within the Jurisdiction of the Court' in Roy S. Lee (ed.), *The International Criminal Court. The Making of the Rome Statute* (The Hague, 1999), 79 at 90–103.
[137] Von Hebel and Robinson, 'Jurisdiction of the Court', 90.
[138] See *Report of the Preparatory Committee*, Volume I at paragraph 86.
[139] *Ibid.*, at paragraphs 88–90.
[140] *Ibid.*, at paragraph 85.
[141] *Ibid.*, at paragraph 87.
[142] See the discussion above at pp. 148–149.

armed conflict'.[143] Nonetheless, the majority view eventually prevailed, and the Rome Statute makes it clear that crimes against humanity can be committed even where no armed conflict exists.

A majority of States also supported the disjunctive test (whereby crimes against humanity refer to attacks which are either widespread or systematic, but need not be both) as having been established as customary law.[144] The ICTY had certainly been clear on this issue, as had the Statute of the ICTR and the International Law Commission (ILC).[145] Again, however, a significant number of States disagreed,[146] arguing that the disjunctive test was too broad, and would lead to the situation where a 'common crime wave' could thereby be included despite there being no connection between the crimes involved. The majority view again prevailed in light of the fact that any such common crime wave would not meet the organisational policy requirements of being an attack directed against a civilian population.

Finally, there is no general requirement in Article 7(1) that crimes against humanity be discriminatory in nature. A number of States had pressed for a provision holding that such crimes must be committed on the grounds of nationality, race, religion, etc.[147] The majority, however, felt that this would make it too difficult to prosecute such crimes and, following the ICTY case law,[148] the Rome Statute confirms that discriminatory intent is required *only* for the inhuman act of persecution under Article 7(1)(h), rather than for all crimes against humanity.

The list of inhuman acts in Article 7(1)(a)–(k) is clearly based upon previous Charters and Statutes. Two new additions appear, however, as does a series of explanations of the various acts in Article 7(2).[149] The two additions, concerning enforced disappearances[150] and apartheid,[151] were

---

[143] This view was proposed by several members of the Arab group, and by a number of other Asian and African delegations. Some even claimed that there must be a nexus to *international* armed conflict. See von Hebel and Robinson, 'Jurisdiction of the Court', 92–93 and n. 43 therein.

[144] *Ibid.*, 94.

[145] See the discussion above at pp. 151–152.

[146] Again several Arab and Asian States, although also including the permanent members of the Security Council. See von Hebel and Robinson, 'Jurisdiction of the Court', 94–95.

[147] Including France. See *ibid.*, 93–94.

[148] See the discussion above at pp. 153–155.

[149] See von Hebel and Robinson, 'Jurisdiction of the Court', 98–103, and Boot, Dixon and Hall, 'Crimes Against Humanity', 129–171.

[150] Article 7(1)(i).

[151] Article 7(1)(j).

accepted by the majority of delegations as being apt for inclusion on the grounds that they had been recognised as crimes against humanity in previous international instruments,[152] and that they would otherwise have been included in Article 7(1)(k) concerning 'other inhuman acts' in any case.

War crimes

Like crimes against humanity, there was general consensus among the participating States that serious violations of the laws and customs applicable in armed conflict should be included within the Rome Statute.[153] Whether violations of the laws of internal armed conflict should be included was much more controversial, remaining a source of real disagreement until late in the day. Indeed, even the final draft placed before the Diplomatic Conference included the option of deleting those sections dealing with internal armed conflict.[154]

Article 20 of the ILC's Draft Statute[155] had provided that:

The Court has jurisdiction in accordance with this Statute with respect to the following crimes:
(a) the crime of genocide;
(b) the crime of aggression;
(c) serious violations of the laws and customs applicable in armed conflict;
(d) crimes against humanity;
(e) crimes, established under or pursuant to the treaty provisions listed in the Annex [including grave breaches of the Geneva Conventions and Additional

---

[152] The Preamble to the 1992 UN Declaration on the Protection of All Persons from Enforced Disappearances provides that such acts have 'the nature of a crime against humanity', and the 1996 ILC Draft Code of Crimes Against the Peace and Security of Mankind includes forced disappearances in Article 18(i). Numerous UN General Assembly resolutions have asserted that apartheid has the character of a crime against humanity, and the 1973 Convention on the Suppression and Punishment of the Crime of Apartheid provides the same in Article I.

[153] See *Report of the Preparatory Committee*, Volume I at paragraph 74.

[154] See Option V ('Delete sections C and D') to the draft Article on war crimes in the Draft Statute, UN Doc. A/CONF.183/2 (April 1998). For discussion of the background and a commentary on the provisions adopted, see von Hebel and Robinson, 'Jurisdiction of the Court', 104–105 and 119–122; and Michael Cottier, William J. Fenrick, Patricia V. Sellers and Andreas Zimmerman, 'Article 8: War Crimes' in Triffterer (ed.), *The Rome Statute*, 173 at 262–286 (Zimmerman).

[155] See *Report of the ILC on the Work of its 46th Session*, 2 May–22 July 1994, GAOR 49th Session, Supp. No. 10, UN Doc. A/49/10, 29. For a commentary on the Draft Statute, see James Crawford, 'The ILC Adopts a Statute for an International Criminal Court' (1995) 89 *AJIL* 404.

Protocol I], which, having regard to the conduct alleged, constitute exceptionally serious crimes of international concern.[156]

No specific mention was made of whether 'serious violations of the laws and customs applicable in armed conflict' was intended to include those violations of humanitarian law committed in the course of internal armed conflicts, although Meron claimed that the Commentary showed this to be the case by stating that Article 20 reflected, at least partly, Article 22 of the ILC Draft Code of Crimes Against the Peace and Security of Mankind, which applies to both international and internal armed conflicts.[157] Greenwood was less convinced, however, and instead believed that the question had been deliberately left open.[158] In fact, the ILC had intended to refer to the customary international law of war crimes in general, whatever it was or would become. The Draft Statute did not provide for jurisdiction over breaches of Additional Protocol II, at least as far as treaty law was concerned.[159] In the wake of *Tadić*, jurisdiction may have been possible over those provisions of the Protocol which reflect custom, although of course the ILC at that time did not have the benefit of the *Tadić* jurisprudence to draw upon.

At any rate, the suggestion that Article 20(c) of the ILC Draft referred only to violations of the laws and customs of international armed conflict, excluding those of an internal character, does not seem easily tenable. This is especially so when one considers that the Commentary attached significance to Article 3 of the ICTY Statute,[160] the application of which to internal armed conflict has been affirmed. The ILC further stated in paragraph 10 of the Commentary to Article 20(c) its opinion that war crimes did indeed exist under customary international law, and the ICTY also stated in *Tadić* that these can and do apply equally to internal armed conflicts.

The majority of States supported the inclusion of internal armed conflict in the Statute of the International Criminal Court, for two main

---

[156] Emphasis added. A commentary on Article 20 can be found at UN Doc. A/49/10, 29 at 70–79.

[157] Meron, 'Criminalization of Internal Atrocities', 574. See also the ILC Commentary, 73–74.

[158] 'The *Tadić* Case', 281.

[159] The Additional Protocol is not listed in the Annex containing those treaties violations of which are crimes within the Court's jurisdiction. Treaties which merely regulate conduct, or which prohibit conduct but only on an inter-State basis, were excluded, and so Additional Protocol II was specifically ruled out since 'it contains no clause dealing with grave breaches, nor any equivalent enforcement provision'. See ILC Commentary, 141 and 145.

[160] ILC Commentary, 73.

reasons – first, 'it was precisely in internal armed conflicts that national criminal justice systems were in all likelihood unable to adequately respond to violations of such norms',[161] and secondly, most of the conflicts since the Second World War had been internal in character, and unless war crimes in those cases were included, the Court would have been unable to act against those violations of humanitarian law which are now the most widespread. As the Lawyers Committee for Human Rights argued in 1998, 'It is untenable to argue that the perpetrators of atrocities committed in non-international armed conflict should be shielded from international justice just because their victims were of the same nationality.'[162]

Despite these arguments, a minority of States[163] continued to campaign against any jurisdiction over internal armed conflicts, claiming that their inclusion would be unrealistic and would undermine the universal acceptance of the Court, that individual criminal responsibility was not clearly established for such violations and that customary law had not changed in this respect since the adoption of the Rwandan Tribunal's Statute.[164] The inclusion of violations of the laws of internal armed conflict eventually won the day, and Article 8(2)(c)–(f) sets out the relevant provisions. Intimately connected to the question of whether internal conflicts should be covered, however, and equally divisive, was the issue of exactly which norms are applicable in such conflicts, and the two proposals initially submitted to the Preparatory Committee's Working Group on the Definition of Crimes reflected this. The first proposal limited crimes in internal armed conflict to violations of common Article 3,[165] whereas the second proposal set out a much more extensive list.[166]

Most delegations were of the opinion that several provisions of Additional Protocol II should be considered customary international law in addition to common Article 3,[167] and accordingly the Statute does more

---

[161] Von Hebel and Robinson, 'Jurisdiction of the Court', 105.
[162] Lawyers Committee for Human Rights, *Establishing an International Criminal Court: Major Unresolved Issues in the Draft Statute* (New York, 1998), section IV.
[163] China, India, the Russian Federation, Turkey, and several Asian and Arab States. See von Hebel and Robinson, 'Jurisdiction of the Court', 105, n. 87.
[164] *Report of the Preparatory Committee*, Volume I at paragraph 78.
[165] See the proposal submitted by the United States, UN Doc. A/AC.249/1997/WG.1/DP.2.
[166] See the proposal which was essentially drawn up by the ICRC, and submitted by New Zealand and Switzerland, UN Doc. A/AC.249/1997/WG.1/DP.1. For an outline of this process, see Cottier *et al.*, 'War Crimes', 262–263, and for the consolidated draft text drawn up by the Working Group, incorporating both proposals (the second as an option), see UN Doc. A/AC.249/1997/WG.1/CRP.2.
[167] Von Hebel and Robinson, 'Jurisdiction of the Court', 105.

than assert jurisdiction over violations of common Article 3 alone. It
provides in Article 8 that:

> 1. The Court shall have jurisdiction in respect of war crimes in particular when
> committed as part of a plan or policy or as part of a large-scale commission of
> such crimes.
> 2. For the purpose of this Statute, 'war crimes' means:
>   . . .
>
>   (c) In the case of an armed conflict not of an international character,
>   serious violations of article 3 common to the four Geneva
>   Conventions of 12 August 1949 . . .
>
>   . . .
>
>   (e) Other serious violations of the laws and customs applicable in armed
>   conflicts not of an international character, within the established
>   framework of international law . . .

Article 8(2)(c) does essentially reproduce common Article 3, but subparagraph (e) goes much further, listing at length other serious violations
of the laws of internal armed conflict. Indeed, most of subparagraph (e)
comes directly from subparagraph (b),[168] which lists violations of the
laws and customs of international warfare other than grave breaches
of the Geneva Conventions.[169] These provisions of Article 8(2)(e) go even
further than those contained in Additional Protocol II, so that the approach taken by the Rome Statute is consistent with 'the gradual blur-
ring of the fundamental differences between international and internal
armed conflicts'.[170]

The Statute also has an impact upon the determination of when an internal armed conflict exists.[171] Subparagraphs (d) and (f) set out the scope

---

[168] Although slightly modified where necessary, references to grave breaches (as in
   Article 8(2)(b)(xxii)) being replaced by references to serious violations of common
   Article 3 (as in Article 8(2)(e)(vi)), for example. Some of the provisions of
   subparagraph (b) are not reproduced in subparagraph (e), either because they are
   simply not relevant to internal armed conflict, or else because they were not
   considered to have attained customary status. See Cottier *et al.*, 'War Crimes', 263.
[169] The majority are, nonetheless, also found in Additional Protocol II.
[170] Von Hebel and Robinson, 'Jurisdiction of the Court', 125. Zimmerman points
   out, however, in Cottier *et al.*, 'War Crimes', 263, that 'the Statute does not
   completely follow the approach by the ICTY which stated that "what is
   inhumane and consequently proscribed, in international wars, cannot but be
   inhumane and inadmissible in civil strife"'. (See *Tadić* (Jurisdiction) at
   paragraph 119.)
[171] See the discussion in von Hebel and Robinson, 'Jurisdiction of the Court',
   119–121.

of application for subparagraphs (c) and (e), subparagraph (d) providing that:

Paragraph 2(c) applies to armed conflicts not of an international character and thus does not apply to situations of internal disturbances and tensions, such as riots, isolated or sporadic acts of violence or other acts of a similar nature.

This is familiar from Additional Protocol II, Article 1(2), and it had initially been intended that the provision would apply equally to subparagraph (e).[172] Instead, however, subparagraph (f) sets out that, in addition to the terms of subparagraph (d), subparagraph (e) *does* apply to 'armed conflicts that take place in the territory of a State when there is protracted armed conflict between governmental authorities and organized armed groups or between such groups'. This represents an important lowering of the threshold from that of Additional Protocol II, and broadens the jurisdiction of the Court significantly.[173]

Finally, Article 8(3) of the Statute is based on Article 3(1) of Additional Protocol II, and provides that subparagraphs (c) and (e) are to have no effect on the 'responsibility of a Government to maintain or re-establish law and order in the State or to defend the unity and territorial integrity of the State, by all legitimate means'. As with the provision in Additional Protocol II, this is merely a sop to worried governments, reassuring them that the inclusion of internal armed conflicts within the jurisdiction of the Court will not allow unjustified interference in the domestic affairs of the State.[174]

The principle of individual criminal responsibility

In the context of the Yugoslav Tribunal, individual criminal responsibility arises primarily under Article 7(1) of the Tribunal's Statute, which provides that:

A person who planned, instigated, ordered, committed or otherwise aided and abetted in the planning, preparation or execution of a crime referred to in

---

[172] *Ibid.*, at 120.
[173] Protocol II has a very strict set of criteria for its application (see above at pp. 103–109), whereas all that is required by the ICC Statute is 'protracted armed conflict'. The Additional Protocol II threshold would have excluded several situations where violations of humanitarian law are common, and yet where the domestic courts would be unable to take any action, as in Somalia. The provisions of Article 8(2)(f) should be warmly welcomed. See von Hebel and Robinson, 'Jurisdiction of the Court', 121.
[174] *Ibid.*, 121–122.

articles 2 to 5 of the present Statute shall be individually responsible for the crime.[175]

Clearly, where an accused has directly engaged in violations of humanitarian law, the application of Article 7(1) is straightforward. The Trial Chamber in *Tadić* (Judgment) was also faced, however, with the more complex issue of participation in, rather than the direct commission of, offences. Drawing on the jurisprudence of the Nuremberg Trials,[176] the Chamber held that:

The accused will be found criminally culpable for any conduct where it is determined that he knowingly participated in the commission of an offence that violates international humanitarian law and his participation directly and substantially affected the commission of that offence through supporting the actual commission before, during, or after the incident. He will also be responsible for all that naturally results from the commission of the act in question.[177]

This approach has subsequently been followed by both the Yugoslav and Rwandan Tribunals.[178]

Throughout the process leading to the adoption of the Rome Statute for the International Criminal Court, it was widely accepted that the concept of individual criminal responsibility for crimes (including the acts of planning, instigating and assisting in the commission of such crimes) was essential, and should accordingly be explicitly stated in the adopted text.[179] The text finally adopted as Article 25 duly reaffirms the principle, although discussion relating to the Article in the Preparatory Committee was far from straightforward.[180] A substantial number of texts were initially proposed, and not until the Working Group had devoted a large proportion of its time during the February 1997 session

[175] That *Prosecutor* v *Tadić* (Judgment) paragraphs 663–668 established a basis in customary law for individual criminal responsibility, and hence for Article 7 of the Statute, was vitally important since 'the...Tribunal is only empowered to apply international humanitarian law that is "beyond any doubt customary law"' (paragraph 662).

[176] *Ibid.*, at paragraphs 670–687, where the requirements were established to be intent, direct contribution, and participation to the extent that the criminal act most probably would not have occurred in the same way had not someone acted in the role assumed by the accused.

[177] Paragraph 692.

[178] See, for example, *Prosecutor* v *Delalić* at paragraph 329, and *Prosecutor* v *Akayesu* at paragraphs 471–485.

[179] See *Report of the Preparatory Committee*, Volume I at paragraph 191.

[180] For an overview, see Per Saland, 'International Criminal Law Principles' in Lee, *The International Criminal Court*, 198–200 and Kai Ambos, 'Article 25: Individual Criminal Responsibility' in Triffterer, *The Rome Statute*, 475–492.

of the Preparatory Committee to the issue was a measure of agreement reached. Even then, however, agreement focused not on the specific content of the provision, but rather on its format and structure: 'i.e., one single article to cover the responsibility of principals and all other modes of participation (except command responsibility), and to cover both completed crimes and attempted ones'.[181] This was, in fact, heavily based on the corresponding Article of the ILC Draft Code of Crimes Against the Peace and Security of Mankind, which had been adopted in 1996.[182]

The exact substance of the Article proved more difficult to resolve. The criminal responsibility of individuals went to the very heart of the proposed Statute, and was therefore accepted throughout negotiations. Much more controversial and divisive was the question of criminal responsibility of legal or juridical persons, and whether it ought to be included in the Statute alongside that of natural persons.[183] It

---

[181] Saland, 'Criminal Law Principles', 198.

[182] UN Doc. A/51/332, 30 July 1996. Article 2 of the ILC Draft Code provided that:

1. A crime against the peace and security of mankind entails individual responsibility.
2. An individual shall be responsible for the crime of aggression in accordance with article 16.
3. An individual shall be responsible for a crime set out in articles 17 [genocide], 18 [crimes against humanity], 19 [crimes against UN personnel] or 20 [war crimes] if that individual:

    (a) intentionally commits such a crime;
    (b) orders the commission of such a crime which in fact occurs or is attempted;
    (c) fails to prevent or repress the commission of such a crime in the circumstances set out in article 6 [responsibility of superiors];
    (d) knowingly aids, abets or otherwise assists, directly and substantially, in the commission of such a crime, including providing the means for its commission;
    (e) directly participates in planning or conspiring to commit such a crime which in fact occurs;
    (f) directly and publicly incites another individual to commit such a crime which in fact occurs;
    (g) attempts to commit such a crime by taking action commencing the execution of a crime which does not in fact occur because of circumstances independent of his intention.

[183] The Preparatory Committee noted that 'There is a deep divergence of views as to the advisability of including criminal responsibility of juridical persons in the Statute. Many delegations are strongly opposed, whereas some strongly favour its inclusion. Others have an open mind.' See *Decisions Taken by the Preparatory Committee at its Session held from 11 to 21 February 1997*, UN Doc. A/AC.249/1997/L.5, 12 March 1997, Annex II (Report of the Working Group on General Principles of Criminal Law and Penalties) at n. 46.

was included as an option in all of the draft versions of the Article, with France particularly fervent in its support for the proposal, believing the inclusion of such responsibility to be vitally important as regards restitution and compensation for the victims of crimes.[184] Nonetheless, when it became evident that consensus could not be reached at the Rome Conference, the proposal was withdrawn, and Article 25 asserts jurisdiction over natural persons only.[185] Article 25(4) provides, however, that the responsibility of States under international law remains unaffected.

The International Criminal Court will accordingly have jurisdiction over individuals who commit any of the crimes enumerated in the Statute. As demonstrated by the *Tadić* Case, however, the commission of a crime is a complex issue, and the Rome Statute recognises that there are different types of perpetration or participation in criminal activity. Article 25(3) provides that:

In accordance with this Statute, a person shall be criminally responsible and liable for punishment for a crime within the jurisdiction of the Court if that person:

(a) Commits such a crime, whether as an individual, jointly with another or through another person, regardless of whether that person is criminally responsible;

(b) Orders, solicits or induces the commission of such a crime which in fact occurs or is attempted;

(c) For the purpose of facilitating the commission of such a crime, aids, abets or otherwise assists in its commission or its attempted commission, including providing the means for its commission;

---

[184] Geoffrey Robertson has expressed the argument in the following terms: 'Why should a multinational chemical corporation not be prosecuted (as well as its directors) for supplying poison gas in the knowledge that it will be used for a crime against humanity? Why should that company, if convicted, not be ordered to pay massive reparations to survivors and to victims' families?' See *Crimes Against Humanity* (London, 2000), 343.

[185] This has been criticised, e.g. by Robertson, *Crimes Against Humanity*, although other commentators have noted its exclusion with approval. Ambos, for example, 'Individual Criminal Responsibility', 478, finds the reasons for its rejection 'as a whole . . . quite convincing. The inclusion of collective liability would detract from the Court's jurisdictional focus, which is on individuals. Furthermore, the Court would be confronted with serious and ultimately overwhelming problems of evidence. In addition, there are not yet universally recognized common standards for corporate liability; in fact, the concept is not even recognized in some major criminal law systems. Consequently, the absence of corporate criminal liability in many States would render the principle of [complementarity] (article 17) unworkable.'

(d) In any other way contributes to the commission or attempted commission of such a crime by a group of persons acting with a common purpose. Such contribution shall be intentional and shall either:

   (i) Be made with the aim of furthering the criminal activity or criminal purpose of the group, where such activity or purpose involves the commission of a crime within the jurisdiction of the Court; or
   (ii) Be made in the knowledge of the intention of the group to commit the crime;

(e) In respect of the crime of genocide, directly and publicly incites others to commit genocide;

(f) Attempts to commit such a crime by taking action that commences its execution by means of a substantial step, but the crime does not occur because of circumstances independent of the person's intentions. However, a person who abandons the effort to commit the crime or otherwise prevents the completion of the crime shall not be liable for punishment under this Statute for the attempt to commit that crime if the person completely and voluntarily gave up the criminal purpose.

Subparagraph (a) deals with three forms of commission, the first of which is the direct commission of a crime contained in the Statute by an individual. This states the obvious, and is uncontroversial. Second is the commission of a crime along with another person, in which case both are criminally responsible.[186] Third is the perpetration of a crime through another person, regardless of whether or not that person (i.e. the actual perpetrator, or agent, rather than the instigator) is criminally responsible. Previous drafts had confirmed that the direct perpetrator in such circumstances is usually 'an innocent agent who is not aware of the criminal nature of the act committed, such as a minor, a person of defective mental capacity or a person acting under mistake of fact or otherwise acting without mens rea'.[187] The dropping of the non-culpability requirement is therefore important, in that the commission of a crime through another can now clearly entail criminal responsibility even where the agent himself is equally culpable. This is likely to be the case where the indirect perpetrator is in a position of control or authority over the agent, and is accordingly closely related to the issues

---

[186] This adopted provision is much tidier than previous drafts, which had dealt with the question of jointly committed crimes and crimes committed through others in various separate sections on the responsibility of principals, and on participation/complicity. See, for example, Draft Article B, *Report of the Preparatory Committee on the Establishment of an International Criminal Court*, Volume II, UN Doc. A/51/22, 13 September 1996.

[187] *Ibid.*, Draft Article B(b)(3).

of ordering the commission of a crime in paragraph 3(b), and command responsibility in Article 28 of the Statute.[188]

Subparagraph (c) is particularly important, in that it deals with the complex issue of when criminal responsibility arises for acts contributing to the commission of a crime, without amounting to direct commission by the individual in question.[189] As outlined above, the Trial Chamber in *Tadić* (Judgment) held that such an act must have 'directly and substantially affected the commission of [the] offence',[190] where 'substantial' means that the contribution has an effect on the commission of the crime.[191] The actual presence of the accused at the commission of the crime is not, however, necessary,[192] and Ambos argues convincingly that, in light of the Trial Chamber's decision that 'aiding and abetting includes all acts of assistance by words or acts that lend encouragement or support',[193] the requirement that a contribution be direct and substantial was not, in fact, taken very seriously.[194]

A slightly different view was taken by the Yugoslav Tribunal in the *Furundžija* Case, where the Trial Chamber chose to differentiate between the nature of the assistance given and its effect on the commission of the crime.[195] With regard to the nature of the assistance, it held that 'aiding and abetting need not be tangible, but may consist of moral support or encouragement'.[196] Indeed, simply being present at the commission of the crime can result in criminal responsibility, provided 'his presence had a significant legitimizing or encouraging effect on the principals'.[197] Article 2(3)(d) of the ILC Draft Code of Crimes[198] was therefore criticised by the Chamber as misleading in that, by requiring the assistance given to be 'direct' as well as 'substantial', it might appear that the assistance must be tangible, or have a causal effect on the commission of the

---

[188] See the discussion in Ambos, 'Individual Criminal Responsibility', 479–480. For a consideration of command responsibility, see below at pp. 180 ff.
[189] See Ambos, 'Individual Criminal Responsibility', 480–486.
[190] At paragraph 692.
[191] *Tadić* (Judgment) at paragraph 688.
[192] *Ibid.*, at paragraph 691.
[193] *Ibid.*, at paragraph 689, a position supported by the Trial Chamber in *Prosecutor v Delalić* at paragraphs 325–329.
[194] Ambos, 'Individual Criminal Responsibility', 481.
[195] *Prosecutor v Furundžija* at paragraphs 190–249.
[196] *Ibid.*, at paragraph 199.
[197] *Ibid.*, at paragraph 232.
[198] Draft Code of Crimes Against the Peace and Security of Mankind, see *Report of the International Law Commission on the Work of its Forty-Eighth Session*, UN Doc. A/51/332 (30 July 1996).

criminal act.[199] This is not the case, and Article 25(3)(c) of the Rome Statute contains no such requirement.

Turning to the effect of the assistance on the commission of the crime, the Trial Chamber did not regard a causal relationship between the assistance and the crime to be necessary.[200] What is required instead is that 'the assistance must have a substantial effect on the commission of the crime'.[201] The Trial Chamber saw this as being very much in line with Article 25(3)(c) of the Rome Statute, and as 'less restrictive than the Draft Code', in that whereas the ILC Draft Code requires the assistance to be 'direct and substantial', the Rome Statute 'clearly contemplates assistance in either physical form or in the form of moral support. Indeed, the word "abet" includes mere exhortation or encouragement.'[202]

Article 25(3)(c) therefore imposes criminal responsibility for any assistance having a substantial effect on the commission of a crime under the Statute. There are, however, two limiting factors, the first of which concerns the requirement that the effect must be 'substantial'. Whether the assistance provided has had a substantial effect can only be determined according to the circumstances of each individual case, although it may be that the further category in paragraph 3(c) of 'otherwise assists' provides a yet lower threshold for responsibility than that required for aiding and abetting.[203] The second limiting factor is that the assistance must be provided 'for the purpose of facilitating such a crime'. The Yugoslav and Rwandan Tribunals have consistently held that an individual must only know that his or her assistance aids the perpetrator in the commission of the crime.[204] This subjective element of the Rome Statute goes further, in that 'purpose generally implies a specific subjective requirement stricter than mere knowledge'.[205]

---

[199] *Prosecutor v Furundžija* at paragraph 232.
[200] *Ibid.*, at paragraph 233.
[201] *Ibid.*, at paragraph 234.
[202] *Ibid.*, at paragraph 231.
[203] See Ambos, 'Individual Criminal Responsibility', 482–483. He accepts, however, at 483 that 'if one follows *Furundžija* and considers the substantial effect of the assistance on the main crime as an independent constituting element of accomplice liability, complicity as an "otherwise assist" would also require a substantial effect within the meaning of sub-paragraph (c)'.
[204] See *Prosecutor v Tadić* (Judgment) at paragraphs 688–692, *Prosecutor v Delalić* at paragraph 328, *Prosecutor v Furundžija* at paragraph 236, and *Prosecutor v Akayesu* at paragraphs 476–479.
[205] Ambos, 'Individual Criminal Responsibility', 483. The requirement would appear to extend even beyond the ordinary *mens rea* criteria contained in Article 30 of the Rome Statute.

Subparagraph (d) deals with the question of group responsibility rather than individual responsibility. There would appear to be no reason, however, why an individual who contributes to a crime under subparagraph (d) would not also be liable or responsible for aiding and abetting an individual crime under subparagraph (c),[206] especially given the wide scope of the latter provision discussed above. Although subparagraph (d) would seem to require a very high level of subjective intent or knowledge of an accused, that would be relevant only for criminal responsibility under that provision – the necessary level of *mens rea* for responsibility under subparagraph (c) would have been met.

Previous incarnations of Article 25 had been unclear as to whether the incitement provision now contained in subparagraph (e) should apply to all crimes within the Court's jurisdiction, or only to that of genocide.[207] The Convention on the Prevention and Punishment of the Crime of Genocide[208] contains such a provision explicitly in Article III(c), and there was a general consensus that incitement ought to apply at least to that specific crime. There was less agreement concerning incitement to commit other crimes under the Statute. Some argued that incitement to commit genocide ought to be contained only in that Article of the Statute dealing specifically with genocide, whereas others felt that incitement to commit other crimes would be covered in any case by solicitation and inducement as already contained in Article 25. This may well be the case, but there is a fundamental difference between incitement to commit genocide as outlined in subparagraph (e) and the alternative forms of liability arising from the preceding provisions – in contrast to the crimes covered in subparagraphs (b), (c) and (d) there is no requirement that the crime of genocide be either committed or attempted. An individual who directly and publicly incites genocide is therefore criminally responsible even if no further action is taken by anybody towards that end. This approach is perfectly consistent with that taken

---

[206] *Ibid.*, 483–486, and 491: 'A person who contributes to a group crime or its attempt will always be liable as an aider and abetter to an individual crime... the significant difference between subparagraphs (c) and (d) lies, if at all, on the subjective level... it is hardly conceivable that a case which entails liability according to subparagraph (d) will not do so according to subparagraph (c).'

[207] The draft placed before the Rome Conference, for example, provided in Article 23(7) as follows: '...a person is criminally responsible and liable for punishment... if that person:... (f) [directly and publicly] incites the commission of [such a crime] [genocide] [which in fact occurs], [with the intention that such crime be commited]'. The question remained controversial throughout the Rome Conference: see Saland, 'Criminal Law Principles', 200, and Ambos, 'Individual Criminal Responsibility', 486–488.

[208] General Assembly Resolution 260A(III), 9 December 1948, 78 UNTS 277.

by the ICTR in *Prosecutor v Akayesu* where, considering the issue of violation of Article 2(3)(c) of the Rwandan Statute, the Trial Chamber held that 'genocide clearly falls within the category of crimes so serious that direct and public incitement to commit such a crime must be punished as such, *even where such incitement failed to produce the result expected by the perpetrator*'.[209]

Finally, subparagraph (f) imposes criminal responsibility for an attempt to commit any crime within the jurisdiction of the Court. This had proved a controversial topic throughout the Preparatory Committee's work, and also for the ILC in drawing up its Draft Code,[210] although it proved relatively unproblematic during the Rome Conference. Japan's proposal to reward an individual who, having decided to commit a crime, later changes their mind by holding that the voluntary abandonment of a criminal act should negate responsibility was accepted with relatively little debate, although no such provision is found in the ILC Draft Code. Difficult questions remain, for example regarding the point in time until which abandonment is possible, when abandonment is truly voluntary, and indeed whether abandonment cannot actually be seen as evidence of an attempt. Nonetheless, Ambos neatly answers any criticisms by explaining that such a provision is absolutely necessary, 'since the possibility of abandonment is recognized in all modern legal systems and can, therefore, be truly considered a general principle of international law. It also makes sense in that it creates an incentive for the perpetrator to withdraw from the commission.'[211]

Importantly, recent case law from the Yugoslav Tribunal has affirmed that reciprocity has no effect on the imposition of individual criminal responsibility for violations of humanitarian law. In the *Kupreskić* Case, the defence relied (albeit indirectly) upon the *tu quoque* principle, whereby the commission of similar offences by the enemy affords a valid defence.[212] The Trial Chamber rejected the argument on two grounds: first, that 'there is in fact no support either in State practice or in the opinions of publicists for the validity of such a defence',[213]

---

[209] *Prosecutor v Akayesu* at paragraph 562. Emphasis added.
[210] At least the issue of what constituted an attempt was controversial. There was a general agreement that attempts to commit crimes should entail responsibility. See Ambos, 'Individual Criminal Responsibility', 488–490, and Saland, 'Criminal Law Principles', 200.
[211] Ambos, 'Individual Criminal Responsibility', 490.
[212] *Prosecutor v Kupreskić* at paragraphs 515–520.
[213] *Ibid.*, at paragraph 516, citing its rejection by the US Military Tribunal following the Second World War, and the Final Report of the Commission of Experts created prior to the establishment of the ICTY.

and secondly that 'the *tu quoque* argument is flawed in principle'.[214] As outlined above with respect to common Article 3 and Additional Protocol II,[215] international humanitarian law is absolute and unconditional. It exists not to protect the interests of States, but rather 'to benefit individuals *qua* human beings', so that compliance with the rules of humanitarian law is not, and cannot be, dependent upon the reciprocal performance of these obligations.[216] Accordingly, 'individual criminal responsibility for serious violations of humanitarian law may not be thwarted by recourse to arguments such as reciprocity'.[217] There would seem to be no reason why this should apply only to those provisions of humanitarian law which are contained in international treaties and conventions; indeed the Trial Chamber in *Kupreskić* alluded to the fact that this was not the case.[218] This is of vital importance, given that the jurisdiction of the International Criminal Court will depend upon its own Statute and on customary international law, rather than treaty crimes.

Article 26 of the Rome Statute provides that the Court has no jurisdiction over those under the age of eighteen at the time of the alleged crime. Agreement on the precise age of criminal responsibility proved extremely difficult to achieve,[219] and the end result has been criticised in some quarters. Robertson, for example, finds the wisdom of Article 26 'questionable' in light of the fact that 'Some appalling atrocities have been committed by "boy soldiers". Article 8 makes it a war crime to enlist persons under fifteen for an active part in hostilities, so why should those of sixteen or seventeen, old enough to participate fully in war, be immune from prosecution for war crimes?'[220]

---

[214] *Ibid.*, at paragraphs 517–518.
[215] See above at p. 41 and pp. 107–108.
[216] *Prosecutor v Kupreskić* at paragraph 518.
[217] *Ibid.*, at paragraph 517.
[218] At paragraph 520, reference is made to the situation '*if* the norms in question are contained in treaties...' (emphasis added).
[219] See the discussions by Saland, 'Criminal Law Principles', 200–202 (where he points out at 201 that proposals ranged from the ages of seven to twenty-one), and Roger S. Clark and Otto Triffterer, 'Article 26: Exclusion of Jurisdiction over Persons under Eighteen' in Triffterer, *The Rome Statute*, 493–499. Article E of the first compilation of proposals had provided in proposal 1 that 'A person under the age of [twelve, thirteen, fourteen, sixteen, eighteen] at the time of the commission of a crime...shall not be criminally responsible under this Statute...' See *Report of the Preparatory Committee*, Volume II at 87. These options remained throughout all of the various drafts until the Statute was eventually adopted.
[220] Robertson, *Crimes Against Humanity*, 343.

With respect, that is a misrepresentation of Article 26. It does not provide those between the ages of fifteen and eighteen with blanket immunity from prosecution. The provision is stated in terms of jurisdiction, not in terms of responsibility, and all that is excluded is the jurisdiction of the International Criminal Court. That is quite different from asserting that persons under the age of eighteen are not responsible for crimes under international law.[221] Indeed, it was suggested in those very terms by several delegations in order to stress that the provision has no effect on whatever age of criminal responsibility exists in national legal systems for such crimes. It should certainly not be interpreted as condoning offences committed by minors.[222]

Criminal responsibility and official capacity

The official capacity or position of individuals can have an important impact on their criminal responsibility in two particular ways – first in terms of claims of immunity, and secondly in terms of command responsibility. Both aspects turn on the importance of recognising criminal responsibility for those involved not only in the direct commission of crimes, but also in the planning and instigation of such crimes at the very highest level.

Regarding the first, it has come to be widely accepted in international law that the official position of the accused cannot prevent individual criminal responsibility. Article VII of the Nuremberg Charter, for example, stated that:

The official position of defendants, whether as Heads of States or responsible officials in Government Departments, shall not be considered as freeing them from responsibility or mitigating punishment.[223]

This position has not always been so widely accepted by domestic law, however, as can be illustrated by the proceedings against the former Chilean dictator, General Augusto Pinochet Ugarte, in the United

---

[221] See Clark and Triffterer, 'Exclusion of Jurisdiction', 499, who go on to state that in fact the opposite is true. However, those under the age of fifteen enlisted to take part in hostilities contrary to Article 8(2)(b)(xxvi) or (e)(vii) are already the victims of crimes under international law – 'they should not be victimized a second time by being brought before a *national* criminal jurisdiction'.

[222] Saland, 'Criminal Law Principles', 201.

[223] See also Article VI of the Tokyo Tribunal Charter, Article 4 of Control Council Law No. 10, and Article IV of the Genocide Convention.

Kingdom.[224] Nonetheless, the House of Lords in its second decision[225] held that Pinochet was not entitled to immunity as a result of his position. The case was concerned mainly with torture under the 1984 Torture Convention, and the situation in Chile never amounted to an armed conflict in terms of common Article 3. Torture is equally relevant to internal armed conflicts, however, both as a violation of the laws and customs of warfare and as a crime against humanity.

The general trend in the House of Lords' decision was to deny Senator Pinochet immunity on the basis of those provisions of the Torture Convention which outline criminal responsibility, while limiting the offences to those committed after 8 December 1988.[226] As Lord Browne-Wilkinson held:

If, as alleged, Senator Pinochet organised and authorised torture after 8 December 1988, he was not acting in any capacity which gives rise to immunity ratione materiae because such actions were contrary to international law, Chile had agreed to outlaw such conduct and Chile had agreed with the other parties to the Torture Convention that all signatory states should have jurisdiction to try official torture ... even if such torture were committed in Chile.[227]

Lord Millett, however, eloquently argued that jurisdiction over torture was not conditional upon the Torture Convention and its incorporation into the law of the United Kingdom:

In my opinion, the systematic use of torture on a large scale and as an instrument of state policy had joined piracy, war crimes and crimes against peace as an international crime of universal jurisdiction well before 1984 [the date of the Torture Convention] ... For my own part, therefore, I would hold that the courts of this country already possessed extra-territorial jurisdiction in respect of torture and conspiracy to commit torture on the scale of the charges in the present

---

[224] For the final judgment of the House of Lords on the matter, see *R v Bartle and the Commissioner of Police for the Metropolis and Others, ex parte Pinochet* and *R v Evans and Another and the Commissioner of Police for the Metropolis and Others, ex parte Pinochet* [1999] 2 All ER 97. For a good discussion of the proceedings, see Neil Boister and Richard Burchill, 'The *Pinochet* Precedent: Don't Leave Home Without It' (1999) 10 *Criminal Law Forum* 405.

[225] The first decision, handed down on 25 November 1998, held by three (Lords Nicholls, Steyn and Hoffmann) to two (Lords Slynn and Lloyd) that Senator Pinochet was not entitled to immunity. This decision was set aside on the grounds that the Committee was not properly constituted as a result of Lord Hoffmann's involvement with Amnesty International (see [1999] 2 WLR 272).

[226] That being the date on which Chile, the United Kingdom and Spain (who were seeking Pinochet's extradition to stand trial) were all bound by the Torture Convention.

[227] *Ex Parte Pinochet* at 115.

case and did not require the authority of statute to exercise it. I understand, however, that your Lordships take a different view.[228]

Lord Millett's opinion seems preferable, and he correctly pointed out that international law has developed even further since the agreement of the Torture Convention in 1984, noting in particular the Criminal Tribunals for the former Yugoslavia and Rwanda, and the Rome Statute of the International Criminal Court, all of which also envisage the prosecution of alleged offenders in domestic courts.[229] The Statutes of these tribunals also rule out the evasion of criminal responsibility on the basis of the official position of the accused.[230]

There was always a broad consensus in the Preparatory Committee that the International Criminal Court should have jurisdiction over persons acting in an official capacity, and by 1997 there was general agreement on a text for the relevant Article.[231] The Rome Statute accordingly provides in Article 27 that:

1. This Statute shall apply equally to all persons without any distinction based on official capacity. In particular, official capacity as a Head of Government, a member of a Government or parliament, an elected representative or a government official shall in no case exempt a person from criminal responsibility under this Statute, nor shall it, in and of itself, constitute a ground for reduction of sentence.

---

[228] *Ibid.*, at 178.

[229] Although the relationships are quite different. The ICTY and ICTR have primacy over national jurisdiction (see Articles 9(2) and 8(2) of the Statutes respectively), whereas the relationship between the ICC and domestic courts is one of complementarity (see Article 1 of the Rome Statute).

[230] The ICTY and ICTR Statutes provide in Articles 7(2) and 6(2) respectively that 'The official position of any accused person, whether as Head of State or Government or as a responsible Government official, shall not relieve such person of criminal responsibility nor mitigate punishment.' The 1996 ILC Draft Code also provides in Article 7 that 'The official capacity of an individual who commits a crime against the peace and security of mankind, even if he acted as head of State or Government, does not relieve him of criminal responsibility or mitigate punishment.'

[231] See *Decisions Taken by the Preparatory Committee at its Session Held from 11 to 21 February 1997*, UN Doc. A/AC.249/1997/L.5, which provided in Article B.e that:

1. This Statute shall be applied to all persons without any discrimination whatsoever: official capacity, either as Head of Government or parliament, or as an elected representative, or as a government official, shall in no case exempt a person from his criminal responsibility under this Statute, nor shall it [per se] constitute a ground for reduction of the sentence.

2. Any immunities or special procedural rules attached to the official capacity of a person, whether under national or international law, may not be relied upon to prevent the Court from exercising its jurisdiction in relation to the person.'

2. Immunities or special procedural rules which may attach to the official capacity of a person, whether under national or international law, shall not bar the Court from exercising its jurisdiction over such a person.[232]

Claims of State or sovereign immunity for violations of the laws of internal armed conflict cannot accordingly be permitted, by either international or municipal law. As Lord Millett concluded, 'In future, those who commit atrocities against civilian populations must expect to be called to account if fundamental human rights are to be properly protected. In this context, the exalted rank of the accused can afford no defence.'[233]

Closely related to the issue of official capacity is that of command responsibility, or the responsibility of those in authority over their subordinates. The Yugoslav Tribunal has held that the principle of command responsibility is 'a well-established norm of customary international law',[234] and that it can arise 'either out of the positive acts of the superior (sometimes referred to as "direct" command responsibility) or from his culpable omissions ("indirect" command responsibility or command responsibility *strictu sensu*)'.[235] The concept is dealt with in Article 7(3) of the ICTY Statute and Article 6(3) of the ICTR Statute, both providing that:

The fact that any of the acts referred to in articles 2 to 5 [2 to 4 in the ICTR Statute] of the present Statute was committed by a subordinate does not relieve his superior of criminal responsibility if he knew or had reason to know that the subordinate was about to commit such acts or had done so and the superior failed to take the necessary and reasonable measures to prevent such acts or to punish the perpetrators thereof.

These provisions apply broadly, to superiors in general, as does Article 6 of the ILC Draft Code of Crimes Against the Peace and Security of Mankind, yet in the debates leading to the adoption of the Rome Statute, there was significant disagreement as to whether command responsibility should apply equally to civilian superiors, or whether the

---

[232] This principle remained uncontested throughout discussions: see Saland, 'Criminal Law Principles', 202. For a more detailed discussion of its development and drafting history, see Otto Triffterer, 'Article 27: The Irrelevance of Official Capacity' in Triffterer, *The Rome Statute*, 501 at 502–514.

[233] *Ex Parte Pinochet* at 180.

[234] *Prosecutor v Delalić* at paragraph 333. Indeed, it was stated in the aftermath of the Second World War that 'a person in a position of superior authority should be held individually responsible for giving the unlawful order to commit a crime, and he should also be held responsible for failure to deter the unlawful behaviour of subordinates if he knew they had committed or were about to commit crimes yet failed to take the necessary and reasonable steps to prevent their commission or to punish those who had committed them'. See *Re Yamashita* (1946) 327 US 1 at 14–16.

[235] *Delalić* at paragraph 333.

concept should be limited to military commanders only.[236] The imposition of criminal responsibility upon military commanders may possibly have been regarded as the more traditional or straightforward option,[237] but the case law from the ICTY and ICTR (and indeed from previous criminal tribunals[238]) is quite unambiguous on this point – command responsibility is *not* limited to those in a position of military authority. Many of those involved in the planning and instigating of violations are routinely non-military, such as political leaders, and as soon as one recognises that the position of Head of State or political leader affords no defence to criminal responsibility, so it must also be the case that command responsibility can attach to those individuals. Instances of political leaders and public officials being held responsible under this principle are now so numerous as to put the issue beyond any doubt.[239]

---

[236] Saland, 'Criminal Law Principles', 202–203. See, for example, *Report of the Preparatory Committee*, Volume II at Article C, which provided as follows:

[In addition to other forms of responsibility for crimes under this Statute, a [commander] [superior] is criminally responsible] [A [commander] [superior] is not relieved of responsibility] [A [commander] [superior] shall be regarded as the perpetrator] for crimes under this Statute committed by [forces] [subordinate[s]] under his command [and effective control] as a result of the [commander's] [superior's] failure to exercise proper control where:

(a) The [commander] [superior] either knew, or [owing to the widespread commission of the offences should have known] [should have known] that the [forces] [subordinate[s]] were committing or intending to commit such crimes; and

(b) The [commander] [superior] failed to take all necessary [and reasonable] measures within his or her power to prevent or repress their commission [or to punish the perpetrators thereof].

[237] As in the case of *Prosecutor v Blaskić*, Case IT-95-14, Judgment of 3 March 2000.

[238] See *Prosecutor v Delalić* at paragraphs 355–363; *Prosecutor v Akayesu* at paragraphs 490–491; *Prosecutor v Kayishema and Ruzindana* at paragraphs 213–216; and *Prosecutor v Musema*, Case ICTR-96-13 (Judgment of 27 January 2000) at paragraphs 127–148, citing evidence from both the Tokyo and Nuremberg Tribunals.

[239] The Appeals Chamber of the ICTY stated in *Prosecutor v Aleksovski*, Case IT-95-14/1 (Judgment of Appeals Chamber, 24 March 2000) that 'it does not matter whether the Appellant was a civilian or military superior. What must be proved is that he had the powers to prevent or to punish the crimes in terms of Article 7(3).' The ICTR has appeared slightly more cautious, however, holding in *Prosecutor v Akayesu*, at paragraph 491, that the application of command responsibility to civilians remains 'contentious', and in *Prosecutor v Musema*, at paragraph 135, that 'it is disputable whether the principle of individual criminal responsibility, articulated in Article 6(3) of the Statute, should be applied to civilians'. The determination of whether or not the accused had the power to take all necessary and reasonable measures to prevent or punish the commission of alleged crimes must accordingly be assessed on a case by case basis. In *Prosecutor v Kayishema and Ruzindana*, however, the ICTR held, at paragraph 213, that 'the application of criminal responsibility to those civilians who wield the requisite authority is *not* a contentious one'.

Indeed, all of those convicted on the basis of command responsibility to date by the ICTR have been civilian, rather than military leaders.[240] All that is required is proof of the superior's effective control over his or her subordinates, in terms of having the ability to prevent or punish violations of the law. Thus:

individuals in positions of authority, whether civilian or within military structures, may incur criminal responsibility under the doctrine of command responsibility on the basis of their *de facto* as well as *de jure* positions as superiors. The mere absence of formal legal authority to control the actions of subordinates should therefore not be understood to preclude the imposition of such responsibility.[241]

The International Criminal Court (ICC) follows this approach,[242] which is confirmed in Article 28 of the Rome Statute. Paragraph (a) provides for the individual criminal responsibility of military commanders, while paragraph (b) provides for responsibility of non-military superiors.

The *mens rea* requirements are slightly different, however. Following the provisions of previous Statutes and case law, military superiors are responsible where they either knew or should have known about the commission or imminent commission of criminal offences.[243] Clearly, where a superior is aware of the commission of an offence, there can be no question regarding command responsibility. More difficult is the question of when a superior should have known about the commission of an offence. Military commanders are deemed to be aware of everything occurring within their sphere of authority, and are criminally responsible for a failure in this regard. This was seen as being unfair to civilian superiors, who may not have the same degree of control

---

[240] Two pleaded guilty on that basis: Jean Kambanda was Prime Minister (see *Prosecutor v Kambanda*, Case ICTR-97-23-S, 37 ILM 1411 (1998)) and Omar Serushago was a businessman and leader of Interahamwe in Gisenyi prefecture (see *Prosecutor v Serushago*, Case ICTR-98-39-S, 38 ILM 854 (1999)). In addition, Jean-Paul Akayesu was bourgmestre of the Taba commune, responsible for the 'performance of executive functions and the maintenance of public order' (see *Prosecutor v Akayesu* at paragraph 4), Clément Kayishema was Prefect of Kibuye (see *Prosecutor v Kayishema and Ruzindana* at paragraphs 473–516), and Alfred Musema was a factory director (see *Prosecutor v Musema* at paragraphs 892–895).

[241] *Prosecutor v Delalić* at paragraph 354.

[242] For a discussion of the development of the concept and its meaning in terms of the ICC Statute, see *Delalić* at paragraphs 333–400; William J. Fenrick, 'Article 28: Responsibility of Commanders and Other Superiors' in Triffterer, *The Rome Statute*, 516–522; and Saland, 'Criminal Law Principles', 202–204.

[243] Article 28(a)(i).

over their subordinates,[244] and so the Rome Statute provides that non-military superiors must meet the higher standard of having either known, or else consciously disregarded, information which clearly indicated that subordinates were committing or about to commit a crime.[245] The ICC formulation has already met with keen support from the ICTR, which finds the distinction 'instructive... insofar that it does not demand a *prima facie* duty upon a non-military commander to be seized of every activity of all persons under his or her control'.[246]

Superior orders

If command responsibility can be considered as one side of a coin, then the opposite side of the same coin deals with the issue of superior orders, and whether such orders have any effect on avoiding, or lessening, criminal responsibility. Just as the official position of an individual should not allow him to escape criminal responsibility, so subordinates should not be permitted to use the responsibility of their superiors to shield themselves from criminal responsibility.[247]

The situation was addressed following the Second World War, with the Nuremberg Charter providing in Article VIII that superior orders did not negate criminal responsibility, but could be considered as a factor in mitigation where the interests of justice so required,[248] a stance upheld more recently by the Statutes of the Yugoslav and Rwandan Tribunals in Articles 7(4) and 6(4) respectively.[249] Triffterer points out, however, that this does not mean that the issue was settled in international law.[250] Indeed, as the Preparatory Committee on the establishment of an International Criminal Court began consideration of the issue, 'the situation

---

[244] A point initially raised by the United States, which met with widespread approval. See Saland, 'Criminal Law Principles', 203. None of the previous drafts, up to and including that placed before the Rome Conference, had included this distinction. See UN Doc. A/CONF.183.2, Article 25.

[245] Article 28(b)(i).

[246] *Prosecutor* v *Kayishema and Ruzindana* at paragraphs 227–228.

[247] At least, not in all cases.

[248] UNTS 288 (1951).

[249] They both provide that 'The fact that an accused person acted pursuant to an order of a Government or of a superior shall not relieve him of criminal responsibility, but may be considered in mitigation of punishment if the International Tribunal determines that justice so requires.'

[250] Otto Triffterer, 'Article 33: Superior Orders and Prescription of Law' in Triffterer, *The Rome Statute*, 573 at 577. For his discussion of the background to the adoption of Article 33 of the Rome Statute and a commentary on its provisions, see 574–588. See also Saland, 'Criminal Law Principles', 210–212.

was open'[251] despite a measure of consensus which held that superior orders should not relieve subordinates from responsibility, at least in cases of genocide and crimes against humanity, and that the defence should be applicable only to specific and limited crimes not contained within either of those categories.[252]

The ILC Draft Statute for an International Criminal Court had contained no provision dealing with superior orders, and the development of the relevant Article by the Preparatory Committee for the Rome Statute was a difficult process. The text finally adopted was the result of two proposals, submitted by Canada and France.[253] Proposal 1 provided that:

> 1. The fact that a person acted pursuant to an order of a Government or of a superior, [whether military or political] shall not relieve that person of criminal responsibility [if the order appears to be manifestly unlawful] [and the person has a greater risk to himself or herself no alternative but to obey, or has no other moral choice].
>
> 2. Where the person has acted pursuant to an order of a government or of a superior in the circumstances as described in paragraph 1, the sentence may be reduced having regard to the circumstances [this fact may be considered in mitigation of punishment if the court determines that justice so requires].[254]

The second proposal introduced the additional concept of prescription by law, and provided that:

> 1. With regard to genocide, crimes against humanity and the crime of aggression, the perpetrator or accomplice in one of these crimes may not be exempted from his criminal responsibility by the sole fact that he carried out an act prescribed or authorized by legislation or regulations or an act ordered by the legitimate authority. However, the court shall take this circumstance into account when determining the sentence and its severity.
>
> 2. With regard to the crimes referred to in articles 31 and 32, a person who carries out an act ordered by the legitimate authority shall not be criminally responsible except where such an act is manifestly unlawful or in conflict with the rules of international law applicable in armed conflicts or with duly ratified or approved international conventions.
>
> 3. However, persons who have carried out acts ordered by the Security Council or who have acted on its behalf and in accordance with a mandate issued

---

[251] Triffterer, 'Superior Orders', 577.
[252] Ibid., citing *Report of the Preparatory Committee*, Volume II, notes to Article Q.
[253] See Saland, 'Criminal Law Principles', 210–212.
[254] *Report of the Preparatory Committee*, Volume II, Article Q, Proposal 1.

by it shall not be criminally responsible and may not be prosecuted before the Court.[255]

Neither of these proposals appeared to be as strict in the imposition of individual criminal responsibility upon subordinates as the corresponding provisions of the Yugoslav and Rwandan Statutes. Whereas Article 7(4) of the Yugoslav Statute, for example, had simply stated that acting pursuant to superior orders would not relieve an individual of criminal responsibility, the proposals placed before the Preparatory Committee both made it a necessary condition of responsibility that the subordinate had a certain degree of knowledge regarding the legality or otherwise of the order which he or she had carried out – the order must have been 'manifestly' unlawful, i.e. the subordinate must have known (or ought to have known) that the order was unlawful. Some commentators regard this development as a backward step in the apportioning of international criminal responsibility,[256] and certain other questions regarding this aspect of the proposals were raised in the course of Preparatory Committee debates.[257]

Nonetheless, the Preparatory Committee proceeded, amalgamating the two proposals into a single draft Article, incorporating the prescription of law into its title. There was still disagreement about the precise form that the final Article should take, however, although the provision regarding subordinates acting on behalf of, or under orders of, the Security Council proved to be generally unpopular, and was discarded.[258] In particular, various opinions existed as to the extent of the knowledge to be required of the subordinate (the various drafts stating only that an unlawful or manifestly unlawful order 'must be understood as an order in conflict with the rules of international law applicable in armed

---

[255] *Ibid.* Article 31 dealt with serious violations of the laws and customs of war, Article 32 with grave breaches of the Geneva Conventions.

[256] See criticism of the Article as finally adopted, below at pp. 187–188.

[257] Such as the questions of whether troops who obey what appears to be a manifestly lawful order should be criminally responsible where it later transpires that their superior had acted unlawfully in giving the order, and whether those troops who received an order which was lawful, although not *manifestly* lawful, should still be criminally responsible where it transpired that the order had in fact been illegal, and no further inquiries had been made by the troops before following the order. See *Report of the Preparatory Committee*, Volume II, note to Article Q, Proposal 1.

[258] There had been 'widespread doubts about the contents and placement' of that particular provision. See, for example, the *Report of the Inter-Sessional Meeting from 19–30 January 1998 in Zutphen, the Netherlands*, UN Doc. A/AC.249/1998/L.13 (4 February 1998) at Article 26[M](2) and n. 51 thereto.

conflict'[259]), and on the issue of whether the Article should be phrased in terms of 'relieving criminal responsibility if...', or else in terms of 'not relieving criminal responsibility unless...'.[260] The draft placed before the Diplomatic Conference in Rome therefore provided that:

1. The fact that a person's conduct was pursuant to an order of a Government or of a superior [whether military or civilian] shall [not] relieve the person of criminal responsibility [[if] [unless] the order [was known to be unlawful or] appeared to be manifestly unlawful].

2. The perpetrator of or an accomplice in a crime of genocide [or a crime against humanity] [or a...] shall not be exempted from criminal responsibility on the sole ground that the person's conduct was pursuant to an order of a Government or a superior, or pursuant to national legislation or regulations.][261]

Saland explains that debates were difficult throughout the Conference, and that in order to agree a text for the Article, he had to ask various interested delegations to discuss the issue informally (with Canada and the United States moderating). Even then, the discussions involved numerous delegations, and were extremely fraught.[262]

The result of this complex and difficult process is that the text of Article 33 as finally agreed differs fairly markedly from the corresponding Articles of the Nuremberg, Yugoslav and Rwandan Tribunals, providing that:

1. The fact that a crime within the jurisdiction of the Court has been committed by a person pursuant to an order of a Government or of a superior, whether military or civilian, shall not relieve that person of criminal responsibility unless:

(a) The person was under a legal obligation to obey orders of the Government or the superior in question;
(b) The person did not know that the order was unlawful; and
(c) The order was not manifestly unlawful.

2. For the purposes of this article, orders to commit genocide or crimes against humanity are manifestly unlawful.

---

[259] See, for example, Article 26[M](1) of the Zutphen Draft, and n. 48 thereto.

[260] See Saland, 'Criminal Law Principles', 211.

[261] Draft Statute for the International Criminal Court, placed before the United Nations Diplomatic Conference of Plenipotentiaries on the Establishment of an International Criminal Court, 15 June–17 July 1998, UN Doc. A/CONF.183/2 (April 1998), Article 32.

[262] Saland, 'Criminal Law Principles', 211. Per Saland was Deputy Head of the Swedish delegation to the Conference, having led it through the Preparatory Committee, and was also Chairman of the Working Group on the General Principles of Criminal Law throughout the entire process from the Preparatory Committee to the Diplomatic Conference.

First, Article 33 sets out the general principle that, irrespective of whether the orders were given by a military or a civilian superior,[263] they do not allow individuals to escape criminal responsibility. More controversial, however, is the rest of paragraph 1, which sets out a list of three preconditions, which, if met, allow the subordinate to avoid criminal responsibility. This has been seen as dangerous, in that, 'any order – by a military, police, governmental or civil authority – may indeed provide a defence to persons who were under a "legal obligation" to obey orders (which soldiers and police invariably are)',[264] provided they were unaware that the order was unlawful, and where the order was not manifestly unlawful. Triffterer answers this criticism by arguing that the crime of the subordinate in those cases is not justified, but rather excused: 'He is free from punishment, because his situation as specified by the elements mentioned under paragraph 1(a)–(c) approximates defences like duress, coercion or error which also may exclude criminal responsibility.'[265]

The effect of this is limited to an extent by paragraph 2, which provides that orders to commit genocide or crimes against humanity are considered to be manifestly unlawful in any case, so that superior orders cannot excuse any such conduct. The possibility remains, however, that Article 33(1) can allow subordinates to escape criminal responsibility for war crimes.[266] As Triffterer points out, this is 'surprising', possibly even shocking, in that crimes against humanity, genocide and war crimes do not differ dramatically in terms of the harm perpetrated by each one, at least in severe cases.[267] He goes on to explain, however, that the reason for the exclusion of war crimes is 'obvious': 'genocide and crimes against humanity can be committed by everybody, while war crimes and crimes against the peace are typically committed by military or paramilitary

---

[263] This follows logically from the previous determination that civilians and the military are equally liable to criminal sanctions on the basis of command responsibility. See above at pp. 180–182.

[264] Robertson, *Crimes Against Humanity*, 343–344.

[265] Triffterer, 'Superior Orders', 586–587. The ICTY has held that even duress does not afford a complete defence to a crime against humanity or a war crime involving the killing of innocent human beings, providing only a degree of mitigation. See *Prosecutor v Erdemović*, IT-96-22 (Sentencing Judgment of 5 March 1998) 37 ILM 1182 (1998) at paragraph 17. The Rome Statute deals, rather unsatisfactorily, with the separate issue of duress in Article 31. For a discussion of the relevant provisions, see Albin Eser, 'Article 31: Grounds for Excluding Criminal Responsibility' in Triffterer, *The Rome Statute*, 537 at 550–552.

[266] And for the crime of aggression, once the Court has the capacity to exercise jurisdiction in that regard.

[267] Triffterer, 'Superior Orders', 587.

persons in whatever actions they may be involved. To protect them obviously is the reason for the limited regulation in paragraph 2.'[268] The reason may indeed be obvious, and also understandable, but the outcome in terms of the avoidance of criminal responsibility does not necessarily merit praise.[269]

Finally, there is no express mention in Article 33 that superior orders, where they do not exclude criminal responsibility altogether, can be considered as a factor in mitigation of the subordinate's punishment. The possibility nonetheless remains. Article 78(1) provides that, in determining the sentence to be imposed upon a convicted individual, the Court shall take into account 'the gravity of the crime and the individual circumstances of the convicted person'.

Contribution of the *Tadić* Case to international law

The judgment of the Appeals Chamber of the International Tribunal in *Prosecutor v Tadić* (Jurisdiction) has made a substantial impression on the law relating to internal armed conflict. The Yugoslav Tribunal not only stated unequivocally that a body of customary international law has developed to regulate the conduct of internal armed conflicts, but went much further by asserting that there are rules applicable to those conflicts based neither upon common Article 3 nor upon Additional Protocol II. This flew in the face of the opinion of the Commission of Experts set up to examine alleged violations of the laws of war in the former Yugoslavia, who believed that:

The treaty-based law applicable to internal armed conflicts is relatively recent and is contained in common Article 3 of the Geneva Conventions, Additional Protocol II, and Article 19 of the 1954 Hague Convention on Cultural Property. It is unlikely that there is any body of customary international law applicable to internal armed conflict which does not find its root in these treaty provisions.[270]

In addition, the Tribunal, for the first time, authoritatively asserted that violations of the laws of internal armed conflict are criminal under international law. Such innovations were of major importance, and have subsequently been endorsed in the case law of both the ICTY and the

---

[268] *Ibid.*

[269] Indeed, Robertson, *Crimes Against Humanity*, 344, sees it as 'another victory for the Pentagon lobby concerned that soldiers should not be emboldened to disobey military edicts of dubious legality'.

[270] UN Doc. S/1994/674 at paragraph 52.

ICTR, and by widespread *opinio juris* as expressed in the Rome Statute of the International Criminal Court.

It is, however, questionable whether the Appeals Chamber was wise to address the issue of the development of customary laws for internal armed conflict in a case concerning the jurisdiction of the Tribunal, where its comments are necessarily *obiter dicta*. This is not the only criticism to have been levelled at the decision. Meron, while agreeing that some of the Hague Rules do apply to internal armed conflict, felt that the Tribunal should nonetheless have taken 'a more prudential course, focusing on specific Hague principles and rules, enumerating means and methods of warfare, listing weapons and avoiding broader conclusions',[271] and suggested that in its interpretation of the extent of its jurisdiction under Article 3 of the Statute, the Tribunal was both under- and over-inclusive.

The Appeals Chamber's decision on jurisdiction is considered to have been under-inclusive in its determination that grave breaches of the Geneva Conventions can be committed only in international armed conflicts, and not during internal armed conflicts as customary international law. It was therefore held that the Tribunal had no jurisdiction in respect of grave breaches through Article 3 of the Statute.[272] This would appear to be the correct conclusion for the Tribunal to have reached, at least as far as the Conventions themselves are concerned, in that the idea of grave breaches under the Geneva Conventions relies on the concept of 'protected' persons and property (i.e. those in the hands of armed forces of a State of which they are not nationals). This is clearly absent from common Article 3, so that grave breaches can in fact only be committed in *international* armed conflict.[273] It may be illogical to demand a different regime of criminal responsibility depending upon the character of the conflict, but this is exactly what was done via the threshold of common Article 2 of the Geneva Conventions.[274] The issue of whether grave breaches can be committed during internal armed conflict as customary law is still, however, to be finally resolved.[275]

---

[271] Meron, 'The Continuing Role of Custom', 243.

[272] *Ibid*. Here he is in conformity with Judge Aldrich, 'Jurisdiction of the Tribunal for Yugoslavia', 68.

[273] *Tadić* (Jurisdiction) at paragraph 81.

[274] Thus in *Public Prosecutor* v *Oie Hee Koi* [1968] 2 WLR 715 (PC), it was held that, 'Convention [III] does not extend the protection given to prisoners of war to nationals of the detaining power . . . [nor] persons who, though not nationals of, owe a duty of allegiance to the detaining power.' Per Lord Hodson at 727–728. See also Warbrick and Rowe, 'Jurisdiction in the *Tadić* Case', 698.

[275] See Aldrich, 'Jurisdiction of the Tribunal for Yugoslavia', 68, and Meron, 'The Continuing Role of Custom', 242.

The Appeals Chamber accepted that its decision in *Tadić* (Jurisdiction) 'may appear not to be consonant with recent trends of both State practice and the whole doctrine of human rights',[276] which could possibly represent a shift in *opinio juris*. In particular, it noted the *amicus curiae* brief submitted by the United States which claimed that, 'the "grave breaches" provisions of Article 2 of the International Tribunal Statute apply to armed conflicts of a non-international character as well as those of an international character'.[277] Nevertheless, the Tribunal asserted that, at the present stage of development of international law, Article 2 of the Statute applied only to those offences committed in the context of international armed conflicts.[278]

Meron has argued that this can only be true if the customary law content of grave breaches corresponds to their treaty content, and that the core offences listed in the grave breaches provisions might in fact have an independent existence in customary law applying also to violations of at least common Article 3.[279] Those grave breaches equally relevant to internal armed conflict (e.g. wilful killing, torture or inhuman treatment) were held to be 'subsumed in the "serious violations of the laws or customs of war"',[280] thus bringing those acts covered by Article 2 of the Statute within the ambit of Article 3 if committed during internal armed conflict. Judge Abi-Saab believed this division of labour to be rather artificial, however, and pressed for the approach suggested by Meron, arguing that there was a strong case for applying Article 2 even to internal conflicts,[281] an approach not accepted by the majority of the Appeals Chamber, or indeed by the Tribunal subsequently.[282]

---

[276] Recent trends stated were the German Military Manual; the agreement between the warring parties in Bosnia that those responsible for grave breaches of the Geneva Conventions and Protocol I should be prosecuted; and a Danish High Court decision regarding crimes committed in a Croatian prison camp in Bosnia, where the Court acted on the basis of the grave breaches provisions without raising the question of the character of the conflict. See *Tadić* (Jurisdiction) at paragraph 83.

[277] US *Amicus Curiae* Brief at 35, as discussed in *Tadić* (Jurisdiction) at paragraph 83.

[278] *Tadić* (Jurisdiction) at paragraph 84.

[279] Meron, 'The Continuing Role of Custom', 243.

[280] *Tadić* (Jurisdiction), Separate Opinion of Judge Abi-Saab, Part IV, (1995) 16 HRLJ 469 at 470. He advocated that a 'strong case can be made for the application of Article 2, even when the incriminated act takes place in an internal conflict', basing this upon a 'teleological interpretation of the [Geneva] Conventions in the light of their object and purpose'. See Warbrick and Rowe, 'Jurisdiction in the *Tadić* Case', 698.

[281] Separate Opinion of Judge Abi-Saab, (1995) 16 HRLJ 469 at 470.

[282] See *Tadić* (Judgment) at paragraphs 607–608, *Prosecutor v Nikolić* at paragraph 30, *Prosecutor v Mrksić* at paragraph 22, *Prosecutor v Karadžić and Mladić* at paragraph 88 and *Prosecutor v Rajić* at paragraph 7. Thus, in *Tadić* (Judgment), since none of the

In *Tadić* (Appeal Judgment) the Appeals Chamber did overturn the Trial Chamber's decision that grave breaches jurisdiction under Article 2 of the Tribunal's Statute was inapplicable to the proceedings, but this was done on the basis that the conflict *was* actually international in character, and that the victims were accordingly protected persons under the Geneva Conventions.[283] The requirement that the conflict be international for the grave breaches regime to operate pursuant to Article 2 of the Statute remained undisputed.[284] It is interesting to note, however, that the Trial Chamber in the *Delalić* Case seemed to agree with the arguments advanced by Professor Meron and Judge Abi-Saab, although the Chamber shied away from actually putting its view into practice:

Recognising that this would entail an extension of the concept of 'grave breaches of the Geneva Conventions' in line with a more teleological interpretation, it is the view of this Trial Chamber that violations of common article 3 of the Geneva Conventions may fall more logically within Article 2 of the Statute. Nonetheless, for present purposes, the more cautious approach has been followed. The Trial Chamber has determined that an international armed conflict existed in Bosnia and Herzegovina during the time-period relevant to the Indictment and that the victims of the alleged offences were 'protected persons', rendering Article 2 applicable. In addition, Article 3 is applicable to each of the crimes charged on the basis that they also constitute violations of the laws or customs of war, substantively prohibited by common article 3 of the Geneva Conventions.[285]

It would therefore appear to be the case that violations of common Article 3 are not currently considered to be grave breaches under customary law, although the future development of the law in that direction certainly cannot be ruled out.

Secondly, the Tribunal's approach has been criticised as being over-inclusive in suggesting that Article 3 of the Statute covers all serious violations of international humanitarian law except for grave breaches, genocide and crimes against humanity, thus applying through customary law nearly the whole of Hague Law to internal armed conflicts.[286]

---

victims were at the relevant time in the hands of a party to the conflict of which they were not nationals, Tadić was found not guilty of all counts under Article 2 of the Statute. This view is shared by Greenwood, who states in 'The *Tadić* Case', 276, that 'It is difficult to escape the conclusion that, at least for the present, the concept of grave breaches ... is confined to international armed conflicts.'

[283] *Tadić* (Appeal Judgment) at paragraphs 83–171. Duško Tadić was accordingly found guilty of six additional counts relating to grave breaches of the Geneva Conventions.

[284] *Ibid.*, at paragraph 83.

[285] *Prosecutor v Delalić* at paragraph 317.

[286] Meron, 'The Continuing Role of Custom', 243.

The Tribunal has certainly adopted a fairly broad approach to the application of Article 3 of the Statute, which it had to do in an effort to assume jurisdiction over violations of common Article 3:

the finding of the Appeals Chamber [in *Tadić* (Jurisdiction)] on the extent of application of Article 2 of the Statute, excluding internal armed conflicts from the ambit of the Tribunal's jurisdiction over 'grave breaches' of the Geneva Conventions, is such that its approach to Article 3 has to be rather broader, in order to achieve this goal of making our jurisdiction 'watertight'.[287]

Fears that the decision would be seen as applying virtually all of the humanitarian laws of armed conflict to internal armed conflict were, however, precisely why the Tribunal was so careful to point out the limitations on the application of customary law mentioned above, namely that only certain rules and principles have been extended to regulate internal armed conflict, and that it is only the general essence of those rules, rather than their detailed regulation, which has become applicable.[288] Nonetheless, the traditional distinction in legal regulation between international and internal armed conflict is becoming ever more blurred.

The International Criminal Court is not yet in existence,[289] but the influence of the ICTR and, more particularly, the ICTY on its development and on the development of customary international law is plain for all to see. As a result, the 'widespread conviction'[290] of the international community as a whole that violations of humanitarian law committed during internal armed conflict can lead to individual criminal responsibility is no longer open to doubt.

[287] *Prosecutor v Delalić* at paragraph 298.

[288] Above at pp. 146–147.

[289] It will come into existence when sixty States have ratified it. At the time of writing, the number of ratifications stands at twenty-two.

[290] *Prosecutor v Delalić* at paragraph 309.

5 Human rights during internal armed conflict

Having examined the humanitarian law governing internal armed conflicts, it remains to consider what alternative or additional protection can be afforded to civilians through international human rights law. A detailed account of the origin and development of human rights is clearly outside the ambit of this book. For present purposes it will suffice to note that human rights essentially became an issue of international concern only after the atrocities of the Second World War.[1]

Human rights and humanitarian law

There is undoubtedly a close relationship between humanitarian law and human rights law.[2] Both are applicable during internal armed conflict – humanitarian law through specific provisions to that effect and

[1] For an exposition of the development of human rights theories see, for example, Jerome J. Shestack, 'The Jurisprudence of Human Rights' in Theodor Meron (ed.), *Human Rights in International Law: Legal and Policy Issues* (Oxford, 1984), vol. I, 69; Gerald I. A. D. Draper, 'Humanitarian Law and Human Rights' (1979) *Acta Juridica* 193 at 196–199; Hersch Lauterpacht, *International Law and Human Rights* (London, 1950), 73–141; Moses Moskowitz, *Human Rights and World Order* (New York, 1958), 13–21; Imre Szabo, 'Historical Foundations of Human Rights and Subsequent Developments' in Karel Vasak (ed.), *The International Dimensions of Human Rights* (Westport, 1982), vol. I, 11; and Paul Sieghart, *The International Law of Human Rights* (Oxford, 1983), 3–23.

[2] There has been extensive doctrinal discussion on the precise nature of the relationship, but academic opinion seems to have crystallised into the view that the two regimes are related, but distinct. See, for example, Jean S. Pictet, *Humanitarian Law and the Protection of War Victims* (Leiden, 1975), 14–15; Mario'n Mushkat, 'The Development of International Humanitarian Law and the Law of Human Rights' (1978) 21 *German YBIL* 150; Dietrich Schindler, 'Human Rights and Humanitarian Law: Interrelationship of the Laws' (1982) 31 *American University LR* 935; Yoram Dinstein, 'Human Rights in Armed Conflict: International Humanitarian Law' in Meron, *Human Rights in International Law*, vol. II, 345; Jacques Meurant, 'Humanitarian Law and Human Rights Law: Alike Yet Distinct' (1993) 293 *Int Rev of the Red Cross* 89; Draper,

through customary law, human rights in so far as they govern relations between a State and its subjects. Indeed, human rights law has had an important, and increasing, influence on the development of humanitarian law.[3] There are, however, important differences.

First, the two legal regimes developed quite separately. International human rights developed in response to the barbarity of the Second World War, whereas humanitarian law first began to be codified at the international level in the nineteenth century. Of course both are considerably older in origin, and Pictet states that both date back as far as the human race, having the same initial objective – to protect the individual against those who would harm him. Pictet goes on to explain, however, that 'that idea has given rise to two distinct aims: to limit the evils of war and to defend man against arbitrary action. Throughout the centuries they have developed along parallel lines.'[4] Their separate development does not mean that the two regimes could not now have merged into one body of law, but it does demonstrate that human rights and humanitarian law have traditionally been seen as distinct, an approach which the weight of modern opinion still tends to support.

A second difference turns upon the relationship between the parties to the conflict. As already explained, the humanitarian laws of internal armed conflict are equally binding upon the government and insurgents, and can also (through common Article 3, although not Additional Protocol II) apply to a conflict between two parties, neither of which is the government of the State concerned. There is therefore a degree of reciprocity as far as the application of humanitarian law is concerned. By contrast, human rights obligations are binding on governments only, and the law has not yet reached the stage whereby, during internal armed conflict, insurgents are bound to observe the human rights of government forces, let alone those of opposing insurgents.[5] Non-government parties are particularly unlikely to have the capacity to uphold certain rights (e.g. the right to due process, being unlikely to have their own legal system, courts, etc.).

'Humanitarian Law and Human Rights', 196–199; and A. H. Robertson, 'Humanitarian Law and Human Rights' in Christophe Swinarski (ed.), *Studies and Essays on International Humanitarian Law and Red Cross Principles in Honour of Jean Pictet* (Geneva, 1984), 793.

[3] For a good discussion of this phenomenon, see Theodor Meron, 'The Humanization of Humanitarian Law' (2000) 94 *AJIL* 239.

[4] Pictet, *Humanitarian Law*, 14–15.

[5] Except, of course, to the extent that these obligations coincide with humanitarian law. See also the discussion above at pp. 44–45 and n. 50.

The extent to which the military are educated on the provisions of each regime also differs. Troops are generally educated to some degree on the content of humanitarian law, representing the rules of engagement by which the military operations of all nations are to be carried out. The level of education afforded on the protection of human rights is significantly lower, and the majority of the world's armed forces probably know relatively little of human rights law except to the extent that it happens to coincide with the laws of war.

Finally, humanitarian law is mandatory, allowing for no exceptions, whereas perhaps one of the major weaknesses of the international human rights regime is that human rights instruments tend to contain clauses allowing derogation from certain provisions in particular circumstances. Article 4(1) of the International Covenant on Civil and Political Rights (ICCPR), for example, provides that:

In time of public emergency which threatens the life of the nation and the existence of which is officially proclaimed, the State Parties to the present Covenant may take measures derogating from their obligations under the present Covenant to the extent strictly required by the exigencies of the situation, provided that such measures are not inconsistent with their other obligations under international law and do not involve discrimination solely on the ground of race, colour, sex, language, religion or social origin.

Similar provisions can be found in Article 15 of the European Convention on Human Rights and Article 27 of the American Convention on Human Rights.[6] War, or in the context of this book civil war, is clearly a situation which could threaten the life of a nation, and the European and American Conventions do explicitly mention it as justifying derogation.[7] Of course, for a public emergency to exist there need not necessarily be an internal armed conflict. The European Court of Human Rights sees derogation as possible only in 'an exceptional situation of crisis or emergency which affects *the whole population* and constitutes a threat to the organised life of the community of which the State is composed'.[8] Accordingly, other situations (e.g. natural disasters, crop failure and subsequent famine, widespread disease, or a concerted terrorist campaign

---

[6] See Subrata R. Chowdhury, *Rule of Law in a State of Emergency* (London, 1989); Jaime Oraà, *Human Rights in States of Emergency in International Law* (Oxford, 1992); Sieghart, *Human Rights*, 110–118, etc.

[7] The European Convention cites 'war or other public emergency', and the American Convention 'war, public danger or other emergency that threatens the independence or security of a State Party'.

[8] *Lawless* Case (*Lawless v Ireland*) (Merits) 1 EHRR 15 at 31. Emphasis added.

as in Northern Ireland) might also threaten the nation and meet the requirements for derogation. Conversely, it does not necessarily follow that an internal armed conflict will meet the derogation criteria,[9] or indeed that a State would necessarily derogate from its human rights obligations where a conflict did meet the requirements.[10] In such situations the relevant human rights instruments remain applicable, along with common Article 3. In the more extreme situations where Additional Protocol II is applicable, its high threshold makes it more likely that the derogation criteria would be met, so that only the non-derogable human rights provisions would apply alongside the Protocol (and of course common Article 3).[11] Between those stages come internal armed conflicts meeting the threshold of application for common Article 3, and where derogation from certain human rights obligations is deemed possible.

Although they may be seen as a limiting factor in the protection of civilians, the inclusion of derogation provisions in human rights instruments actually serves to underline that human rights continue to apply in times of armed conflict. As the International Court of Justice has stated, 'the protection of the International Covenant on Civil and Political Rights does not cease in times of war, except by operation of Article 4 of the Covenant'.[12] Furthermore, derogations must not be 'inconsistent with their [i.e. States'] other obligations under international law'.[13] This is clearly of fundamental importance during internal conflict, and means that even human rights provisions which are in principle derogable according to the particular instrument cannot validly be derogated from if those human rights are restated in, or otherwise protected by, the applicable humanitarian law.

Human rights instruments therefore remain valuable in several ways during internal conflict. First, and perhaps most importantly, they can be used as an interpretative device to expand upon and clarify the various protections afforded by humanitarian law, imposing human rights obligations upon insurgents by equating those obligations placed upon

---

[9] A conflict confined to part of a State's territory, for example, may not endanger the life and security of the whole nation. Conversely, a terrorist campaign might trigger derogation without crossing the threshold of common Article 3, as in the UK with respect to Northern Ireland.

[10] See *Cyprus* v *Turkey* 4 EHRR 482.

[11] Assuming that the State did derogate from its obligations.

[12] *Advisory Opinion on the Legality of the Threat or Use of Nuclear Weapons*, ICJ Reports 1996, 225 at paragraph 25.

[13] See ICCPR Article 4(1), European Convention Article 15(1) and American Convention on Human Rights Article 27(1).

governments with provisions found in common Article 3, etc.; secondly, human rights can apply fully alongside humanitarian law, providing more detailed protection in many circumstances, should the affected State decide not to derogate from its obligations (or else find that it cannot validly derogate due to the other international obligations incumbent upon it, as discussed above); thirdly, several human rights provisions remain non-derogable and thus operational regardless, although these vary from one instrument to another; and finally, the enforcement mechanisms contained in human rights instruments can possibly be used as alternative methods of implementing and enforcing humanitarian protection during armed conflicts.[14]

To what extent, then, do the provisions of common Article 3 and Additional Protocol II represent, and interrelate with, human rights protection?

Human rights law and common Article 3

Humane treatment

Common Article 3 begins by requiring that those not involved in hostilities be treated humanely in all circumstances. Phrased as a positive obligation, this contrasts with international human rights instruments to a degree, in that they are largely addressed to various distinct aspects of humane treatment in particular circumstances,[15] rather than a basic or blanket requirement. The American Convention on Human Rights does contain a non-derogable duty of humane treatment in Article 5, but what exactly is meant by 'humane treatment' can only be discovered by examining the rest of common Article 3 and international human rights law.

Non-discrimination

The humane treatment required by common Article 3 must be afforded 'without any adverse distinction founded on race, colour, religion or faith, sex, birth or wealth, or any other similar criteria'. Clearly influenced by the Universal Declaration of Human Rights adopted the previous year,[16] the requirement of non-discrimination is echoed in other

[14] See chapter 6 below at pp. 255 ff. for a more detailed discussion of this final aspect.
[15] E.g. Article 10(1) of the ICCPR, requiring humane treatment for those whose liberty has been restricted.
[16] UN Doc. A/811.

human rights treaties, ICCPR Article 2(1), for example, providing that:

Each State Party to the present Covenant undertakes to respect and ensure to all individuals within its territory and subject to its jurisdiction the rights recognized in the present Covenant, without distinction of any kind, such as race, colour, sex, language, religion, political or other opinion, national or social origin, property, birth or other status.

Similar provisions exist in Article 14 of the European Convention and Article 1(1) of the American Convention, where the prohibited grounds of discrimination are virtually identical, apart from the European Convention's inclusion of 'association with a national minority'. Human rights law can thus be valuable in determining when adverse distinctions have been made in the context of common Article 3, perhaps especially those on the basis of 'any other similar criteria'.

Although Article 3 prohibits discrimination on fewer grounds than human rights law (omitting language, political or other opinion, and national or social origin), in times of internal armed conflict it may be perceived to be necessary, or indeed desirable, for the government to treat insurgents in a discriminatory fashion, much as enemy nationals would be treated during international armed conflict. This may justify the exclusion of political or other opinion and national or social origin,[17] and can be linked to the fact that derogations from human rights obligations are permissible provided they do not involve discrimination 'solely on the ground of race, colour, sex, language, religion or social origin'.[18] Again, this is a reduced list compared to ICCPR Article 2(1), accepting that discrimination against the enemy may be necessary in time of conflict, and so striking a balance by excluding political or other opinion and national origin. Perhaps more important, however, is the word 'solely'.[19] Only derogations where one of those grounds is the *exclusive* reason for discrimination are prohibited. Derogations aimed at suppressing specific problems encountered during internal armed conflict, but indirectly affecting some section of the population (e.g. a religious minority), are accordingly still permitted.[20]

---

[17] On nationality as a basis for discrimination, see above at pp. 60–61.

[18] Article 4(1) of the ICCPR. See also Article 27(1) of the ACHR. The ECHR has no such caveat.

[19] See *Summary Records of the Commission on Human Rights, Sixth Session*, UN Doc. E/CN.4/SR.195 at 22 (1950); UN Doc. E/CN.4/SR.196 at 3, 6 (1950); and UN Doc. E/CN.4/SR.331 at 6 (1952).

[20] The American Convention does not include the word 'solely', but otherwise the discrimination provision regarding derogations contained in Article 27 is identical.

Violence to life and person

Turning to consider those acts specifically prohibited by common Article 3, paragraph 1(a) outlaws 'violence to life and person, in particular murder of all kinds, mutilation, cruel treatment and torture'. This clearly reaffirms several human rights which, along with the surrounding case law, can be used to elaborate and clarify the humanitarian law obligation. '[V]iolence to life and person, in particular murder of all kinds' can uncontroversially be equated with the non-derogable and inherent right to life of every human being found in ICCPR Article 6(1), Article 2(1) of the European Convention and Article 4(1) of the American Convention. These Articles also contain provisions on the death sentence,[21] preventing the use of arbitrary or unlawful executions to put down insurrection by eliminating those who have committed 'crimes against the State' (provided that those crimes were not punishable by death before the conflict began). Common Article 3 also prohibits this.

The right to life as protected by human rights law is, however, rather vague and general. As a consequence it can 'add little or nothing to the detailed provisions of the laws of war'.[22] In such circumstances, the previously suggested roles of human rights and humanitarian law can in fact be reversed, with the laws of war assisting in the interpretation of the human rights provision protecting the right to life. Thus, the ICJ has accepted that the right not to be arbitrarily deprived of life continues to apply during armed conflict, but:

The test of what is an arbitrary deprivation of life... falls to be determined by the applicable *lex specialis*, namely the law applicable in armed conflict... Thus whether a particular loss of life, through the use of a certain weapon in warfare, is to be considered an arbitrary deprivation of life contrary to Article 6 of the Covenant, can only be decided by reference to the law applicable in armed conflict and not deduced from the terms of the Covenant itself.[23]

See Oraà, *States of Emergency*, 124–125; Thomas Buergenthal, 'To Respect and to Ensure: State Obligations and Permissible Derogations' in Louis Henkin (ed.), *The International Bill of Rights: The Covenant on Civil and Political Rights* (New York, 1981), 413 n. 22; and Joan Fitzpatrick, *Human Rights in Crisis* (Philadelphia, 1994), 61–63.

[21] ICCPR Article 6(2), (4) and (5), ECHR Article 2(1), ACHR Article 4(2)–(6).

[22] Christopher J. Greenwood, *International Humanitarian Law and the Laws of War*, (Preliminary Report for the Centennial Commemoration of the First Hague Peace Conference 1899) (The Hague, 1999), 23 at paragraph 49.

[23] ICJ *Advisory Opinion on the Use of Nuclear Weapons* at paragraph 25. The Inter-American Commission on Human Rights has also held that since 'the American Convention contains no rules that either define or distinguish civilians from combatants and other military targets, much less, specify when a civilian can be lawfully attacked

The specific prohibition of mutilation by humanitarian law is interesting. Human rights instruments do not mention it explicitly, but this is not a protection secured only by humanitarian law. The prohibition on mutilation is instead subsumed in other human rights provisions – mutilation resulting in death clearly contravenes the right to life, while mutilation without fatal consequences must violate the prohibition on cruel and inhuman treatment, perhaps even torture (if inflicted for a purpose[24]). Article 5(1) of the American Convention also provides that 'Every person has the right to have his physical . . . integrity respected.'

The distinction between mutilation and medical experiments also deserves consideration. Obviously, extreme acts upon the human body such as the removal of organs or skin, amputation, etc., must be classed as mutilation, whereas the administering of drugs for experimental purposes is not. That mutilation may be distinguished from other medical experiments in this way can be seen by contrasting ICCPR Article 7 with Article 11(2) of Additional Protocol I. Article 7 of the ICCPR stands alone in providing that 'no one shall be subjected without his free consent to medical or scientific experimentation'. Additional Protocol I prohibits the carrying out on prisoners of war, even with their consent, of physical mutilations, medical or scientific experiments, and the removal of tissue organs for transplantation, except where these acts are justified in conformity with Article 11(1), requiring the protection of the physical and mental health of prisoners of war. The equivalent provision in Protocol II for prisoners during internal armed conflict fails to make such distinctions, requiring simply that prisoners not be treated in any way not indicated by their state of health (although mutilation is prohibited separately in Article 4(2)(a)).[25]

The prohibition of 'cruel treatment and torture' can also be equated to non-derogable human rights provisions, human rights law again elaborating upon common Article 3. ICCPR Article 7, Article 3 of the European Convention and Article 5(2) of the American Convention are all apposite, and the 1984 Convention Against Torture and Other Cruel, Inhuman or

or when civilian casualties are a lawful consequence of military operations . . . the Commission must necessarily look to and apply definitional standards and relevant rules of humanitarian law as sources of authoritative guidance in its resolution of this and other kinds of claims alleging violations of the American Convention in combat situations'. *Abella* v *Argentina*, Report No. 55/97, Annual Report of the Inter-American Commission on Human Rights 1997, at paragraph 161.

[24] See below at pp. 201–202.

[25] Article 5(2)(e). See discussion of this provision below at p. 224.

Degrading Treatment or Punishment[26] is particularly helpful, defining torture in Article 1(1) as:

any act by which severe pain or suffering, whether physical or mental, is intentionally inflicted on a person for such purposes as obtaining from him or a third person information or a confession, punishing him for an act he or a third person has committed or is suspected of having committed, or intimidating or coercing him or a third person, or for any reason based on discrimination of any kind, when such pain or suffering is inflicted by or at the instigation of or with the consent or acquiescence of a public official or other person acting in an official capacity. It does not include pain or suffering arising only from, inherent in or incidental to lawful sanctions.[27]

This area serves as perhaps one of the clearest examples of the importance of human rights in the interpretation of humanitarian law. Thus, in discussing torture under Article 3 of the Tribunal's Statute, the Yugoslav Tribunal has applied the definition provided by international human rights law, holding that 'International humanitarian law, while outlawing torture in armed conflict, does not provide a definition of the prohibition. Such a definition can instead be found in Article 1(1) of the 1984 Torture Convention.'[28]

Common Article 3(1)(c), outlawing 'outrages upon personal dignity, in particular humiliating and degrading treatment', can be read in conjunction with the 'cruel treatment and torture' provision of Article 3(1)(a), since degrading treatment is also mentioned expressly in the non-derogable torture provisions above. The relevant case law can also be helpful in determining what torture, cruel, inhuman or degrading treatment are. European human rights case law in particular distinguishes between various degrees of treatment, establishing a hierarchy

[26] UN Doc. A/RES/39/46. Despite the title of the Convention and its extensive definition of torture, no definition is offered for acts of cruel, inhuman or degrading treatment not amounting to torture. There is also a European Convention for the Prevention of Torture and Inhuman or Degrading Treatment or Punishment, 1987, 27 ILM 1152 (1988), and an Inter-American Convention to Prevent and Punish Torture, 1985, 25 ILM 519 (1986).

[27] This definition falls down by failing to include physical suffering inflicted for no apparent reason or for mere amusement. See *Prosecutor v Tadić* (Indictment) 34 ILM 1028 (1995).

[28] *Prosecutor v Furundžija* 38 ILM 317 (1999) at paragraph 159. See also *Prosecutor v Delalić*, Case IT-96-21-T (Judgment of 16 November 1998) at paragraph 459, where it was held that 'the definition of torture contained in the Torture Convention...reflects a consensus which the Trial Chamber considers to be representative of customary international law'; and *Prosecutor v Akayesu* 37 ILM 1399 (1998) at paragraph 593, where the ICTR also defined torture in terms of the Torture Convention.

with torture at the top and degrading treatment at the bottom. The process began in the *Greek* Case,[29] which held:

> that there may be treatment to which all these descriptions apply, for all torture must be inhuman and degrading treatment, and inhuman treatment also degrading. The notion of inhuman treatment covers at least such treatment as deliberately causes severe suffering, mental or physical, which, in the particular situation, is unjustifiable.
>
> The word 'torture' is often used to describe inhuman treatment, which has a purpose, such as the obtaining of information or confessions, or the infliction of punishment, and it is generally an aggravated form of inhuman treatment. Treatment or punishment of an individual may be said to be degrading if it grossly humiliates him before others or drives him to act against his will or conscience.[30]

Subsequent cases have followed these distinctions,[31] although it would appear that no real legal consequences follow. There is undoubtedly a stigma attached to torture, but beyond this, all of the acts are prohibited at all times, and the only valid reason for the distinction may be for the purposes of Conventions applying *only* to torture. Nevertheless, interpreting common Article 3(1)(a) and (c) in European human rights terms would add much greater clarity to the meaning of the words used therein.

The taking of hostages

Common Article 3(1)(b) prohibits the taking of hostages during internal armed conflict. Article 9(1) of the ICCPR could be seen as relevant in this regard, stating that:

> Everyone has the right to liberty and security of person. No one shall be subject to arbitrary arrest or detention. No one shall be deprived of his liberty except on such grounds and in accordance with such procedures as are established by law.[32]

---

[29] *Denmark, Norway, Sweden and Netherlands* v *Greece*, (1969) Ybk ECHR at 186.

[30] *Ibid.*, at paragraph 2.

[31] E.g. *Republic of Ireland* v *United Kingdom* 2 EHRR 25, especially paragraph 167, where various interrogation methods used by the UK (known as the 'five techniques', and consisting of wall-standing, hooding, subjection to noise, deprivation of sleep and deprivation of food and drink) against several detainees in order to compile information about the IRA were held to be inhuman and degrading treatment but, despite the fact that they were used systematically to extract information or confessions, did not cause suffering of the particular intensity and cruelty necessary for them to be seen as torture.

[32] Article 5(1) of the European Convention and Article 7(1)–(3) of the American Convention cover the same subject, although in none of the instruments is the provision non-derogable.

The provisions of the ICCPR are primarily aimed, however, at the ostensibly lawful detention of individuals by the government or public authorities, rather than at the taking of hostages *per se*. Common Article 3(1)(b) is based instead on humanitarian principles, as expressed in Article 34 of Geneva Convention IV.

Taking the approach that human rights law can add clarity to humanitarian law provisions, one might have considered that the Hostages Convention of 1979[33] would also be relevant.[34] Article 13 of the Convention, however, states that it is inapplicable where (a) the offence is committed within a single State, (b) both the hostage and the alleged offender are nationals of that State, and (c) the alleged offender is found in that State's territory. This is likely to be the situation existing under common Article 3, so that in effect there is no legally binding obligation to prosecute or extradite hostage-takers during internal armed conflict in either human rights or humanitarian law. Rather, all that exists is a basic and cursory prohibition on hostage-taking.[35]

Judicial guarantees

Common Article 3(1)(d) prohibits 'the passing of sentences and the carrying out of executions without previous judgement pronounced by a regularly constituted court, affording *all the judicial guarantees which are recognized as indispensable by civilized peoples*'. Clearly, the best way to identify these judicial guarantees is to look not at individual legal systems, but rather at what States have agreed upon in widely accepted international instruments. These demonstrate protection to be twofold, covering due process and freedom from the application of *ex post facto* laws. The latter is included in the human rights instruments under consideration

[33] International Convention Against the Taking of Hostages, 18 ILM 1456 (1979).

[34] Article 12 states that: 'In so far as the Geneva Conventions of 1949 for the protection of war victims or the Additional Protocols to those conventions are applicable to a particular act of hostage-taking, and in so far as States Parties to this Convention are bound under those conventions to prosecute or hand over the hostage-taker, the present Convention shall not apply to an act of hostage-taking committed in the course of armed conflicts as defined in the Geneva Conventions of 1949 and the Protocols thereto, including armed conflicts mentioned in article 1, paragraph 4, of Additional Protocol I of 1977, in which peoples are fighting against colonial domination and alien occupation and against racist regimes in the exercise of their right of self-determination, as enshrined in the Charter of the United Nations and the Declaration of Principles of International Law Concerning Friendly Relations and Co-operation Among States in accordance with the Charter of the United Nations.'

[35] Joseph J. Lambert, *Terrorism and Hostages in International Law – A Commentary on the Hostages Convention 1979* (Cambridge, 1990), 263–298, especially 280–282.

separately from the rights regarding a fair trial,[36] but is undoubtedly an indispensable judicial guarantee, and so is contained within common Article 3. Non-derogable in all three instruments, its application is assured even in times of grave national emergency.

ICCPR Article 14 can usefully serve as a basis for the examination of the right to due process (reference being made where relevant to the corresponding provisions of the European and American Conventions), and it starts with the general premise that 'all persons shall be equal before the courts and tribunals'. There is no corresponding provision in the other two instruments, and this does little more than require in general terms that all human beings are equal in rights, and that access to the courts is equally available to all.

Article 14 goes on to provide that 'everyone shall be entitled to a fair and public hearing by a competent, independent and impartial tribunal established by law'. Article 6(1) of the European Convention and Article 8(1) of the American Convention provide the same. Even in peacetime, however, the right to a public trial can be limited for reasons of public order or national security, or in the interests of justice or the private lives of the parties involved.[37] Clearly considerations of national security apply *a fortiori* in situations of internal armed conflict, so that the right may not always be applicable in such cases. The requirement that the tribunal be independent and impartial was designed to ensure a separation of powers between the judiciary and the executive, but during internal armed conflict governments may opt to transfer the trial of civilians from civil to military courts, or even create special *ad hoc* tribunals for the trial of offences against State security.[38] Where the normal court machinery remains in operation there is no need for such action, but even where these steps are taken, human rights obligations need not be violated provided the other guarantees of due process are met. It should not be automatically assumed that military courts would fail to provide an accused with a fair trial.[39]

---

[36] ICCPR Article 15, ECHR Article 7, ACHR Article 9.
[37] ICCPR Article 14(1), ECHR Article 6(1).
[38] Examples of this are numerous. See IACHR, *Report on the Situation of Human Rights in the Republic of Nicaragua*, OEA/Ser.L/V/II.53, doc. 25, 30 June 1981 (in Thomas Buergenthal and Robert E. Norris, *Human Rights: The Inter-American System, vol. 5*, Booklet 22 (1983) 117 at 120) and *Report on the Situation of Human Rights in Chile*, OAS Doc. OEA/Ser.L/V/II.66, doc. 17, September 1985 (*ibid.* Booklet 22.2 (1986) 51 at 69–71).
[39] *Fals Borda v Colombia*, Comm. No. 46/1979, UN Doc. A/37/40, 193, paragraphs 9.2 and 13.3: the mere fact of being tried by a military tribunal does not breach ICCPR Article 14 if due process is respected.

Article 14(2) states the fundamental presumption of innocence,[40] before Article 14(3) lists the minimum guarantees to ensure a fair trial: the right to be informed promptly and in detail in a language which one understands of the nature and cause of the charge;[41] the right to adequate time and facilities for the preparation of one's defence and to communicate with counsel of one's choosing;[42] the right to be tried without undue delay;[43] the right to be present at one's own trial and to defend oneself in person or through legal assistance of one's own choosing, or to have legal assistance assigned and paid for if possessing insufficient means;[44] the right to examine prosecution witnesses, and to have defence witnesses examined under the same conditions;[45] the right to a free interpreter if one does not understand or speak the language used in court;[46] and the right not to be compelled to testify against oneself or to confess guilt.[47]

Problems can arise in the context of internal armed conflict for several of these requirements. First, it must be appreciated that in times of emergency or conflict there may well be longer delays in the trial process than in peacetime. Of course, delays justified by the circumstances are not undue delays. What cannot be justified is the indefinite postponement of trials, leaving people in detention for substantial periods of time without trial.[48] The right to the defence of one's choosing may also be controversial in times of conflict, where lawyers could conceivably be involved with terrorists or insurgents, thus endangering State security.[49] The alternative suggested, namely the elaboration of a list of lawyers vetted by the State,[50] may serve to alleviate the problem, but with tensions running high, mistrust could easily arise over the fairness

---

[40] ECHR Article 6(2), ACHR Article 8(2).
[41] ECHR Article 6(3)(a), ACHR Article 8(2)(b).
[42] ECHR Article 6(3)(b), ACHR Article 8(2)(c) and (d).
[43] ECHR Article 6(1), ACHR Article 8(1).
[44] ECHR Article 6(3)(c), ACHR Article 8(2)(d) and (e).
[45] ECHR Article 6(3)(d), ACHR Article 8(2)(f).
[46] ECHR Article 6(3)(d), ACHR Article 8(2)(a).
[47] ACHR Article 8(2)(g). The ECHR surprisingly has no corresponding provision.
[48] The IACHR has stated that in its opinion, 'the indefinite prolonging of trials for crimes against public order and state security, which give rise in some instances to deprivation of the freedom of the accused for a longer period than the longest sentence he could receive, is a violation of the right to a fair trial'. See OAS, *The IACHR: Ten Years of Activities (1971–1981)* (Washington, 1982), 320.
[49] Oraà, *States of Emergency*, 117–118.
[50] Or at least those not permitted to visit prisoners charged with security offences. International Commission of Jurists, *States of Emergency: Their Impact on Human Rights* (Geneva, 1983), 428; Oraà, *States of Emergency*, 117–118.

or political aims of such a system. A problem also exists as regards the examination of witnesses, particularly the attendance of prosecution witnesses, who could be the subjects of threats, dissuading potential witnesses from giving evidence and endangering the whole system of justice. To obtain their attendance may not therefore be possible, or desirable, in all cases. Evidence must still be available for examination, however, in order to maintain the fairness of the trial process.[51]

Article 14(4) requiring that procedures should be such as to take account of juveniles' ages and the desirability of promoting their rehabilitation has no corresponding provision in the other human rights instruments, and is of no particular relevance to internal conflict. Article 14(5) provides for the right to appeal, which is undoubtedly viewed as a fundamental tenet of the right to a fair trial,[52] and Article 14(6) covers the situation where a conviction has been obtained wrongly and is overturned, or a pardon is granted, in which case compensation shall be paid to the victim.[53] This would tend to arise after the end of hostilities, however, when the convictions attained were reviewed, rather than at the stage of protecting judicial guarantees during the conflict *per se*. Finally, Article 14(7) states that nobody is to be tried or punished again for an offence for which he has already been finally acquitted or convicted.[54]

Most problematic in this area, however, is the fact that common Article 3 protects only those guarantees considered *indispensable*. International human rights instruments treat guarantees of due process as derogable, and thus *not* indispensable at all. The right to a fair trial is one of the most basic human rights,[55] and it is therefore surprising that it was not entrenched. The rights are given great importance in the laws of war, and it might be that guarantees considered applicable in time of international war could reasonably be expected to apply in times of a lesser threat to the nation.[56] Certainly, during discussions

---

[51] The International Commission of Jurists expressed the desire that the testimony of prosecution witnesses not appearing at trial still be admitted, while making all possible efforts to permit the defence to test the veracity of such testimony and preserving the right to examine all those who do not appear, although quite how this is to be achieved is left unclear. It is also suggested that this be derogable. *States of Emergency*, 429.

[52] ACHR Article 8(2)(h) guarantees this, as does ECHR Protocol 7, Article 2.

[53] ACHR Article 10, ECHR Protocol 7, Article 3.

[54] ACHR Article 8(4), ECHR Protocol 7, Article 4 (which is non-derogable).

[55] Certainly in the *Lawless* and *Ireland* v *UK* cases this protection was treated with great importance, and subjected to the strictest controls as regards derogation.

[56] E. J. de Arechaga, International Commission of Jurists, *States of Emergency*, 427.

on whether to incorporate the right to a fair trial into the list of the ICCPR's non-derogable provisions, it was opposed as unnecessary on the basis that a list of the rights of due process was already contained in the Geneva Conventions of 1949,[57] so that these rights at least should be guaranteed in emergencies according to the ICCPR. Unfortunately, this is not necessarily so. As stated above, an emergency can exist *without* there being an armed conflict (and certainly without there being an international armed conflict to which the Geneva Conventions apply in their entirety). The principle that if these guarantees are applicable in wartime then they should logically apply in lesser situations is sound, but only serves to strengthen the case for those rights to be listed as non-derogable, and there is certainly a strong current of opinion that a core of the rights to a fair trial should be entrenched.[58] The UN Human Rights Committee has stated that derogations should not exceed those strictly required by the exigencies of the actual situation, and that the rest of the ICCPR Article 14(1) should be respected.[59]

The principle of consistency with other international obligations offers little assistance, since common Article 3 lists no rights of due process itself. That a list of rights of due process based on human rights instruments has now been included in both Additional Protocols[60] does, however, lend weight to the assertion that at least those rights must be seen as indispensable, having been considered so fundamental by the international community as to merit enumeration in instruments regulating armed conflicts, including those of an internal character. It would

---

[57] Convention III Articles 82–108, and Convention IV Articles 43, 65, 67, 71–76, 78, 117 and 126.

[58] Several authorities led Oraà to elaborate twelve rights to be protected during internal conflict or public emergency: the right to be informed promptly and in detail of charges; to all rights and means of defence necessary; to be present at one's trial; the presumption of innocence; not to be forced to give incriminatory evidence or to confess; to a tribunal which offers essential guarantees of independence and impartiality; to appeal; non-retroactivity of penal laws; to obtain the attendance and examination of defence witnesses; not to be retried after a final judgment; to a lawyer of one's choice; and to free legal assistance if necessary. See *States of Emergency*, 115–116, drawing upon International Commission of Jurists, *States of Emergency*, 428; International Law Association, *Minimum Standards of Human Rights Norms in a State of Exception*, Report of the Committee on the Enforcement of Human Rights Law to the 61st Conference, Paris, 1984 (London, 1985), 56–96; 'The Siracusa Principles on the Limitation and Derogation Provisions in the ICCPR', (1985) 7 *HRQ* at 3–130; and Theodor Meron, 'Draft Model Declaration on Internal Strife' (1988) 262 *Int Rev of the Red Cross* 59–76.

[59] GC 13/21, GAOR Doc. A/39/40 at 144.

[60] Additional Protocol I Article 75(4) and Additional Protocol II Article 6.

thus seem reasonable to consider Protocol II, Article 6 as interpreting common Article 3(1)(d), and outlining what those rights are.[61]

Human rights protection of civilians beyond common Article 3

As can be seen, then, the provisions of common Article 3 correspond to a large extent with various human rights obligations. International human rights instruments, however, contain other non-derogable provisions which remain applicable during internal armed conflict despite not being contained within, or equivalent to, provisions of common Article 3. The ICCPR, European and American Conventions include a variety of these, some – but not all – of which are common.

Only four non-derogable provisions are stated by all three treaties to be indispensable, three of which are also contained in common Article 3: the right to life; the prohibition against torture and other inhuman or degrading treatment or punishment; and freedom from the retroactive application of penal laws. All three treaties additionally prohibit slavery and servitude,[62] which finds no place in common Article 3, and which therefore represents protection afforded by human rights law beyond the scope of humanitarian law. These are the only non-derogable provisions contained in the European Convention, but the ICCPR and American Convention include several others.

Common to both are the right to recognition as a person before the law,[63] and the freedom of conscience and religion.[64] The ICCPR alone lists as non-derogable the right to be free from imprisonment for the failure to fulfil a contractual obligation,[65] while the American Convention also protects as non-derogable the right to raise a family,[66] the right to a name,[67] the rights of children,[68] the right to a nationality[69] and the right to participate in government.[70] None of these rights find any place in common Article 3, largely due to the fact that many of them

---

[61] The majority of rights enumerated in n. 58 above are contained in the Additional Protocols.
[62] ICCPR Article 8(1) and (2), ECHR Article 4(1), ACHR Article 6.
[63] ICCPR Article 16, ACHR Article 3.
[64] ICCPR Article 18, ACHR Article 12.
[65] This is also provided for in derogable ACHR Article 7(7). Article 1 of Protocol 4 to the ECHR also secures this right, but again derogably.
[66] Article 17.
[67] Article 18.
[68] Article 19.
[69] Article 20.
[70] Article 23.

are not particularly relevant to national emergencies, so that it could not be considered reasonably necessary to derogate from them in order to overcome the situation. This certainly appears to be true of the right to be recognised as a person before the law, the right to be free from imprisonment for the inability to fulfil a contractual obligation, rights of the family, children, and to a name.

Several of these provisions, however, could conceivably have an effect during internal armed conflict, particularly the right to freedom of conscience and religion, and the right to participate in government. The freedom of conscience or religion includes the freedom to manifest such beliefs 'in community with others'.[71] It is easy to appreciate that during internal conflict, perhaps based on religious differences, this could have a serious effect on State security, leading to an escalation in hostilities (although such problems can be avoided through the limitation clauses contained in both instruments,[72] which state that the freedom is 'subject... to such limitations as are prescribed by law and are necessary to protect public safety [or] order').[73] The right to participate in government could also be relevant during internal armed conflict, in that the failure to provide this right to a significant group of the population would clearly represent a breach of the American Convention, and could incite those disenfranchised to take up arms against the State. Equally, the right appears rather vulnerable during times of emergency or conflict in two respects. First, unrest and disorganisation caused by armed conflict can make elections unworkable, leading to their postponement and a suspension of the right to vote contained in Article 23(1)(b). This would not, however, amount to a violation of the treaty provided the conduct of public affairs continued through freely chosen representatives as required by Article 23(1)(a), and an election was held as soon as the state of emergency was over.[74] Secondly, the right in Article 23(1)(c) to have equal access to the State's public services will inevitably fall by the wayside, as indeed might many of the public services themselves.

Remaining is the issue of the right to a nationality. Simply possessing a nationality cannot reasonably be regarded as threatening the security of the State, but, 'on the other hand, as nationality is the prerequisite

---

[71] ICCPR Article 18(1). The ACHR also provides in Article 12 the 'freedom to profess or disseminate one's religion... together with others, in public'.

[72] ICCPR Article 18(3) and ACHR Article 12(3).

[73] ICCPR, Article 18(3).

[74] Oraà, *States of Emergency*, 101, citing IACHR, *Report on Nicaragua* (1981) at 139, where the Commission stated that the postponement of elections until after the emergency was not *per se* a violation of Articles 27(2) and 23(1)(b).

for the enjoyment of all the rights and guarantees recognized in the legislation of the State, deprivation of nationality has been used by governments as a means of depriving political opponents to the regime of all the rights and benefits to which nationality entitles them'.[75] All that is prohibited by Article 20(3), however, is the *arbitrary* deprivation of nationality. The removal of an individual's nationality for reasons of State security would accordingly seem to be permissible in a situation of emergency, despite the fact that the provision is non-derogable in principle. The right of a State to expel its nationals or to refuse them entry to the country also remains unaffected despite the apparent contravention of Article 22(5) of the American Convention, as Article 22 is susceptible to derogation.

Human rights law and Additional Protocol II

By 1977, a link between human rights law and humanitarian law had been firmly established, perhaps mainly due to efforts of the United Nations from the 1968 Tehran Conference onwards,[76] 'purporting to weld human rights with the humanitarian law of armed conflict'.[77] In fact, the two regimes were converging to the extent that the protection of human rights found explicit mention in the Preamble to Additional Protocol II, an essentially humanitarian law instrument. It provides:

THE HIGH CONTRACTING PARTIES,
RECALLING that humanitarian principles enshrined in Article 3 common to the Geneva Conventions of 12 August 1949, constitute the foundation of respect for the human person in cases of armed conflict not of an international character,
RECALLING furthermore that international instruments relating to human rights offer a basic protection to the human person . . .

---

[75] Oraà, *States of Emergency*, 98.
[76] A resolution was adopted there called 'Human Rights in Armed Conflict', stating in the Preamble that certain acts ('massacres, summary executions, torture, inhuman treatment of prisoners, the murder of civilians in armed conflict and the use of chemical and biological weapons, including napalm bombs') served to 'undermine human rights'. See *Final Act of the International Conference on Human Rights*, UN Doc. A/Conf32/41 (1969). Several resolutions in the following years reiterated the close relationship between human rights and humanitarian law, e.g. UN General Assembly Resolution 2675 (XXV) of 9 December 1970, asserting that in order to protect civilians, 'Fundamental Human Rights as accepted in international law and established in international instruments remain manifestly applicable in an armed conflict.' See Schindler, 'Interrelationship of the Laws', 936–937, and Draper, 'Humanitarian Law and Human Rights', 194–196.
[77] Draper, 'Humanitarian Law and Human Rights', 194.

An increased number of human rights thus find more detailed protection in Additional Protocol II than in common Article 3. This is perhaps not surprising, the Protocol being an entire instrument to develop and supplement the single Article 3.

The human rights provisions of Additional Protocol II are found largely in Part II (Humane Treatment), where Article 4 enumerates various fundamental guarantees, Article 5 addresses the rights of persons whose liberty has been restricted, and Article 6 deals with penal prosecutions, i.e. the rights of due process. That these provisions do indeed concern human rights is further underlined by the ICRC Commentary on the Additional Protocols, which states that:

> These are inalienable and fundamental rights, inherent in the respect due to the human person...bear[ing] the mark of international human rights law...inspired by the Covenant on Civil and Political Rights.
>
> These fundamental guarantees constitute a minimum standard of protection which anyone can claim at any time, and they underlie the whole system of human rights.[78]

Fundamental guarantees

Humane treatment

Article 4(1) of Additional Protocol II states that all those who do not take part in hostilities, or else have ceased to do so, and whether or not their liberty has been restricted, 'are entitled to respect for their person, honour and convictions and religious practices'. An element of the required standard of humane treatment set out later in the paragraph, this provision is taken (although in a slightly modified form) from Article 27 of Geneva Convention IV,[79] the Commentary to which states that: 'The right of respect for the person must be understood in its widest sense: it covers all the rights of the individual, that is, the rights and qualities which are inseparable from the human being by the very fact of his existence and his mental and physical powers.'[80]Quite what these inseparable rights

---

[78] Yves Sandoz, Christophe Swinarski and Bruno Zimmerman (eds.), *Commentary on the Additional Protocols of 8 June 1977 to the Geneva Conventions of 12 August 1949* (Geneva, 1987), 1365.

[79] Article 27 states that 'Protected persons are entitled, in all circumstances, to respect for their persons, their honour, their family rights, their religious convictions and practices, and their manners and customs. They are at all times to be humanely treated.'

[80] Jean S. Pictet, *Commentary to the Geneva Conventions of 12 August 1949, volume IV* (Geneva, 1958), 201.

and qualities of the human being are is not elaborated upon, so we must again turn to international human rights law in order to shed light on the meaning of the humanitarian law requirement.

Respect for the person is a blanket term, including all of the human rights thereafter enumerated in Additional Protocol II, along with any non-derogable human rights not mentioned therein. No human rights treaty states this obligation explicitly, it being instead the underlying purpose of *all* such instruments, whether they be general in nature, or else aimed at perhaps one specific aspect.[81] Respect for the person can therefore be understood in light of provisions such as the prohibition of torture, freedom of religion, and the like, and the broad terms of Article 4(1) make it possible (if not necessary) to refer to international human rights law to assist in its interpretation.

The concept of one's 'honour' seems rather more difficult to define. Again it seems a general idea, akin perhaps to an individual's personal reputation and dignity. Certainly the ICCPR states in Article 17(1) that 'No one shall be subjected to arbitrary or unlawful interference with his privacy, family, home or correspondence, nor to unlawful attacks on his honour and reputation', and a similar provision exists in Article 11 of the American Convention.[82] As far as the word can be said to encompass the idea of dignity, it must also cover rights prohibited more explicitly by both human rights law and other provisions of Additional Protocol II, such as the rights to be free from slavery and from degrading treatment.

Respect for convictions and religious practices is not mentioned by common Article 3, but is covered by human rights treaties. The ICCPR provides in Article 18 that 'everyone shall have the right to freedom of thought, conscience and religion. This right shall include freedom to...manifest his religion or belief in worship, observance, practice and teaching', and in Article 19 that 'Everyone shall have the right to hold opinions without interference.' Similar provisions can be found in Articles 9 and 10 of the European Convention, and Articles 12 and 13 of the American Convention.[83]

---

[81] E.g. one's physical and mental integrity, protected in instruments such as the 1984 Convention Against Torture and Other Cruel, Inhuman or Degrading Treatment or Punishment.

[82] It states: '(1) Everyone has the right to have his honor respected and his dignity recognized. (2) No one may be the object of arbitrary or abusive interference with his private life, his family, his home, or his correspondence, or of unlawful attacks on his honor or reputation.'

[83] Although only ICCPR Article 18 and ACHR Article 12 are non-derogable.

An interesting issue arises as to whether 'convictions' can include opinions and beliefs other than those of a religious nature. The *travaux préparatoires* of the 1974–1977 Conference show that the question gave rise to much discussion,[84] leading to the modification mentioned above with respect to Article 27 of Convention IV. Article 27 refers to 'religious convictions and practices', whereas Article 4(1) of Protocol II refers to 'convictions and religious practices'. This change was quite deliberate, and results in religion being relevant only to the word 'practices'. The Protocol therefore ensures respect also for philosophical and political convictions.[85] Article 19 of the ICCPR does extend protection to non-religious views, but the provision is derogable,[86] and human rights instruments subject the freedom of religion and conscience, even if the right is non-derogable, to such limitations as may be necessary in order to protect public order, etc.[87] This is clearly of great importance where the internal conflict could be caused by (or causing) religious tensions, and Protocol II's protection of the right to manifest one's religious beliefs, while also having one's other convictions respected, makes it more stringent in the protection of these rights than human rights law despite the intensity of conflict necessary for the Protocol's application.

Article 4(1) continues by requiring that all those not taking a direct part in hostilities 'shall in all circumstances be treated humanely, without any adverse distinction'. Adverse distinctions can be explained by reference to Article 2(1) of the Protocol, requiring the instrument to be applied without any adverse distinction 'founded on race, colour, sex, language, religion or belief, political or other opinion, national or social origin, wealth, birth, or other status, or on any other similar criteria'.[88]

Finally, Article 4(1) prohibits orders that there are to be no survivors.[89] Although based on the traditional law of The Hague,[90] rather than human rights law, it clearly came into being through some fundamental notion of respect for human life, and is of great importance. It is, after all, 'a precondition governing the application of all the rules of protection laid down in the Protocol, for any guarantees of humane treatment,

---

[84] E.g. CDDH/407/Rev.1, paragraph 43; XV at 461.

[85] Sandoz, Swinarski and Zimmerman, *Commentary on the Additional Protocols*, 1370.

[86] *Perdoma and De Lanza v Uruguay*, UN Doc. A/35/40, at 111.

[87] ICCPR Article 18(3), ECHR Article 9(2) and ACHR Article 12(3).

[88] Adverse distinction clauses are also contained in common Article 3 and various human rights instruments. See the discussion above at pp. 197–198.

[89] See above at p. 111.

[90] Article 23(d) of the 1907 Hague Regulations annexed to Convention IV states that it is forbidden to declare that no quarter will be given.

any rule on care to be given the wounded and sick, and any judicial guarantees would remain a dead letter if the struggle were conducted on the basis of orders to exterminate the enemy'.[91]

Violence to life and person

Like common Article 3, Article 4(2) proceeds from the general requirement of humane treatment to list various acts which are prohibited specifically and absolutely, rather than relying upon the blanket requirement of humane treatment. The phrase 'without prejudice to the generality of the foregoing' means, however, that these explicit prohibitions cannot limit the scope of the overall principle.

Article 4(2)(a) prohibits 'violence to the life, health and physical or mental well-being of persons, in particular murder as well as cruel treatment such as torture, mutilation or any form of corporal punishment', much of which represents a restatement of the protections contained in common Article 3(1)(a).[92] The two provisions differ, however, in that firstly, the Protocol's provision proscribes 'violence to the life, health and physical or mental well-being of persons' compared to common Article 3's prohibition on 'violence to life and person', and secondly, Protocol II contains a new provision on corporal punishment.

Turning to the former, despite assertions that 'The scope of the prohibition was considerably strengthened; "violence to the life, health, and physical or mental well-being" is further-reaching in protection than the sole mention of violence to life and person, as contained in Article 3',[93] it would appear that the new term is simply an elaborate replacement for that contained in common Article 3. One's 'person' can be seen as comprising one's 'health and physical or mental well-being' and, as such, the provision continues to outlaw violence to life and person, neither increasing nor diminishing the protection previously afforded. Legal protection is not extended merely by stating the rights to be protected in a more long-winded fashion. Given the protection of health, the additional protection of physical and mental well-being seems superfluous.

The addition of a prohibition on corporal punishment also seems unnecessary since corporal punishment must, by its very nature, be likely to inflict violence upon the physical (or indeed mental) well-being of a

---

[91] Sandoz, Swinarski and Zimmerman, *Commentary on the Additional Protocols*, 1371.

[92] On how common Article 3(1)(a) reaffirms several human rights (and thus on how Additional Protocol II does likewise), see above at pp. 197 ff.

[93] Sandoz, Swinarski and Zimmerman, *Commentary on the Additional Protocols*, 1373.

person. Human rights treaties already deal with this issue under the ambit of cruel and inhuman or degrading treatment, as seen in the case of *Tyrer v UK*,[94] but several delegations at the Diplomatic Conference were keen that corporal punishment be specifically included,[95] and it seems churlish to argue against detailed and specific protection for civilians in conflict situations.

Article 4(2)(b) is a new provision as regards internal armed conflicts, and prohibits collective punishments. Based on the humanitarian law[96] aim to prohibit 'penalties of any kind inflicted upon persons or entire groups of persons in defiance of the most elementary principles of humanity, for acts that these persons have not committed',[97] it reiterates Article 5(3) of the American Convention, a non-derogable provision requiring that, 'Punishment shall not be extended to any person other than the criminal.' Whilst it might have been thought that such acts would be covered by the judicial guarantees sections of human rights treaties, and so by Article 6 of Additional Protocol II, the Diplomatic Conference was at great pains to ensure that the provision would prohibit not only judicial penalties, but any other type of sanction taken against the civilian population. The term 'collective penalty' found in Geneva Convention IV was therefore changed to 'collective punishment'. A laws of war measure has thus been extended to internal armed conflict, broadening the protection previously afforded both by common Article 3 and by human rights law.[98]

Article 4(2)(c) simply restates common Article 3(1)(b) by prohibiting the taking of hostages,[99] while Article 4(2)(d) is another new provision, prohibiting 'acts of terrorism'. This again extends the protection afforded to civilians during internal armed conflict through the application of a provision previously applicable only during international conflicts.[100] A prohibition on terrorism is not found explicitly in human rights treaties, although human rights law does impact on the provision in

---

[94] 2 EHRR 1. For corporal punishment to be degrading the level of physical violence is likely to be relatively low. More damaging acts will be contained within the more general prohibition on violence to health and well-being.

[95] E.g. France and Poland. See CDDH/I/GT/65; CDDH/I/287/Rev.1, X at 104; and CDDH/I/SR.39, VIII at 411.

[96] See Hague Regulations IV Article 50, Geneva Convention III Article 87 with respect to prisoners of war, Geneva Convention IV Article 33, and Additional Protocol I Article 75(2)(d).

[97] Pictet, *Commentary IV*, 225.

[98] Sandoz, Swinarski and Zimmerman, *Commentary on the Additional Protocols*, 1374.

[99] See above at pp. 202–203.

[100] Geneva Convention IV Article 33. See also Additional Protocol I Article 51(2).

that the right to life must be relevant to the extent that it is threatened by terrorist attacks. Terrorist attacks on the civilian population can be seen as being prohibited by Article 13(2) of the Protocol, there being no reason to differentiate in that respect between attacks of a terrorist nature and those of the 'normal' military type. Nevertheless, Article 13(2) also states specifically that 'Acts or threats of violence the primary purpose of which is to spread terror among the civilian population are prohibited.' Such acts, i.e. those designed not to injure, but only to terrorise, must also contravene the general protection afforded by Article 4(1) regarding mental well-being.[101]

Article 4(2)(e) prohibits 'outrages upon personal dignity, in particular humiliating and degrading treatment, rape, enforced prostitution and any form of indecent assault'. The first part of the provision is identical to the corresponding part of common Article 3(1)(c), but the additions regarding rape, prostitution and indecent assault merit further consideration. Inspired by Article 27 of Geneva Convention IV,[102] they represent the feeling of the Conference that the protection of women and children during internal armed conflict had to be strengthened.[103] The question is how far this additional humanitarian protection is underpinned by international human rights law. As discussed in relation to common Article 3, human rights law prohibits cruel, inhuman or degrading treatment, Article 5(1) of the American Convention, for example, stating that, 'Every person has the right to have his physical, mental, and moral integrity respected.' The ICCPR, European and American Conventions all fail expressly to mention the right to be free from sexual attacks, but the right must nevertheless be contained within the inhuman and degrading treatment provisions, none of which may be derogated from. As has been stated by the ICTY, 'No international human rights instrument specifically prohibits rape or other serious sexual assaults. Nevertheless, these offences are implicitly prohibited by the provisions safeguarding physical integrity.'[104]

---

[101] Article 4(2)(d) in fact goes beyond the prohibition of terrorist attacks against civilians, and sets out a fairly general prohibition also covering acts of terrorism directed against other targets or installations which would result in victims as a consequence. See Sandoz, Swinarski and Zimmerman, *Commentary on the Additional Protocols*, 1375.

[102] Stating that 'Women shall be especially protected against any attack on their honour, in particular against rape, enforced prostitution, or any form of indecent assault.' This is now also included in Additional Protocol I: see Articles 75(2)(b) and 76(1).

[103] At one point a separate Article specifically aimed at this was sought. See CDDH/I/287/Rev.1; X at 105, and CDDH/I/SR.39 paragraphs 15–18; VIII at 413.

[104] *Prosecutor v Furundžija* at paragraph 170.

Rape has been commonplace in many recent armed conflicts, both of an internal and international character[105] and, as has been demonstrated, is explicitly prohibited by conventional international law, including common Article 3 which 'implicitly refers to rape'.[106] The prohibition of rape as well as other serious sexual assault has furthermore been held by the ICTY to have 'evolved in customary international law'.[107] There can be no doubt, then, that rape is a violation of humanitarian law as well as human rights law. Neither body of legal regulation, however, has provided a definition of what constitutes rape in international law. Faced with this problem, the International Criminal Tribunal for Rwanda had to arrive at its own definition. It held in *Prosecutor v Akayesu* that:

Like torture, rape is used for such purposes as intimidation, degradation, humiliation, discrimination, punishment, control or destruction of a person. Like torture, rape is a violation of personal dignity, and rape in fact constitutes torture when inflicted by or at the instigation of or with the consent or acquiescence of a public official or others acting in an official capacity. The Chamber defines rape as a physical invasion of a sexual nature, committed on a person under circumstances which are coercive.[108]

This approach has since been reaffirmed by the Yugoslav Tribunal.[109] Nevertheless, there has been little consistency of approach when it came to judgments with respect to prosecution of the offence of rape. As outlined by the Trial Chamber in the *Furundžija* Judgment:

The prosecution of rape is explicitly provided for in Article 5 of the Statute of the Tribunal as a crime against humanity. Rape may also amount to a grave breach of the Geneva Conventions, a violation of the laws or customs of war or an act of genocide, if the requisite elements are met, and may be prosecuted accordingly.[110]

Rape can therefore be prosecuted as a crime against humanity in its own right,[111] or as a crime against humanity amounting to torture; as a violation of laws and customs of war in its own right, or amounting

---

[105] As demonstrated by the conflicts in the former Yugoslavia and in Rwanda. See, for example, *Tadić* (Indictment) at 1030; *Prosecutor v Nikolić* 108 ILR 21 at 37; *Prosecutor v Furundžija*; and *Prosecutor v Delalić*. From the ICTR case law, see *Prosecutor v Akayesu*. See also *Aydin v Turkey* ECHR Reports 1997-VI, No. 50, 1866.

[106] *Prosecutor v Furundžija* at paragraph 166.

[107] *Ibid.*, at paragraph 168.

[108] *Prosecutor v Akayesu* at paragraphs 597–598.

[109] *Prosecutor v Furundžija* at paragraphs 176–186, and *Prosecutor v Delalić* at paragraphs 478–479.

[110] *Prosecutor v Furundžija* at paragraph 172.

[111] *Prosecutor v Akayesu* at paragraphs 685–697.

to torture;[112] and as an element of genocide, providing the necessary intent can be proved. The trend does seem, however, to have been in the direction of finding rape to amount to torture. In *Aydin* v *Turkey*, the European Court of Human Rights found in the context of serious internal disturbances in South East Turkey (no finding was made as to whether the situation was one of internal armed conflict) that 'the accumulation of acts of physical and mental violence inflicted on the applicant and the especially cruel act of rape to which she was subjected amounted to torture in breach of Article 3 of the Convention'.[113] Likewise, in the case of *Fernando and Raquel Mejia* v *Peru*, the Inter-American Commission on Human Rights has held that rape can constitute torture,[114] and both of these regional human rights cases were cited as support for the finding of the Trial Chamber in *Delalić*.[115]

Article 4(2)(f) deals with one of the most fundamental human rights, listed as non-derogable in all of the relevant human rights treaties, by prohibiting 'slavery and the slave trade in all its forms'.[116] It therefore fills a gap left by common Article 3, as does the prohibition of pillage contained in Article 4(2)(g), although the latter is not really a human rights provision. The American Convention on Human Rights does protect property rights in Article 21, but this is derogable, and the ICCPR fails to mention property rights. This is, therefore, another provision imported from the law of international armed conflict.[117]

Finally, Article 4(2)(h) also breaks new ground as far as the regulation of internal conflicts is concerned, by prohibiting 'threats to commit any

---

[112] *Prosecutor* v *Furundžija* at paragraphs 264–275 and *Prosecutor* v *Delalić* at paragraphs 925–965. See also *Delalić* at paragraphs 1062–1066, where it was held that forcing detainees to perform fellatio upon each other 'could constitute rape for which liability could have been found if pleaded in the appropriate manner'. (It was instead held to be inhuman treatment under Article 2 of the Statute, and cruel treatment under Article 3 of the Statute.)

[113] At paragraph 86. It is not, of course, open to the European Court of Human Rights to find a violation of the laws of war, or the commission of crimes against humanity. In the course of the proceedings Amnesty International made a submission relying on indictments before the ICTY (see paragraph 51).

[114] Report No. 5/96, Case No. 10.970 at 187.

[115] As were reports of the UN Special Rapporteur on Torture and the UN Special Rapporteur on Contemporary Forms of Slavery, Systematic Rape, Sexual Slavery and Slavery-like Practices during Armed Conflict. See *Delalić* at paragraphs 491–493.

[116] See also the 1926 Slavery Convention, UKTS 16 (1927) Cmnd 2910, and the Supplementary Convention on the Abolition of Slavery, the Slave Trade and Institutions and Practices Similar to Slavery of 1956, UKTS 59 (1957) Cmnd 257.

[117] Inspired by Articles 28 and 47 of the 1907 Hague Regulations and Article 33 of Geneva Convention IV. The European Convention protects property rights in Protocol 1, Article 1.

of the foregoing acts'. Additional Protocol I has a similar provision in Article 75, but this concept emerged only at the 1974–1977 Conference. No human rights treaty offers protection from the threat of a breach of one's rights, and this is perhaps difficult to equate with the idea of humane treatment, since a mere threat to treat somebody inhumanely involves no actual inhumane treatment. It could be argued, however, that widely publicised threats to treat the civilian population in the above-mentioned ways may be damaging to their mental well-being.

Rights of the child

Article 4(3) details certain measures for the protection of children, who are particularly vulnerable during armed conflict, and is accordingly a huge advance on common Article 3, which makes no special provision whatsoever. Very little protection of this kind had previously been set out in humanitarian instruments, although some inspiration was clearly drawn from Article 50 of Geneva Convention IV, addressed to the needs of children in occupied territories. It is therefore necessary to turn again to human rights law as an interpretative device.

Article 24(1) of the ICCPR and Article 19 of the American Convention both secure the overall protection of children in very general terms. Thus the ICCPR Article 24(1) states that:

Every child shall have, without any discrimination as to race, colour, sex, language, religion, national or social origin, property or birth, the right to such measures of protection as are required by his status as a minor, on the part of his family, society and the state.

This is very broad, however, and makes no effort to describe what sort of protection may be necessary. Are there more detailed provisions corresponding to the requirements of Protocol II?

Turning first to consider Article 4(3)(a) of the Protocol, protecting the right of children to be educated in accordance with the wishes of their parents or guardians, the general right to an education is set out in Article 13 of the International Covenant on Economic, Social and Cultural Rights (ICESCR) and the Convention on the Rights of the Child, Articles 28 and 29. Closer to Article 4(3)(a), however, are Article 18(4) of the ICCPR, Article 2 of the First Protocol to the European Convention and Article 12(4) of the American Convention. Article 18(4) of the ICCPR, for example, provides that 'The States Parties to the present Covenant undertake to have respect for the liberty of parents and, when applicable, legal guardians to ensure the religious and moral education of their children in conformity with their own convictions.' The provisions of the ICCPR and the American Convention are non-derogable, and Protocol II underlines their continuing applicability in situations of high-intensity internal armed conflict.[118]

Subparagraph (b), requiring all appropriate steps to be taken to reunite families temporarily separated, has its basis in Article 26 of Geneva Convention IV, and is not a provision which would find any place in human rights treaties, owing to the particular circumstances of the armed conflict causing the split.[119] Article 4(3)(c) prohibits those under fifteen years of age from being recruited into the armed forces and from taking part in hostilities.[120] It has no basis in human rights law other than the general protection of minors,[121] but the fact that even if this provision is not respected, children continue to receive the benefits of the rest of Article 4(3) (as provided in Article 4(3)(d)) serves to strengthen the level of protection.[122]

The temporary movement of children to safe areas may appear to conflict with freedom of movement and the right to stay in the area of choice within the territory of one's State, as protected by the ICCPR Article 12(1), Article 2(1) of the Second Protocol to the European Convention, and Article 22(1) of the American Convention. Articles 12(3), 2(3)

---

[118] Surprise has been expressed that the provision was universally accepted, the relevant provision in the European Convention being the object of more reservations than any other: see Michael Bothe, Karl J. Partsch and Waldemar A. Solf, *New Rules for Victims of Armed Conflicts: Commentary on the Two 1977 Protocols Additional to the Geneva Conventions of 1949* (The Hague, 1982), 642. For East German and Ukrainian objections to Article 4(3)(a) see CDDH/III/SR.46; XV, 80 (paragraph 17); CDDH/SR.50; VII, 90 (paragraph 39); and CDDH/SR.53; VII, 145 (paragraph 21).

[119] Although see below at pp. 227–228 on the obligation to search for those missing, and human rights obligations in the context of disappearances.

[120] See Howard Mann, 'International Law and the Child Soldier' (1987) 36 *ICLQ* 32, and Ilene Cohn and Guy S. Goodwin-Gill, *Child Soldiers* (Oxford, 1994).

[121] Article 38(1) of the Convention on the Rights of the Child provides that 'States Parties undertake to respect and ensure respect for rules of international humanitarian law applicable to them in armed conflicts which are relevant to the child.'

[122] This is the case despite initial fears that subparagraph (d) might serve to weaken the text. See Sandoz, Swinarski and Zimmerman, *Commentary on the Additional Protocols*, 1380. The absolute nature of Article 4(3)(c) is qualified, however, by Article 38(2) of the Convention on the Rights of the Child, which requires only that States parties take 'all feasible measures to ensure that persons who have not attained the age of fifteen years do not take a direct part in hostilities', although where the State is a party to both this Convention and Additional Protocol II, Article 41 provides that, 'Nothing in the present Convention shall affect any provisions which are more conducive to the realization of the rights of the child and which may be contained in: (a) The law of the State Party; or (b) International law in force for that State.'

and (4), and 22(3) respectively, however, contain the proviso that such freedom can be restricted for reasons of national security, public order, etc. Additional Protocol II clearly only permits this course of action for the benefit of children, and with the consent of those responsible for the child's welfare where possible,[123] which is not open to criticism.[124] Article 4(3) is, then, a clear attempt to advance the protection of human rights and their application to children during internal armed conflict, previously afforded in such a comprehensive fashion by neither human-itarian law nor human rights law. The circumstances of the conflict, however, may make them difficult to ensure.[125]

Persons whose liberty has been restricted

All of the protections in Article 4 are also applicable to those who have had their liberty restricted for reasons related to the armed conflict. Common Article 3 contains no specific protection for these people, and although the provisions of Protocol II are based largely on Geneva Conventions III and IV,[126] it is important to consider the relationship between these requirements and the standards required by human rights law.

Article 5 is split into two sets of requirements, one of which must be respected as a minimum (Article 5(1)), the other of which need only be respected by those responsible for the internment or detention 'within the limits of their capabilities' (Article 5(2)). Article 5(1)(a) requires that the wounded and sick be dealt with according to Article 7 of Protocol II, which is itself an elaboration of common Article 3(2), allowing only medical distinctions to be made between victims, whilst Article 5(1)(b) requires that those interned or detained shall, 'to the same extent as the local civilian population, be provided with food and drinking water and be afforded safeguards as regards health and hygiene and protection against the rigours of the climate and the dangers of the armed conflict'. This is simply an aspect of humane treatment, required more generally by Protocol II elsewhere, and in human rights law by Article 10(1) of the ICCPR, for example, which provides that 'All persons deprived of

[123] Of course it may be impossible to trace those responsible for the child.
[124] Additional Protocol II, unlike Article 27 of Geneva Convention IV, permits only their removal to a safe place within the same country.
[125] Indeed, Bothe, Partsch and Solf have stated in *Commentary on the 1977 Protocols*, 643, that, 'In some cases . . . it may seem questionable whether this attempt is really realistic and feasible.'
[126] See especially Convention III Articles 22, 26 and 27, and Convention IV Articles 82, 85, 89 and 90.

their liberty shall be treated with humanity and with respect for the inherent dignity of the human person.' Several of these obligations could also be said to be covered by the rather more vague provisions of the ICESCR – Article 11 protects the right to an adequate standard of living 'including adequate food, clothing and housing',[127] and Article 12 the right to the highest possible standards of health (both physical and mental).[128] Those rights contained in the ICESCR are, however, notoriously difficult to enforce, and the provisions of Article 5(1)(b) of Protocol II are a welcome improvement on the general provision of the ICCPR. Of course, the standard of treatment need only be as high as that of the local civilian population, which is dangerous where they themselves have a fairly poor standard of living, perhaps deprived of several human rights by their government, as is often the case in civil conflict.[129]

The right to receive relief as contained in Article 5(1)(c) is clearly a humanitarian rather than a human rights provision,[130] whilst Article 5(1)(d) in contrast is clearly a human rights provision in that it outlines the freedom of religion, protected by Article 18 of the ICCPR and Article 12 of the American Convention as non-derogable, and also by Article 9 of the European Convention. Article 5(1)(e) provides that if detainees are made to work, then they are to receive the same safeguards as the local civilian population. This may seem to contradict various human rights provisions stating that 'No one shall be required to perform forced or compulsory labour',[131] but only the American Convention lists this as non-derogable, and all three treaties do list situations in which 'compulsory labour' is permissible.[132] Article 5(1)(e) is thus to be applauded, at least for affording some measure of protection for those made to work during detention, although, again, the fact that the protection is tied to the conditions of the local civilian population renders it weaker than the more absolute rights commonly contained in human rights instruments.

Turning to Article 5(2), that these provisions are to be respected only within the limits of the capabilities of those in charge of the detainees

---

127 The provision of food as required by Article 5, and protection against the rigours of the climate being covered by clothing and shelter.

128 For which food and water are essential, as are the safeguards as regards health and hygiene, and the protection against the climate and the armed conflict detailed in Article 5 of Protocol II.

129 See above at pp. 112–114.

130 See Article 72 of Geneva Convention III, and Article 108 of Geneva Convention IV. The right to relief has no effect on the requirement of adequate food and water, etc.

131 ICCPR Article 8(3)(a), ECHR Article 4(2) and ACHR Article 6(2).

132 By defining certain activities as not being compulsory labour. See the ICCPR Article 8(3)(b) and (c), ECHR Article 4(3) and the ACHR Article 6(2) and (3).

leaves open to question their true value, although in a situation meriting the application of Additional Protocol II, the high level of organisation required of the insurgent party ought to ensure that both sides are capable of observing at least some of these measures. The lack of a competent authority to decide whether or not such provisions are within the capabilities of the parties will, of course, leave the issue to the perhaps dubious judgement of the parties themselves.

Article 5(2)(a) deals with the segregation of men and women, and is clearly based upon human rights provisions requiring respect for the dignity of detainees,[133] and prohibiting degrading or humiliating treatment. Special provisions with respect to women detainees can also be found in Geneva Conventions III and IV.[134] It is perhaps surprising, however, that Protocol II does not insist upon the segregation of juveniles from adults, as required by the ICCPR Article 10.[135] Article 5(2)(b) sets out the freedom of correspondence, also found in human rights law,[136] although the right may be derogated from, and interference with correspondence is permitted provided it is not arbitrary or unlawful. The ability to communicate with friends and family can be important for the mental health of detainees, however,[137] as protected by Article 4(2)(a), in that a lack of knowledge regarding the well-being of loved ones could cause a great deal of anguish. The inclusion of the right in Protocol II is therefore an improvement in the protection of detainees (always provided, of course, that the relevant party felt such measures to be within their capabilities).

Article 5(2)(c), requiring that detainees be located away from the conflict zone, is clearly a laws of war provision,[138] and subparagraph (d), requiring medical examinations, is another facet of the general requirement of humane treatment. The ICESCR Article 12 requirement that everyone has the right to the highest possible standards of health must

---

[133] ICCPR Article 10(1), ACHR Article 5(2).

[134] E.g. Geneva Convention III Article 14 and Convention IV Article 27.

[135] Bothe, Partsch and Solf find this 'astonishing' and suggest that the duty to segregate should be respected in situations governed by Additional Protocol II. See *Commentary on the 1977 Protocols*, 647. See also Additional Protocol I Article 77(4).

[136] See Article 17(1) of the ICCPR, Article 8(1) of the ECHR and Article 11(2) of the ACHR.

[137] Sandoz, Swinarski and Zimmerman, *Commentary on the Additional Protocols*, 1390; Bothe, Partsch and Solf, *Commentary on the 1977 Protocols*, 647.

[138] Although virtually all of these provisions could be said to impinge upon humane treatment – being located close to hostilities would render it more likely that breaches could occur to the right to life and health. Bothe, Partsch and Solf also consider this requirement to be important to the psychological well-being of detainees, *Commentary on the 1977 Protocols*, 647.

entail medical examination, but none of the other human rights instruments contain such explicit requirements. Finally, subparagraph (e) requires that:

[the] physical or mental health and integrity [of detainees] shall not be endangered by any unjustified act or omission. Accordingly, it is prohibited to subject the persons described in this Article to any medical procedure which is not indicated by the state of health of the person concerned, and which is not consistent with the generally accepted medical standards applied to free persons under similar medical circumstances.

This can be seen as a prohibition on medical experimentation, clearly also linked to the general rights of physical and mental health, and possibly even to Article 4(2)(a) of the Protocol, dealing with the prohibition on mutilations. That this is so makes it difficult to appreciate why it should be placed in Article 5(2), rather than in the list of obligations to be respected at all times.[139] Finally, Article 5(3) and (4), dealing with those detained for reasons of the conflict but not covered by paragraph 1, and with the release of detainees, are not human rights law provisions.

It must always be remembered, however, that only those detained *for reasons connected with the armed conflict* receive the protection of Article 5. Those detained during internal armed conflict for unconnected breaches of domestic criminal law must rely solely on international human rights law for their protection.

Penal prosecutions

The provisions on the right to a fair trial are obviously based on international human rights law, although Protocol II takes a different approach from that of common Article 3. As already outlined, common Article 3 provides only that 'the passing of sentences and carrying out of executions are prohibited without previous judgment pronounced by a regularly constituted court, affording all the judicial guarantees which are recognized as indispensable by civilized peoples'. An examination of human rights law is therefore necessary in order to discover what these indispensable guarantees are, and problems then arise on discovery of the fact that most such guarantees are not, in fact, considered indispensable at all.

Additional Protocol II instead sets out the general requirement that 'No sentence shall be passed and no penalty shall be executed on a

[139] See above at p. 200.

person found guilty of an offence except pursuant to a conviction pronounced by a court offering the essential guarantees of independence and impartiality',[140] before proceeding to give a non-exhaustive list of these guarantees.[141] Article 6(2)(a) requires that the accused be informed without delay of the offence alleged, and be provided with all necessary rights and means of defence, i.e.:

> the accused must be informed as quickly as possible of the particulars of the offence alleged against him, and of his rights, and he must be in a position to exercise them and be afforded the rights and means of defence 'before and during his trial', i.e. at every stage of the procedure. The right to be heard, and, if necessary, the right to call on the services of an interpreter, the right to call witnesses for the defence and produce evidence; these constitute the essential rights and means of defence.[142]

This reiterates the human rights set out by the ICCPR in Article 14(3)(a), (b), (d), (e) and (f), the European Convention in Article 6(3)(a)–(e), and the American Convention in Article 8(2)(a)–(f). That no one is to be convicted of an offence except on the basis of individual penal responsibility is not actually contained within the human rights instruments,[143] but the non-retroactivity of penal laws in Article 6(2)(c) restates the ICCPR Article 15(1) virtually *verbatim*.[144] Human rights law can also be seen in Article 6(2)(d) which restates the presumption of innocence,[145] Article 6(2)(e) which requires that everyone charged with an offence has the right to be tried in his presence,[146] and Article 6(2)(f) which states that nobody shall be compelled to testify against himself nor to confess guilt.[147] These measures clearly do not exhaust the rights of due process as set out in the human rights treaties,[148] but they do form only the *absolute minimum* to be respected.

---

[140] A court offering the guarantees of independence and impartiality replaced the requirement of a regularly constituted court contained in common Article 3, since it was felt by some experts that it was unlikely that a court could be regularly constituted under national law by an insurgent party. See Sandoz, Swinarski and Zimmerman, *Commentary on the Additional Protocols*, 1398.

[141] The requirements are only listed 'in particular'.

[142] Sandoz, Swinarski and Zimmerman, *Commentary on the Additional Protocols*, 1398.

[143] Although it is stated in Article 33 of Geneva Convention IV.

[144] See also ECHR Article 7 and ACHR Article 9.

[145] See ICCPR Article 14(2), ECHR Article 6(2) and ACHR Article 8(2).

[146] ICCPR Article 14(3)(d), but not explicitly provided by the European or American Conventions.

[147] See ICCPR Article 14(3)(g) and ACHR Article 8(3)(g).

[148] For example, the right to be tried without undue delay, and the principle of *non bis in idem*.

Article 6(3) provides that a convicted person shall be advised on conviction of his judicial and other remedies, and of the time limits within which they may be exercised. This is similar to Article 14(5) of the ICCPR, Article 2 of Protocol 7 to the European Convention and Article 8(3)(h) of the American Convention, all of which protect the right to appeal to a higher court according to law. The slight difference in Protocol II was a deliberate choice, however, since 'It was not considered realistic in view of the present state of national legislation in various countries to lay down a principle to the effect that everyone has a right of appeal against a sentence pronounced upon him, i.e. to guarantee the availability of such a right.'[149]

Under Article 6(4), the death penalty 'shall not be pronounced upon persons who were under the age of eighteen years at the time of the offence and shall not be carried out on pregnant women or mothers of young children'. Human rights law also requires that the death penalty not be imposed upon persons under the age of eighteen or on pregnant women,[150] but by extending the prohibition to include the mothers of young children Protocol II has significantly increased the human rights protection afforded in times of conflict.[151] Finally, Article 6(5) is an amnesty provision unique in the context of Article 6 in that it is relevant only to situations of armed conflict.

What is vitally important, however, is that, as with Article 5(1), Article 6 applies only to the prosecution and punishment of criminal offences *related to the armed conflict*. Persons subjected to judicial proceedings during the conflict for unconnected reasons do not, therefore,

---

[149] Sandoz, Swinarski and Zimmerman, *Commentary on the Additional Protocols*, 1400–1401.

[150] ICCPR Article 6(5). The American Convention, in Article 4(5), goes further by including those over the age of seventy. Article 1 of Protocol 6 to the European Convention actually abolishes the death penalty non-derogably, although Article 2 states that provision may still be made for the death penalty in time of war or imminent threat of war. The American reservation to the ICCPR Article 6(5), reserving the right to 'impose capital punishment on any person (other than a pregnant woman) duly convicted under existing or future laws permitting the imposition of capital punishment, including such punishment for crimes committed by persons below eighteen years of age' (UN Doc. ST/LEG/SER.E/13 at 175), has been widely criticised, and the Human Rights Committee has stated it to be incompatible with the object and purpose of the Article (UN Doc. CCPR/C/79/Add.50 (1995) paragraph 14), which has been seen as good evidence that this is now the position in customary law. See William A. Schabas, *The Abolition of the Death Penalty in International Law*, 2nd edn (Cambridge, 1997), 305–307.

[151] Nothing actually outlines how young children must be to exempt their mother from execution, but Article 14(1) of Geneva Convention IV might provide some guidance in this respect by mentioning mothers of children under seven years of age.

benefit from its provisions. What protection do they receive? The protections contained in the human rights treaties are still applicable, although, as has been explained, these can in principle be derogated from. In all cases where Additional Protocol II is applicable, however, common Article 3 is also applicable, offering the protection of Article 3(1)(d). That is *not* dependent on the crime being related to the conflict and, as outlined above, is likely to correspond to the provisions of Article 6 of the Protocol.

Remaining provisions of Additional Protocol II

Part III, dealing with the wounded, sick and shipwrecked, merely elaborates common Article 3(2), although it does extend protection to medical and religious personnel. As mentioned in the context of common Article 3, this therefore tends to represent protection afforded only by humanitarian law. Article 8 of the Protocol, however, requires that 'Whenever circumstances permit... all possible measures shall be taken, without delay, to search for and collect the wounded, sick and shipwrecked.' This obligation may seem relevant to the human rights measures taken with respect to the missing and disappeared by the UN Working Group on Disappearances.

Created in 1980 by UN Commission on Human Rights Resolution 20 (XXXVI) to 'examine questions relevant to enforced or involuntary disappearances of persons', the role of the Group in times of internal armed conflict is open to some debate. When confronted by the problem of widespread disappearances in the former Yugoslavia, the Working Group explained that:

From the very early years of its existence, the Working Group has consistently taken the view that cases occurring in the context of an international armed conflict should not be taken up by the Group. That position was occasioned by the Iran–Iraq war. The Group argued at the time that taking up all cases of disappearance occurring in international armed conflicts, including the disappearance of combatants, would be a task far surpassing the resources of the Group...

...As regards the situation in the former Yugoslavia, the Working Group is not aware of any authoritative position within the United Nations system which might give it guidance as to whether the armed conflict in that area is of an international or an internal character... The Working Group has no independent means of establishing the character of the conflict and acting accordingly.[152]

---

[152] Report of the UN Working Group on Disappearances, UN Doc. E/CN.4/1993/25 at paragraphs 38–39.

Although apparently declining to take any action, this statement clearly gives the impression that the Working Group does consider internal armed conflicts to be within its mandate. The Group may therefore be prepared to take action with respect to the missing provided that (a) the conflict is internal rather than international in character, and (b) the scale of the conflict is such that the Group can do justice to the problems of the missing and disappeared, bearing in mind its rather limited resources.[153]

Part IV outlines specific protection for the civilian population and, although based more upon the laws of war, several provisions do appear to have underpinnings in particular human rights. First, Article 13(1) states that the civilian population and individual civilians are to enjoy general protection against the dangers of military operations. More specifically, Article 13(2) requires that:

> The civilian population as such, as well as individual civilians, shall not be the object of attack. Acts or threats of violence the primary purpose of which is to spread terror among the civilian population are prohibited.

This would seem to cover essentially the same ground, and have the same human rights basis, as Article 4(2)(a), (d) and (h) of the Protocol – attacks upon the civilian population are necessarily measures of violence towards their life and health, while terrorist attacks and threats to attack the civilian population are also prohibited.

Article 14 of the Protocol prohibits starvation of the civilian population as a means of combat, protecting crops, agricultural areas for the production of foodstuffs, livestock, drinking water supplies, etc. from attack or destruction. Article 11(1) of the ICESCR outlines the right of everyone to adequate food, and Article 11(2) the 'fundamental right of everyone to be free from hunger'. Starvation would clearly also endanger the Article 12(1) right of everyone to enjoy the highest attainable standard of health. It has already been noted, however, that these rights

---

[153] In fact, the Working Group adopted the following approach with respect to the former Yugoslavia: '(a) All cases of missing persons in any part of the former Yugoslavia should be considered under the same special procedure, geared to the exigencies of the situation; (b) That special procedure should be implemented as a joint mandate by one member of the Working Group... and the Special Rapporteur on the situation of human rights in the former Yugoslavia, resulting in joint reports to be submitted to the Commission on Human Rights; (c) The Secretary-General should provide sufficient financial and personnel resources to the special procedure in order to guarantee its effective functioning.' See Report of the UN Working Group on Disappearances, UN Doc. E/CN.4/1994/26 at paragraph 43.

are difficult to place on the same level as those contained in the ICCPR, at least as regards effective enforcement, and Article 14 can equally be seen as restating a particular aspect of the humane treatment required by Article 4(1) and (2)(a) of the Protocol. Starvation could also represent inhuman treatment, prohibited by human rights instruments, and extreme cases of starvation must also endanger the right to life. The same is true of Article 15, outlawing attacks on works or installations containing dangerous forces, if such attacks would cause the release of these forces and, as a consequence, severe losses among the civilian population.

Article 16 protects 'historic monuments, works of art or places of worship which constitute the cultural or spiritual heritage of peoples'. A human rights law equivalent of this provision might be found in Article 15(1)(a) of the ICESCR, which recognises the general right to take part in cultural life. Only that part of Article 16 relating to places of worship, however, finds any measure of protection in the ICCPR, European or American Conventions, through provisions protecting the freedom of religion and the right to practise it with others in public or in private,[154] although even these rights may not be particularly apposite here, since damage to places of worship or their use for military purposes may not necessarily prevent people from practising their religion. It may be perfectly possible to practise one's religion without attending a place of worship.

Article 17 prohibits the forced movement of civilians, paragraph (1) stating that displacement of the population is not to be ordered for reasons related to the conflict unless their security or military reasons require it. This reiterates to a large extent the provisions in human rights treaties[155] which state that everyone lawfully within the territory of a State has liberty of movement and is free to choose his residence unless it is necessary to protect national security, public order, public health, etc. These provisions are all derogable, however, and so could be disregarded in time of conflict without Additional Protocol II's insistence. Of course, displacement of civilians for reasons unconnected with the conflict remains to be regulated by human rights law only. Article 17(2) further states that civilians shall not be forced to leave their own territory for reasons related to the conflict. This again restates human rights law, which is equally applicable when it is sought to expel civilians for

---

[154] ICCPR Article 18, ECHR Article 9 and ACHR Article 12.
[155] ICCPR Article 12(1), ECHR Protocol 4 Article 2(1) and ACHR Article 22(1).

reasons unconnected to the conflict, prohibited by Article 3(1) of Protocol 4 to the European Convention and Article 22(5) of the American Convention.[156] These provisions are derogable, and so Protocol II has considerably strengthened the protection afforded.

Finally, Article 18 deals with relief societies and their ability to afford services to civilians affected by the conflict. Although, as with all humanitarian law, the provision of relief itself is undoubtedly inspired by a concern for human rights and dignity, and the desire to prevent suffering, these provisions arose from the ICRC's involvement in the development of international humanitarian law, and do not reflect specific provisions of international human rights law. Far fewer non-derogable provisions of human rights law are not protected by Protocol II in comparison with common Article 3. The prohibition on imprisonment for failure to meet a contractual obligation is omitted from Additional Protocol II for the same reason as its omission from common Article 3[157] and, as with common Article 3, Articles 17, 18, 20 and 23 of the American Convention find no place in the Protocol.

From the preceding examination of the human rights content of common Article 3 and Additional Protocol II, it is clear that there is a great deal of overlap between the humanitarian laws of internal armed conflict and international human rights law. Indeed, much of the relevant humanitarian law simply reiterates human rights obligations, so that the two regimes regularly apply at the same time. As Schindler states:

The convergence of humanitarian law and human rights shows that war and peace, civil wars and international wars as well as international law and domestic law, are increasingly intertwined. Consequently, the law of war and the law of peace, as well as humanitarian law and human rights, which were originally clearly distinct in scope, are now often applicable simultaneously.[158]

The legal position can perhaps best be described as a continuum of protection for civilians, ranging from the complete application of human rights law and the inapplicability of humanitarian law at the bottom end of the spectrum (i.e. in time of peace), to the complete

---

[156] The ICCPR states only in Article 12(4) that nobody is to be *arbitrarily* deprived of the right to enter his own country.

[157] I.e. its irrelevance to situations of armed conflict.

[158] 'Interrelationship of the Laws', 938. Hans-Peter Gasser also sees Article 3 and Additional Protocol II as a codification of fundamental human rights law for civil war situations. See 'International Humanitarian Law' in Hans Haug (ed.), *Humanity for All: The International Red Cross and Red Crescent Movement* (Berne, 1993), 491 at 566.

application of the laws of war, with only the barest of respect for human rights law at the other end (i.e. where the State is involved in international armed conflict).[159] Between these two extremes come two more stages, the first of which arises where public order has broken down to an extent, but not such that the position can be seen as amounting to internal armed conflict. This situation is commonly called civil or internal strife, and such difficulties might warrant limitations being placed upon human rights law by the State (through derogation from some of its provisions) in an effort to restore public order. Internal disturbances along these lines fall short of armed conflict, however, and so there can be no role for common Article 3. The question of exactly which legal regime should apply to such circumstances is an interesting and controversial one, but outside the scope of the present study, dealing as it does only with the issue of internal armed conflict. Others have addressed the issue in much greater detail.[160]

The second intermediate stage is that of internal armed conflict, where a basic minimum of both humanitarian law and human rights law is applicable, as has been demonstrated throughout the course of this chapter. During internal armed conflict, common Article 3 outlines the irreducible minimum of humanitarian protection, and includes a residue of human rights protection guaranteeing most of the non-derogable rights along with a few others. Additional Protocol II develops the protection afforded by common Article 3 in both spheres, although it is rarely applied. International human rights law clearly, then, has an important role to play during internal armed conflict. Perhaps the most important, however, is in the actual enforcement of the legal protection of civilians, to which the final chapter is dedicated.

---

[159] Although many of the provisions of humanitarian law regulating international armed conflict can be seen to have their basis in human rights.

[160] See, for example, Theodor Meron, *Human Rights in Internal Strife: Their International Protection* (Cambridge, 1987); Asbjörn Eide, 'Internal Disturbances and Tensions' in ICIHI, *Modern Wars* (London, 1986), 102; Eide, 'Internal Disturbances and Tensions' in UNESCO, *International Dimensions of Humanitarian Law* (Dordrecht, 1988), 241; Hans-Peter Gasser, 'A Measure of Humanity in Internal Disturbances and Tensions: A Proposal for a Code of Conduct' (1988) 262 *Int Rev of the Red Cross* 38.

6   Implementation and enforcement of the laws of internal armed conflict

A considerable body of international law exists to protect civilians during internal armed conflict. The main problem lies not in the content of those rules, but rather in their enforcement. The enforcement of humanitarian law in international conflicts has been extensively studied,[1] but much less has been written on how this is to be achieved where the conflict is not international in character.[2] Neither common Article 3 nor Additional Protocol II contains provisions governing their enforcement. In fact, 'The system as a whole has been devised for international conflicts; it cannot simply be switched over to non-international conflicts, whose basic data are completely different.'[3] Enforcement and implementation of the humanitarian laws of internal armed conflict will thus be examined in terms of (a) sanctions against lawbreakers, and (b) other means of securing compliance.

---

[1] See, for example, Georges Abi-Saab, 'The Implementation of Humanitarian Law' in Antonio Cassese (ed.), *The New Humanitarian Law of Armed Conflict* (Naples, 1979), 310; Yves Sandoz, 'Implementing International Humanitarian Law' in UNESCO, *International Dimensions of Humanitarian Law* (Dordrecht, 1988), 259; Edward Kwakwa, *The International Law of Armed Conflict: Personal and Material Fields of Application* (Dordrecht, 1992), 159; and George H. Aldrich, 'Compliance with the Law: Problems and Prospects' in Hazel Fox and Michael A. Meyer (eds.), *Armed Conflict and the New Law, Volume II: Effecting Compliance* (London, 1993), 3.

[2] Indeed, to Sir Hersch Lauterpacht's famous statement that: 'If international law is, in some ways, at the vanishing point of law, the law of war is, perhaps even more conspicuously, at the vanishing point of international law' (Lauterpacht, 'The Problem of the Revision of the Law of War' (1952) 29 *BYIL* 382) could be added the further caveat that the law of internal armed conflict is at the vanishing point of the vanishing point.

[3] Sandoz, 'Implementing Humanitarian Law', 259.

Sanctions against lawbreakers

Individual criminal responsibility

Enforcement measures against individuals alleged to have violated humanitarian law primarily entail their trial following hostilities. The clearest example is that of the Nuremberg Tribunal following the Second World War where many leading Nazis were tried for crimes against peace, war crimes and crimes against humanity. The trials at Nuremberg, and those of other war criminals since,[4] have, however, tended to be concerned with violations of the laws of international conflict. The establishment by the United Nations of Criminal Tribunals for the trial of those alleged to have violated the law in the context of conflicts in Rwanda and the former Yugoslavia, and the adoption of a Statute for an International Criminal Court with jurisdiction over crimes committed during internal armed conflicts, are therefore of great importance.[5]

It is not enough in itself, however, that crimes against humanity and violations of the laws and customs of war committed during internal conflict are recognised as entailing individual criminal responsibility. International law must be effectively applied against individuals, and those responsible must be convicted. In that respect, although the establishment and pronouncements of the Yugoslav and Rwandan Tribunals are undoubtedly vital as regards the development of international law, an examination of their practical enforcement of the law makes slightly more disappointing reading. As at September 2000, the Rwandan Tribunal had handed down eight judgments,[6] and of ninety-four individuals publicly indicted by the ICTY, only eighteen judgments had been handed down.[7]

---

[4] E.g. *A-G of the Government of Israel v Eichmann* 36 ILR 5, and *Fédération Nationale des Déportés et Internés Résistants et Patriotes and Others v Barbie* 78 ILR 124.

[5] Although the ICTY has tended to consider the conflict in the former Yugoslavia as international (see chapter 2 above at pp. 47–50), it is accepted that the Tribunal would have jurisdiction were any of the constituent conflicts held to be internal.

[6] *Prosecutor v Akayesu*, Case ICTR-96-4-T (Judgment of 2 September 1998) 37 ILM 1399 (1998); *Prosecutor v Kambanda*, Case ICTR-97-23-S (Judgment of 4 September 1998) 37 ILM 1411 (1998); *Prosecutor v Serushago*, Case ICTR-98-39-S (Judgment of 5 February 1999) 38 ILM 854 (1999); *Prosecutor v Kayishema and Ruzindana*, Case ICTR-95-1, ICTR-96-10 (Judgment of 21 May 1999); *Prosecutor v Rutaganda*, Case ICTR-96-3 (Judgment of 6 December 1999) 39 ILM 557 (2000); *Prosecutor v Musema*, Case ICTR-96-13 (Judgment of 27 January 2000); and *Prosecutor v Ruggiu*, Case ICTR-97-32 (Judgment of 1 June 2000).

[7] *Prosecutor v Erdemović*, Case IT-96-22-Tbis (Sentencing Judgment of 5 March 1998) 37 ILM 1182 (1998); *Prosecutor v Delalić, Mucić, Delić and Landžo*, Case IT-96-21-T (Judgment of

Many of those perceived as the main perpetrators of humanitarian violations in the former Yugoslavia have yet to be brought to trial, with sixty-seven indictments outstanding, and twenty-six of those indicted still at large.[8] There have been several additional Rule 61 decisions, but the accused in these cases are not in the Tribunal's custody, and the judgments are of a purely provisional nature.[9]

There can be no doubt that the crimes committed by Duško Tadić, Dražen Erdemović and the like merited prosecution,[10] and their convictions and sentences demonstrate that the Yugoslav and Rwandan Tribunals can function effectively, and that international justice is indeed possible. They are, however, 'small fry' in the overall scheme of things, and the failure to arrest others indicted has been widely criticised.[11] Judge Richard Goldstone, then Chief Prosecutor of the Tribunal, warned that the failure to arrest Radovan Karadžić and Ratko Mladić in particular 'could prove a fatal blow to this tribunal and to the future of international justice'.[12] He is not alone in having reservations about the efficacy of the Tribunals, and Meron shares his concern regarding how effective such *ad hoc* tribunals might prove to be. While supporting the establishment of the Tribunals for Yugoslavia and Rwanda, Meron remains:

concerned about the selectivity involved in a system where the establishment of a tribunal for a given conflict situation depends on whether consensus to apply chapter VII of the UN Charter can be obtained. What is needed is a uniform and definite corpus of international humanitarian law that can be applied

16 November 1998); *Prosecutor v Tadić*, Case IT-94-1-A (Appeal Judgment of 15 July 1999) 38 ILM 1518 (1999); *Prosecutor v Jelisić*, Case IT-95-10 (Judgment of 14 December 1999); *Prosecutor v Kupreškić et al.*, Case IT-95-16 (Judgment of 14 January 2000); *Prosecutor v Blaskić*, Case IT-95-14 (Judgment of 3 March 2000); *Prosecutor v Aleksovski*, Case IT-95-14/1 (Appeal Judgment of 24 March 2000); and *Prosecutor v Furundžija*, Case IT-95-17/1-A (Appeal Judgment of 21 July 2000). The *Delalić, Jelisić, Kupreškić* and *Blaskić* cases are currently subject to appeal.

8 ICTY figures (as at 25 September 2000).
9 See Christopher J. Greenwood, 'War Crimes Proceedings Before the International Criminal Tribunal for the Former Yugoslavia' [1997] *Military LJ* 15.
10 See *Tadić* Indictment, 34 ILM 1028 (1995).
11 The action taken by SAS/NATO troops on 10 July 1997 in arresting the indicted Bosnian Serb, Kovacević, and the killing of Drljaca whilst attempting to do likewise (*The Times*, 11 July 1997, 1), was hoped at the time to represent a renewed determination on the part of the international community to enforce the law and bring those indicted to justice. Unfortunately this does not seem to have been the case.
12 Robert Fisk, 'Bosnia Judge Condemns West', *Independent*, 17 September 1996, 1.

apolitically to internal atrocities everywhere, and that recognizes the role of all states in the vindication of such law.[13]

The creation of the permanent International Criminal Court, with jurisdiction over violations of the law committed during internal armed conflict,[14] should signal the end for *ad hoc* criminal tribunals. It is nevertheless difficult to see how problems concerning the actual apprehension of those believed to be responsible for violations would disappear. Given the lack of political will evident in bringing those accused to justice, even where a tribunal has been established specifically for that purpose, there would appear to be no reason for attitudes to change merely because the ultimate place of trial would be different. The enforcement of the laws of internal armed conflict at the international level is clearly not straightforward. Can domestic courts, therefore, offer effective assistance in this area?

Crimes against humanity are subject to universal jurisdiction,[15] and with the acceptance that breaches of common Article 3 and the laws and customs of war entail international criminal responsibility must also come the acceptance that these acts are equally subject to universal jurisdiction. All States have the right to exercise jurisdiction over offenders.[16] That violations of common Article 3 are not grave breaches[17] does not therefore mean that they cannot be punished by any State party, an approach complementing the requirement in common Article 1 of the Geneva Conventions that all States must seek to ensure respect for the Conventions, achieving this through the prosecution of alleged violators.[18]

The success of universal jurisdiction is dependent upon individual States enacting the relevant laws and taking the necessary steps to implement them. Sadly, 'the record of national prosecutions of violators of such international norms as the grave breaches is disappointing, even when the obligation to prosecute or extradite violators is unequivocal. A lack of resources, evidence and, above all, political will has stood in the

---

[13] Theodor Meron, 'International Criminalization of Internal Atrocities' (1995) 89 *AJIL* 554 at 555.

[14] See Rome Statute of the International Criminal Court, UN Doc. A/CONF.183/9, 17 July 1998, Articles 5–8, and the discussion above at pp. 160–188.

[15] Meron, 'Criminalization of Internal Atrocities', 569 and the authorities listed at n. 82 therein.

[16] This is in contrast, however, to grave breaches of the Geneva Conventions, where States have an *obligation* to deal with offenders.

[17] Although see above at pp. 189–191 on this point.

[18] On common Article 1 see below at pp. 245–250.

way.'[19] Most States have neither the necessary resources nor sufficient interest to prosecute offenders unless actually involved in the situation in question,[20] a dangerous position following internal armed conflict where the victors dispense justice to the vanquished, risking degeneration into an atmosphere of revenge. Some degree of amnesty would clearly be preferable for the good of the country.[21] Nevertheless, those who have committed atrocities ought to be brought to justice, and a truly independent judiciary ought to represent a safeguard against unfair trials. State organs, however, bring those people before the courts in the first place, not the judiciary. Influenced by the newly triumphant government, it is therefore unlikely that excesses committed by the victors will be addressed as thoroughly.

Two other important factors have been highlighted in proceedings against the former Chilean dictator, Augusto Pinochet Ugarte, in the United Kingdom.[22] Although the situation in Chile never amounted to an armed conflict under common Article 3, the case was concerned mainly with torture, which *is* equally relevant to internal armed conflicts, both as a violation of the laws and customs of warfare and as a crime against humanity.[23] First, as outlined previously and confirmed by the Statute of the International Criminal Court,[24] the *Pinochet* Case affirmed that there can be no question of sovereign immunity as regards the commission (or ordering) of torture, and therefore for the commission of other war crimes or crimes against humanity. Secondly, the *Pinochet* Case is a reminder that, despite the importance of discussions relating to the customary law regulating internal armed conflict and criminal responsibility for its violation, individual criminal responsibility can also arise for offences under *conventional* international law.

Torture is specifically rendered criminal by the 1984 UN Convention Against Torture and Other Cruel, Inhuman or Degrading Treatment or Punishment. Each State party to the Convention must ensure that all acts of torture are offences under their own criminal law (Article 4). Article 5 requires States to take such measures as are necessary to establish

[19] Meron, 'Criminalization of Internal Atrocities', 555–556.
[20] *Ibid.*, 573.
[21] See above at p. 67, n. 145.
[22] *R v Bartle and the Commissioner of Police for the Metropolis and Others, ex parte Pinochet* and *R v Evans and Another and the Commissioner of Police for the Metropolis and Others, ex parte Pinochet* [1999] 2 All ER 97.
[23] See chapter 4.
[24] See above at pp. 177 ff.

jurisdiction over instances of torture where the offences are committed in territory under the State's jurisdiction, where the alleged offender is a national of the State, or where the victim is a national of the State (if considered appropriate), and Article 5(2) further provides that all States party shall take all necessary measures to establish jurisdiction where an individual accused of torture is present within the State's jurisdiction, and where the State does not extradite him. Conventional international law therefore places States under an obligation to prosecute individuals accused of having committed torture in any circumstances. The obligation must continue to apply where the torture was committed during an internal armed conflict.

Belligerent reprisals

Belligerent reprisals exist as sanctions to enforce the laws of war during hostilities.[25] Although the doctrine of *pacta sunt servanda* ought to mean that common Article 3 and Additional Protocol II are applied in good faith, insurgents may not accept these provisions (and by definition they will have played no part in deciding to accede to them), making it more difficult to rely on this concept in their case.[26] At any rate, practice has shown that good faith is rarely present and in that case, apart from continued requests that the law be respected, belligerent reprisals are essentially all that remain for either party to enforce the obligations under common Article 3 and Additional Protocol II in the course of hostilities. The legality of armed reprisals, however, is a subject of considerable debate.[27]

Traditionally, reprisals were ostensibly unlawful measures taken in response to a prior breach of international law, transforming their unlawful nature provided the reprisal was necessary and intended to make the

---

[25] For an examination of the topic see Frits Kalshoven, *Belligerent Reprisals* (Leiden, 1971), especially 266–270, and Christopher J. Greenwood, 'The Twilight of the Law of Belligerent Reprisals' (1989) 20 *NYIL* 35, dealing with reprisals in internal conflict at 67–68.

[26] For a discussion of the juridical basis upon which they are nevertheless bound see above at pp. 52–58 and pp. 96–99.

[27] See Derek W. Bowett, 'Reprisals Involving Recourse to Armed Force' (1972) 66 *AJIL* 1; Robert W. Tucker, 'Reprisals and Self-Defense: The Customary Law' (1972) 66 *AJIL* 586; Remigiusz Bierzanek, 'Reprisals as a Means of Enforcing the Laws of Warfare: The Old and the New Law' in Cassese, *New Humanitarian Law*, 232; and R. Barsotti, 'Armed Reprisals' in Antonio Cassese (ed.), *The Current Legal Regulation of the Use of Force* (Dordrecht, 1986), 79.

opposing party comply with the law, and reasonably proportionate to the original wrongdoing.[28] This is clearly dangerous, and, 'While the threat of reprisals has sometimes been effective in ending violations, the actual reprisal has much less often had the desired effect and, on the contrary, has often led to counter-reprisals which, in turn, can lead to a downward spiral into greater savagery.'[29] There has accordingly been a trend to limit, if not prohibit altogether, the use of armed reprisals in international relations, and other factors have also served to render reprisals an unsatisfactory means of enforcing humanitarian law.[30] First, progress in the techniques of war, particularly the development of weapons of mass destruction, makes an escalation of hostilities dangerous by encouraging progressively more cruel reprisal and counter-reprisal, inevitably harming the civilian population. Against this, it could be argued that 'smart' missiles developed by modern technology can be accurate to the extent of precise hits on military targets (as demonstrated by Allied troops in the 1991 Gulf Conflict), minimising collateral impact upon the civilian population. Secondly, in contrast to most classical wars, many armed conflicts are now asymmetrical, with one party having large numbers of troops and access to a full array of weaponry, and the other being forced to resort to guerrilla warfare. This imbalance inevitably renders retaliation in kind a limited possibility since comparisons between the losses and damage caused by the initial offence and reprisals will be difficult. Proportionality can thus be called into question as a pretext for further reprisals. This is particularly relevant to the present study, such inequality being even more apparent during many internal armed conflicts.

Although the resort to force as a measure of reprisal is clearly contrary to international law,[31] resort to belligerent reprisals *during* a conflict is not, and the Geneva Conventions seek to regulate them by prohibiting

---

[28] *Naulilaa* Arbitration (*Germany* v *Portugal*) 31 July 1928, 2 Int. Arb. Awards 1013. While the case no longer represents international law, the criteria have remained important in assessing whether reprisals are deemed to be acceptable.

[29] Aldrich, 'Compliance with the Law', 8.

[30] Bierzanek, 'Reprisals', 244. He also asserts that reprisals are contrary to the fundamental respect of the human being. This is addressed below in the context of reprisals and common Article 3. See also above at p. 61.

[31] Any use of force not amounting to an act of self-defence is prohibited by Article 2(4) of the UN Charter, while the Declaration on Principles of International Law Concerning Friendly Relations (UNGA Resolution 2625/XXV of 24 October 1970) asserts that States have a duty to refrain from acts of reprisal including the use of armed force. See also *ICJ Advisory Opinion on the Legality of the Threat or Use of Nuclear Weapons* [8 July 1996] 35 ILM 809 (1996).

their use against the wounded and sick, medical personnel, buildings or equipment,[32] the shipwrecked and vessels for the amelioration of the condition of the wounded and sick in the field and at sea,[33] prisoners of war,[34] and civilian persons and their property.[35] In addition, Article 4 of the 1954 Hague Convention on Cultural Property prohibits reprisals with respect to such objects, Article 51(6) of Additional Protocol I prohibits reprisals against civilians, and the UN General Assembly has reiterated that reprisals against civilian populations in armed conflicts are prohibited.[36] None of these provisions, however, expressly apply to internal armed conflict. Some delegates at the Diplomatic Conference of 1974–1977 even argued that rules on reprisals were not relevant to internal conflicts, concerning only relations between States.[37] The ICRC, however, disagreed, explaining that the:

application of common Article 3 has no legal effect on the status of the parties confronting each other, and consequently does not imply in any way recognition of belligerency. The same applies for application of Protocol II. But... the parties to the conflict are still subjects of international law in the limited context of humanitarian rights and obligations resting upon them under these two instruments. Whenever there is the possibility of rules of international law not being respected, there may be reprisals.[38]

There is no logical reason why belligerent reprisals should occur during international armed conflict, and yet not during internal armed conflict. The question therefore arises as to how common Article 3 and Additional Protocol II deal with them.

The failure of common Article 3 to mention reprisals could be taken to mean that they are permitted during internal armed conflict, especially since certain types of reprisal are explicitly prohibited elsewhere in the Conventions. Inhumane treatment of those protected by common Article 3 is impermissible, and clearly this must include armed attack. Of course, belligerent reprisals are ordinarily unlawful, so are attacks

---

[32] Convention I Article 46.

[33] Convention II Article 47.

[34] Convention III Article 13.

[35] Convention IV Article 33. This only relates, however, to civilians who are 'protected persons' under the Convention – i.e. those in the hands of a power of which they are not nationals. Clearly, this is not the position during internal conflict.

[36] Resolution 2675/XXV of 1970.

[37] Yves Sandoz, Christophe Swinarski and Bruno Zimmerman (eds.), *Commentary on the Additional Protocols of 8 June 1977 to the Geneva Conventions of 12 August 1949* (Geneva, 1987), 1372, n. 18.

[38] *Ibid.*

on the civilian population by way of reprisal permitted? The absolute
nature of common Article 3 would appear to render any belligerent
reprisal against the civilian population or those placed *hors de combat*
unlawful, and the ICRC supports such an assertion: 'The acts referred
to under items (a) to (d) are prohibited absolutely and permanently, no
exception or excuse being tolerated. Consequently, any reprisal which
entails one of these acts is prohibited, and so…is any reprisal incompatible with the "humane treatment" demanded unconditionally in the
first clause of sub-paragraph (1).'[39] The protection afforded by common
Article 3 would thus accord with the position in international armed
conflicts.

Again, no mention is made of reprisals in Additional Protocol II, although the ICRC Commentary offers both legal and political reasons
for this.[40] First, the lack of a reference to reprisals in common Article
3 might give rise to *a contrario* interpretations of that provision should
they be specifically prohibited by Additional Protocol II. Secondly, the list
of prohibited acts in Additional Protocol II is fuller than that contained
in common Article 3 (specifically including in Article 4(2)(b) a prohibition on collective punishments[41]). Coupled with the fact that common
Article 3's prohibitions are absolute, there can accordingly be no room
left at all for the carrying out of belligerent reprisals against civilians.
They may not be mentioned expressly, but the ICRC considered them to
be implicitly prohibited. Given that common Article 3 has crystallised
into customary international law, representing elementary standards of
humanity applicable to *all* armed conflicts,[42] it must therefore be the
case that customary international law prohibits the carrying out of belligerent reprisals against civilian populations.

The International Criminal Tribunal for the former Yugoslavia supported such a proposition in the *Martić* (Rule 61) Case,[43] holding that
'the rule which states that reprisals against the civilian population as
such, or individual civilians, are prohibited in all circumstances, even
when confronted by wrongful behaviour of the other party, is an integral
part of customary international law and must be respected in all armed

---

[39] Jean S. Pictet, *Commentary on the Geneva Conventions of 12 August 1949, Volume IV* (Geneva, 1958), 39–40.
[40] Sandoz, Swinarski and Zimmerman, *Commentary on the Additional Protocols*, 1372–1373.
[41] Seen as 'virtually equivalent to prohibiting "reprisals" against protected persons', *ibid.*, 1374.
[42] *Military and Paramilitary Activities In and Against Nicaragua (Nicaragua v US)* (Merits), 76 ILR 5 at paragraphs 218–219.
[43] *Prosecutor v Martić* 108 ILR 40 at 46–48.

conflicts'.[44] This decision was criticised,[45] but it has nonetheless proved influential in forming an authoritative legal position. Indeed, the ICTY has since held in *Prosecutor v Kupreskić* that 'a customary rule of international law has emerged on the matter',[46] arguing that its formation can be evidenced through 'a widespread *opinio necessitatis* in international dealings'.[47]

The Trial Chamber in that case pointed to the vast majority involved in the adoption of UN General Assembly Resolution 2675,[48] the large number of States having ratified Additional Protocol I,[49] the opinion of the ICRC as expressed in 1983 to the parties to the 1949 Geneva Conventions,[50] and to the *Martić* Case. This position was further strengthened by the fact that those States which have participated in recent internal and international armed conflicts have, in the vast majority of cases, resisted the claim that belligerent reprisals against civilians are permitted.[51] The International Law Commission has also stated that common Article 3 'prohibits any reprisals in non-international armed conflicts with respect to the expressly prohibited acts as well as any other reprisals incompatible with the absolute requirement of humane treatment',[52] an opinion which the Trial Chamber in *Kupreskić* saw as authoritative confirmation of the rule.[53] The weight of opinion in favour of the prohibition of belligerent reprisals against civilian populations in all armed conflicts would accordingly seem to be overwhelming, and it certainly ought to be the case that such

---

[44] *Ibid.*, paragraph 17.

[45] See Greenwood, 'War Crimes Proceedings', 23–24.

[46] *Prosecutor v Kupreskić et al.* at paragraph 531.

[47] *Ibid.*, at paragraphs 532–533.

[48] See above at n. 36 and accompanying text.

[49] And therefore accepting the prohibition of reprisals against civilians in international conflicts. The UK, however, has lodged a fairly sweeping reservation to the relevant Article. See below at n. 56.

[50] See the memorandum of 7 May 1983 on the Iran–Iraq war in M. Sassoli and A. A. Bouvier (eds.), *How Does Law Protect in War?* (Geneva, 1999), 982.

[51] Indeed, only Iraq has made such a claim in practice (see *ibid.*). France and the UK have made the claim in abstract terms – France at the Diplomatic Conference leading to the Additional Protocols in 1974, where it voted against the provision on reprisals as 'contrary to existing international law' (*Diplomatic Conference on the Reaffirmation and Development of International Humanitarian Law Applicable in Armed Conflict, Official Records* (Berne, 1977), vol. VI, 162), and the UK in lodging its reservation to Additional Protocol I in 1998 (see below at n. 56).

[52] ILC's comments on former Article 14 of Part II of the Draft Articles on State Responsibility, 1995 *Yearbook of the International Law Commission*, vol. II at paragraph 18.

[53] At paragraph 534.

reprisals against civilians are prohibited even during internal armed conflict.[54]

Nonetheless, it must be difficult for those involved in armed conflict to disregard the possibility of belligerent reprisals where violations of the law are occurring, and Judge Aldrich has expressed concern, in the context of international conflicts under Additional Protocol I, that, given the inadequacy of existing oversight mechanisms, States have been so reluctant to lodge reservations regarding the limitations on reprisals contained in the instrument. He feels that, 'States are agreeing to sweeping prohibitions of reprisal which they will find it impossible to respect when faced with serious violations of the law by an enemy.'[55] The United Kingdom, however, upon ratification of Additional Protocol I in January 1998, made a full-blooded reservation to Articles 51–55 on the basis of reciprocity, which seems to imply the right to take belligerent reprisals against the civilian population.[56] This is clearly contrary to the views outlined above,[57] although to date there have been no objections by other States.

The parties to an armed conflict will inevitably find it difficult to resist the resort to belligerent reprisals in practice, and there is no reason

[54] The Trial Chamber in *Kupreskić* argued against them in principle by virtue of their barbaric and arbitrary nature, their characterisation as a blatant infringement of fundamental human rights, and the fact that they are no longer the only effective means of compelling compliance with international law since the prosecution and punishment of war criminals by national and international courts became more available and effective. See paragraphs 528–530.

[55] Aldrich, 'Compliance with the Law', 8–9.

[56] It provides in paragraph (m) that: 'The obligations of Articles 51 and 55 are accepted on the basis that any adverse party against which the United Kingdom might be engaged will itself scrupulously observe those obligations. If an adverse party makes serious and deliberate attacks, in violation of Article 51 or Article 52 against the civilian population or civilians or against civilian objects, or, in violation of Articles 53, 54 and 55, on objects or items protected by those Articles, the United Kingdom will regard itself as entitled to take measures otherwise prohibited by the Articles in question to the extent that it considers such measures necessary for the sole purpose of compelling the adverse party to cease committing violations under those Articles, but only after formal warning... Any measures thus taken by the United Kingdom will not be disproportionate to the violations giving rise thereto and will not involve any action prohibited by the Geneva Conventions of 1949...' Corrected letter of 28 January 1998 sent to the Swiss Government by Christopher Hulse, the UK Ambassador.

[57] Indeed, Pictet has clearly stated that 'a belligerent who disregarded the ban [on reprisals against civilians contained in Protocol I] and engaged in reprisals... would be committing a violation just like that of his adversary, and both parties would be equally guilty'. See Jean S. Pictet, *Development and Principles of International Humanitarian Law* (Dordrecht, 1985), 67–68.

to suppose that this will not also be the case during internal armed conflict. As with any system of self-help, even permissible reprisals are a dangerous mechanism, which ought to be discouraged. The possibility of their use in certain circumstances nevertheless remains.

Alternative means of securing compliance

Dissemination

Humanitarian law is inapplicable in peacetime.[58] Steps can nevertheless be taken to ensure the implementation of humanitarian law should armed conflict arise. There must be more likelihood of the relevant laws being observed if those involved in the conflict are aware in advance of their legal obligations. Steps towards encouraging such a 'culture of compliance'[59] will therefore involve the dissemination of that law as required by both Additional Protocol II and the Geneva Conventions of 1949. Each of the Geneva Conventions requires that:

The High Contracting Parties undertake, in time of peace as in time of war, to disseminate the text of the present Convention as widely as possible in their respective countries, and, in particular, to include the study thereof in their programmes of military and, if possible, civil instruction, so that the principles thereof may become known to the entire population.[60]

This must include the provisions of common Article 3, so that a degree of knowledge of the laws governing internal armed conflict ought to be imparted to a State's entire population. Article 19 of Additional Protocol II additionally requires that the Protocol be 'disseminated as widely as possible'. Neither of these provisions is particularly demanding, however, leaving the High Contracting Parties considerable leeway to decide how much education is given in this field, particularly as regards the civilian population. As such they are never likely to be adequate to ensure the education of *all* in the laws of internal armed conflict. Even so far as military instruction is concerned, the degree of dissemination provided varies immensely from State to State.[61] A significant level of training

---

[58] Although it can be *enforced* in peacetime through trials for war crimes and crimes against humanity.

[59] Christopher J. Greenwood, *International Humanitarian Law and the Laws of War*, (Preliminary Report for the Centennial Commemoration of the First Hague Peace Conference 1899) (The Hague, 1999), at paragraph 163; Louis Henkin, 'International Law: Politics, Values and Functions' (1989-iv) 216 *Rec des Cours* 67–87.

[60] Geneva Conventions Articles 47/48/127/144.

[61] Hilaire McCoubrey, *International Humanitarian Law* (Aldershot, 1990), 206–207.

may be given to the armies of the UK and USA, for example, with more detailed instruction being given to officers than to other ranks, but in some other States training is either inadequate or else non-existent. The armed forces of El Salvador, for example, received such poor education in humanitarian law that eventually the ICRC was called upon to give the necessary training.[62] It is not always in expected quarters, however, that instruction in humanitarian law falls short of the desired standard. A surprising example is Sweden, where instruction was given in 1984 at the Military School of Interpretation on torture techniques, the instructors openly believing humanitarian law to be unreal and of limited value in actual armed conflict.[63]

As regards education of the civilian population in the laws of war, very little takes place despite the aims of the Geneva Conventions and Additional Protocol II.[64] In the UK, humanitarian law is not taught in school, and the same is true of university (unless the student studies law, or international relations, including international law as an option). Judge Aldrich writes that he had the same experience in the USA.[65] This does not appear to be a wholly unsatisfactory situation, however, in that education of the entire population in the details of humanitarian law is probably unnecessary. More important is that the military and their legal advisers be highly educated in this regard. An entirely 'civilian' insurgent party to an internal armed conflict might have a dangerous ignorance of the laws governing the conflict, but in order for common Article 3 and Additional Protocol II to be applicable (i.e. in order for there to be an armed conflict at all), the relevant degree of organisation on their part[66] could, in all likelihood, be achieved only with the co-operation and guidance of several people with military experience in positions of authority.

Measures taken by third parties

Pictet described humanitarian norms in the following terms: 'not [as] an engagement concluded on the basis of reciprocity...[but] rather a series of unilateral engagements solemnly contracted before the world

---

[62] Ibid., 207, drawing from ICRC, Dissemination, no. 6, April 1987, 3–4.

[63] Ibid., See also Göran Melander, 'Torture Education During Military Service' in Christophe Swinarski (ed.), Studies and Essays on International Humanitarian Law and Red Cross Principles in Honour of Jean Pictet (Geneva, 1984), 411.

[64] Although, ironically, Yugoslavia always won plaudits from the ICRC for the extent to which its civilian population was educated in international humanitarian law.

[65] Aldrich, 'Compliance with the Law', 4–5.

[66] See above at pp. 36–38 and 103–105.

as represented by other Contracting Parties'.[67] This assertion might initially appear to be inconsistent with his opinion that humanitarian law is stronger than ordinary norms of international law, but Gasser has explained that acceptances by parties of humanitarian treaties are not mere unilateral declarations of doubtful legal effect, open to revocation at any time.[68] He believes instead that Pictet was seeking to underline the fundamental character of humanitarian obligations, i.e. that as moral values they transcend legal obligations and require the individual and unilateral commitment of each State, so that humanitarian norms can be seen as obligations *erga omnes*:[69] 'Obligations toward the international community as a whole [they are, by] their nature ... the concern of all States. In view of the importance of the rights involved, all States can be held to have a legal interest in their protection.'[70] How does this affect the regulation of internal armed conflict? Do the relevant provisions have the same character, or are obligations *erga omnes* confined to the international arena? The *Nicaragua* Case[71] stated that common Article 3 reflects 'elementary considerations of humanity' within the meaning of the *Corfu Channel* Case[72] and, to that extent, it must be said to represent an obligation *erga omnes*. Additional Protocol II must accordingly have the same status, in so far as it merely develops and supplements the provisions of common Article 3.[73] The entire community of States therefore has an interest in ensuring respect for the fundamental rules of internal armed conflict. Thus, States not involved in an internal armed conflict can, and should, take steps to ensure that the conflicting parties respect the humanitarian rules applicable.[74]

Other High Contracting Parties

Notwithstanding the status of the humanitarian laws of internal armed conflict as obligations which all States have an interest in seeing applied,

---

[67] Pictet, *Commentary IV*, 15.

[68] Hans-Peter Gasser, 'Ensuring Respect for the Geneva Conventions and Protocols: The Role of Third States and the United Nations' in Fox and Meyer, *Effecting Compliance*, 15 at 21.

[69] *Ibid.*

[70] *Barcelona Traction Light and Power Company Limited*, Judgment, ICJ Rep (1970) 4 at paragraphs 33–34.

[71] At paragraph 218.

[72] *Corfu Channel* Case, Merits, ICJ Rep (1949) 4 at 22.

[73] Gasser agrees: 'Ensuring Respect', 22–23.

[74] *Ibid.*, 23. The ICJ held the same view in the *Nicaragua* Case at paragraph 220. See also the Dissenting Opinion of Judge Schwebel at paragraph 259.

common Article 1 of the Geneva Conventions specifically requires those States party not only to respect the Conventions, but also to *'ensure respect'* for them.[75] As explained by the ICRC Commentaries, 'The proper working of the system of protection provided by the Convention demands in fact that the Contracting Parties should not be content merely to apply its provisions themselves, but should do everything in their power to ensure that the humanitarian principles underlying the Conventions are applied universally.'[76] This opinion was subsequently confirmed by a resolution of the 1968 Tehran Conference on Human Rights, which pointed out that 'States parties to the Red Cross Geneva Conventions sometimes fail to appreciate their responsibility to take steps to ensure the respect of these humanitarian rules in all circumstances by other States, even if they are not themselves directly involved in an armed conflict.'[77] Yet further strength was added to the obligation by the inclusion of a similar provision in Article 1 of Additional Protocol I. No corresponding provision is, however, found in Additional Protocol II. The enforcement of its provisions by third States accordingly rests entirely upon the extent to which they are obligations *erga omnes*. What steps may, then, legitimately be taken by third States to ensure respect for humanitarian norms during internal armed conflict?

As already stated, the primary obligation arising through humanitarian law in peacetime is that of dissemination. High Contracting Parties ought, therefore, to be examining each other's readiness to ensure respect for humanitarian law, e.g. through courses of education or the adoption of national legislation setting out the obligation to comply with humanitarian law. There is some evidence that States have shown a degree of willingness to take multilateral action in this respect, under the aegis of the Red Cross. Gasser points to the example of Resolution V of the 25th International Conference of the Red Cross and Red Crescent (Geneva, 1986),[78] which 'urges the governments of States Parties ... to fulfil entirely their obligation to adopt or supplement the relevant national legislation'.[79] States are, however, less keen to take measures on a

---

[75] Emphasis added.
[76] Jean S. Pictet, *Commentary on the Geneva Conventions of 12 August 1949, Volume III* (Geneva, 1960), 18.
[77] Resolution XXIII, International Conference on Human Rights, Tehran 1968.
[78] Gasser, 'Ensuring Respect', 26.
[79] Resolution V: National Measures to Implement International Humanitarian Law (1986) 255 *Int Rev of the Red Cross* 344 at 346–347.

bilateral basis.[80] This is not surprising, States being naturally reluctant to criticise other States lest they come under such scrutiny themselves.

When an armed conflict is in progress, the situation becomes much more dangerous as regards action by third States to enforce humanitarian law – such steps could easily be construed as interference, leading to an escalation of hostilities. The exact content of the obligation to ensure respect in such cases is therefore vital and, not surprisingly, a matter of some debate. The International Court of Justice sought to clarify the issue in the *Nicaragua* Case, holding that the United States, not being a party to the conflict between the Nicaraguan Government and the insurgent *Contras*, was obliged to ensure respect for the Geneva Conventions (in this case, common Article 3) by the parties to the conflict, but, more especially, by that party which it was supporting (i.e. the *Contras*).[81] The United States was thus required not to encourage violations of humanitarian law, an obligation clearly breached by the distribution of a manual on methods of non-conventional warfare, containing advice on how to violate basic rules of humanitarian law.[82] Third States are therefore required not to encourage those involved in armed conflict to violate humanitarian law, an obligation which grows stronger as regards ensuring respect for humanitarian law by an ally or a party with which the State has close links.[83]

Beyond this, there are more active measures available to third States in seeking to ensure the application of humanitarian law by parties to an internal armed conflict, although how far they can go in this regard is controversial. The first, and most obvious, step is to exert diplomatic pressure upon the party (or parties) violating humanitarian law, either by lodging protests with ambassadors present in the third State, or through representatives in the area of conflict. Formal diplomatic channels are ordinarily available only with respect to government parties, but States with influence over insurgents are nevertheless likely to have channels of communication sufficient to bring pressure to bear upon the insurgent party as regards their legal obligations. Of course, the extent to which such action occurs is difficult to discover, diplomatic representations being typically confidential.

Where diplomatic action fails to achieve the observance of humanitarian law, States might opt to mobilise shame by publicly denouncing

---

[80] Gasser, 'Ensuring Respect', 26, finds no evidence of such scrutiny.
[81] *Nicaragua* Case at paragraph 220.
[82] *Ibid.*, paragraphs 254–256.
[83] Gasser, 'Ensuring Respect', 28.

violations of the law by the party responsible.[84] Further, more force-ful, measures on the basis of common Article 1 are considered by San-doz to be, at best, inadvisable and, at worst, legally impermissible: 'the most that can be done is to take diplomatic measures or publicly de-nounce violations. It would be improper, and probably dangerous, to impose non-military sanctions (and still more obviously, to impose mil-itary sanctions or any form of intervention).'[85] Other writers disagree, asserting that a range of more coercive measures may be taken unilat-erally by third States under the guise of either retortion or (unarmed) reprisal.[86]

Retortion is an unfriendly, even damaging, act. In contrast to reprisals, however, it is perfectly valid under international law,[87] although where such an act breaches an existing international agreement between the two States it would amount to a reprisal, and so must be proportionate to the original violation. Most acts of retortion can only be aimed at governmental parties, but steps to promote compliance may neverthe-less be possible against insurgents, e.g. restrictions on aid in the form of arms or finance, other forms of trade, or the threat that they will not be dealt with favourably should they ultimately triumph (although this last option is unlikely where the State in turmoil is important to the third State as a trade partner, or through ownership of valuable nat-ural resources, for example). At any rate, it is unusual for third States individually to go beyond diplomacy and public denunciation.[88]

There are, of course, limits to the action which may be taken by third States, and it is impermissible to resort unilaterally to armed force in order to enforce humanitarian law. This would not only be a clear intervention in the conflict, risking a transformation of its character and an escalation of hostilities, but is strictly prohibited by Article 2(4)

---

[84] See statements made by the European Union in the context of conflicts in Liberia and Chechnya as cited in *Tadić* (Jurisdiction) at paragraphs 113 and 115.

[85] Sandoz, 'Implementing Humanitarian Law', 266.

[86] See, for example, Gasser, 'Ensuring Respect', 29, and Umesh Palwankar, 'Measures Available to States for Fulfilling their Obligation to Ensure Respect for International Humanitarian Law' (1994) 298 *Int Rev of the Red Cross* 9.

[87] E.g. the expulsion of diplomats and breaking of diplomatic relations, or restrictions on exports and imports, etc. See Palwankar, 'Measures Available to States', 16–17.

[88] The lack of a Protecting Power system for internal armed conflict is also relevant here, in that no third party other than the ICRC is available to scrutinise the application of humanitarian law and safeguard the interests of the parties to the conflict. This is in contrast to the system employed in international armed conflict (see Geneva Conventions Articles 8/8/8/9), although the system of Protecting Powers has been virtually ignored in any case.

of the UN Charter. Allowing such action would, furthermore, be contrary to everything humanitarian law stands for: 'international humanitarian law starts off from the premise that any armed conflict results in human suffering, and proceeds to elaborate a body of rules *meant precisely to alleviate this very suffering*. It would indeed be logically and legally indefensible to deduce that that same law *itself allows*, even in extreme cases, for the use of armed force.'[89] Common Article 1 of the Geneva Conventions cannot therefore constitute any basis for the use of force to ensure respect for humanitarian law. In fact, it has been argued that there is no support at all, either in the *travaux préparatoires* or in State practice, for the broad interpretation placed on common Article 1 by some writers. Rather, Article 1 was intended merely as a requirement that States ensure that those subject to their authority comply with the Conventions and, more recently, as a basis on which third States can make representations to the belligerents regarding their conduct.[90]

Despite common Article 1, the wide range of measures available to third States, and the status of the fundamental aspects of humanitarian law as obligations *erga omnes*, it is difficult to reach any firm conclusion on how third States have applied the obligation during internal armed conflicts. Academic opinion is firmly divided. Sandoz, for example, claims that States have not been keen to implement common Article 1, and make little effort to monitor the extent to which it is observed.[91] In contrast, Gasser argues that, although no clear evidence is available, there is reason to believe that governments do act to support a better respect for humanitarian law by State parties to armed conflict, confidentially and on a bilateral level. He makes no judgement, however, as to whether efforts are as strenuous regarding internal armed conflict and non-State parties.[92] Although arguing that States do take action, Gasser significantly accepts that:

A brief look at the behaviour of governments leaves no doubt that they do not feel themselves to be under a legal obligation to act if humanitarian law is being flouted by a party to an armed conflict. If third parties actually do act, they do so if and when they feel that a *démarche* is also in their own interest or if public

---

[89] Palwankar, 'Measures Available to States', 20–21.
[90] Greenwood, 'War Crimes Proceedings', 23, referring to Adam Roberts, 'The Laws of War: Problems of Implementation' in European Commission, *Law in Humanitarian Crises* (Luxembourg, 1996), vol. I, 13 at 30–32.
[91] 'Implementing Humanitarian Law', 266.
[92] 'Ensuring Respect', 31.

pressure at home is such that to act seems wiser than to run counter to public opinion.[93]

The International Committee of the Red Cross

The ICRC plays an important role during internal armed conflict, although this is more through encouragement than actual enforcement.[94] No effective sanction is practically available to the organisation to ensure the application of humanitarian law except perhaps the withdrawal of humanitarian aid, which would never be used as a threat or a bargaining counter. The protection and assistance of those affected by armed conflict is, after all, the *raison d'être* of the organisation. To use aid as a tool for the enforcement of the law would thus be indefensible.

ICRC action to implement the law moves instead along other lines,[95] the first of which is through dissemination. While the primary responsibility in this regard lies with States, the ICRC is nevertheless very active in assisting the process, producing a range of teaching materials and running courses on humanitarian law. It also shares its expertise with nationals of the country in which it is working, enabling them to spread the humanitarian message in the local language and having regard for local culture and tradition. Its impact is accordingly made as broad as possible. Secondly, as far as encouragement to implement the law is concerned, the ICRC prefers confidential approaches to the conflicting parties in an effort to persuade them to apply the law: 'Most of the time, when ICRC representatives engage public authorities in discussion, they do not argue law at all, whether humanitarian law or general human rights law. They try to create a confidential climate in which moral reasoning can make an impact on the situation.'[96] The ICRC might also make approaches to particular third States, asking that they use their influence to achieve observance of humanitarian law.

Where violations are particularly serious and continue despite such confidential efforts, the ICRC may opt to publicise those facts, in the hope that this will shame the parties concerned into moderating their

---

[93] *Ibid.*, 32.

[94] On ICRC and United Nations action, see Hilaire McCoubrey and Nigel D. White, *International Organizations and Civil Wars* (Aldershot, 1995), especially chapters 2 and 10.

[95] Marion Harroff-Tavel, 'Action Taken by the International Committee of the Red Cross in Situations of Internal Violence' (1993) 294 *Int Rev of the Red Cross* 195; Gasser, 'Ensuring Respect', 44–48; David P. Forsythe, 'The International Committee of the Red Cross' in Fox and Meyer, *Effecting Compliance*, 83; and Hans Haug (ed.), *Humanity for All: The International Red Cross and Red Crescent Movement* (Berne, 1993).

[96] Forsythe, 'The ICRC', 93.

behaviour, possibly also reminding the international community of their collective responsibility under common Article 1 to ensure compliance with the law.[97] Public statements, however, are not readily made by the ICRC. The organisation prefers to work quietly and confidentially if possible, in order to gain the trust of the parties to the conflict. A 1981 policy document in fact provided that public statements should only be made (a) if the violations are major and repeated; (b) if steps taken confidentially have not succeeded in putting an end to the violations; (c) if such publicity is in the interest of the persons or populations affected or threatened; and (d) if the ICRC delegates have witnessed the violations with their own eyes, or if the existence and extent of the breaches have been established by reliable and verifiable sources.[98] The mobilisation of shame may be an effective tool, bringing widespread condemnation and pressure to bear upon violators of the law, but much of the ICRC's valuable work would be impossible absent the confidential approach which it favours.

Finally, the ICRC may provide good offices in order to promote the adoption of agreements between the parties under common Article 3(2). As already explained, however,[99] this suffers from the defect that such offers need not be accepted by the parties to the conflict. As a result, any such agreements are truly exceptional. The ICRC, then, does little actively to *enforce* humanitarian law. That is not its purpose. Rather, it seeks to persuade and cajole the parties involved into observing the relevant humanitarian provisions, or else to persuade third States to ensure respect for the law.

The United Nations

The United Nations, representing the international community, also has an important role to play in ensuring respect for humanitarian law. Despite Article 2(7) of the UN Charter, prohibiting interference in the internal affairs of Member States, the United Nations clearly does have the ability to act in relation to internal armed conflicts. Article 2(7) itself provides that the prohibition contained therein is not prejudicial to

---

[97] E.g. the appeal made to parties in Bosnia-Herzegovina on 13 August 1992 to respect their humanitarian obligations. At the same time the ICRC reminded the community of States that they also were responsible for making sure that the law was applied. See Gasser, 'Ensuring Respect', 47.

[98] 'Action by the International Committee of the Red Cross in the Event of Breaches of International Humanitarian Law' (1981) 221 *Int Rev of the Red Cross* 76 at 81.

[99] See above at pp. 63–65.

enforcement action which may be taken under Chapter VII. The organisation is therefore free to act where an internal armed conflict is deemed by the Security Council to threaten international peace and security.[100] Given that many conflicts will have an effect on neighbouring States, this situation is not difficult to envisage. The vital question in situations where the United Nations does become involved in an internal armed conflict through this process is just what steps can be legitimately undertaken by the organisation for the enforcement of humanitarian law. The primary responsibility for the maintenance of international peace and security lies with the Security Council,[101] which has various measures available to it under Chapter VII with the aim of maintaining or restoring international peace and security, i.e. an end to hostilities. Ending hostilities is not, however, necessarily the same as ensuring that ongoing hostilities are conducted in accordance with humanitarian law. A conflict conducted entirely within the regulation of the relevant humanitarian laws could nevertheless constitute a threat to international peace and security. Where hostilities are conducted without regard for the law, however, the Security Council may act to promote the application of humanitarian law in an effort to minimise the danger to the international community.[102] To that end, certain non-forceful measures may be employed under Article 41 of the UN Charter (e.g. interruption of economic relations, severing of diplomatic relations, etc.), which Member States are bound to apply if called upon to do so.[103] Where such action is unsuccessful, the use of armed force can ultimately be authorised by the Security Council. The action taken by Allied troops in the 1991 Gulf Conflict was authorised in this way,[104] and although that situation was international in nature, there would appear to be

---

[100] Under Article 39 of the UN Charter. See SC Resolution 688 of 5 April 1991 dealing with protection of the Kurds in Northern Iraq. The resolution was also seen as a call to Iraq to observe its obligations under common Article 3, the application of which was taken for granted, as discussed by Gasser, 'Ensuring Respect', 39. Another example is SC Resolution 770 of 13 August 1992, dealing with the conflict in the former Yugoslavia.

[101] Article 24(1).

[102] Gasser feels that 'Ensuring compliance with humanitarian law by parties to an ongoing armed conflict is certainly part of that responsibility [i.e. the responsibility to restore international peace and security].' See 'Ensuring Respect', 37.

[103] Article 25 of the Charter states that UN Members agree to accept and carry out the decisions of the Security Council. Examples are SC Resolution 713 of 1991 imposing an arms embargo on the whole former Yugoslavia region, and SC Resolution 757 of 1992 imposing economic sanctions on the Federal Republic of Yugoslavia.

[104] Through SC Resolution 678 of 29 November 1990.

no obstacle to such measures in the context of internal armed conflicts where it was deemed to be necessary.[105]

In the aftermath of the Gulf Conflict, concern arose about the situation of internal unrest in Iraq, particularly the repression of the Kurdish and Shiite minorities. The coalition States therefore requested the UN Secretary-General to establish a UN force to deal with the problem. He had no authority to do this, however, and Iraq refused consent for a peacekeeping force. The Security Council also refused to create the force, certain members being opposed to humanitarian action within a State. Instead, the Security Council adopted Resolution 688,[106] condemning the repression of the Iraqi civilian population and characterising it as a threat to international peace and security in the region. The resolution further insisted that Iraq allow humanitarian organisations access and appealed to Member States to contribute to the humanitarian relief efforts, in response to which certain coalition States created safety zones in Iraq and enforced a 'no-fly' policy against Iraqi aircraft in those areas. It would therefore appear that humanitarian intervention is possible under the general umbrella of Security Council action, but only where the situation threatens international peace and security.[107]

Of course, force used in the above ways differs from peacekeeping projects aimed solely at *maintaining* peace rather than actively restoring it or protecting sections of the population, and must be based upon the UN Charter rather than humanitarian law.[108] Any forcible measures, however, may result in an escalation of hostilities, and it seems advisable to abstain from the use of force if at all possible in what are already volatile situations. What more peaceful avenues are open to the United Nations?

Both the Security Council and the General Assembly have the capacity to make official statements and appeals to the parties to armed

---

[105] In the civil conflict in Somalia, for example, the Security Council authorised the use of force to protect the delivery of humanitarian aid, having already determined that the conflict was a threat to international peace and security. See SC Resolution 794 (1992).

[106] SC Resolution 688, 5 April 1991, 30 ILM 858 (1991).

[107] Rosalyn Higgins, *Problems and Process: International Law and How We Use it* (Oxford, 1994), 254–257. On humanitarian intervention in international law generally, see Robert Y. Jennings and Arthur Watts (eds.), *Oppenheim's International Law, Volume 1*, 9th edn (London, 1992), 442–444.

[108] As Palwankar elaborates, 'Measures Available to States', 20: 'The lawfulness of the use of force in such circumstances is strictly limited to this goal, and *cannot be derived* from any rule or provision of *international humanitarian law* . . . ' See the explanation for this above at pp. 109–110 and 248–249.

conflicts regarding the applicability of humanitarian law, calling for its respect and denouncing violations.[109] The General Assembly can, under Article 11 of the UN Charter, furthermore recommend its Members to adopt sanctions or countermeasures against those parties failing to meet their humanitarian obligations. Alternatively, it can draw the attention of its Members to specific situations without making any explicit recommendation, which could amount to an implicit authorisation of countermeasures.[110] The General Assembly is prevented from taking any such action, however, where the Security Council is dealing with the situation.[111] In the most pressing of conflict situations it is therefore unlikely that the General Assembly will be called upon to act unless the Security Council requests it. The Security Council and General Assembly may instead prefer simply to draw the attention of third States to their duty to ensure respect for international humanitarian law, as in the contexts of the conflict in the former Yugoslavia[112] and the Israeli Occupied Territories.[113] It seems unlikely, however, that States which show no desire to observe this duty in the normal course of affairs will be any more likely to do so following a reminder from the United Nations, especially given the appalling record of compliance with most UN requests and appeals on humanitarian law.

Other United Nations organs may also seek to promote the observance of humanitarian law. First, the Secretary-General can act upon requests from the Security Council or General Assembly,[114] organising enquiries into specific situations before reporting back.[115] He also has a right of initiative as set out in Article 99 of the Charter, allowing him to bring any matter which he perceives as a threat to international peace and

---

[109] The Security Council acting under Article 39 of the Charter, and the General Assembly under Article 11(2). The Security Council has made several such appeals in the context of the Yugoslav conflict, as well as in international situations such as the Israeli Occupied Territories. As for the General Assembly, see UNGA Resolutions 40/137 of 31 December 1985, 43/139 of 8 December 1988, 44/161 of 15 December 1989, and 45/174 of 18 December 1990 on the conflict in Afghanistan, and Resolutions 43/145 of 8 December 1988 and 44/165 of 15 December 1989 on the civil conflict in El Salvador.

[110] Palwankar, 'Measures Available to States', 21, citing Resolution A/RES/ES.6/2 of 14 January 1980 which dealt with the Soviet armed intervention in Afghanistan, but without naming the USSR.

[111] UN Charter Article 12.

[112] SC Resolution 770 of 13 August 1992.

[113] UNGA Resolution 45/69 of 6 December 1990.

[114] UN Charter Article 98.

[115] As in the process leading to the creation of the International Criminal Tribunals for the former Yugoslavia and Rwanda.

security to the attention of the Security Council. His role can therefore be important, but actual enforcement is ultimately left to the Security Council. The United Nations Commission on Human Rights and the Human Rights Committee also have important roles to play in protecting civilians during internal armed conflict,[116] and the International Court of Justice can pass judgments and opinions on matters relevant to armed conflicts in both its contentious[117] and its advisory jurisdiction.[118] Of course, no judgment can be made on the factors underlying the armed conflict by the Court acting in the latter function, and an advisory opinion alone cannot enforce the application of humanitarian law. It may, however, persuade the Security Council to take action.

The above steps have had only limited effect for internal armed conflicts, and the United Nations has proved sadly ineffective at ensuring the application of humanitarian law. The establishment by the Security Council, acting under Chapter VII, of International Criminal Tribunals to try those responsible for breaches of humanitarian law in the conflicts in Rwanda and the former Yugoslavia,[119] however, represented important steps in the UN's fight to enforce international humanitarian law,[120] and the effectiveness of the Tribunals has been addressed above.[121] Nonetheless, the consistent and effective enforcement of humanitarian law still presents the international community with substantial problems.

Enforcement of human rights law

In seeking to ensure respect for humanitarian values in armed conflict, however, the international community is not limited to humanitarian law. The more developed machinery for the enforcement of human rights law also has an important role to play. The United Nations is bound to promote and encourage respect for human rights,[122] and Member States are required to take relevant action in this regard.[123] To

[116] As discussed below in the context of the enforcement of human rights law during internal armed conflict. Of course, human rights law mirrors humanitarian law in some aspects, as discussed in chapter 5.

[117] As in the *Nicaragua* Case.

[118] Available to UN organs under Article 96 of the Charter. See, for example, *Advisory Opinion on the Threat or Use of Nuclear Weapons* 35 ILM 809 (1996).

[119] See chapter 4.

[120] Steps built upon by the adoption of a Statute for the International Criminal Court.

[121] At pp. 233–235 and chapter 4.

[122] UN Charter Articles 1(3) and 55.

[123] UN Charter Article 56.

the extent that human rights coincide with the humanitarian law of internal armed conflict, this is dealt with in the preceding sections of this chapter. Indeed, since 'Many of the humanitarian law rules applicable to internal armed conflicts are indistinguishable from human rights provisions',[124] the enforcement of human rights can in some respects be equated to, or even contained within, the enforcement of humanitarian law. Separate enforcement mechanisms nevertheless exist for human rights, and it is to these that we now turn.

United Nations enforcement and supervision

Broadly speaking, the United Nations has two methods of promoting compliance with human rights law – through the UN Commission on Human Rights and the Human Rights Committee. Turning first to the more political avenue of the Commission on Human Rights and its Subcommission on the Prevention of Racial Discrimination and the Protection of Minorities,[125] the main supervision measures available are ECOSOC Resolutions 1235[126] and 1503[127] which establish public and confidential procedures for dealing with alleged human rights violations.[128] The system has, however, had relatively little success, and is particularly

---

[124] Gasser, 'Ensuring Respect', 35.

[125] Established in 1946 by ECOSOC under its general powers in Article 62 of the UN Charter and, more specifically as regards the setting up of Commissions, Article 68. On the Commission in general, see Philip Alston, 'The Commission on Human Rights' in Philip Alston (ed.), *The United Nations and Human Rights* (Oxford, 1992), 126, and Howard Tolley Jr, *The United Nations Commission on Human Rights* (Boulder, 1987). Despite its name, the Subcommission deals with all aspects of human rights violations, and its members serve (at least theoretically) in an independent capacity, although nominated by their governments, and many are equally instruments of their government as their counterparts on the Commission itself. See Tom J. Farer, 'The United Nations and Human Rights: More than a Whimper, Less than a Roar' in Richard P. Claude and Burns H. Weston (eds.), *Human Rights in the World Community: Issues and Action*, 2nd edn (Philadelphia, 1992), 227 at 231. It has consistently been accepted that, 'When experts have to deal with problems in which political considerations are deeply embedded, it is quixotic to suppose that their views will not be tinged with attitudes which reflect their national affiliations more than their technical qualifications.' (Inis L. Claude Jr, 'The Nature and Status of the Subcommission on Prevention of Discrimination and Protection of Minorities' (1951) 5 *International Organization* 300 at 303.) On the Subcommission see Tolley, *The UN Commission*, 163–186 and Asbjörn Eide, 'The Subcommission on Prevention of Discrimination and Protection of Minorities' in Alston, *The UN and Human Rights*, 211.

[126] ECOSOC Resolution 1235 (XLII) of 6 June 1967.

[127] ECOSOC Resolution 1503 (XLVIII) of 27 May 1970.

[128] For a detailed account of these procedures see Tolley, *The UN Commission*, 55–82 and Alston, 'The Commission on Human Rights', 126 ff.

poor in the context of internal armed conflict. The investigation process takes too long, and the schedule of Subcommission Working Group meetings[129] renders the system impotent to protect those in life-and-death situations. Furthermore, only exposure after the fact can be threatened, unless the situation is grave enough to warrant action under Chapter VII. The governmental nature of the Commission, envisaged as an enticement for States to co-operate, instead serves only to make enforcement through that route virtually impossible. Often no action is taken in even the most extreme situations, and complaints have inevitably triggered divisions along political and ideological lines.[130] As Farer explains:

> The United Nations is now a participant, however ambivalent, in the defense of human rights. That is indisputable. Equally indisputable is its highly selective attitude toward enforcement and its refusal in all cases other than Rhodesia and South Africa to recommend sanctions.
>
> There is not much sympathy among UN members for unauthorized humanitarian intervention. Being weak and vulnerable states, most members see themselves only as objects of intervention. Moreover, being former colonies or *de facto* dependencies of powerful states, most recall the many occasions in the past when the words 'humanitarian intervention' served as a fig-leaf for the crass thrust of imperial interests. Anxious to build walls of precedent behind which to shelter, they have condemned intervention even by other Third World states against irredeemably barbarous regimes.[131]

Perhaps more effective has been the role of the UN Commission on Human Rights in undertaking investigations into the human rights situation in selected States, particularly through the appointment of Special Rapporteurs, a procedure which has been applied to States undergoing internal armed conflict.[132] In a demonstration of the close relationship between human rights and humanitarian law, and illustrating the role that human rights mechanisms have to play in the implementation of humanitarian law, the Special Rapporteurs have not confined themselves to statements on the respect for human rights law. They have been more than willing to venture also into the sphere of the laws of armed conflict. Felix Ermacora, for example, stated in his 1994 report on the situation of human rights in Afghanistan that 'Several thousand civilians

---

[129] To whom initial Resolution 1503 complaints must be addressed.

[130] Tolley, *The UN Commission*, 67–70. See also Amnesty International, '1997 UN Commission on Human Rights – 50 Years Old' (Amnesty International, 1997).

[131] Farer, 'The UN and Human Rights', 240.

[132] See, for example, the reports of the Special Rapporteurs on human rights in Afghanistan (from 1985) and the former Yugoslavia (from 1992).

have been killed and many more injured since 1994 in fierce military conflict . . . there is a failure to observe even the most basic elements of humanitarian law as applied to civilians.'[133] Tadeusz Mazowiecki likewise drew attention to violations of humanitarian law perpetrated in various parts of the former Yugoslavia in his reports.[134]

Alternative United Nations action comes through enforcement of the International Covenant on Civil and Political Rights by the Human Rights Committee.[135] It has been suggested that:

The activities of Convention-based systems . . . are in a way building on firmer ground. In terms of law they are usually more tidy, the obligations of states and the mandates of organs are explicit, international measures of implementation are prescribed, and the process of negotiation and ratification gives reason to hope that once states have committed themselves they are serious about it, even in the absence of direct enforcement.[136]

This would seem to be a rather weak assumption,[137] and just how effective the Human Rights Committee is in encouraging States to respect their human rights obligations under the Covenant is worthy of examination.

The Human Rights Committee is an impartial organisation,[138] performing three supervisory functions under the Covenant – the examination of State reports, and the settlement of inter-State and individual complaints. The reporting procedure under Article 40 is compulsory, with reports submitted by States being studied by the Committee, which then makes general comments and submits these to the States parties

[133] Report of Special Rapporteur: Situation of Human Rights in Afghanistan, UN Doc. A/49/650, 8 November 1994, at paragraph 91.

[134] See, for example, Report of Special Rapporteur, Situation of Human Rights in the former Yugoslavia, UN Doc. A/49/641; S/1994/1252, 4 November 1994, at paragraphs 25–34, outlining military attacks upon civilians in Bosnia-Herzegovina. Violations of humanitarian law as well as human rights law have continued to be reported by subsequent Special Rapporteurs. See, for example, UN Doc. A/53/322, 11 September 1998, at paragraph 86, where Special Rapporteur Jiri Dienstbier denounces abductions in Kosovo as 'grave violations of basic principles of international human rights and humanitarian law'.

[135] ICCPR Article 28. See Torkel Opsahl, 'The Human Rights Committee' in Alston, *The UN and Human Rights*, 369, and Dominic McGoldrick, *The Human Rights Committee* (Oxford, 1994), 44.

[136] Torkel Opsahl, 'Instruments of Implementation of Human Rights' (1989) 10 *HRLJ* 13 at 19.

[137] Accepted as such by Opsahl, *ibid.*, n. 20.

[138] Although again members are nominated by States. Wages are paid by the UN, however, which might serve to distance the members from any overwhelming sense of national fidelity.

and to ECOSOC.[139] Reports must be made in a specific form, setting out the legal framework in place in the State (i.e. whether there is a constitution or bill of rights, etc.), then stating the legal measures being taken to protect the rights set out in the Covenant. Further periodic reports must update this Article by Article, paying particular attention to the response of the Committee to previous reports. The underlying idea is that State reports are studied through a process of 'constructive dialogue', with the State parties being invited to present the report, and to answer questions posed by the Committee with respect to it.

The procedure is deeply flawed as regards the protection of human rights during internal conflict. It had been hoped that the system would lead to compliance through internal as well as international accountability, with States being encouraged to publish the report, thus promoting debate at the domestic level. Reporting is, however, an extremely partial method of divulging information, the authors commonly being the perpetrators of abuse.[140] Furthermore, many States undergoing internal armed conflict simply do not report at all. Reports from Angola, Haiti, the Philippines, Rwanda and Somalia are currently well overdue,[141] and although Uruguay submitted its third periodic report on 26 March 1991, none were submitted in the 1970s or early 1980s when that State was gripped by internal turmoil. Some governments do make an effort to submit reports to the Committee despite internal conflict,[142] although the value of this exercise is open to doubt in light of their typical quality.

El Salvador's initial report of 2 June 1983 admitted that as long as military action continued, there would be violations of human rights (especially the right to life), and that excesses had been committed by both sides.[143] When the second report[144] was considered, the Human

---

[139] Article 40(4). See Bernhard Graefrath, 'Reporting and Complaint Systems in Universal Human Rights Treaties' in Allan Rosas and Jan E. Helgesen (eds.), *Human Rights in a Changing East–West Perspective* (London, 1990) 290; McGoldrick, *The Human Rights Committee*, 62; and Michael O'Flaherty, *Human Rights and the UN: Practice Before the Treaty Bodies* (London, 1996), 32–45.

[140] Of course abuses are equally likely to be perpetrated by insurgents, but there is no mechanism for them to be bound by the Covenant or to report on their human rights record. See above at p. 44 and n. 50.

[141] For example, Angola currently has reports overdue from 31 January 1994 and 9 April 1998; Bosnia-Herzegovina from 5 March 1993 and 1998; Rwanda from 10 April 1992, 31 January 1995 and 10 April 1997; and Somalia from 23 April 1991 and 1996.

[142] E.g. El Salvador, Afghanistan, Iraq and Sri Lanka.

[143] *Report of the Human Rights Committee*, UN Doc. A/39/40 (1984), 12 at paragraph 72.

[144] Received 26 August 1993.

Rights Committee found that it:

neither accurately nor candidly represent[ed] the actual human rights situation in El Salvador in the period covered by the report, during which armed conflict and massive violations of human rights have been followed by a peace process...In particular, it provide[d] little relevant information on such key areas as the protection of the right to life under Article 6 of the Covenant, the prohibition of torture under Article 7, the right to liberty and security of person under Article 9 and the guarantee of due process under the law in accordance with Article 14.[145]

Many of the questions put to the delegation during discussions were felt by the Committee to have been left unanswered.[146]

Afghanistan's report considered in 1985 was held to be unrealistic and too concise,[147] the Human Rights Committee openly questioning how laws and remedies could be successfully implemented given the situation in the country. One member even suggested that the motivation for Afghanistan's acceptance of the Covenant had been the protection of its public image rather than its population.[148] Iraq has also been the subject of criticism by the Human Rights Committee, and when it submitted its third periodic report in June 1991, following the Gulf Conflict and during internal difficulties involving Kurdish and Shiite sections of its population, the Committee 'had hoped that a constructive dialogue between [it] and Iraq would be possible, [but] unfortunately that had not proven to be the case. Rather, the representative of the State party had engaged in a kind of monologue or "stonewalling" and had sought constantly to evade certain issues.'[149] The report was simply an attempt to present the Iraqi Government's views on the Gulf crisis and its aftermath without addressing the issue of Iraq's compliance with human rights law. Violations committed after 2 August 1990 were not addressed, and the Committee expressed serious concern over the repressive action being taken against Kurds and Shiites.[150]

Sri Lanka, in contrast, has submitted three reports during its internal armed conflict, discussions of which have seen the Human Rights Committee voice its concern over human rights violations and shortcomings of the reports,[151] but which have nevertheless yielded

---

[145] *Report of the Human Rights Committee*, UN Doc. A/49/40 (1994), 38 at paragraph 210.
[146] *Ibid.*, paragraph 211.
[147] *Report of the Human Rights Committee*, UN Doc. A/40/40 (1985), 114 at paragraph 590.
[148] *Ibid.*, paragraph 592.
[149] *Report of the Human Rights Committee*, UN Doc. A/46/40 (1991), 150 at paragraph 651.
[150] *Ibid.*, paragraphs 652–653, and *Report of the Human Rights Committee*, UN Doc. A/47/40 (1992), 41 at paragraph 214.
[151] *Report of the Human Rights Committee*, UN Doc. A/46/40 (1991), 114 at paragraph 490.

'fruitful' discussions.[152] The most recent was received by the Committee in July 1994 and considered the following year.[153] Although the report was submitted late, and was considered unsatisfactory 'in that it failed to provide detailed information on the actual implementation in practice of the provisions of the Covenant', the Human Rights Committee nevertheless expressed its 'gratitude to the delegation for the supplementary information it provided orally in answer to both the written and oral questions posed by members of the Committee', and 'welcome[d] the initiatives being undertaken by the Government to further the promotion and protection of human rights'.[154]

The reporting procedure of the Human Rights Committee is clearly ineffective. States disregard their obligation to report at no penalty, and those reports submitted are frequently unacceptable. Furthermore, representatives are often uncooperative during discussions of the reports, and the Committee lacks the power to make States observe its suggestions or directions. Aimed at the promotion of human rights rather than their enforcement, in situations of internal conflict the system has so far failed.

Two further procedures are available to enforce the obligations in the Covenant – inter-State complaints under Articles 41–43, and individual communications under the first Optional Protocol. Turning first to inter-State complaints, under Article 41 a State party may declare that it recognises the competence of the Human Rights Committee to receive communications to the effect that another State is failing to fulfil its obligations under the Covenant. This optional process has been accepted by only a relatively small proportion of High Contracting Parties.[155] States are naturally reluctant to condemn the human rights record of others, leaving themselves open to criticism in the future, and the politically sensitive nature of such accusations would inevitably prove problematical. The situation is different as regards individual complaints. Governed by the first Optional Protocol to the Covenant,[156] many more States have accepted its application,[157] although few have been in the arena of internal armed conflict, and even the majority of those States which *have* been in that position have had no claims brought against

---

[152] *Ibid.*, paragraph 491.
[153] See UN Doc. A/50/40 (1995).
[154] *Ibid.*, paragraphs 436 ff.
[155] Of 144 States party, 47 had made Article 41 declarations as at 9 December 1999.
[156] For its background and an explanation of the various requirements to be met for a communication to be admissible, see McGoldrick, *The Human Rights Committee*, 120 and O'Flaherty, *Human Rights and the UN*, 47–52.
[157] Ninety-five as at 9 December 1999.

them.[158] One State stands out, however, in the jurisprudence of the Human Rights Committee under the Optional Protocol.

For several years prior to 1985, there was a total breakdown of law and order in Uruguay. Whether the situation ever reached one of true internal armed conflict so as to be governed by humanitarian law is a difficult question, but the Government declared a state of 'internal war' in April 1972, implementing emergency legislation the operation of which was extended annually.[159] Nevertheless, Uruguay had ratified the Optional Protocol to the ICCPR in 1970 and it entered into force on 23 March 1976, since when the State has been the subject of countless individual complaints. Most have involved people arrested and detained, often incommunicado, for subversive activities contrary to State security under the 'prompt security measures' adopted to combat the situation. As a result, the Human Rights Committee has found Uruguay to have committed many violations of the Covenant – mainly of the right to life (Article 6),[160] the right to be free from torture and cruel, inhuman or degrading treatment (Article 7),[161] the right to liberty (Article 9),[162] and guarantees of due process (Article 14).[163] These would clearly correspond to provisions of humanitarian law if committed during armed conflict, although violations of purely human rights provisions were also found, for example of Articles 22(1)[164] and 25.[165]

Finding Uruguay to have breached certain of its human rights obliga-tions does not, however, necessarily equate to actual enforcement of the law. Final decisions of the Human Rights Committee are given in the form of 'views' which, although quasi-judicial in style, were intended

---

[158] To date, and which have been publicised by the Human Rights Committee. Examples are Angola (Optional Protocol in force from 10 April 1992), the Philippines (22 November 1989) and Somalia (24 April 1990). The Optional Protocol came into force for Nicaragua on 12 June 1980, and it has since been the subject of one published complaint. This criticism is less easy to level at the European human rights system in light of the numerous cases brought against Turkey.

[159] This did not necessarily represent an admission by the Government that the situation was an armed conflict. Rather it provided for the suspension of individual liberties and the imposition of martial law in certain areas. See *Keesing's Contemporary Archives of World Events* (1973), 25411.

[160] E.g. *Dermit v Uruguay* 71 ILR 354.

[161] E.g. *López v Uruguay* 68 ILR 29; *Bleier v Uruguay* 70 ILR 259; and *Estrella v Uruguay* 78 ILR 40.

[162] E.g. *López v Uruguay*; *Altesor v Uruguay* 70 ILR 248; and *Drescher Caldas v Uruguay* 79 ILR 180.

[163] E.g. *Altesor v Uruguay*; *Bleier v Uruguay*; and *Estrella v Uruguay*.

[164] *López v Uruguay*.

[165] *Altesor v Uruguay*.

to suggest a non-binding decision. No enforcement or implementation mechanisms are contained in the Optional Protocol, and pressure to observe the views of the Committee comes only from the 'inherent authority as emanating from an independent body's objective assessment and from the accompanying publicity. Unfortunately, effective publicity for the Human Rights Committee's work has been sadly lacking.'[166] As a result, pressure to implement the views of the Committee has been easy to resist, and the 'degree of co-operation afforded by the Uruguayan government . . . varied from minimal to non-existent'.[167]

Protection of civilians during internal armed conflict by the Human Rights Committee is therefore disappointing in its effectiveness. United Nations machinery does not stand alone in the field of human rights law 'enforcement',[168] however, and comparable procedures also exist under regional systems.

Regional human rights enforcement

The European system

It is unnecessary to go into detail as regards the specific machinery and procedural requirements of the European Convention's enforcement mechanisms for present purposes.[169] What is more important is the application of the European Convention to situations of internal armed conflict. Armed conflict has been rare in Europe since the adoption of the Convention, and questions of its enforcement during such situations are, as a result, largely absent.[170] The issue was first touched upon under Article 24 procedure in the case of *Cyprus* v *Turkey*.[171] Although not dealing with internal armed conflict, the application of human rights to the situation is important from the point of view of their value and enforcement in situations of armed conflict in general.

---

[166] McGoldrick, *The Human Rights Committee*, 201.
[167] *Ibid.*, 202.
[168] To the extent that the United Nations can be said to enforce human rights law at all.
[169] See P. van Dijk and G. J. H. van Hoof, *Theory and Practice of the European Convention on Human Rights*, 2nd edn (Deventer, 1990), 32–52 and chapters 2 and 3; David J. Harris, Michael O'Boyle and Chris Warbrick, *Law of the European Convention on Human Rights* (London, 1995), chapters 22–24.
[170] The most obvious European armed conflict(s) occurred in the former Yugoslavia, particularly Bosnia-Herzegovina, and Yugoslavia never became a party to the Convention. Of the new States which arose from the break-up of Yugoslavia, only Slovenia has since become a party, ratifying the Convention on 28 June 1994.
[171] 4 EHRR 482.

Following Turkey's invasion and subsequent occupation of Northern Cyprus in 1974, Cyprus alleged various breaches of the European Convention by Turkey, unconnected with military operations. The Commission largely found in Cyprus' favour, and invited the parties to make observations on the applicability of the Convention to a situation of military action, as in this case, paying particular attention to Article 15.[172] Turkey refuted the capacity of the Greek Cypriot Government to bring the claim before the Commission, and refused to co-operate.[173] For its part, the Commission made no statement on the subject, deciding that Article 15 was inapplicable, Turkey having made no formal or public declaration of derogation.[174] Cyprus, however, did address the question, asserting that the Convention continued to apply irrespective of the military situation for several reasons.[175]

First, it claimed that the Convention's application was unaffected by Turkey's concurrent responsibility under other international instruments (particularly Geneva Convention IV), since:

in belligerent operations a State [is] bound to respect not only the humanitarian law laid down in the Geneva Conventions . . . but also the fundamental human rights.

Resolution 2675 (XXV) of the United Nations General Assembly of 9 December 1970 provided that human rights, as accepted by international law and laid down in international instruments, 'continue to apply fully in situations of armed conflict'.[176]

It was also asserted that the Convention must apply to situations of armed conflict since Article 15(1) makes provision for the case of 'war', presupposing that the Convention applies to armed conflicts irrespective of the applicability of other obligations under international law. Furthermore, the reference to 'deaths resulting from lawful acts of war' in Article 15(2) means that the Convention must apply simultaneously with humanitarian law, since there may be deaths during an armed conflict which do not result from such lawful acts (as alleged in this case).

It is interesting to hear a State making such assertions, and the arguments are very persuasive. There is undoubtedly a broad acceptance that human rights law applies alongside humanitarian law in armed

[172] Ibid., 552.
[173] Ibid., 554.
[174] Ibid., 556.
[175] Ibid., 552–553.
[176] Ibid., 552.

conflicts, and the findings of the Commission in *Cyprus v Turkey* that violations of human rights (several of which are also contained in common Article 3 and Additional Protocol II[177]) had been committed during what it itself called a 'situation of military action' serves to strengthen this assertion.

Those aspects of humanitarian law coinciding with human rights can therefore be enforced through the European human rights system, alongside other human rights not affected by armed conflict.[178] Indeed, the European human rights system has more recently dealt with several incidents which arguably arose in the context of internal armed conflict and concerned military activity. Thus, under Article 25 procedure, Turkey has been found by the European Court of Human Rights to have violated several human rights obligations in the context of the conflict in South East Turkey between Government security forces and Kurdish separatists.[179] European human rights jurisprudence can also be valuable in that it has dealt with incidents which, although not arising out of an internal armed conflict, are nevertheless potentially relevant to such situations. This is particularly true of some of the cases which have arisen in the context of the troubles in Northern Ireland.[180]

[177] The Commission found breaches of Article 2(1) (the right to life), Article 3 (freedom from torture, etc.), Article 5(1) (the right to liberty), Article 1 of Protocol No. 1 (the peaceful enjoyment of possessions), and Articles 13 and 14 with respect to these breaches.

[178] Provided steps have not been taken to derogate from obligations. Turkey was also held to have violated Article 1 of Protocol No. 1 in the context of northern Cyprus in *Loizidou v Turkey* 23 EHRR 513.

[179] A situation described by the Court as 'civil strife', however, rather than armed conflict (*Akdivar v Turkey* 23 EHRR 143 at 186). There breaches of Article 8 and Article 1 of Protocol No. 1 were found, whereas violations of Articles 3, 5(3) and 13 were found in *Aksoy v Turkey* 23 EHRR 553. See also *Kaya v Turkey* ECHR Reports 1998-I, No. 65, 297; *Güleç v Turkey* ECHR Reports 1998-IV, No. 80, 1698; and *Ergi v Turkey* ECHR Reports 1998-IV, No. 81, 1751. And see the more recent cases of *Ogur v Turkey* (Application No. 21594/93), Judgment of 20 May 1999; *Tanrikulu v Turkey* (Application No. 23763/94), Judgment of 8 July 1999; *Cakici v Turkey* (Application No. 23657/94), Judgment of 8 July 1999; *Mahmut Kaya v Turkey* (Application No. 22535/93), Judgment of 28 March 2000; *Kiliç v Turkey* (Application No. 22492/93), Judgment of 28 March 2000; *Sevtap Veznedaroglu v Turkey* (Application No. 32357/96), Judgment of 11 April 2000; and *Timurtas v Turkey* (Application No. 23531/94), Judgment of 13 June 2000, where violations of Articles 2 and 3 were found to have been committed. These later cases are available at the European Court of Human Rights website, http://www.echr.coe.int/Eng/Judgments.htm.

[180] See, for example, *McCann and Others v UK* ECHR Series A, vol. 324 (1996), concerning the shooting of three IRA terrorists by British security forces on the Island of Gibraltar; *Farrell v UK* 5 EHRR 466, concerning a shooting by British security forces in

The Inter-American system

The Americas, and Latin American States in particular, have for some time been characterised by systematic human rights abuses occurring in situations of internal unrest, typified by disappearances and violations of the rights of due process, freedom from detention and from torture. Two bodies are involved in the implementation process of the American Convention – the Commission and the Court.[181] The Inter-American Commission on Human Rights[182] provides three options in this respect.

First, it can receive communications from individuals under Article 44 of the Convention. As mentioned, several of the parties to the Convention have suffered internal armed conflict, and complaints brought against them before the Commission have been numerous. El Salvador serves well as an example, and in a series of decisions on complaints relating to the conduct of Government troops, the Commission found several violations of Articles 4 and 7.[183] Demonstrating the importance of human rights mechanisms during internal armed conflict, however, the Inter-American Commission has gone further than simply examining

Northern Ireland; and *Stewart* v *UK*, Communication 10044/82, European Commission on Human Rights Decisions and Reports, No. 39 (1984) 162, concerning death caused by a plastic bullet fired by British security forces in Northern Ireland. Increasing emphasis is also being placed on the obligation of States to investigate serious human rights violations, independently of any right the applicant may have to a remedy, and even in relation to emergency situations. As the European Court of Human Rights stated at paragraph 161 of *McCann* v *UK*: 'The obligation to protect the right to life under [Article 2], read in conjunction with the State's general duty under Article 1 of the Convention to "secure to everyone within their jurisdiction the rights and freedoms defined in [the] Convention", requires by implication that there should be some form of effective official investigation when individuals have been killed as a result of the use of force by, *inter alios*, agents of the State.' See also *Kaya* v *Turkey* at paragraph 86.

[181] On the American system in general see Thomas Buergenthal, 'The Inter-American System for the Protection of Human Rights' in Theodor Meron (ed.), *Human Rights in International Law: Legal and Policy Issues* (Oxford, 1984), vol. II, 439.

[182] Comprising members sitting in their personal capacity, the Commission was originally created in 1959. See Thomas Buergenthal, Robert E. Norris and Dinah Shelton, *Protecting Human Rights in the Americas* (Strasbourg, 1982), 18–22.

[183] E.g. Cases 6717–6720 (El Salvador) in IACHR, *Annual Report of the Inter-American Commission on Human Rights 1983–1984*, OAS Doc. OEA/Ser.L/V/II.63, doc. 10, 24 September 1984 at 35–41, reproduced in Thomas Buergenthal and Robert E. Norris, *Human Rights: The Inter-American System, vol. 4*, Booklet 21.1 (1986) at 71–78; and Case 6724 (El Salvador) in IACHR, *Report 1984–1985*, OAS Doc. OEA/Ser.L/V/II.66, doc. 10, rev. 1, 1 October 1985, reproduced in Buergenthal and Norris, *ibid.*, 211–212.

the protection of human rights, and has also explicitly applied human-itarian law.[184]

The second possibility is that of inter-State claims under Article 45(1) of the Convention. This procedure, however, is not compulsory and re-quires the further consent of the respondent State. Like the correspond-ing ICCPR procedure, it has proved unattractive to States, and ultimately ineffective.

Finally, the Commission can undertake studies to address widespread violations of human rights in particular States under Article 41 of the Convention, resulting in a country report.[185] This has been done with rel-ative frequency when faced with large-scale breakdowns of public order and internal armed conflict. A good example is the report on Nicaragua dealing with the conflict which culminated in the Sandanista Govern-ment taking control.[186] Therein the Commission addressed various hu-man rights violations, unequivocally stating that:

[the] contending parties have the duty of respecting the unarmed population which is unable to protect itself. Such duty . . . was not observed by the National Guard.

Moreover, the Government of Nicaragua assumed the solemn obligation of respecting international norms of humanitarian law, especially those set forth in the Geneva Convention on the Protection of Civilians in Time of War . . . which is also applicable in armed conflicts not of an international character.[187]

The report concluded that the Government had been responsible for serious attempts against the right to life in violation of international humanitarian norms and various other human rights violations. In the context of the civil war in El Salvador, the Commission also issued a report outlining the State's responsibility for a massacre committed in 1983 by security forces, concluding that the events constituted a viola-tion of Articles 4, 5, 8 and 25 of the American Convention.[188]

The Inter-American Court of Human Rights, unlike the Commis-sion, was created by the American Convention on Human Rights. Its

---

[184] In the case of *Abella* v *Argentina*, Report No. 55–97, OAS Annual Report 1997 (1998). See discussion above at p. 199, n. 23 and accompanying text.

[185] Buergenthal, Norris and Shelton, *Human Rights in the Americas*, 140–192.

[186] IACHR, *Report on the Situation of Human Rights in Nicaragua*, OEA/Ser.L/V/II.45, doc. 16, rev. 1, 17 November 1978, reproduced in part in Buergenthal and Norris, *The Inter-American System*, vol. 5, Booklet 22 (1983) 66.

[187] *Ibid.*, 67–68.

[188] IACHR, *El Salvador Report* (Report No. 26/92 – Case 10.287, 24 September 1992) in (1993) 14 *HRLJ* 167.

jurisdiction is available only to States and the Commission,[189] and is subject to the consent of the respondent State. Until the late 1980s, the Court was called upon only to give advisory opinions under Article 54. In 1986, however, it heard its first case relating to a disappearance during the internal unrest in Honduras,[190] finding breaches of Articles 4, 5 and 7 of the American Convention. This has been followed by other cases which also have relevance for the protection of human rights during internal armed conflict, e.g. against Surinam in the context of the insurgency there in the late 1980s.[191] The Court tries to take more direct enforcement action than is available to the Commission, and has actually decided upon the amount of compensation due to the families of victims, undertaking to supervise indemnification and close its files only when it has been paid.[192]

The African system

The African system of human rights protection is significantly less mature and established than the European and American models, having come into force as recently as 1986.[193] Its supervisory mechanisms, presently consisting solely of the African Commission on Human and Peoples' Rights,[194] are less developed and, as a result, commonly regarded as being less effective. This is particularly unfortunate, as the issue of human rights violations arising from internal armed conflict is vitally important to Africa, where ethnic rivalry, violence and civil war are presently commonplace.

---

[189] Article 61.

[190] *Velásquez Rodríguez Case* (1988) 9 *HRLJ* 212.

[191] Such as the murder of seven civilians by armed forces in *Aloeboetoe et al.* v *Surinam* (1993) 14 *HRLJ* 413.

[192] In *Velásquez Rodríguez* it awarded 750,000 lempiras in compensatory damages. (1990) 11 *HRLJ* 127 at 133.

[193] For a general, but brief, overview of the African human rights system, see, for example, Richard Gittleman, 'The Banjul Charter on Human and Peoples' Rights: A Legal Analysis' in Claude E. Welch Jr and Ronald I. Meltzer (eds.), *Human Rights and Developments in Africa* (New York, 1984), 152; U. Oji Umozurike, 'The African Charter on Human and Peoples' Rights' (1983) 77 *AJIL* 902; and Edem Kadjo, 'The African Charter on Human and Peoples' Rights' (1990) 11 *HRLJ* 271. A more detailed account can be found in Umozurike, *The African Charter on Human and Peoples' Rights* (The Hague, 1997).

[194] A Protocol to establish an African Court of Human and Peoples' Rights was adopted in 1998, but has yet to enter into force. Its potential effectiveness has, in any case, been called into question. See Makau Mutua, 'The African Human Rights Court: A Two-Legged Stool?' (1999) 21 *HRQ* 342.

Under Article 45 of the African Charter on Human and Peoples' Rights, the Commission is entrusted with the promotion and protection of human rights in Africa. It is probably fair to say that most of the Commission's activity to date has been taken up with the former rather than the latter. The Commission does, however, have the role of examining State reports under Article 62, and of dealing with communications from States,[195] or from individuals or other interested parties,[196] which allege violations of the rights contained in the Charter. As with the corresponding mechanisms under the ICCPR, the inter-State complaint procedure has never been used, and the State reporting procedure is widely abused and, as a result, ineffective. Many States are in arrears as regards the submission of reports, with a significant number still to submit any reports whatsoever for consideration by the Commission.[197] As the Human Rights Committee also finds, those States encountering severe internal difficulties tend to be particularly errant in this regard. The initial report by Algeria, for example, originally due on 20 June 1989, was not examined by the Commission until its 19th Session in March–April 1996.[198] Likewise, the initial report from Sudan, due on 21 October 1988, was not examined by the Commission until its 21st Session in April 1997.[199]

The most concrete mandatory protective measure available to the Commission is the handling of communications from individuals and from national or international organisations.[200] Although the number of cases finally decided on their merits is still relatively small, over 200 complaints have been lodged with the Commission,[201] which demonstrates a growing awareness in Africa of the procedure. Individual communications before the African Commission suffered in the past,

---

[195] Under Article 47 of the Charter.
[196] Under Article 55, and simply classed as 'other communications'.
[197] See the table on the status of submission of reports in the *Twelfth Annual Activity Report of the African Commission on Human and Peoples' Rights, 1998–1999*, 24th and 25th Ordinary Sessions, 26 April–5 May 1999, Banjul, The Gambia, at Annex III.
[198] See *Final Communiqué of the 19th Ordinary Session of the African Commission on Human and Peoples' Rights*, 26 March–4 April 1996, Ouagadougou, Burkina Faso.
[199] See *Final Communiqué of the 21st Ordinary Session of the African Commission on Human and Peoples' Rights*, 15–24 April 1997, Nouakchott, Mauritania.
[200] See Chidi Anselm Odinkalu, 'The Individual Complaints Procedures of the African Commission on Human and Peoples' Rights: A Preliminary Assessment' (1998) 8 *Transnational Law and Contemporary Problems* 359, and Rachel Murray, 'Decisions by the African Commission on Individual Communications under the African Charter on Human and Peoples' Rights' (1997) 46 *ICLQ* 412.
[201] Odinkalu, 'Individual Complaints Procedures', 366.

however, from a lack of publicity and transparency. Not until the Seventh Annual Activity Report of the Commission in 1994[202] were the details of individual communications included, although details of the legal reasoning behind those decisions made was scant. More recent reports have improved a great deal in this regard. As is perhaps inevitable, the Commission has dealt with a number of communications concerning States in the throes of internal armed conflict.[203] Nonetheless, such cases have not tended to centre upon military activity. As a result, although they may relate to human rights which are also protected by humanitarian law, the Commission has offered little in terms of the explicit treatment of humanitarian norms through its case law.

The African Commission has not been afraid, however, to assert the relevance of humanitarian law to the human rights problems faced by many States. In 1994, for example, the Commission passed a resolution on the Promotion and Respect of International Humanitarian Law and Human and Peoples' Rights,[204] and a resolution on Rwanda which called on all parties to respect the principles of humanitarian law.[205] In 1995, a resolution was passed, 'Recalling that Sudan is legally bound to comply with international human rights and international humanitarian law treaties it has ratified ... [and further calling] on all factions of the SPLA and the SSIA to respect international humanitarian law, particularly Article 3 common to the four Geneva Conventions of 1949'.[206] At the same session, the Commission also adopted a resolution on anti-personnel mines, which:

1. Encourages African States to ratify, within the shortest possible time, the 1980 United Nations Convention on prohibitions or restrictions on the use of certain conventional weapons which may be deemed to be excessively injurious or to have indiscriminate effects;

---

[202] *Seventh Annual Activity Report of the African Commission on Human and Peoples' Rights, 1993–1994*, 30th Ordinary Session, 13–15 June 1994, Tunis, Tunisia.

[203] Such as Rwanda, Angola and Sudan.

[204] Adopted by the Commission at its 14th Ordinary Session (1–10 December 1993) in Addis Ababa. See *Seventh Annual Activity Report*. The resolution included an invitation to all African States parties to the African Charter to 'adopt appropriate measures at the national level to ensure the promotion of the provisions of international humanitarian law', and stressed the need for the armed forces and forces of law and order to be instructed in international humanitarian law as well as human rights.

[205] Adopted at the 15th Ordinary Session of the Commission (18–27 April 1994) in Banjul, The Gambia. See *Seventh Annual Activity Report*.

[206] Resolution on Sudan adopted by the African Commission on Human and Peoples' Rights at its 17th Ordinary Session, 13–22 March 1995, at Lomé in Togo. See *Eighth Annual Activity Report of the Commission on Human and Peoples' Rights, 1994–1995*, 31st Ordinary Session, 26–28 June 1995, Addis Ababa, Ethiopia.

2. Urgently requests African States to participate in large numbers in the review conference to press for the introduction of a clause on the prohibition or restriction of the use of mines in that convention;...[and]

3. Requests that the provisions of the above Convention be extended to situations of internal conflict.[207]

Following the adoption of the Ottawa Convention on the Prohibition of the Use, Stockpiling, Production and Transfer of Anti-Personnel Mines and on Their Destruction in 1997,[208] the Commission adopted a resolution calling on all African States to sign and ratify the treaty[209] and, at the same time, adopted another resolution calling on all parties to the African Charter to sign and ratify the Rome Treaty on the International Criminal Court.[210]

It is to be hoped that, as the African human rights system continues to develop, the Commission and the Court – when it comes into existence – will continue to strive for the application and enforcement of humanitarian norms throughout the continent.

Problems with the enforcement of human rights during internal armed conflict

The human rights conventions...provide a system allowing complaints to be made by a contracting party or by the individuals whose rights have been infringed. The procedures to be followed before the international tribunals created for this purpose will normally be unsuitable for the conditions of armed conflicts. Insofar as individual complaints are admissible, the conventions, moreover, require the exhaustion of domestic remedies before a complaint may be lodged with the international tribunal. Persons protected by humanitarian law usually are helpless and defenseless and not in a position to resort to any legal process. The rights of victims of armed conflicts are, therefore, better secured by an impartial body which acts on its own initiative than by a system in which the persons whose rights are violated have to institute legal proceedings.[211]

---

[207] See *Eighth Annual Activity Report*.

[208] See 36 ILM 1507 (1997).

[209] Resolution on the Ratification of the Convention on Anti-Personnel Mines, adopted by the African Commission on Human and Peoples' Rights at its 24th Ordinary Session, 22–31 October 1998, in Banjul, The Gambia. See *Twelfth Annual Activity Report*, Annex IV.

[210] Resolution on the Ratification of the Treaty on the International Criminal Court, adopted by the African Commission on Human and Peoples' Rights at its 24th Ordinary Session, 22–31 October 1998 in Banjul. See *Twelfth Annual Activity Report*.

[211] Dietrich Schindler, 'Human Rights and Humanitarian Law: Interrelationship of the Laws' (1982) 31 *American University LR* 935 at 941.

All of the human rights supervision mechanisms suffer from defects in terms of enforcement during internal conflict. While political considerations make action difficult in many cases, the European system has shown that this need not be a major stumbling block. European States are perhaps more confident and comfortable with their sovereignty, however, having largely been colonial powers rather than colonies. In any case, more practical problems also arise.

First, as outlined above, human rights are enforceable only against the government and not against all parties to an internal armed conflict.[212] It is therefore only to the extent that those rights overlap with provisions of humanitarian law that insurgents can be held accountable for their actions.

Secondly, the time-frame for human rights supervision means that violations are only addressed long after the fact, which is clearly unacceptable as regards the civilian right to life threatened during armed conflict. As Doswald-Beck and Vité explain:

We can appreciate straight away the inconvenience of having to wait for decisions as to whether every action which takes place is justifiable or not, as the protection of people in armed conflict is usually literally a matter of life or death at that very moment. What is needed, therefore, is a code of action applicable in advance. Human rights lawyers have consequently turned to humanitarian law because, despite its different origins and formulation, compliance with it has the result of protecting the most essential human rights of both the 'civil' and the 'economic and social' types.[213]

This, however, is a defect shared with humanitarian law enforcement. Violations of the laws of war are also addressed only after the fact, typically after the conflict has ended. It is accordingly difficult to accept prosecutions for war crimes as representing effective protection rather than simply punishment for wrongdoing, but the same is true of any law enforcement measure which is not pre-emptive. Protection hopefully comes from the fact that such prosecutions will dissuade parties from committing the same acts in the future.

Thirdly, it has been shown that little supervision in the field of human rights actually amounts to 'enforcement' of the laws. Many of the procedures are optional, and States frequently disregard decisions

---

[212] At least up to a point. See above at p. 44, n. 50.
[213] Louise Doswald-Beck and Sylvain Vité, 'International Humanitarian Law and Human Rights Law' (1993) 293 *Int Rev of the Red Cross* 94 at 107.

and directions.[214] The enforcement of humanitarian law, in contrast, tends to entail the application of penal sanctions to those individuals who commit violations of its provisions. Sadly, the effectiveness of even this is not readily apparent. The convictions obtained at Nuremberg proved unable to prevent the barbaric excesses which continue to be committed during the course of armed conflicts, and the process depends entirely upon States both having custody of alleged offenders *and* being willing to try them. The International Criminal Tribunals for Rwanda and the former Yugoslavia, coupled with the imminent International Criminal Court, perhaps represent a change in attitude and a renewed determination on the part of the international community to deal more effectively with the perpetrators of atrocities. They offer States yet another chance to demonstrate that the application and enforcement of international humanitarian law and the protection of civilians during armed conflict can be achieved both consistently and effectively.

Summary and conclusions

Laws protecting civilians during internal armed conflict have been in place for fifty years, and now comprise both conventional and customary humanitarian law, along with international human rights protection. The conventional law is contained in Article 3 common to the Geneva Conventions of 1949 and Additional Protocol II of 1977, with common Article 3 being the first internationally agreed provision on internal conflict. It sets out minimum obligations for the protection of those taking no part in hostilities which are equally binding upon States and insurgents. The provisions of common Article 3 have come to be considered as 'elementary considerations of humanity', applicable in *all* armed conflicts, be they either internal or international in character,[215] and, as a result, common Article 3 can be regarded as a customary international legal norm, binding even upon those States not party to the Geneva Conventions.

Nevertheless, it is not adhered to sufficiently in practice. Despite its presence in the Conventions and its status as customary law, breaches continually occur. When faced with internal difficulties, States tend to

---

[214] Although this defect is less apparent in the European Convention system. Turkey, for example, has complied with every adverse judgment except that in *Loizidou*.

[215] *Nicaragua* Case at paragraph 218.

disregard the provisions of common Article 3, often denying that the situation is an armed conflict at all. Article 3 may assert that its application has no effect on the legal status of the parties to the conflict, but States fear the opposite, and to an extent they are right to do so – the insurgents must receive some measure of legal personality to the extent that they gain rights and obligations under the Article. States are furthermore not inclined to apply the Article immediately, as it may impair their ability to crush rebellion swiftly. Equally, insurgents are unlikely to feel any compulsion to comply with common Article 3 where the government disregards its obligations.[216] Where internal conflict continues for a substantial period, however, States do tend to accept some form of regulation. This may not necessarily entail the application of common Article 3 *per se*,[217] being more likely instead to involve the acceptance of some vague set of 'humanitarian principles' or ICRC initiatives. The situation is therefore better than may have been feared, but the protection afforded by common Article 3 was nevertheless considered to be inadequate in any event.

As a result, Additional Protocol II was adopted in 1977 to develop and supplement Article 3.[218] Again binding on both governments and insurgents, it sets out many of Article 3's provisions in more detail, extending the protection afforded to civilians, detainees and medical personnel. Unfortunately, given the reasons behind its adoption, it regulates only the most extreme internal conflicts, leaving the majority regulated by common Article 3 as before. It is accordingly doubtful that many of its provisions beyond those also contained in common Article 3 have customary status. Accepted by fewer States than the Geneva Conventions,[219] instances of the Protocol's application have been rare indeed.[220]

---

[216] Insurgents may nevertheless accept the application of humanitarian law in order to gain international credibility, as the FLN did during the Algerian conflict: see above at pp. 68–74. Of course, such acceptance of the law does not necessarily equate to its application in practice.

[217] Although, of course, explicit references to the Geneva Conventions and common Article 3 are not unheard of (e.g. the Nigerian Government during the Biafran struggle: see above at pp. 79–83).

[218] But without superseding it, common Article 3 retaining its independent legal existence. See above at pp. 100–103.

[219] Although only slightly fewer than Additional Protocol I. In April 2001 there were 189 States party to the Geneva Conventions, 158 to Additional Protocol I, and 150 to Additional Protocol II (ICRC figures).

[220] El Salvador and the Philippines are still the only examples where both government and insurgent parties to a non-international armed conflict have accepted its application. See above at p. 131.

In addition to conventional international law, it has recently been affirmed by the International Criminal Tribunal for the former Yugoslavia that a substantial body of customary law exists to regulate internal armed conflict, and that breaches of the laws of war (either conventional or customary) during internal armed conflict result in individual criminal liability. The customary rules principally protect civilians and civilian property from direct attack and from unnecessary harm; but also contain some rules on methods and means of warfare, in particular a prohibition on the use of chemical weapons and perfidious means of warfare. There is also a degree of protection for certain other objects, for example cultural property.[221]

The protection of civilians during internal armed conflict is not, however, limited to humanitarian law. Although primarily designed for peacetime, human rights continue to be relevant in such situations. In fact, much of the humanitarian law applicable to internal conflict mirrors human rights provisions, requiring humane treatment at all times and protecting the right to life, freedom from torture, rights of due process, etc. There are problems, however, with the application of human rights to internal armed conflict. First, human rights law binds only States in current international law. Insurgents are required to respect human rights only to the extent that they coincide with their humanitarian obligations. Secondly, the possibility also exists for governments to derogate from several human rights obligations in times of national emergency, including internal armed conflict, although any such derogation must not be contrary to the State's other obligations under international law. Thus, during internal armed conflict it is unlawful to derogate from human rights which also have a place in common Article 3 or Additional Protocol II. In addition, certain other human rights obligations are always non-derogable. Human rights law therefore offers a valuable alternative avenue for the protection of many humanitarian obligations.

The above constitutes a fairly extensive corpus of law, undoubtedly capable of offering civilians adequate protection were it to be applied. Further development or codification of the laws of internal armed conflict is not required so much as a wider acceptance and more effective implementation of the existing law. Traditionally, two options were thought to exist in this regard – either to persuade more States to accept humanitarian law in advance, or else to improve the methods of

---

[221] See *Tadić* (Jurisdiction) 35 ILM 32 (1996) and chapter 4 above.

enforcement. As regards the first method, there is already largely universal acceptance of the Geneva Conventions of 1949 (and thus of common Article 3). Those States typically affected by internal armed conflict are developing nations, but those same States, having obtained the inclusion of wars of national liberation in Additional Protocol I as international conflicts, have consistently avoided ratification of Protocol II. Nevertheless, while there are still significantly fewer States party to Additional Protocol II than to the Geneva Conventions, there are almost the same number as States party to Additional Protocol I. Efforts at wider ratification of Protocol II could still be made, but acceptances of humanitarian law often amount to little more than lip service, and are of little importance unless the law is applied in practice. The answer must therefore lie in more effective enforcement of the law.

While the enforcement mechanisms of human rights are more developed than those of humanitarian law, several problems exist as regards their application in armed conflict. As outlined above, they are available only against States, so that breaches by insurgents can be addressed only through humanitarian law. In addition, much of the supervision machinery is optional, relying on the consent of the State concerned, and so making sanctions against the perpetrators a limited possibility.[222] Human rights mechanisms can nonetheless prove valuable in the protection of civilians during internal armed conflict, and even to enforce humanitarian law where it happens to coincide with international human rights obligations.[223]

The effective enforcement of humanitarian law itself is vital, however. Ten years ago this did not seem to be a viable option – the international community was simply unwilling to take the necessary steps. States had shown little inclination towards accepting their obligation under common Article 1 of the Geneva Conventions to ensure that their provisions were applied by the other High Contracting Parties, and although collective measures were occasionally taken under the umbrella of the UN in the context of ensuring humanitarian relief,[224] this tended to occur without addressing the question of enforcing humanitarian law and human rights. Any such steps had been virtually non-existent since Nuremberg. The creation by the United Nations Security Council of International Criminal Tribunals to deal with violations of international

---

[222] This is perhaps particularly true of United Nations supervision. The European system, as already discussed, would appear to be more effective.

[223] Or, in some circumstances, even to enforce humanitarian law directly.

[224] As taken in Somalia, Rwanda, Iraq and Bosnia-Herzegovina.

law committed in Rwanda and the former Yugoslavia has nevertheless demonstrated that enforcement action is possible, and the pronouncements of those Tribunals have had a great effect on the development of international law.

The actual administering of justice will, however, be rendered impossible unless and until the international community accepts its obligation to arrest those indicted and deliver them to the Tribunals. Despite the relatively widespread fears expressed during the formative stages of the International Criminal Tribunals,[225] both have had a degree of success to date, and demonstrate that international justice is indeed possible, although many of the main offenders remain at large in the former Yugoslavia. Nevertheless, the signs are hopeful that the international community is beginning to face up to its responsibilities as regards the enforcement of international law – the adoption of a Statute for the permanent International Criminal Court, the proceedings in the United Kingdom against Senator Pinochet and NATO action against Serbia in the context of the Kosovo crisis can be seen as part of this process. It can only be hoped that States will reflect this shift in attitude in a more concrete fashion, by actually taking the steps necessary to administer international justice, rather than providing mere lip service to the concept. In this respect, the final decade of the twentieth century may well represent a true turning point in international law.

[225] See, for example, the rather pessimistic views of Judge Richard Goldstone, then Chief Prosecutor, in Fisk, 'Bosnia Judge Condemns West'.

Bibliography

Abdy, John T. (ed.), *Kent's Commentary on International Law*, 2nd edn (Deighton, Bell & Co., Cambridge, 1866)

Abi-Saab, Georges, 'Wars of National Liberation in the Geneva Conventions and Protocols' (1979-iv) 165 *Recueil des Cours* 353

'The Implementation of Humanitarian Law' in Antonio Cassese (ed.), *The New Humanitarian Law of Armed Conflict* (Editoriale Scientifica, Naples, 1979), 310

'Non-international Armed Conflicts' in UNESCO, *International Dimensions of Humanitarian Law* (Henry Dunant Institute/UNESCO/Martinus Nijhoff, Dordrecht, 1988), 217

Abi-Saab, Rosemary, Droit humanitaire et conflits internes. Origines et évolution de la reglementation internationale (Henry Dunant Institute/Editions Pedone, Paris, 1986)

'The "General Principles" of Humanitarian Law According to the International Court of Justice' (1987) 259 *International Review of the Red Cross* 367

'Humanitarian Law and Internal Conflicts: The Evolution of Legal Concern' in Astrid J. M. Delissen and Gerard J. Tanja (eds.), *Humanitarian Law of Armed Conflict: Challenges Ahead: Essays in Honour of Frits Kalshoven* (Martinus Nijhoff, Dordrecht, 1991), 209

African Commission on Human and Peoples' Rights, *Seventh Annual Activity Report, 1993–1994, 30th Ordinary Session, 13–15 June 1994, Tunis, Tunisia*

Eighth Annual Activity Report, 1994–1995, 31st Ordinary Session, 26–28 June 1995, Addis Ababa, Ethiopia

Twelfth Annual Activity Report, 1998–1999, 24th and 25th Ordinary Sessions, 26 April–5 May 1999, Banjul, The Gambia

Final Communiqué of the 19th Session, 26 March–4 April 1996, Ouagadougou, Burkina Faso

Final Communiqué of the 21st Session, 15–24 April 1997, Nouakchott, Mauritania

Akpan, Ntieyong U., *The Struggle for Secession 1966–1970* (Frank Cass, London, 1971)

Aldrich, George H., 'Compliance with the Law: Problems and Prospects' in
    Hazel Fox and Michael A. Meyer (eds.), *Armed Conflict and the New Law,
    Volume II: Effecting Compliance* (British Institute of International and
    Comparative Law, London, 1993), 3
    'Jurisdiction of the International Criminal Tribunal for the Former
    Yugoslavia' (1996) 90 *American Journal of International Law* 64
Alexidze, L., 'Legal Nature of Jus Cogens in Contemporary International Law'
    (1981-iii) 172 *Recueil des Cours* 218
Allen, Rodney G., Cherniack, Martin and Andreopoulos, George J., 'Refining
    War: Civil Wars and Humanitarian Controls' (1996) 18 *Human Rights
    Quarterly* 747
Alston, Philip (ed.), *The United Nations and Human Rights* (Clarendon Press,
    Oxford, 1992)
    'The Commission on Human Rights' in Philip Alston (ed.), *The United Nations
    and Human Rights* (Clarendon Press, Oxford, 1992), 126
Ambos, Kai, 'Article 25: Individual Criminal Responsibility' in Otto Triffterer
    (ed.), *Commentary on the Rome Statute of the International Criminal Court.
    Observers' Notes, Article by Article* (Nomos Verlagsgesellschaft, Baden-Baden,
    1999), 475
Amnesty International, '1997 UN Commission on Human Rights – 50 Years Old'
    (Amnesty International, 1997)
Arsanjani, Mahnoush H., 'The Rome Statute of the International Criminal
    Court' (1999) 93 *American Journal of International Law* 22
Askin, Kelly D., 'Sexual Violence in Decisions and Indictments of the Yugoslav
    and Rwandan Tribunals: Current Status' (1999) 93 *American Journal of
    International Law* 97
Barsotti, R., 'Armed Reprisals' in Antonio Cassese (ed.), *The Current Legal
    Regulation of the Use of Force* (Martinus Nijhoff, Dordrecht, 1986), 79
Bassiouni, M. Cherif, 'Russia's War in Chechnya is an Internal Armed Conflict
    Governed by International Conventions on War, Top Experts Say' (Crimes
    of War Project, http://www.crimesofwar.org/chechnya/bassiouni.
    html)
Baty, Thomas and Morgan, John H., *War: Its Conduct and Legal Results* (John
    Murray, London, 1915)
Baxter, Richard R., 'Multilateral Treaties as Evidence of Customary
    International Law' (1965–1966) 41 *British Yearbook of International Law*
    275
    'Ius in Bello Interno: The Present and Future Law' in John N. Moore (ed.), *Law
    and Civil War in the Modern World* (Johns Hopkins University Press,
    Baltimore, 1974), 518
Bedjaoui, Mohammed, *Law and the Algerian Revolution* (International Association
    of Democratic Lawyers, Brussels, 1961)
Best, Geoffrey, *War and Law Since 1945* (Clarendon Press, Oxford, 1994)

Bierzanek, Remigiusz, 'Reprisals as a Means of Enforcing the Laws of
    Warfare: The Old and the New Law' in Antonio Cassese (ed.),
    The New Humanitarian Law of Armed Conflict (Editoriale Scientifica, Naples,
    1979), 232
Binyon, Michael, 'Impact of World Outrage will be Limited', *The Times*, 8
    December 1999, 16
Boals, Kathryn, 'The Relevance of International Law to the Internal War in
    Yemen' in Richard A. Falk (ed.), *The International Law of Civil War* (Johns
    Hopkins Press, Baltimore, 1971), 303
Boister, Neil and Burchill, Richard, 'The *Pinochet* Precedent: Don't Leave Home
    Without It' (1999) 10 *Criminal Law Forum* 405
Bond, James E., 'Internal Conflict and Article 3 of the Geneva Conventions'
    (1971) 48 *Denver Law Journal 263*
    The Rules of Riot: Internal Conflict and the Law of War (Princeton University Press,
    Princeton, 1974)
Boot, Machteld, Dixon, Rodney and Hall, Christopher K., 'Article 7: Crimes
    Against Humanity' in Otto Triffterer (ed.), *Commentary on the Rome Statute of
    the International Criminal Court. Observers' Notes, Article by Article* (Nomos
    Verlagsgesellschaft, Baden-Baden, 1999), 118
Bordwell, Percy, *The Law of War Between Belligerents* (Callaghan and Co., Chicago,
    1908)
Bothe, Michael, 'Conflits armes internes et droit international humanitaire'
    (1978) 82 *Revue Generale de Droit International Public* 82
    'Article 3 and Protocol II: Case Studies of Nigeria and El Salvador' (1982) 31
    American University Law Review 899
Bothe, Michael, Partsch, Karl J. and Solf, Waldemar A., *New Rules for Victims of
    Armed Conflicts: Commentary on the Two 1977 Protocols Additional to the Geneva
    Conventions of 1949* (Martinus Nijhoff, The Hague, 1982)
Bowett, Derek W., *United Nations Forces* (Stevens & Sons, London, 1964)
    'Reprisals Involving Recourse to Armed Force' (1972) 66 *American Journal of
    International Law* 1
Brierly, James L., *The Law of Nations*, 6th edn, edited by H. Waldock (Clarendon
    Press, Oxford, 1963)
Briggs, Herbert W., 'Relations Officeuses and Intent to Recognise: British
    Recognition of Franco' (1940) 34 *American Journal of International Law* 47
    The Law of Nations, 2nd edn (Appleton-Century-Crofts, Inc., New York,
    1952)
Brownlie, Ian, *Principles of Public International Law*, 4th edn (Clarendon Press,
    Oxford, 1990)
Buergenthal, Thomas, 'To Respect and to Ensure: State Obligations and
    Permissible Derogations' in Louis Henkin (ed.), *The International Bill of
    Rights: The Covenant on Civil and Political Rights* (Columbia University Press,
    New York, 1981), 413

'The Inter-American System for the Protection of Human Rights' in Theodor Meron (ed.), *Human Rights in International Law: Legal and Policy Issues* (Clarendon Press, Oxford, 1984), vol. II, 439

Buergenthal, Thomas and Norris, Robert E., *Human Rights: The Inter-American System* (Oceana Publications, New York, 1993)

Buergenthal, Thomas, Norris, Robert E. and Shelton, Dinah, *Protecting Human Rights in the Americas* (International Institute of Human Rights/NP Engel, Strasbourg, 1982)

Cassese, Antonio, 'The Status of Rebels Under the 1977 Geneva Protocol on Non-international Armed Conflicts' (1981) 30 *International and Comparative Law Quarterly* 416

'The Geneva Protocols of 1977 and Customary International Law' (1984) 3 *UCLA Pacific Basin Law Journal* 55

'Respect for Humanitarian Norms in Non-international Armed Conflict' in ICIHI, *Modern Wars* (Zed Books, London, 1986) 86

(ed.), *The New Humanitarian Law of Armed Conflict* (Editoriale Scientifica, Naples, 1979)

(ed.), *The Current Legal Regulation of the Use of Force* (Martinus Nijhoff, Dordrecht, 1986)

Castren, Erik, *Civil War* (Suomalainen Tiedeakatemia, Helsinki, 1966)

Chowdhury, Subrata R., *Rule of Law in a State of Emergency* (Pinter, London, 1989)

Ciobanu, Dan, 'The Concept and Determination of the Existence of Armed Conflicts not of an International Character' (1975) 58 *Rivista di Diritto Internazionale* 43

'The Attitude of the Socialist Countries' in Antonio Cassese (ed.), *The New Humanitarian Law of Armed Conflict* (Editoriale Scientifica, Naples, 1979), 399

Clapham, Andrew, *Human Rights in the Private Sphere* (Clarendon Press, Oxford, 1993)

Clark, Roger S. and Sann, Madeleine (eds.), *The Prosecution of International Crimes* (Transaction, New Brunswick, 1996)

Clark, Roger S. and Triffterer, Otto, 'Article 26: Exclusion of Jurisdiction over Persons under Eighteen' in Otto Triffterer (ed.), *Commentary on the Rome Statute of the International Criminal Court. Observers' Notes, Article by Article* (Nomos Verlagsgesellschaft, Baden-Baden, 1999), 493

Claude, Inis L. Jr, 'The Nature and Status of the Subcommission on Prevention of Discrimination and Protection of Minorities' (1951) 5 *International Organization* 300

Claude, Richard P. and Weston, Burns H. (eds.), *Human Rights in the World Community: Issues and Action*, 2nd edn (University of Pennsylvania Press, Philadelphia, 1992)

Clendenen, Clarence C., 'Tribalism and Humanitarianism: The Nigerian–Biafran Civil War' in Robin D. S. Higham (ed.), *Civil Wars in the Twentieth Century* (Kentucky University Press, Lexington, 1972), 164

Cockburn, Patrick, 'Russia Rattled by Torture Claims at Chechen Camps',
    Independent, 18 February 2000, 14
Cohn, Ilene and Goodwin-Gill, Guy S., *Child Soldiers* (Clarendon Press, Oxford,
    1994)
Condorelli, Luigi, 'Les Pays afro-asiatiques' in Antonio Cassese (ed.), *The New
    Humanitarian Law of Armed Conflict* (Editoriale Scientifica, Naples, 1979),
    386
Condorelli, Luigi, La Rosa, Anne-Marie and Scherrer, Sylvie (eds.), *The United
    Nations and International Humanitarian Law* (Editions Pedone, Paris, 1996)
Cottier, Michael, Fenrick, William J., Sellers, Patricia V. and Zimmerman,
    Andreas, 'Article 8: War Crimes' in Otto Triffterer (ed.), *Commentary on the
    Rome Statute of the International Criminal Court. Observers' Notes, Article by
    Article* (Nomos Verlagsgesellschaft, Baden-Baden, 1999), 173
Crawford, James, *The Creation of States in International Law* (Clarendon Press,
    Oxford, 1979)
    'The ILC Adopts a Statute for an International Criminal Court' (1995) 89
    American Journal of International Law 404
Crozier, Brian, *The Rebels* (Chatto & Windus, London, 1960)
Davis, George B., *The Elements of International Law*, 3rd edn (Harper & Brothers,
    New York, 1908)
Delissen, Astrid J. M. and Tanja, Gerard J. (eds.), *Humanitarian Law of Armed
    Conflict: Challenges Ahead: Essays in Honour of Frits Kalshoven* (Martinus Nijhoff,
    Dordrecht, 1991)
Delk, James D., *Fires and Furies: The LA Riots: What Really Happened* (ETC
    Publications, Palm Springs, 1995)
De Visscher, Charles, *Theory and Reality in Public International Law*, trans. P. E.
    Corbett (Princeton University Press, Princeton, 1957)
Dhokalia, R. P., 'Civil Wars and International Law' (1971) 11 *Indian Journal of
    International Law* 219
Dinstein, Yoram, 'Human Rights in Armed Conflict: International
    Humanitarian Law' in Theodor Meron (ed.), *Human Rights in International
    Law: Legal and Policy Issues* (Clarendon Press, Oxford, 1984), vol. II, 345
Doswald-Beck, Louise and Vité, Sylvain, 'International Humanitarian Law and
    Human Rights Law' (1993) 293 *International Review of the Red Cross* 94
Draper, Gerald I. A. D., *The Red Cross Conventions of 1949* (Stevens & Sons, London,
    1958)
    'The Legal Limitations Upon the Employment of Weapons by the United
    Nations Force in the Congo' (1963) 12 *International and Comparative Law
    Quarterly* 387
    'The Geneva Conventions of 1949' (1965-i) 114 *Recueil des Cours* 63
    'Wars of National Liberation and War Criminality' in Michael Howard (ed.),
    Restraints on War (Oxford University Press, Oxford, 1979), 135
    'Humanitarian Law and Human Rights' (1979) *Acta Juridica* 193

'Humanitarian Law and Internal Armed Conflicts' (1983) 13 *Georgia Journal of International and Comparative Law* 253

Dunlop, John B., *Russia Confronts Chechnya* (Cambridge University Press, Cambridge, 1998)

Durand, André, *History of the International Committee of the Red Cross, Volume I: From Sarajevo to Hiroshima* (Henry Dunant Institute, Geneva, 1984)

Editorial, 'Rights and Responsibilities: It is Time for a Real Human Rights Clean-up in Chechnya', *The Times*, 31 March 2000, 23

Eide, Asbjörn, 'The New Humanitarian Law in Non-international Armed Conflict' in Antonio Cassese (ed.), *The New Humanitarian Law of Armed Conflict* (Editoriale Scientifica, Naples, 1979), 277

'Internal Disturbances and Tensions' in ICIHI, *Modern Wars* (Zed Books, London, 1986), 102

'Internal Disturbances and Tensions' in UNESCO, *International Dimensions of Humanitarian Law* (Henry Dunant Institute/UNESCO/Martinus Nijhoff, Dordrecht, 1988), 241

'The Subcommission on Prevention of Discrimination and Protection of Minorities' in Philip Alston (ed.), *The United Nations and Human Rights* (Clarendon Press, Oxford, 1992), 211

Elder, David A., 'The Historical Background of Common Article 3 of the Geneva Convention of 1949' (1979) 11 *Case Western Reserve Journal of International Law* 37

Elliott, H. Wayne, 'Russia's War in Chechnya is an Internal Armed Conflict Governed by International Conventions on War, Top Experts Say' (Crimes of War Project, http://www.crimesofwar.org/chechnya/elliott.html)

Eser, Albin, 'Article 31: Grounds for Excluding Criminal Responsibility' in Otto Triffterer (ed.), *Commentary on the Rome Statute of the International Criminal Court. Observers' Notes, Article by Article* (Nomos Verlagsgesellschaft, Baden-Baden, 1999), 537

Falk, Richard A., 'Janus Tormented: The International Law of Internal War' in James N. Rosenau (ed.), *International Aspects of Civil Strife* (Princeton University Press, Princeton, 1964), 185

The International Law of Civil War (Johns Hopkins Press, Baltimore, 1971)

Farer, Tom J., 'The Humanitarian Laws of War in Civil Strife: Towards a Definition of "International Armed Conflict"' (1971) 7 *Revue Belge du Droit International* 20

'The United Nations and Human Rights: More than a Whimper, Less than a Roar' in Richard P. Claude and Burns H. Weston (eds.), *Human Rights in the World Community: Issues and Action*, 2nd edn (University of Pennsylvania Press, Philadelphia, 1992), 227

Farina, Niccolò, 'The Attitude of the People's Republic of China' in Antonio Cassese (ed.), *The New Humanitarian Law of Armed Conflict* (Editoriale Scientifica, Naples, 1979), 445

Fenrick, William J., 'The Development of the Law of Armed Conflict through
    the Jurisprudence of the International Criminal Tribunal for the Former
    Yugoslavia' (1998) 3 *Journal of Armed Conflict Law* 197
  'Article 28: Responsibility of Commanders and Other Superiors' in Otto
    Triffterer (ed.), *Commentary on the Rome Statute of the International Criminal
    Court. Observers' Notes, Article by Article* (Nomos Verlagsgesellschaft,
    Baden-Baden, 1999), 516
Final Record of the Diplomatic Conference of Geneva of 1949 (Federal Political
    Department, Berne, 1951), 4 vols.
Final Report of the Commission of Experts Established Pursuant to Security
    Council Resolution 780 (1992), UN Doc. S/1994/674
Fiore, Pasquale, *International Law Codified*, trans. E. M. Borchard (Baker, Voorhis
    & Co., New York, 1918)
Fisk, Robert, 'Bosnia Judge Condemns West', *Independent*, 17 September 1996, 1
Fitzpatrick, Joan, *Human Rights in Crisis* (University of Pennsylvania Press,
    Philadelphia, 1994)
Fleck, Dieter (ed.), *The Handbook of Humanitarian Law in Armed Conflicts* (Oxford
    University Press, Oxford, 1995)
Fletcher, M., 'EU Tries War of Words to Help Chechnya', *The Times*, 11 December
    1999, 18
Forsythe, David P., 'Legal Management of Internal War: The 1977 Protocol on
    Non-international Armed Conflicts' (1978) 72 *American Journal of
    International Law* 272
  'The International Committee of the Red Cross' in Hazel Fox and Michael A.
    Meyer (eds.), *Armed Conflict and the New Law, Volume II: Effecting
    Compliance* (British Institute of International and Comparative Law,
    London, 1993), 83
Fox, Hazel and Meyer, Michael A. (eds.), *Armed Conflict and the New Law, Volume II:
    Effecting Compliance* (British Institute of International and Comparative Law,
    London, 1993)
Fraleigh, Arnold, 'The Algerian Revolution as a Case Study in International
    Law' in Richard A. Falk (ed.), *The International Law of Civil War* (John Hopkins
    Press, Baltimore, 1971), 179
Gall, Carlotta and De Waal, Thomas, *Chechnya* (New York University Press, New
    York, 2000)
Garner, James W., 'Recognition of Belligerency' (1938) 32 *American Journal of
    International Law* 106
Gasser, Hans-Peter, 'International Non-international Armed Conflicts: Case
    Studies of Afghanistan, Kampuchea and Lebanon' (1982) 31 *American
    University Law Review* 911
  'An Appeal for Ratification by the United States' in 'AGORA: The US Decision
    Not to Ratify Protocol I to the Geneva Conventions on the Protection of
    War Victims' (1987) 81 *American Journal of International Law* 910

'A Measure of Humanity in Internal Disturbances and Tensions:
  A Proposal for a Code of Conduct' (1988) 262 *International Review of the
  Red Cross* 38
'Ensuring Respect for the Geneva Conventions and Protocols: The Role of
  Third States and the United Nations' in Hazel Fox and Michael A. Meyer
  (eds.), *Armed Conflict and the New Law, Volume II: Effecting Compliance*
  (British Institute of International and Comparative Law, London,
  1993), 15
'International Humanitarian Law' in Hans Haug (ed.), *Humanity for All: The
  International Red Cross and Red Crescent Movement* (Henry Dunant
  Institute/Paul Haupt, Berne, 1993), 491
Gentleman, Amelia, 'Flee or Die, Chechens Warned', *Guardian*, 7 December
  1999, 1
Gentleman, Amelia and MacAskill, Ewen, 'West Threatens Sanctions against
  Russia', *Guardian*, 8 December 1999, 15
Gittleman, Richard, 'The Banjul Charter on Human and Peoples' Rights:
  A Legal Analysis' in Claude E. Welch Jr and Ronald I. Meltzer (eds.), *Human
  Rights and Developments in Africa* (State University of New York Press, New
  York, 1984), 152
Graefrath, Bernhard, 'Reporting and Complaint Systems in Universal
  Human Rights Treaties' in Allan Rosas and Jan E. Helgesen (eds.),
  Human Rights in a Changing East–West Perspective (Pinter, London, 1990), 290
Greenberg, Eldon van C., 'Law and the Conduct of the Algerian Revolution'
  (1970) 11 *Harvard International Law Journal* 37
Greenspan, Morris, *The Modern Law of Land Warfare* (University of California
  Press, Berkeley and Los Angeles, 1959)
Greenwood, Christopher J., 'The Twilight of the Law of Belligerent Reprisals'
  (1989) 20 *Netherlands Yearbook of International Law* 35
  'Customary Law Status of the 1977 Additional Protocols' in Astrid J. M.
  Delissen and Gerard J. Tanja (eds.), *Humanitarian Law of Armed Conflict:
  Challenges Ahead: Essays in Honour of Frits Kalshoven* (Martinus Nijhoff,
  Dordrecht, 1991), 93
  'The International Tribunal for Former Yugoslavia' (1993) 69 *International
  Affairs* 641
  'Scope of Application of Humanitarian Law' in Dieter Fleck (ed.), *The
  Handbook of Humanitarian Law in Armed Conflicts* (Oxford University Press,
  Oxford, 1995), 39
  'International Humanitarian Law and the *Tadić* Case' (1996) 7 *European Journal
  of International Law* 265
  'Protection of Peacekeepers: The Legal Regime' (1996) 7 *Duke Journal of
  Comparative and International Law* 185
  'War Crimes Proceedings Before the International Criminal Tribunal for the
  Former Yugoslavia' [1997] *Military Law Journal* 15

International Humanitarian Law and the Laws of War, Preliminary Report for the Centennial Commemoration of the First Hague Peace Conference 1899, pursuant to UN GA Res. 52/154 of 15 December 1997 and UN Doc. A/C.6/52/3 (The Hague, 1999)

Gutman, Roy and Rieff, David (eds.), *Crimes of War: What the Public Should Know* (Norton, New York, 1999)

Hackworth, Green H., *Digest of International Law* (Government Printing Office, Washington, 1940), vol. I

Halleck, H. W., *International Law* (H. H. Bancroft & Co., San Francisco, 1861), vol. II

Hampson, Françoise, 'Russia's War in Chechnya is an Internal Armed Conflict Governed by International Conventions on War, Top Experts Say' (Crimes of War Project, http://www.crimesofwar.org/chechnya/ hampson.html)

Haraszti, György (ed.), *Questions of International Law* (Akadémiai Kiadó, Budapest, 1981)

Harris, David J., O'Boyle, Michael and Warbrick, Chris, *Law of the European Convention on Human Rights* (Butterworths, London, 1995)

Harroff-Tavel, Marion, 'Action Taken by the International Committee of the Red Cross in Situations of Internal Violence' (1993) 294 *International Review of the Red Cross* 195

Haug, Hans (ed.), *Humanity for All: The International Red Cross and Red Crescent Movement* (Henry Dunant Institute/Paul Haupt, Berne, 1993)

Helsinki Watch, *War Crimes in Bosnia-Hercegovina* (Human Rights Watch, New York, 1992)

Henkin, Louis, 'International Law: Politics, Values and Functions' (1989-iv) 216 *Recueil des Cours* 67

  (ed.), *The International Bill of Rights: The Covenant on Civil and Political Rights* (Columbia University Press, New York, 1981)

Herczegh, Géza, 'Protocol Additional to the Geneva Conventions on the Protection of Victims of Non-international Armed Conflicts' in György Haraszti (ed.), *Questions of International Law* (Akadémiai Kiadó, Budapest, 1981), 71

Higgins, Rosalyn, 'International Law and Civil Conflict' in Evan D. T. Luard (ed.), *The International Regulation of Civil Wars* (Thames & Hudson, London, 1972), 169

  United Nations Peacekeeping 1946–1967 (Oxford University Press, Oxford, 1980), vol. III

  'The European Convention on Human Rights' in Theodor Meron (ed.), *Human Rights in International Law: Legal and Policy Issues* (Clarendon Press, Oxford, 1984), vol. II, 495

  Problems and Process: International Law and How We Use It (Clarendon Press, Oxford, 1994)

Higham, Robin D. S. (ed.), *Civil Wars in the Twentieth Century* (Kentucky University Press, Lexington, 1972)

Hilsman, Roger and Good, Robert C. (eds.), *Foreign Policy in the Sixties* (Johns Hopkins Press, Baltimore, 1965)

Horne, Alistair A., *A Savage War of Peace* (Macmillan, London, 1977)

Howard, Michael (ed.), *Restraints on War* (Oxford University Press, Oxford, 1979)

Human Rights Watch, 'Civilian Killings in Staropromyslovski District of Grozny', vol. 12, No. 2(D) (February 2000)

'No Happiness Remains: Civilian Killings, Pillage and Rape in Alkhan-Yurt, Chechnya', vol. 12, No. 5(D) (April 2000)

'February 5: A Day of Slaughter in Novye Aldi', vol. 12, No. 9(D) (June 2000)

'Welcome to Hell: Arbitrary Detention, Torture and Extortion in Chechnya' (October 2000)

Hyde, Charles C., *International Law Chiefly as Interpreted and Applied by the United States*, 2nd edn (Little, Brown & Co., Boston, 1945), vol. I

Ijalye, David A., 'Was "Biafra" at Any Time a State in International Law?' (1971) 65 *American Journal of International Law* 551

Independent Commission on International Humanitarian Issues, *Modern Wars* (Zed Books, London, 1986)

Inter-American Commission on Human Rights, *Report on the Situation of Human Rights in Nicaragua*, OAS Doc. OEA/Ser.L/V/II.45, doc. 16, rev. 1, 17 November 1978

Report on the Situation of Human Rights in the Republic of Nicaragua, OAS Doc. OEA/Ser.L/V/II.53, doc. 25, 30 June 1981

Report on the Situation of Human Rights in Chile, OAS Doc. OEA/Ser.L/V/II.66, Doc. 17, September 1985

El Salvador Report (Report No. 26/92 - Case 10.287, 24 September 1992) in (1993) 14 *Human Rights Law Journal* 167

Interim Report of the Commission of Experts Established Pursuant to Security Council Resolution 780 (1992), UN Doc. S/25274

International Commission of Jurists, *States of Emergency: Their Impact on Human Rights* (International Commission of Jurists, Geneva, 1983)

International Committee of the Red Cross, *Annual Reports* (ICRC, Geneva)

'The ICRC in the Congo' (1961) *International Review of the Red Cross*, Supplement 14

The ICRC and the Algerian Conflict (ICRC Doc. D766b: Geneva, 1962)

'The Red Cross Action in the Congo' (1962) 10 *International Review of the Red Cross* 3

'The United Nations and the Application of the Geneva Conventions' (1962) 10 *International Review of the Red Cross* 29

'The New African States and the Geneva Conventions' (1962) 13 *International Review of the Red Cross* 207

'External Activities: Nigeria' (1967) 79 *International Review of the Red Cross* 535
'External Activities in Nigeria' (1967) 80 *International Review of the Red Cross* 591
'Help to War Victims in Nigeria' (1968) 92 *International Review of the Red Cross* 571
'Help to War Victims in Nigeria' (1969) 94 *International Review of the Red Cross* 3
'Help to War Victims in Nigeria' (1969) 95 *International Review of the Red Cross* 81
'Help to War Victims in Nigeria' (1969) 96 *International Review of the Red Cross* 119
Report on the Work of the Conference of Government Experts on the Reaffirmation and Development of International Humanitarian Law Applicable in Armed Conflict (ICRC, Geneva, 1972), 2 vols.
'Action by the International Committee of the Red Cross in the Event of Breaches of International Humanitarian Law' (1981) 221 *International Review of the Red Cross* 76
'25th International Conference of the Red Cross' (1986) 255 *International Review of the Red Cross* 340
Angola (Special Brochure, Doc. 0575/0020, 05/94 (ICRC, Geneva, May 1994)
Afghanistan (Special Brochure, Doc. 0579/002 (ICRC, Geneva, July 1994)
Declarations of the ICRC re the Former Yugoslavia 29/7/92–25/11/94, Doc. DP (1994) (ICRC, Geneva, 1994).
Press Releases and Communications to the Press re the Former Yugoslavia 2/7/91–2/12/94, Doc. DP (1994) 51b (ICRC, Geneva, 1994)
Public Statements Issued by the ICRC on its Activities in Rwanda: Collection of News Releases and Press Communications (ICRC, Geneva, 7 December 1994)
Symposium on Humanitarian Action and Peace-Keeping Operations (ICRC, Geneva, 1994)
International Law Association, *Minimum Standards of Human Rights Norms in a State of Exception,* Report of the Committee on the Enforcement of Human Rights Law to the 61st Conference, Paris, 1984 (International Law Association, London, 1985)
Jennings, Robert Y. and Watts, Arthur (eds.), *Oppenheim's International Law,* Volume I, 9th edn (Longman, London, 1992)
Jones, John R. W. D., *The Practice of the International Criminal Tribunals for the Former Yugoslavia and Rwanda* (Transnational, New York, 1998)
Junod, Sylvie S., 'Additional Protocol II: History and Scope' (1983) 33 *American University Law Review* 29
Kadjo, Edem, 'The African Charter on Human and Peoples' Rights' (1990) 11 *Human Rights Law Journal* 271.
Kalshoven, Frits, *Belligerent Reprisals* (A. W. Sijthoff, Leiden, 1971)
Constraints on the Waging of War (ICRC, Geneva, 1992)
Keesing's Contemporary Archives of World Events (from 1986: *Keesing's Record of World Events*) (Longman, London)

Kelegama, Saman, 'Economic Costs of Conflict in Sri Lanka' in Robert I. Rotberg
    (ed.), *Creating Peace in Sri Lanka: Civil War and Reconciliation* (World Peace
    Foundation/Belfer Center for Science and International Affairs/Brookings
    Institution Press, Washington, 1999), 71
Kilgore, K. Edwin, 'Geneva Convention Signatories Clarify Applicability of Laws
    of War to Internal Armed Conflict' (1978) 8 *Georgia Journal of International
    and Comparative Law* 941
Kirk-Greene, Anthony H. M., *Crisis and Conflict in Nigeria, A Documentary
    Sourcebook* (Oxford University Press, London, 1971), 2 vols.
Kwakwa, Edward, *The International Law of Armed Conflict: Personal and Material
    Fields of Application* (Kluwer, Dordrecht, 1992)
Lambert, Joseph J., *Terrorism and Hostages in International Law – A Commentary on
    the Hostages Convention 1979* (Grotius Publications, Cambridge,
    1990)
Landale, James, 'Russia Told it Faces Aid Cuts over Grozny', *The Times*, 8
    December 1999, 14
Lauterpacht, Hersch, *Recognition in International Law* (Cambridge University
    Press, Cambridge, 1947)
    International Law and Human Rights (Stevens & Sons, London, 1950)
    'The Problem of the Revision of the Law of War' (1952) 29 *British Yearbook of
    International Law* 382
    (ed.), *Oppenheim's International Law, Volume I*, 8th edn (Longmans, Green & Co.,
    London, 1955)
    (ed.), *Oppenheim's International Law, Volume II*, 7th edn (Longmans, Green & Co.,
    London, 1952)
Lawrence, Thomas J., *The Principles of International Law*, 7th edn, revised by P. H.
    Winfield (Macmillan, London, 1923)
Lawyers Committee for Human Rights, *Establishing an International Criminal
    Court: Major Unresolved Issues in the Draft Statute* (New York, 1998)
Lee, Roy S. (ed.), *The International Criminal Court. The Making of the Rome Statute*
    (Kluwer, The Hague, 1999)
Lefever, Ernest W., 'The UN as a Foreign Policy Instrument: The Congo Crisis' in
    Roger Hilsman and Robert C. Good (eds.), *Foreign Policy in the Sixties* (Johns
    Hopkins Press, Baltimore, 1965), 153
Levi, Werner, *Contemporary International Law: A Concise Introduction* (Westview
    Press, Boulder, 1979)
Levie, Howard S. (ed.), *The Law of Non-international Armed Conflict* (Martinus
    Nijhoff, Dordrecht, 1987)
Lijnzaad, Liesbeth, *Reservations to UN-Human Rights Treaties: Ratify and Ruin?*
    (Martinus Nijhoff, Dordrecht, 1995)
Luard, Evan D. T., 'Civil Conflicts in Modern International Relations' in Evan
    D. T. Luard (ed.), *The International Regulation of Civil Wars* (Thames & Hudson,
    London, 1972), 7
    (ed.), *The International Regulation of Civil Wars* (Thames & Hudson, London, 1972)

Lysaght, Charles, 'The Attitude of Western Countries' in Antonio Cassese (ed.), *The New Humanitarian Law of Armed Conflict* (Editoriale Scientifica, Naples, 1979), 349

'The Scope of Protocol II and its Relation to Common Article 3 of the Geneva Conventions of 1949 and Other Human Rights Instruments' (1989) 33 *American University Law Review* 9

MacIntyre, Ben, 'UN Accuses Russia of Failing on Rules of War', *The Times*, 9 November 1999, 20

Mann, Frederick A., *Further Studies in International Law* (Clarendon Press, Oxford, 1990)

Mann, Howard, 'International Law and the Child Soldier' (1987) 36 *International and Comparative Law Quarterly* 32

Marks, Stephen P., 'Principles and Norms of Human Rights Applicable in Emergency Situations: Underdevelopment, Catastrophes and Armed Conflicts' in Karel Vasak (ed.), *The International Dimensions of Human Rights* (UNESCO/Greenwood Press, Westport, 1982), vol. I, 175

McCoubrey, Hilaire, *International Humanitarian Law* (Dartmouth, Aldershot, 1990)

'War Crimes Jurisdiction and a Permanent International Criminal Court: Advantages and Difficulties' (1998) 3 *Journal of Armed Conflict Law* 9

McCoubrey, Hilaire and White, Nigel D., *International Law and Armed Conflict* (Dartmouth, Aldershot, 1992)

International Organizations and Civil Wars (Dartmouth, Aldershot, 1995)

McGoldrick, Dominic, *The Human Rights Committee* (Clarendon Press, Oxford, 1994)

McNair, Arnold D., *The Law of Treaties* (Clarendon Press, Oxford, 1938)

International Law Opinions (Cambridge University Press, Cambridge, 1956), vol. I

McNemar, Donald W., 'The Postindependence War in the Congo' in Richard A. Falk (ed.), *The International Law of Civil War* (Johns Hopkins Press, Baltimore, 1971), 244

Melander, Göran, 'Torture Education During Military Service' in Christophe Swinarski (ed.), *Studies and Essays on International Humanitarian Law and Red Cross Principles in Honour of Jean Pictet* (ICRC/Martinus Nijhoff, Geneva, 1984), 411

Merignhac, A., *Droit public international* (Librairie Générale de Droit et de Jurisprudence, Paris, 1912), vol. III

Meron, Theodor, *Human Rights in Internal Strife: Their International Protection* (Grotius Publications, Cambridge, 1987)

'Draft Model Declaration on Internal Strife' (1988) 262 *International Review of the Red Cross* 59

Human Rights and Humanitarian Norms as Customary Law (Clarendon Press, Oxford, 1989)

'International Criminalization of Internal Atrocities' (1995) 89 *American Journal of International Law* 554

'The Continuing Role of Custom in the Formation of International Humanitarian Law' (1996) 90 *American Journal of International Law* 238

'War Crimes Law Comes of Age' (1998) 92 *American Journal of International Law* 462

'The Humanization of Humanitarian Law' (2000) 94 *American Journal of International Law* 239

(ed.), *Human Rights in International Law: Legal and Policy Issues* (Clarendon Press, Oxford, 1984), 2 vols.

Meurant, Jacques, 'Humanitarian Law and Human Rights Law: Alike Yet Distinct' (1993) 293 *International Review of the Red Cross* 89

Möller, Axel, *International Law in Peace and War* (Levin & Munksgaard, Copenhagen, 1935), part II

Moore, John B., *History and Digest of the International Arbitrations to which the US has been a Party* (Government Printing Office, Washington, 1898), vol. I

A Digest of International Law (Government Printing Office, Washington, 1906), vol. I

Moore, John N. (ed.), *Law and Civil War in the Modern World* (Johns Hopkins University Press, Baltimore, 1974)

Morison, Samuel E., *The Oxford History of the American People* (Oxford University Press, London, 1965)

Moskowitz, Moses, *Human Rights and World Order* (Oceana Publications, New York, 1958)

Murphy, Sean D., 'Progress and Jurisprudence of the International Criminal Tribunal for the Former Yugoslavia' (1999) 93 *American Journal of International Law* 57

Murray, Rachel, 'Decisions by the African Commission on Individual Communications under the African Charter on Human and Peoples' Rights' (1997) 46 *International and Comparative Law Quarterly* 412

Mushkat, Mario'n, 'The Development of International Humanitarian Law and the Law of Human Rights' (1978) 21 *German Yearbook of International Law* 150

Mutua, Makau, 'The African Human Rights Court: A Two-Legged Stool?' (1999) 21 *Human Rights Quarterly* 342

Nwogugu, E. I., 'The Nigerian Civil War: A Case Study in the Law of War' (1974) 14 *Indian Journal of International Law* 13

O'Ballance, Edgar, *Civil War in Bosnia, 1992–1994* (St Martin's Press, New York, 1995)

Odinkalu, Chidi Anselm, 'The Individual Complaints Procedures of the African Commission on Human and Peoples' Rights: A Preliminary Assessment' (1998) 8 *Transnational Law and Contemporary Problems* 359

Odinkalu, Chidi Anselm and Christensen, Camilla, 'The African Commission on Human and Peoples' Rights: The Development of its Non-State Communication Procedures' (1998) 20 *Human Rights Quarterly* 235

Official Records of the Diplomatic Conference on the Reaffirmation and Development of International Humanitarian Law Applicable in Armed Conflicts, Geneva (1974–1977) (Federal Political Department, Berne, 1978)

O'Flaherty, Michael, *Human Rights and the UN: Practice Before the Treaty Bodies* (Sweet & Maxwell, London, 1996)

Oppenheim, Lassa F. L., *International Law, Volume I* (Longmans, Green & Co., London, 1905)

    International Law, Volume II (Longmans, Green & Co., London, 1906)

Opsahl, Torkel, 'Instruments of Implementation of Human Rights' (1989) 10 *Human Rights Law Journal* 13

    'The Human Rights Committee' in Philip Alston (ed.), *The United Nations and Human Rights* (Clarendon Press, Oxford, 1992), 369

Oraà, Jaime, *Human Rights in States of Emergency in International Law* (Clarendon Press, Oxford, 1992)

Organization of American States, *The IACHR: Ten Years of Activities (1971–1981)* (OAS, Washington, 1982)

O'Rourke, Vernon A., 'Recognition of Belligerency in the Spanish Civil War' (1937) 31 *American Journal of International Law* 398

Padelford, Norman J., *International Law and Diplomacy in the Spanish Civil Strife* (Macmillan, New York, 1939)

Palwankar, Umesh, 'Applicability of International Humanitarian Law to United Nations Peacekeeping Forces' (1993) 294 *International Review of the Red Cross* 227

    'Measures Available to States for Fulfilling their Obligation to Ensure Respect for International Humanitarian Law' (1994) 298 *International Review of the Red Cross* 9

Perham, Margery, 'Reflections on the Nigerian Civil War' (1970) 46 *International Affairs* 231

Pictet, Jean S., *Commentary on the Geneva Conventions of 12 August 1949, Volume I* (ICRC, Geneva, 1952)

    Commentary on the Geneva Conventions of 12 August 1949, Volume IV (ICRC, Geneva, 1958)

    Commentary on the Geneva Conventions of 12 August 1949, Volume II (ICRC, Geneva, 1960)

    Commentary on the Geneva Conventions of 12 August 1949, Volume III (ICRC, Geneva, 1960)

    Humanitarian Law and the Protection of War Victims (A. W. Sijthoff, Leiden, 1975)

    Development and Principles of International Humanitarian Law (Martinus Nijhoff, Dordrecht, 1985)

Pinto, R., 'Le Drame algerien et la Croix-Rouge Internationale', *Le Monde*, 20 November 1957, 5

Plattner, Denise, 'La Portée juridique des déclarations de respect du droit
international humanitaire qui émanent de mouvements en lutte
dans un conflit armé' (1984) 18 *Revue Belge du Droit International*
298
'The Penal Repression of Violations of International Humanitarian Law
Applicable in Non-international Armed Conflicts' (1990) 278 *International
Review of the Red Cross* 409
Project Ploughshares, *Armed Conflict Report 2000* (Institute of Peace and Conflict
Studies, Ontario, 2000)
Ratner, Steven R. and Abrams, Jason S., *Accountability for Human Rights Atrocities
in International Law* (Oxford University Press, Oxford, 1997)
Renfrew, Barry, 'Chechnya' in Roy Gutman and David Rieff (eds.), *Crimes of War:
What the Public Should Know* (Norton, New York, 1999), 68
Report of the International Law Commission on the Work of its 46th Session,
2 May–22 July 1994. GAOR 49th Session, Supplement No. 10, UN Doc.
A/49/10
Report of the Observer Team to Nigeria, 24 September to 23 November 1968,
Cmnd 3878 (HMSO, London, 1969)
Roberts, Adam and Guelff, Richard (eds.), *Documents on the Laws of War*
(Clarendon Press, Oxford, 1989)
Robertson, A. H., 'Humanitarian Law and Human Rights' in Christophe
Swinarski (ed.), *Studies and Essays on International Humanitarian Law and
Red Cross Principles in Honour of Jean Pictet* (ICRC/Martinus Nijhoff, Geneva,
1984), 793
Robertson, Geoffrey, *Crimes Against Humanity* (Penguin, London, 2000)
Robinson, Darryl, 'Defining "Crimes Against Humanity" at the Rome
Conference' (1999) 93 *American Journal of International Law* 43
Rogers, A. P. V., 'Russia's War in Chechnya is an Internal Armed Conflict
Governed by International Conventions on War, Top Experts Say' (Crimes
of War Project, http://www.crimesofwar.org/chechnya/rogers.html)
Rosas, Allan and Helgesen, Jan E. (eds.), *Human Rights in a Changing East–West
Perspective* (Pinter, London, 1990)
Rosenau, James N., *International Aspects of Civil Strife* (Princeton University Press,
Princeton, 1964)
Rotberg, Robert I. (ed.), *Creating Peace in Sri Lanka: Civil War and Reconciliation*
(World Peace Foundation/Belfer Center for Science and International
Affairs/Brookings Institution Press, Washington, 1999)
Rowe, Peter, *Defence: The Legal Implications: Military Law and the Laws of War*
(Brassey's Defence, London, 1987)
Saland, Per, 'International Criminal Law Principles' in Roy S. Lee (ed.), *The
International Criminal Court. The Making of the Rome Statute* (Kluwer, The
Hague, 1999), 198

Sandoz, Yves, 'Implementing International Humanitarian Law' in UNESCO,
    International Dimensions of Humanitarian Law (Henry Dunant
    Institute/UNESCO/Martinus Nijhoff, Dordrecht, 1988), 259
Sandoz, Yves, Swinarski, Christophe and Zimmerman, Bruno (eds.), *Commentary
    on the Additional Protocols of 8 June 1977 to the Geneva Conventions of 12 August
    1949* (ICRC/Martinus Nijhoff, Geneva, 1987)
Sassoli, M. and Bouvier, A. A. (eds.), *How Does Law Protect in War?* (ICRC, Geneva,
    1999)
Schabas, William A., *The Abolition of the Death Penalty in International Law*,
    2nd edn (Cambridge University Press, Cambridge, 1997)
Schindler, Dietrich, 'The Different Types of Armed Conflicts According to the
    Geneva Conventions and Protocols' (1979-ii) 163 *Recueil des Cours* 117
    'Human Rights and Humanitarian Law: Interrelationship of the Laws' (1982)
    31 *American University Law Review* 935
Schindler, Dietrich and Toman, Jirí (eds.), *The Laws of Armed Conflicts. A Collection
    of Conventions, Resolutions and Other Documents*, 3rd edn (Martinus Nijhoff,
    Dordrecht, 1988)
Schlögel, Anton, 'Civil War' (1970) 108 *International Review of the Red Cross* 123
Schmidt, Dana A., *Yemen: The Unknown War* (The Bodley Head, London, 1968)
Schwarz, Walter, *Nigeria* (Pall Mall Press, London, 1968)
Schwarzenberger, Georg, *International Law* (Stevens & Sons, London, 1968), vol. II
Secretary General's Report on Aspects of Establishing an International Tribunal
    for the Prosecution of Persons Responsible for Serious Violations of
    International Humanitarian Law Committed in the Territory of Former
    Yugoslavia (3 May 1993), UN Doc. S/25704, reproduced in (1993) 32
    International Legal Materials 1159
Shestack, Jerome J., 'The Jurisprudence of Human Rights' in Theodor Meron
    (ed.), *Human Rights in International Law: Legal and Policy Issues* (Clarendon
    Press, Oxford, 1984), vol. I, 69
Shraga, Daphna, 'The United Nations as an Actor Bound by International
    Humanitarian Law' in Luigi Condorelli *et al.* (eds.), *The United Nations and
    International Humanitarian Law* (Editions Pedone, Paris, 1996), 317
Sieghart, Paul, *The International Law of Human Rights* (Clarendon Press, Oxford,
    1983)
Silber, Laura and Little, Allan, *The Death of Yugoslavia* (Penguin/BBC, London,
    1995)
Sinclair, I. M., *The Vienna Convention on the Law of Treaties*, 2nd edn (Manchester
    University Press, Manchester, 1984)
'Siracusa Principles on the Limitation and Derogation Provisions in the ICCPR',
    (1985) 7 *Human Rights Quarterly* 3
'Sixth Annual Red Cross–Washington College of Law Conference on
    International Humanitarian Law: A Workshop on Customary
    International Law and the 1977 Protocols Additional to the 1949 Geneva

Conventions', (1987) 2 *American University Journal of International Law and Policy* 419

Smith, Chris, 'South Asia's Enduring War' in R. I. Rotberg (ed.), *Creating Peace in Sri Lanka: Civil War and Reconciliation* (World Peace Foundation/Belfer Center for Science and International Affairs/Brookings Institution Press, Washington, 1999), 17

Smith, Dan, *The State of War and Peace Atlas*, 3rd edn (Penguin/International Peace Research Institute, Oslo, London, 1997)

Smith, Herbert A., 'Some Problems of the Spanish Civil War' (1937) 18 *British Yearbook of International Law* 17

(ed.), *Great Britain and the Law of Nations* (P. S. King & Son, London, 1932; reprinted Kraus Reprint Co., New York, 1975), vol. I

Solf, Waldemar A., 'Commentary on International Non-international Armed Conflicts: Case Studies of Afghanistan, Kampuchea and Lebanon' (1982) 31 *American University Law Review* 927

Stone, Julius, *Legal Controls of International Conflict*, revised impression (Stevens & Sons, London, 1959)

Swinarski, Christophe (ed.), *Studies and Essays on International Humanitarian Law and Red Cross Principles in Honour of Jean Pictet* (ICRC/Martinus Nijhoff, Geneva, 1984)

Szabo, Imre, 'Historical Foundations of Human Rights and Subsequent Developments' in Karel Vasak (ed.), *The International Dimensions of Human Rights* (UNESCO/Greenwood Press, Westport, 1982), vol. I, 11

Taubenfeld, Howard J., 'The Applicability of the Laws of War in Civil War' in John N. Moore (ed.), *Law and Civil War in the Modern World* (Johns Hopkins University Press, Baltimore, 1974), 499

Taylor, Hannis, *A Treatise on International Public Law* (Callaghan & Co., Chicago, 1901)

Taylor, Telford, *Nuremberg and Vietnam: An American Tragedy* (Quadrangle Books, Chicago, 1970)

Thomas, Ann van W. and Thomas, A. J. Jr, 'International Legal Aspects of the Civil War in Spain, 1936–1939' in Richard A. Falk (ed.), *The International Law of Civil War* (Johns Hopkins Press, Baltimore, 1971), 111

Thomas, Hugh, 'The Spanish Civil War' in Evan D. T. Luard (ed.), *The International Regulation of Civil Wars* (Thames & Hudson, London, 1972), 26

Tolley, Howard Jr, *The United Nations Commission on Human Rights* (Westview Press, Boulder, 1987)

Traynor, Ian, 'US Accuses Russia of Flouting International Law in Chechnya', *Guardian*, 24 December 1999, 9

Triffterer, Otto, 'Article 27: The Irrelevance of Official Capacity' in Otto Triffterer (ed.), *Commentary on the Rome Statute of the International Criminal Court. Observers' Notes, Article by Article* (Nomos Verlagsgesellschaft, Baden-Baden, 1999), 501

'Article 33: Superior Orders and Prescription of Law' in Otto Triffterer (ed.), *Commentary on the Rome Statute of the International Criminal Court. Observers' Notes, Article by Article* (Nomos Verlagsgesellschaft, Baden-Baden, 1999), 573

(ed.), *Commentary on the Rome Statute of the International Criminal Court. Observers' Notes, Article by Article* (Nomos Verlagsgesellschaft, Baden-Baden, 1999)

Truth and Reconciliation Commission of South Africa, *Truth and Reconciliation Commission Report* (Macmillan, Basingstoke, 1999), vol. I

Tucker, Robert W., 'Reprisals and Self-Defense: The Customary Law' (1972) 66 *American Journal of International Law* 586

Turns, David, 'Russia's War in Chechnya is an Internal Armed Conflict Governed by International Conventions on War, Top Experts Say' (Crimes of War Project, http://www.crimesofwar.org/chechnya/turns.html)

Tuzmukhamedov, Bakhtiyar, 'Russia's War in Chechnya is an Internal Armed Conflict Governed by International Conventions on War, Top Experts Say' (Crimes of War Project, http://www.crimesofwar.org/chechnya/tuzmukhamedov.html)

Umozurike, U. Oji, 'The African Charter on Human and Peoples' Rights' (1983) 77 *American Journal of International Law* 902

The African Charter on Human and Peoples' Rights (Martinus Nijhoff, The Hague, 1997)

UNESCO, *International Dimensions of Humanitarian Law* (Henry Dunant Institute/UNESCO/Martinus Nijhoff, Dordrecht, 1988)

UNHCR, *The State of the World's Refugees* (Oxford University Press, Oxford, 1997)

Van Dijk, P. and van Hoof, G. J. H., *Theory and Practice of the European Convention on Human Rights*, 2nd edn (Kluwer, Deventer, 1990)

Vasak, Karel (ed.), *The International Dimensions of Human Rights* (UNESCO/Greenwood Press, Westport, 1982), 2 vols.

Vattel, Emmerich de, *The Law of Nations* (Newbery, Richardson, Crowder, Caslon, Longman, Law, Fuller, Coote & Kearsly, London, 1760)

Von Hebel, Herman and Robinson, Darryl, 'Crimes Within the Jurisdiction of the Court' in Roy S. Lee (ed.), *The International Criminal Court. The Making of the Rome Statute* (Kluwer, The Hague, 1999), 79

Waldock, C. H. M., 'The Regulation of the Use of Force by Individual States in International Law' (1952-ii) 81 *Recueil des Cours* 455

Walker, Wyndham L., *Pitt Cobbett's Leading Cases on International Law*, 5th edn (Sweet & Maxwell, London, 1937), vol. II

Walzer, Michael, *Just and Unjust Wars*, 2nd edn (Basic Books, New York, 1992)

Warbrick, Colin and Rowe, Peter, 'The International Criminal Tribunal for Yugoslavia: The Decision of the Appeals Chamber on the Interlocutory Appeal on Jurisdiction in the *Tadić* Case' (1996) 45 *International and Comparative Law Quarterly* 691

Wehberg, Hans, 'La Guerre civile et le droit international' (1938-i) 63 *Recueil des Cours* 7

Welch, Claude E. Jr, 'The African Commission on Human and Peoples' Rights: A Five-Year Report and Assessment' (1992) 14 *Human Rights Quarterly* 43

Welch, Claude E. Jr and Meltzer, Ronald I. (eds.), *Human Rights and Developments in Africa* (State University of New York Press, New York, 1984)

Wells, Donald A., *War Crimes and Laws of War*, 2nd edn (University Press of America, Lanham, 1991)

Wharton, Francis (ed.), *A Digest of the International Law of the United States*, 2nd edn (Government Printing Office, Washington, 1887), vol. I

Wheaton, Henry, *Elements of International Law*, 8th edn, edited by R. H. Dana (Sampson Low, Son & Co., London, 1866)

Whittell, Giles, 'Bomb Raid "Kills 50 Chechnya Refugees"', *The Times*, 30 October 1999, 15

'Chechens Told to Abandon Grozny or Die', *The Times*, 7 December 1999, 16

Wilson, A. Jeyaratnam, *Sri Lankan Tamil Nationalism* (Hurst & Co., London, 1999)

Wilson, Heather A., *International Law and the Use of Force by National Liberation Movements* (Clarendon Press, Oxford, 1988)

Womack, Helen, 'Kremlin Orders Inquiry into Mass Chechen Graves', *Independent*, 26 February 2000, 15

Wood, Paul, 'Chechnya's Civilians Put to the Sword', *Independent*, 6 February 2000, 20

Woolsey, Theodore D., *Introduction to the Study of International Law*, 4th edn (Sampson Low, Marston, Low & Searle, London, 1875)

Wright, Quincy, 'The American Civil War, 1861–65' in Richard A. Falk (ed.), *The International Law of Civil War* (Johns Hopkins Press, Baltimore, 1971), 30

Index

Abi-Saab, Georges, 100–101, 106,
    119–120, 190, 191
Additional Protocol I
    Algeria, 69, 71
    belligerent reprisals, 242
    customary law, 90
    Former Yugoslavia, 79–80
    Gulf Conflict, 47
    national liberation, 89–90, 99, 102
    territorial control, 106
Additional Protocol II
    aims, 91
    application, 14, 91–92, 97–98,
        99–109
    belligerent reprisals, 240
    binding nature for insurgents, 96–99
    Bosnia-Herzegovina, 125–127
    Chechnya, 127–131
    and common Article 3, 52, 95, 96–97,
        100–103
    customary law, 108–109, 136,
        143–144, 165
    drafting process, 91–96
    El Salvador, 120–122, 131
    human rights, 109, 133
    humane treatment, 110–115
    humanitarian relief, 95, 118–119
    ICRC activity, 95
    intervention, 109–110
    jus cogens, 109
    methods and means of warfare, 94,
        117–118
    protection of civilians, 94, 116–119
    reciprocity, 86, 107–108
    Rwanda, 122–125
    territorial control, 38, 105–106

    wounded, sick and shipwrecked,
        115–116
Afghanistan, 44, 51, 69, 84, 120,
    257–258, 260
Africa
    colonialism, 1
    human rights, 268–271
African Commission on Human and
    Peoples' Rights, 268, 269–271
Ago, Roberto, 140
Aldrich, George H., 242, 244
Algeria
    acceptance of common Article 3, 66,
        71–72, 78
    application of common Article 3,
        72–74
    casualties, 69, 72–73
    character of armed conflict, 69–71
    Commission de Sauvegarde des
        Droits et des Libertés Individuels, 74
    ICRC activity, see ICRC
Ambos, Kai, 172, 175
Amnesty, 67, 99
Amnesty International, 114, 178
Angola, 84, 104, 120, 146, 259
Annan, Kofi, 1
Armed conflict
    definition, 25, 32–34, 42–45, 88, 91, 101
    existence, 5–6, 14–16, 34–43, 45, 167
    geographical location, 9, 31
    intensity, 4, 15, 39, 43, 106–107
    internationalised, 46–52, 69–71
    parties to, 39–40, 103–105
Armed forces
    definition, 104–105
    governmental use, 38–40

Asia, colonialism, 1
Australia, 24, 25, 26

Bassiouni, M. Cherif, 128
Baxter, Richard R., 139
Belgium
    Additional Protocol II, 52, 96
    Congo, 70, 74
    war crimes jurisdiction, 159
Belligerency, see Recognition of
        belligerency
Belligerent reprisals, 61, 62, 237–243
Biafra
    application of common Article 3, 81–83
    blockade, 79–80
    character of armed conflict, 79–81
    ICRC activity, see ICRC
    Observer Team, 82–83
    statehood, 80
Blockade, 9, 12, 15–16, 79–80
Boer War, 19
Bombardment, 129
Bond, James E., 87
Bosnia-Herzegovina
    application of Additional Protocol II,
        125–127
    application of common Article 3, 84–85
    character of armed conflict, 47–50,
        136–137
    recognition of belligerency, 42, 79–80
    see also Yugoslavia
Bowett, Derek W., 77–78
Brazil, 9, 19
Browne-Wilkinson, Lord, 178
Burma, 25, 29, 61

Canada, 24, 25, 82
Cassese, Antonio, 51, 52, 54, 97, 98, 99
Chamberlain, Neville, 139–140
Chechnya, 84, 127–131, 142
    see also Russia
Chemical weapons, 145–146
    see also Methods and means of warfare
Children, 111, 219–221
Chile, 18, 177–178, 236
China, 24
Civilians
    and combatants, 2–3, 58–59
    protection of, 2, 58–59, 94, 116–119,
        139–144, 228–230
Cold War, 2, 46

Collective punishment, 215
Colombia, 19
Colonialism, 1, 68–70, 74, 90
Common Article 3
    and Additional Protocol II, 95,
        97, 100–103
    automatic application, 27, 41, 85–86
    belligerent reprisals, 61, 62, 239–240
    binding nature for insurgents, 37,
        44–45, 52–58
    broad application, 36–38, 43–44
    criteria for application, 31–32, 34–36,
        43–45
    customary law, 42, 56, 140–141, 165
    drafting history, 23–29
    effect on legal status, 65–67
    Former Yugoslavia, 79–80
    humane treatment, 58–63
    individual criminal responsibility,
        157–160
    jus cogens, 56–57
    personal application, 58–60
    principles of humanity, 42, 56,
        86–87, 140
    prisoners of war, 60
    recognition of belligerency, 40–42, 65
    special agreements, 42, 46–47, 63–65,
        71, 79–80, 141
    State reluctance, 86–88
    territorial control, 38
Congo
    application of common Article 3,
        75–78, 141–142
    casualties, 78
    character of armed conflict, 75–76
    ICRC activity, see ICRC
    State succession, 55, 75
    UN involvement, see United
        Nations
Control, 48–50
    see also International armed
        conflict
Corporal punishment, 214–215
Cretan Insurrection, 14
Crimes against humanity
    attack on civilian population, 150–153
    collective character, 151–152
    discriminatory intent, 153–155
    ICC Statute, 161–163
    motive, 155–156
    nexus to armed conflict, 148–150

Crimes against humanity (*cont.*)
  policy requirement, 152–153
  universal jurisdiction, 235
  see also Customary law;
    Individual criminal
    responsibility; ICC; ICTY
Crimes of War Project, 128
Croatia, 48, 79, 125, 126
  see also Bosnia-Herzegovina;
    Yugoslavia
Cuba, 9, 13, 18, 20
Customary law
  Additional Protocol II, 108–109,
    136, 143–144, 165
  belligerent reprisals, 240
  codification, 18
  common Article 3, 42, 56, 140–141, 165
  effect on character of conflict, 51–52,
    137, 190–192
  ICC Statute, 160–167
  ICTY, 51, 133–134, 188–192
  individual criminal responsibility,
    156–160
  methods and means of warfare,
    145–147
  opinio juris, 138–139
  protection of civilians, 139–144
  treaties, 53
Cyprus, 264
Czechoslovakia, 60, 64

Death penalty, 226
Denmark, 24
Detainees, *see* Prisoners of war
Disappearances, 227–228
Dissemination, 243–244
Distinction, 2–3, 18, 87, 116–117
Domestic law, 54–55
Domestic security, 3
Doswald-Beck, Louise, 272
Draper, Gerald I. A. D., 38, 41

Egypt, 46, 69, 84
Eide, Asbjörn, 109, 115
El Salvador
  Additional Protocol II, 120–122,
    131, 143–144
  armed conflict, 84
  casualties, 121–122
  dissemination, 244
  human rights 259–260, 267

Truth Commission, 122
  US involvement, 122
Enforcement
  human rights mechanisms, 255–273
  ICRC, 250–251
  third States, 244–250
  United Nations, 251–255, 256–263
  see also Belligerent reprisals; Individual
    criminal
    responsibility; ICC; ICTR; ICTY
Ermacora, Felix, 257
ETA (Euskadi Ta Askatasuna), 105
  see also Spain; Terrorism
Ethnic cleansing, 2
European Court of Human Rights, 195,
    263–265
European Union
  Chechnya, 129–130, 142
  Iraq, 145
  Liberia, 142

Fair Trial, *see* Judicial guarantees
Farer, Tom J., 46, 257
FLN (Algerian National Liberation Front),
  see Algeria
FMLN (Farabundo Martí National
  Liberation Front), *see* El Salvador
Former Yugoslavia, *see* Bosnia-Herzegovina;
  ICTY; Yugoslavia
Forsythe, David P., 94
France
  Additional Protocol II, 90
  Algeria, 1, 68–74
  American Civil War, 9
  common Article 3, 24, 25, 26, 27, 28, 60
  Greek Insurrection, 9
  Rwanda, 123
Franco, General, 20

Gabon, 80
Gasser, Hans-Peter, 246, 249–250
Geneva Conventions
  agreements to apply, 26, 27, 28,
    42, 46–47, 63–65
  Biafra, 80–81
  common Article 1, 246–250
  common Article 2, 41, 81
  Congo, 75, 78
  Former Yugoslavia, 79–80, 84
  grave breaches, 50, 164, 166,
    189–191, 235

internal armed conflict, 25–29, 63–65
level of acceptance, 31, 88
principles of, 22, 26, 31, 75, 77, 83,
    86–87
travaux préparatoires, 41, 53
UN forces, 76–78
Genocide, 2, 82, 174–175
Georgia, 143
Germany
  chemical weapons, 145
  military manual, 143, 159
  Spanish Civil War, 20
Goldstone, Richard, 234
Greece, 9, 12, 13, 24, 25
Greenberg, Eldon van C., 66
Greenwood, Christopher J., 103, 147
Guerrilla warfare, 3, 58–59, 66, 72,
    83, 106
Gulf Conflict, 47, 253

Haiti, 19, 80, 120, 259
Herczegh, Géza, 117
Hoffmann, Lord, 178
Honduras, 268
Hostages, 202–203
Human rights law
  Additional Protocol II, 109, 133, 210–230
  Africa, 268–271
  Americas, 266–268
  binding nature for insurgents, 44–45
  children, 219–221
  civilian population, 228–230
  common Article 3, 44, 197–208
  derogation, 37, 44, 195–196
  enforcement, 255–273
  Europe, 263–265
  humane treatment, 62, 197, 211–214
  and humanitarian law, 193–197,
      230–231
  judicial guarantees, 203–208, 224–227
  jus cogens, 57
  non-derogable provisions, 208–210, 230
  non-discrimination, 197–198, 213
  obligations *erga omnes*, 57, 245
  violence to life and person, 199–202,
      214–219
Humane treatment
  children, 111
  meaning, 61–62
  nationality, 60–61
  non-discrimination, 60–61

personal application, 58–61, 110,
    111, 112
  prisoners of war, 60, 111–114
Humanitarian law
  codification, 18–19
  customary law, 18, 42
  development, 21–23, 89
  Diplomatic Conference 1949, 23–29
  dissemination, 243–244
  historical application, 3–4, 11–18
  and human rights law, 193–197,
      230–231
  jus cogens, 56–57
  obligations *erga omnes*, 57, 245
  prior to 1949, 18–19
Humanitarian relief, 21–22, 95,
    118–119, 230
Humanitarianism, 17
Hungary, 13, 22, 24, 25

Immunity, *see* Individual criminal
    responsibility; ICC; Pinochet, Augusto
India, 92
Individual criminal responsibility, 148,
    156–160, 167–177, 233–237
  age limit, 176–177
  assistance with crimes, 172–173
  attempted crimes, 175
  command responsibility, 180–183
  commission of crimes, 170–172
  group responsibility, 174
  incitement, 174–175
  official capacity, 177–180
  superior orders, 183–188
Indonesia, 69
Insurgency, *see* Recognition
Insurgents
  legal status, 3, 5, 10, 17, 24, 60,
      65–67, 95–96
  obligations, 52–58
  organisation, 36–38, 43, 59, 104–105
  territorial control, 38, 105–106
Inter-American Commission on Human
    Rights, 44, 59, 199–200, 205, 266–267
Inter-American Court of Human Rights,
    267–268
Internal armed conflict
  Additional Protocol I, 89–90
  asymmetry, 3, 58, 66
  and international armed conflict, 3,
      46–52, 137

Internal armed conflict (*cont.*)
  international regulation, 2–3, 21–23
  regional regulation, 19
Internal disturbances, 24, 25, 37, 43–44,
  101–102, 231
International armed conflict, 46–52,
  89–90
  see also Armed conflict; Control;
  National liberation
International Commission of Jurists, 206
International Committee of the Red Cross
  (ICRC)
  Afghanistan, 51, 84
  Algeria, 71, 72, 73
  Angola, 84
  belligerent reprisals, 239, 240
  Biafra, 80, 81, 82
  Bosnia-Herzegovina, 84
  Chechnya, 84
  Congo, 75, 77
  development of humanitarian law,
    21–23
  dissemination, 244
  drafting Additional Protocol II, 91
  drafting common Article 3, 26, 29
  enforcement, 250–251
  humane treatment, 62, 113
  humanitarian initiative, 26, 27, 63,
    95, 113, 118
  Rwanda, 84, 123–125
  Sri Lanka, 84, 85
  State succession, 55, 75
  status, 82
  threshold of common Article 3,
    35–36
  Yemen, 83
International Court of Justice (ICJ)
  character of armed conflict, 47
  common Article 3, 56, 57, 87, 140
International Criminal Court (ICC)
  adoption of Statute, 160
  crimes against humanity, 161–163
  definitions of crimes, 32
  individual criminal responsibility, 161,
    167–177, 235
  national liberation, 90
  official capacity, 177–183
  responsibility of legal persons,
    169–170
  superior orders, 183–188
  war crimes, 163–167

International Criminal Tribunal for
  Rwanda (ICTR)
  command responsibility, 181, 182
  definition of armed conflict, 45
  effectiveness, 233, 277
International Criminal Tribunal for the
  Former Yugoslavia (ICTY)
  belligerent reprisals, 240–241
  character of armed conflict, 47–50
  command responsibility, 180
  crimes against humanity, 147–156
  customary law, 51, 134, 137–147, 275
  definition of armed conflict, 42–43,
    45, 104
  effectiveness, 233–234, 277
  grave breaches, 50, 189–191
  individual criminal responsibility,
    156–160, 167–168, 233
  reciprocity, 108, 175–176
  Rule 61 procedure, 234
International Monetary Fund (IMF),
  130
International peace and security, 2,
  109–110, 252
International Peace Institute, 1
Internees, *see* Prisoners of war Intervention
  Additional Protocol II, 109–110
  character of armed conflict, 46–51
  on behalf of government, 36
  Spanish Civil War, 20
IRA (Irish Republican Army), 105,
  202, 265
  see also Northern Ireland; Terrorism;
  United Kingdom
Iran, 69
Iraq
  Algeria, 69
  chemical weapons, 145
  common Article 3, 68
  human rights, 260
  Kuwait, 47
  United Nations action, 253
Israel, 254
Italy
  Additional Protocol II, 95–96
  common Article 3, 24, 25, 27
  Spanish Civil War, 20
Ivory Coast, 80

Jennings, Robert Y., 140
Jordan, 69

Judicial guarantees
  Additional Protocol II, 114–115,
    224–227
  common Article 3, 203–208
  see also Human rights law; Humane
    treatment
Jus cogens, 56–57, 109

Katanga, see Congo
Kosovo, 258, 277
  see also NATO; Yugoslavia
Kuwait, 47

Landmines, 146, 270–271
  see also Methods and means of warfare
Lauterpacht, Sir Hersch, 40, 41
Lawyers Committee for Human Rights,
  165
League of Nations, 140
Lebanon, 69, 104
Legislative jurisdiction, 53–55,
  96
Liberia, 104, 142, 143
Libya, 69
Lieber, Dr Francis, 19
Lieber Code, 12, 19
Lincoln, Abraham, 13, 16
Los Angeles Riots, 37

Marshall Islands, 31
Martens Clause, 133
Mazowiecki, Tadeusz, 258
McDonald, Gabrielle Kirk, 49, 50
McNair, Lord Arnold, 17
Medical experiments, 200, 224
Meron, Theodor, 133–134, 164,
  189, 190, 191, 234–235
Methods and means of warfare,
  18, 81, 83–84, 87, 94, 117–118,
  145–147
  see also Additional Protocol II; Customary
    law
Mexico, 18, 24
Military manuals, 19, 138–139,
  143, 157, 159
Millett, Lord, 178–179
Monaco, 25, 26, 27
Montenegro, see Yugoslavia
Morocco, 69
Mozambique, 120
Mutilation, 200

Namibia, 120
National liberation, 89–90, 99, 102,
  106
  see also Additional Protocol I;
    International armed conflict
NATO, 126, 234, 277
  see also Kosovo; Yugoslavia
Nauru, 31
Netherlands, 9
Neutrality, 7, 8, 15, 20
  see also Recognition of belligerency
New Zealand, 159
Nicaragua, 47, 48, 120, 247
Nigeria, see Biafra
Non bis in idem, 114
Northern Ireland, 35, 38, 87, 105, 196,
  265–266
  see also IRA; Terrorism; United Kingdom
Norway, 24, 25, 92
Nullum crimen sine lege, 114, 135, 148
Nuremberg Tribunal, 57, 149, 153, 158,
  168, 177, 183, 233

Obligations erga omnes, 57, 245
Official capacity, see Individual criminal
  responsibility; Pinochet, Augusto
Organisation of African Unity, 82

Pairings, 47, 76
Pakistan, 69, 93
Perfidy, 146
  see also Methods and means of warfare
Peru, 7, 18
Philippines
  Additional Protocol I, 90
  Additional Protocol II, 90, 131
  human rights, 259
Pictet, Jean S., 32, 35, 36, 37–38, 43,
  64, 70, 109, 194, 244–245
Pinochet, Augusto, 177–178, 236,
  277
  see also Chile; Individual criminal
    responsibility; Torture
Poland, 35, 82
Police, 38–39, 80
Political will, 88, 235–236, 276–277
Portugal, 20
Prisoners of war
  exchanges, 82, 83
  humane treatment, 60, 73, 78,
    81–82, 83, 111–114, 221–224

Prisoners of war (*cont.*)
   insurgent treatment, 3
   see also Humane treatment
Proportionality, 18, 87

Rape, 216–218
   see also Crimes against
      humanity; Torture; War crimes
Rebellion, 4, 24
Reciprocity
   Additional Protocol II, 86,
      107–108
   criminal responsibility, 175–176
   Geneva Conventions, 23, 26, 41,
      85–86
   humanitarian law, 23, 53
   recognition of belligerency, 10
Recognition
   belligerency, *see* Recognition of
      belligerency
   governments, 5–6, 20
   insurgency, 4–5, 20
Recognition of belligerency
   American Civil War, 9, 11, 12–13,
      15–16
   common Article 3, 40–42, 65
   criteria, 13–15
   decline, 19–21, 41, 79
   discretion, 10, 13, 15, 17, 18
   effects, 7–8, 10–11, 41
   Former Yugoslavia, 79–80
   Great Britain, 6–7, 9, 14–17, 20,
      21–22
   parent States, 10–11
   Spanish Civil War, 20, 79, 80.
   State practice, 11–18
   tacit, 13, 17, 79
   third States, 7–9
   traditional international law, 5–11,
      86
   United States of America, 6, 14,
      15–16, 20
Refugees, 2
Religious freedom, 212–213
   see also Additional Protocol II; Human
      rights law; Humane treatment
Reprisals, *see* Belligerent reprisals
Robertson, Geoffrey, 176, 188
Romania, 24
RPF (Rwandan Patriotic Front), see
   Rwanda

Russia
   ICRC activity, 22
   internal conflict, 22, 127–131
   recognition of belligerency, 9
   see also Chechnya; Soviet Union
Rwanda
   Additional Protocol II,
      122–125
   atrocities, 2, 84
   French involvement, 123
   human rights, 259, 270
   ICRC activities, *see* ICRC
   United Nations involvement,
      77, 123
   see also ICTR

Saland, Per, 186
San Domingo, 16
Sandoz, Yves, 248, 249
SAS, 234
Saudi Arabia, 46, 69
Schindler, Dietrich, 230
Secession, 66, 75, 79
Self-determination, 66, 89–90
Self-interest, 8, 17, 18, 20, 45
Serbia, *see* Yugoslavia
Shahabuddeen, Mohamed, 48, 49
Sierra Leone, 44
Slavery, 208, 218
   see also Human rights law
Smith, Herbert A., 6
Solf, Waldemar A., 121
Somalia, 39, 104, 120, 143, 159–160,
   167, 259
South Africa, 67
   see also Amnesty
Sovereignty, 24, 92, 272
Soviet Union
   Additional Protocol II, 96
   Afghanistan, 51
   common Article 3, 24, 25, 26, 27,
      28, 29, 63, 64
   see also Russia
Spain
   American Civil War, 9
   American colonies, 6–7, 9, 12,
      16–17
   Basque separatism, 105
   Civil War, 13, 19–20, 22, 79, 80,
      138, 139, 140
   common Article 3, 24, 25

Sri Lanka
  human rights, 260-261
  internal conflict, 84, 85, 120
State responsibility, 48, 50, 55
State succession, 55, 75, 125
Statehood, 80
Sudan, 44-45, 270
Superior orders, see Individual criminal
  responsibility
Sweden, 82, 244
Switzerland, 25, 29, 42
Syria, 69

Tamil Tigers (Liberation Tigers of Tamil
  Eelam), see Sri Lanka
Tanzania, 80
Territorial control, 38, 54, 105-106
Terrorism, 66, 105, 215-216
  see also Algeria; IRA; Northern Ireland;
  Spain
Thailand, 69
Thant, U, 76-77
Threats, 218-219
Tokyo Tribunal, 161, 177
Torture, 200-202, 236-237
  see also Crimes against
    humanity; Human rights law; War
    crimes
Treaty law, 52-53, 97-99
Triffterer, Otto, 183, 187
Tu quoque, 175-176
Tunisia, 69
Turkey, 264, 265
Turns, David, 128
Tutu, Archbishop Desmond, 67
Tuzmukhamedov, Bakhtiyar, 128

United Kingdom
  American Civil War, 9,
    15-16
  belligerent reprisals, 242
  Biafra, 82
  chemical weapons, 145
  civil disturbances, 34
  common Article 3, 24, 25,
    26, 27
  dissemination, 244
  military manual, 159
  police, 34, 38
  recognition of belligerency, 6-7, 9,
    14, 15-17, 20

Spanish Civil War, 20
  see also IRA; Northern Ireland;
    Pinochet, Augusto
United Nations
  Algeria, 69-71
  Commission on Human Rights, 130-131,
    227, 256-258
  Congo, 75-78
  enforcement, 251-255, 256-263
  Human Rights Committee, 114, 207,
    226, 258-263
  humanitarian law, 76-77
  intervention, 109-110
  Iraq, 252-253
  Rwanda, 77, 123
United States of America
  Chechnya, 129, 130
  chemical weapons, 145-146
  Civil War, 1-2, 9, 10, 11, 12-13,
    15-16, 19
  common Article 3, 24, 25, 26, 60, 63
  dissemination, 244
  El Salvador, 122
  military manual, 159
  Nicaragua, 47, 48, 247
  recognition of belligerency, 6, 10, 14,
    15, 18, 19, 20
  War of Independence, 12
Universal jurisdiction, 235
Upper Silesia, 22
Uruguay, 25, 28, 259, 262-263

Vattel, Emmerich de, 3, 11
Vité, Sylvain, 272

War crimes, 163-167
  see also Customary law; Geneva
    Conventions; Individual criminal
    responsibility; ICC; ICTY
Wirtz, Captain Henry, 12-13
World War I, 21
World War II, 2, 22, 117, 183, 193, 233
Wounded, sick and shipwrecked
  Additional Protocol II, 115-116, 118
  common Article 3, 28
  insurgent treatment of, 3

Yemen
  Algeria, 69
  application of common Article 3, 31,
    46, 83-84

Yemen (*cont.*)
  common Article 3 agreement, 141
  ICRC activity, *see* ICRC
Yugoslavia
  character of armed conflict, 47–50,
      136–137
  common Article 3 agreement, 42, 141

recognition of belligerency, 42,
    79–80
United Nations action, 254
see also ICTY; Kosovo

Zaire, 96
Zambia, 80

CAMBRIDGE STUDIES IN INTERNATIONAL AND COMPARATIVE LAW

Books in the series

1 *Principles of the institutional law of international organisations*
C. F. Amerasinghe

2 *Fragmentation and the international relations of micro-states*
Jorri Duursma

3 *The polar regions and the development of international law*
Donald R. Rothwell

4 *Sovereignty over natural resources*
Nico Schrijver

5 *Ethics and authority in international law*
Alfred P. Rubin

6 *Religious liberty and international law in Europe*
Malcolm D. Evans

7 *Unjust enrichment*
Hanoch Dagan

8 *Trade and the environment*
Damien Geradin

9 *The changing international law of high seas fisheries*
Francisco Orrego Vicuña

10 *International organizations before national courts*
August Reinisch

11 *The right to property in commonwealth constitutions*
Tom Allen

12 *Trusts*
Maurizio Lupoi and Simon Dicks

13 *On civil procedure*
J. A. Jolowicz

14 *Good faith in European contract law*
Reinhard Zimmermann and Simon Whittaker

15 *Money laundering*
Guy Stessens

16 *International law in antiquity*
David J. Bederman

17 *The enforceability of promises in European contract law*
James Gordley

18 *International commercial arbitration and African states*
Amazu Asouzu

19 *The law of internal armed conflict*
Lindsay Moir